COLLECTING IMPRESSIONISM

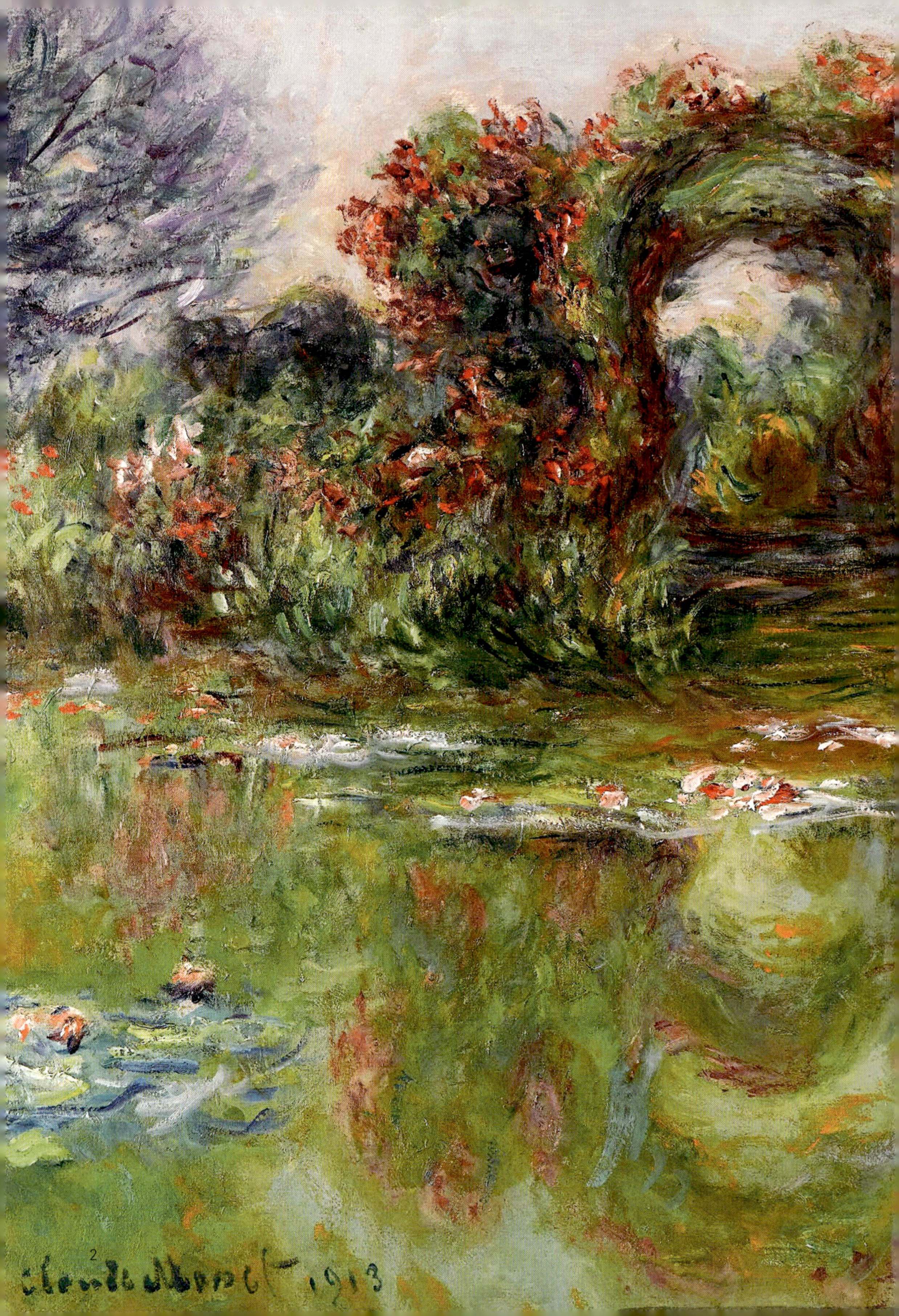

COLLECTING IMPRESSIONISM

A Reappraisal of the Role of Collectors in the History of the Movement

edited by Ségolène Le Men
and Félicie Faizand de Maupeou

SilvanaEditoriale

Foreword

The State and the Île-de-France and Normandy regions are committed to supporting research on Impressionism, thanks to the Interregional Project (CPIER) for the Seine Valley, the cradle and source of inspiration for Impressionism.
For tourists and amateurs from all over the world, this region is an iconic destination, the "Impressionist destination".
As symbolic as it is, this region, too, has been affected by the COVID crisis and must adapt to the current changes in tourism more than ever before. It has realised the increasing need to assert its cultural legitimacy through high quality scientific research.
The *Collecting Impressionism* international symposium has played an important role in this regard, not focusing exclusively on tourism, but also seeking to develop a network of specialists on Impressionism and mobilising teaching and research institutions. Both local and international, this event has contributed to supporting research on Impressionism in its historical homeland.

The Impressionists were the first instigators of a "Seine route" stretching from Paris to its estuary, at Le Havre and Honfleur, and passing through Argenteuil, Chatou, Bougival, Giverny or Rouen. Ambassadors of the Seine Valley, these exceptional painters were able to spread their art thanks to the collectors presented at the symposium.

Thus, Impressionism was not just the great artistic movement we all know today, but equally the testimony of artists supported by collectors who were aware of the transformation of their region caused by the Industrial Revolution.

We hope that the vision of these talented painters will be a source of learning and inspiration, helping us to adapt to the transformations of the Seine Valley linked to ecological transitions.

That is why the State, who supported the symposium through the CPIER, hopes that this new scientific momentum will continue to grow and consolidate this iconic "Impressionist destination" even further.

Pascal Sanjuan
Interministerial Delegate for the Development of the Seine Valley

Acknowledgements

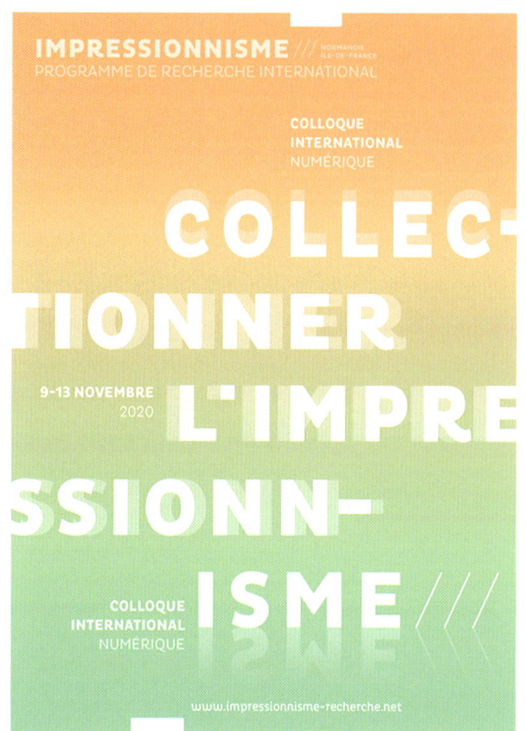

This collective book stems from the international conference entitled *Collecting Impressionism*, held online from 9 to 13 November 2020, within the framework of the "Normandie – Paris Île-de-France : Destination impressionnisme" Destination Contract,[1] as part of a programme supporting new research on Impressionism that is transversal, interdisciplinary and international.

It was organised by the Fondation de l'Université Paris Nanterre, in partnership with the French Cluster (LABEX) "The Pasts in the Present" and the research team "Histoire des arts et des representations" of the Université Paris Nanterre, as well as the Université de Rouen, on the occasion of the fourth edition of *Normandie impressioniste*. It was originally intended to be held in Rouen, having been designed in connection with the exhibition at the Musée des Beaux-Arts de Rouen on the collector-donor François Depeaux, who was involved in the genesis of Monet's *Cathedrals* series.[2] Due to the unforeseen circumstances of the pandemic, however, the symposium was entirely digital: a recorded bilingual version is still accessible as a supplement to the present revised publication.[3]

We would like to thank all those who made the symposium, as well as the publication of the present volume, possible: first of all the authors, the members of the scientific committee – Sylvain Amic, Frédéric Cousinié, Marina Ferretti, Frances Fowle, Xavier Greffe, Jacques-Sylvain Klein, Géraldine Lefebvre, Marianne Mathieu, Sylvie Patry, Hadrien Viraben – as well as Philippe Piguet and Selma Toprak, and the members of the organisation committee. A real collaboration has been going on for two years between the Destination Contract team – Nathalie Lecerf, Raphaëlle Guillou, Isabelle Lebreton – and the university team with Ghislaine Glasson Deschaumes and Marina Egidi. We would particularly like to thank our financial partners, the Normandy region, as well as the Delegation for the Development of the Seine Valley and the Prefect Mr François Philizot, who provided his ongoing support to this original scientific chapter of the Destination Contract within the framework of the development of the Seine Valley, which he was in charge of up until the spring of 2021, and which he hoped to see come to life along the banks of the Seine, a river so much loved by the Impressionists.

We extend our warmest thanks to everyone who contributed, as well as the publisher Laurianne Barban who helped in preparing the book, and the collectors who made their documentation available and authorised the reproductions.

Ségolène Le Men and Félicie Faizand de Maupeou

1 Since 2014, Île-de-France and Normandy have joined forces around the Impressionism Destination Contract, bringing together more than fifty cultural and tourist partners to make these regions a unique tourist destination of excellence.

2 Sylvain Amic and Joanne Snrech (eds.), *François Depeaux: collectionneur des impressionnistes*, exhibition catalogue, Musée des Beaux-Arts, Rouen, 3 April – 7 September 2020 (Paris: In Fine and Réunion des Musées Métropolitains Rouen Normandie, 2020).

3 https://impressionnisme-recherche.net/programme-2020/

Contents

COLLECTING IMPRESSIONISM: HERE OR THERE?

SÉGOLÈNE LE MEN
AND FÉLICIE FAIZAND DE MAUPEOU

Art collecting is a cultural practice, both social and individual, that spread across different spheres of society in the late nineteenth century, and not just among businessmen and entrepreneurs.[1] It developed in parallel to Impressionism, following Manet's "symbolic revolution".[2] This encounter is the focus of this collective book that came out of a symposium organised in 2019 and which brought together art historians, academics and curators. Before we start, let us not forget that the word "*collectionneur*", in its masculine form, along with its feminine equivalent "*collectionneuse*", appeared in the first volume of the *Littré* in 1866, and in the fourth volume of the *Grand dictionnaire universel du XIXᵉ siècle* by Pierre Larousse in 1869. It entered dictionaries as a neologism derived from the verb "*collectionner*" in the years that preceded its invention, linked to the title of the painting shown by Monet in 1874, from the word "impressionism", which was immediately recorded by the *Littré*, not unlike the term "japonism", coined by the art critic Philippe Burty in 1872. This simultaneousness of Impressionism and a taste for collecting was not just expressed through vocabulary but also through painting itself: it is one of the arguments in Monet's portrait of his first wife Camille Doncieux, shown at the second Impressionist exhibition in 1877 (it was where the group first appropriated, the initially satirical name, of Impressionists) and entitled *Japonnerie*, which today can be found in the collection at the Boston Museum of Fine Arts (fig. 1). His model posed in an interior, dressed as a Japanese woman holding a fan. We can see a section of wall in the background, decorated with a collection of *ushiwa*, which were small fans exported to Europe and could be "picked up" at the World Fair in 1867. Each of these painted fans seems, with a self-parodying Jap-

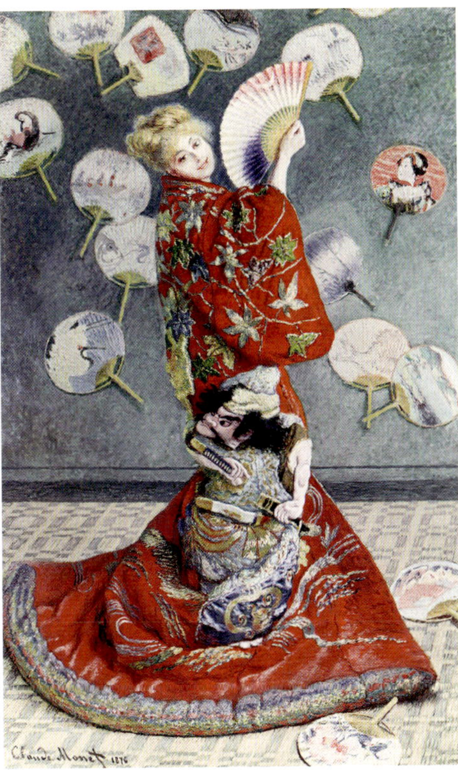

1. Claude Monet, *Camille Monet in Japanese Costume* (*La Japonaise*), 1875, oil on canvas, Museum of Fine Arts, Boston

anese-inspired note, to represent a small imaginary museum of Impressionist painting and Monet's landscapes, while at the same time depicting motifs from Bracquemond's tableware.

General Concerns: Three Levels of Interaction

The interactions between "collectionism" and Impressionism were played out on three levels. The first is a structural level and concerns both the sociology of those involved and the history of tastes: the redefinition of the art world led to the emergence of the figure of the modern art collector, which began around 1850 in the École de Barbizon, attached both to the notion of the avant-garde that came out of Saint-Simonianist theories and applied to Impressionism by the critic-collector Théodore Duret,[3] as the expansion of the "art dealer-critic system"[4] that opposed, and simultaneously existed alongside, the "academic system", founded on training at the École des Beaux-Arts, exhibitions at the Salon and public commissions, and which was in the process of being broken down. Duret had underlined their importance and, as early as 1878, provided a list of the first art enthusiasts which included: "Messrs. d'Auriac, Etienne Baudry,

de Belio [*sic*], Charpentier, Choquet [*sic*], Deudon, Dollfus, Faure, Murer, de Rasty, among others".[5] It was from this list that Anne Distel's founding work, *Les Collectionneurs des impressionnistes*,[6] supported by numerous sources, was constructed. The Impressionists themselves were close to the collectors, some of them being painters like Caillebotte or Rouart, and sometimes became collectors, like Monet (supported by Hoschedé whose wife became his own, and by his chemist brother, Léon Monet[7]) or Degas.[8] The number of collectors rapidly increased, not just in Paris, but also in the provinces and overseas. Why did these collectors – in relation to a whole network of intermediaries, art dealers and gallery owners, but also advisors to collectors, critics, experts, auctioneers – choose to buy Impressionist paintings, pastels and prints and thus support the group of artists who exhibited together in Paris, even though Impressionism, at its debuts, was still a relatively limited enterprise, mocked by the critics and the public? Where did they discover these works that they brought into the world of collectibles, and which from one collection to another, from auction to auction, increased in value, and reinforced their pedigree? How did they get hold of them? Was it at an exhibition, when they visited a studio, in the galleries of art dealers, at the auction house? What role did reproductions play in the expansion of the market? The role of photographs and illustrated sale catalogues, art magazines, but also monographs and books, in French or translated?
The second level is spatio-temporal and takes into account the way in which the collectors, on different scales, from the regional to the transcontinental, contributed to the spread and progressive universalisation of Impressionism, while at the same time standing out from the styles of the movement's protagonists once the group exhibitions were over, and the definition of Impressionism widened according to its artistic appropriations, whether it was beyond borders, or, nationally, on a more local level, in "small clusters", beginning with Normandy: through Impressionism, the collector François Depeaux established a modern school of landscape in his hometown which would later take the name of the École de Rouen. Although the role of art dealers, such as Durand-Ruel, and intermediaries like Mary Cassatt or Count Harry Kessler,[9] are well-known today, how did collectors participate in the spread and globalisation of the movement? Although other transnational vectors could also have been mentioned, the present volume offers an in-depth look at the how Impressionism was promoted in Europe and on the other side of the Atlantic, as well as its relationship with Asia.
The third level of interaction is an institutional one, pertaining to the role of collectors in accessing public collections and bringing works into the museum of Impressionism: depending on the places and cultural traditions,

their patronage expressed itself with different modalities whose extremes opposed the French situation, whereby museums, which emerged after the Revolution, managed inalienable state collections – divided up in Paris between the Louvre, a posthumous museum, and the Luxembourg for living artists, while in the provinces, museums were also being created[10] – to those of other countries like the United States, where museums were private foundations, and Japan, where the National Museum of Tokyo was created after the Second World War. Nobody has forgotten the polemic around the bequest of one of the group's painters, Gustave Caillebotte (1848–1894), who was also a keen collector of Impressionism: bequeathed in 1894, his collection struggled to get into the Luxembourg in 1896, and was exhibited there in 1897.[11] A decade later, the donations of Isaac de Camondo (1851–1911) to the Louvre, in 1897 and 1903, subject to usufruct and which had become part of the national collections after his death, were more easily accepted.[12] This was also the case with the donation of Étienne Moreau-Nélaton's (1859–1927) art collections in 1906 and 1919.[13] Other bequests were made in the provinces, like the one from François Depeaux (1853–1920), previously mentioned, or from Henry Vasnier (1832–1907) in 1907, an associate of the champagne house Pommery, who had created a private gallery inspired by the layout of the Georges Petit gallery, and who gave his collection to Reims so that his hometown could boast an ambitious and modern museum.[14]

The Poetics of Display and the Issues Surrounding Seriality

A fourth level can be added to these three, what we might call the "poetic" dimension of Impressionist collections in transposing an idea already posited by Dominique Pety on the intrinsic relationship between collections and nineteenth-century literature into the visual arts.[15] It is perfectly represented by the iconic catalogue-book by Edmond de Goncourt, *La Maison d'un artiste* (1880), which recorded room by room lists of collected objects in Goncourt's home. "Colligere" means bringing together in the same place a group of objects, which, once reunited have meaning, and highlight the choices and preferences of a collector: collecting involves the gathering of disparate elements, picked up here and there, to unite a group which takes its meaning from its exhibition value (which can also be seen as its domestic decorative value), and provides harmonious parallels between the elements of the collection: "I myself see in the simultaneous presence, in the thought-provoking and harmonious juxtaposition of *Lady in Blue* (*Dame bleue*) by Corot and the *Lady in Blue* (*Dame bleue*) by Renoir, a striking symbol of the whole collection and the spirit behind it",[16]

wrote Arsène Alexandre about the Rouart collection, whose monograph, published by Goupil in 1912, paralleled its dispersion, although he had just explained that "when you look over the collection in one glance, an astonishing relationship is established between two precious landmarks of an artistic evolution with an amateur art enthusiast who remained faithful to his former admirations, while at the same time opening up to his new admirations".[17] Such relationships, also allow collections to be juxtaposed with others because they often blend perfectly into the collector's house, as the display in Étienne Moreau-Nélaton's interior shows. Another well-known example is the recently renovated Barnes Foundation in Baltimore, with its display of paintings and ironwork.[18] This private exhibition in the collector's home equivalent can go as far as resembling a whole work of art – Camondo spoke about his collection like an "opera".
And so, through the problematic of series, it aligns itself with the poetry of Impressionism, in Monet's work in particular. The well-known article "Révolution de cathedrals", published by Clemenceau in May 1895 on the front pages of *La Justice*, deploring the fact that the State had not acquired the paintings as an ensemble, highlighted the importance of this serial phenomenon which he qualified as a "revolution without gunshots". The *Cathedrals* (*Cathédrales*) were exhibited as a simultaneous ensemble, based on repetition and variation, of paintings that formed a work reunited in a collection, but which remained distinct: each of them exists on its own, and today, the group is dispersed throughout museums and collections around the world, in Paris (at the Musée d'Orsay and at the Musée Marmottan Monet) and in Rouen, but also in Cardiff, Belgrade, Moscow, Washington, New York and Hakone. When Monet carefully planned this exhibition at Durand-Ruel's in 1895, he oversaw the creation of a catalogue (fig. 2) in order to show both the series, entitled *The Rouen Cathedral* (*La Cathédrale de Rouen*), and each of the twenty or so paintings exhibited, whose listed titles varied, and which, even when separated, individually continued to represent the ensemble as a whole. The order and the wording of the five descriptions in the catalogue put together by Monet designating those who lent the works for this first exhibition are very interesting: number 2, *The Portal* (*Le Portail*) and *The Court of Albania* (*La Cour d'Albane*) are listed as "*Belonging to Mr Depeaux*", the "coal merchant" and logistical assistant during the genesis of the ensemble, who had the privilege, as a form of gratitude, to choose one of the works from the series, and accepting the high price demanded by Monet; numbers 8, 11 and 14, belonging to the banker Isaac de Camondo, who acquired four paintings from the series via his agent Maurice Joyant; number 20, which was the last in the series, belonged to the representative of the American Art Association James Fountain Sutton, whose Parisian agent at that time

LA CATHÉDRALE DE ROUEN

1 — *Le Portail* (*Effet du matin*).

2 — *Le Portail et la tour d'Albane.*
Appartient à M. Depeaux.

3 — *La Cour de la maîtrise.*

4 — *Le Portail* (*Soleil*).

5 — *Idem.* *Idem.*

6 — *Idem.* *Idem.*

7 — *La Cathédrale dans le brouillard.*

8 — *Le Portail* (*Temps gris*).
Appartient à M. le comte de Camondo.

9 — *Le Portail vu de face.*

10 — *La Cour de la maîtrise* (*Temps gris*).

11 — *Le Portail.*
Appartient à M. le comte de Camondo.

12 — *Le Portail* (*Effet du matin*).

13 — *Idem.* *Idem.*

2. Exhibition of paintings by Claude Monet, exhibition catalogue, Durand-Ruel, Paris, 10–31 May 1895 (Paris: s.n., 1895), p. 3

was Montaignac. The names of these three lenders were listed according to a significant grading system which marked the three levels of distribution of Monet's work, local, national and international, and through it, Impressionism, via three profiles of collectors linked to industry and the coal trade for the first, banking for the second and the art market for the third, while the same time highlighting the serial mode of acquisition of Count Isaac de Camondo, continued by Sutton in the United States.
In this convergence between the serial phenomenon and the effect of collecting, we find the nature of the collection, as analysed Jean Baudrillard in *Le Système des objets. La consommation des signes* in 1968 in relation to objects of industrial consumption, one year before Roy Lichtenstein's lithographic pop art remake of Monet's *Rouen Cathedral* (*La Cathédrale de Rouen*) in 1969: his writings show the tension between the one and the multiple – "a serial game" (p. 109) then "from quantity to quality: the unique object" (p. 110) – and then he comes to the time of "watches" – "objects and habits: watches" (p. 113) – and the time of collecting which is "in the fullest sense of the term a *pastime*" that "represents the perpetual renewal of an orchestrated cycle ... It is, he continues, the environment of private objects and their possession – of which the collection is the extreme point – a dimension as essential as imaginary in our lives. As essential as dreams"[19] (pp. 115–16). Further on, the paragraph "from

serial motivation to the real motivation" finally comes to the way in which the collection "emerges towards culture": "it targets differentiated objects which often have an exchange value, and which are also 'objects' of conservation, trade, social rites, exhibition, perhaps even the source of profits. These objects are paralleled with projects. Without ever ceasing to refer to each other, they involve social exteriorisation, human relationships in this play".

A Prolific Field of Research

Similarly to the earlier international symposium, this book provides an opportunity to bring together the points of view of art historians working on the field of collecting, a fast-growing subject which is linked not just to anthropological questions but also historical, sociological, cultural, aesthetic, literary and economical ones. The very numerous conferences, study days, seminars or publications on this theme[20] perfectly reflect this plurality of approaches by treating in a more or less transversal manner[21] the passage from private to public,[22] the construction of identities through collections,[23] their presentation,[24] how they were constituted,[25] or by focusing on a period,[26] a geographical area,[27] the types of collectors or specific objects,[28] or further still on a particular collector.[29] Dedicated research centres have also been developed in recent years, notably the Center for the History of Collecting at the Frick Collection in New York which, among other actions, is developing an online repertoire to "to help researchers locate primary source material about American art collectors, dealers, agents and advisors, and the repositories that hold these records." [30] The Society for the History of Collecting belongs to this same movement but adopts a broader stance because it is not limited to a period or geographical area. In France, the MO.CO. Montpellier Contemporain has developed a research centre on collectors of contemporary art, posing a question that is directly linked to those raised by the various contributors to the research: "What was the contribution of collectors in producing and modifying values, whether they were economic, social, symbolic, aesthetic or historic and, more widely, to the life of the works themselves? What impact has the content of collections had and still has at a local, regional or international level?".[31] In the nineteenth century, the rise of "collectionism" is inseparable from the development of a private art market. This field of investigation has then also benefitted from the multiplication of studies on the art market.[32]

Since 2010, research on Impressionism has seen a new momentum that has been reflected in numerous exhibitions and publications. One of the most prominent features of this impetus is the question of the internationalisation of the movement whose analysis and interpretation have been highly controversial. From the movement's initial exportation to England at the time of the 1870 war,[33] to the major American exhibitions in the 1890s, and up to the increasingly visible presence of Impressionist works in European capitals in the late nineteenth century, the history of the spread of the movement on a planetary scale in the last decades of the nineteenth century has been well established. By highlighting, for example, the transnational dynamics[34] or the dominant role of intermediaries, up until recently lesser-known, such as Mary Cassatt[35] or the American Art Association,[36] recent research has proven that many aspects of this diffusion still remain to be explored. Today, the propagation of the movement is being looked at in a new light. Its internationalisation is no longer understood merely as the circulation of works by a few painters, with a clearly identifiable aesthetic within a specific time period, but as its true appropriation, different depending on the country, the period or even the artists, to the extent of considering Impressionism not just as a French movement but as a resolutely international one.

Collections: A Vector of Universalisation of Impressionism

In their introduction to the collective work *Globalizing Impressionism: Reception, Translation, and Transnationalism*,[37] Alexis Clark and Frances Fowl remind us that although it might seem new to some, this interpretation is actually firmly anchored in history. From the early twentieth century, far from referring just to the Parisian movement, the term "Impressionist" became polysemic. Designating either at the same time or in turn a style, a naturalist aesthetic, landscape painting or an avant-gardist stance, it was freely employed by critics and contemporary commentators to refer to paintings by artists of all nationalities. This interpretation was then progressively erased to make Impressionism a well-defined moment in time – essentially centred around eight Impressionist exhibitions (1874–86) but generally extending to the World Fair in 1900 – uniquely French and focusing on just a few artists, commonly designated as "the central core of Impressionism". In the 1960s and then especially in the 1970s and 1980s, research was concentrated on national and regional schools to highlight their specificities without any reference to the French model. While this approach allowed these schools to be given due prominence, it also isolated them from the international context. In the 1990s – and Norma Broude's *L'impressionnisme dans le monde*,[38] has been the most accomplished expression – it was the international reception of Impressionism and the different national reactions that were studied. A great number of publications, often stemming from exhibitions, sought to show the existence of a Scottish, Irish, Greek, Italian, German, Swedish, Belgian, Canadian, American, Brazilian, Turkish, Australian, Japanese, etc. Impressionism.[39] They were qualified as national Impressionist schools for having developed the same tendencies of painting daily life, working directly from the motif, capturing the effects of natural light, adopting a light colour palette, etc. However, in their most recent book on this subject matter, Clark and Fowle posit that Impressionism must no longer be considered as an international but truly a global movement. In the broader context of multiplying studies on the circulation of works and people and a geographical extension of studies on the art market,[40] today the aim of Impressionist studies is to consider the different Impressionist currents, without inevitably referring to the French model and above all without erasing their specificities. Moreover, it is not just about studying the spread of Impressionism from an aesthetic viewpoint but to highlight its processes and mechanisms, the people involved and the overall context. Impressionism will no longer designate a group of artists having developed a personal aesthetic vocabulary in a defined place and time, but a much broader movement that spread from France, but also emerged independently.

The Benefits of Case Studies and Monographic Exhibitions

Far from being uniquely theoretical, these historiographic evolutions are based on real case studies, whether they focus on a country, a period or the people involved in this expansive dynamic. Although art dealers, with Durand-Ruel at the forefront,[41] and sometimes the artists themselves crafted this international success,[42] collectors equally played an essential role. there has been an increasing number of exhibitions devoted to them in recent years. Without claiming to be exhaustive, we have counted no less than thirty since 1989, with a very large majority (twenty-three) having been held since 2005. We have only taken into account French exhibitions, even if most of these exhibitions also travelled to other countries.[43] Since its opening, the Fondation Vuitton has stood out by showing the Courtauld, Chtchoukine and Morozov collections, reflecting the underlying identity of the museum as a collector's museum.[44] Adopting an original viewpoint initiated by Marianne Mathieu, the Musée Marmottan Monet has managed on two occasions to exhibit works that are today still in private collections.[45] This cycle was completed by an exhibition bringing together works owned by Monet,[46] highlighting the importance of this figure of artist-collector, and which this book refers to in several essays. At the time of writing this introduction, the exhibition *Julie Manet* was on display,[47] while the Musée d'Orsay hosted an exhibition devoted to Signac as a collector.[48] The vast majority of these exhibitions adopt a monographic standpoint. They are concerned with retracing the biography of a celebrity, their encounter with Impressionism, the creation and management of their collection and, in the case of foreign collectors, these exhibitions generally touch on their role and that of the works in the propagation of Impressionism in their home country. These exhibitions participate in an individual approach to Impressionist collecting, a point of view often favoured. The challenge of this volume is to go beyond this monographic approach, not by rejecting case studies but by adding each and every one and confronting them with more global studies. It is by multiplying this analysis of collector profiles, their trajectories and of course their collections that the importance of their role in the different phases of the movement, its constitution, its development, its diffusion can be revealed.

Contributions to the Volume

Rather than being extras, collectors were key players in the Impressionist movement, involved right from the beginning by the artists themselves. Similarly to art dealers or critics, but according to different modalities, they equally contributed to defining the movement. However, it was the painters who initially ensured the circulation of their works among a limited circle of artists through a system of trade, gifts or purchases, as examined in-depth by Gwendoline Corthier-Hardouin. Some of them took on the role of collectors to such an extent that we might wonder if they were really artist-collectors or collector-artists, as Fausto Minervini elaborates with the case of Giuseppe De Nittis and Alexandre d'Andoque for Gustave Fayet, the latter gradually establishing a veritable strategy in developing his collection through a process of buying and selling. The importance of collectors in defining the Impressionist movement can be seen right from the group's very first exhibition, as highlighted by the first version of the catalogue, analysed here by Anne Distel, which is all the more precious as it is hand-annotated by the exhibitors themselves. Catherine Méneux perfectly illustrates the involvement of collectors during the fourth Impressionist exhibition, an involvement which, while not outwardly publicised by the artists, was nonetheless determining. Whether through exhibition catalogues or other mediums, like the directories studied by Léa Saint Raymond, collectors reveal something about their relationship with the movement in the way they showed their attachment to it.

The collectors and the works they brought together have equally played a major role in the widespread of Impressionism on a regional, national and international scale. Paris was the nerve centre of the art world where collectors came to find the latest trends which they took back to their own countries. In his essay, Lukas Gloor highlights how several generations of Swiss collectors maintained a unique relationship with France and Impressionism. Carolyn Kinder Carr recounts how, on the other side of the Atlantic, Americans developed a taste for Impressionism very early on, like the Palmers, who travelled to Paris on several occasions to make their purchases, advised by Sara Tyson Hallowell. In Hollywood, it was actors and film directors who developed this passion for Impressionism which, as Théo Esparon cleverly shows, was even transposed into their films by using some of these collections as a backdrop or by adopting a similar artistic language. Although for a long time, China remained untouched by the spread of Impressionism, except for a few attempts like those by Sun Peicang who came close, it entered the field in a rather impressive manner in the second half of the twentieth century thanks to the transformation of its economy. Marie Laureillard traces this evolution in an essay that sheds light on a little-known geography of the reception of Impressionism. Finally, collectors played a determining role in transferring works from the private to the public sphere. Many contemporary art museums were built around a core of Impressionist works donated by private collectors. Yet, this shift from an individual to a collective vision played out in the transition to museum collections equally contributed to defining the movement. And so, the different scales of how Impressionism was received had an impact on the construction of identities, private or collective, whether they were regional, as Noémie Picard demonstrates with the Depeaux collection and the École de Rouen, or national, as Samuel Raybone evokes in his essay showing the nationalistic dimension of the reception of Impressionism in Wales. Based on well-known facts, Chikako Takaoka links the original way in which Impressionism was received in Japan to the nation's identity in the early twentieth century.

Ségolène Le Men touches on the layout and formation of Impressionist collections "at home", taking the example of Étienne Moreau-Nélaton in 1907, just before it entered the national collections.

The last essay in the book, by Anne Higonnet, opens up some fascinating perspectives by proposing new museographies, placing Impressionism at the heart of a true international history of art and not just a Western one.

1 Albert Boime, "Les hommes d'affaire et les arts en France au XIXe siècle", *Actes de la recherche en Sciences sociales*, no. 28, 1979, pp. 57–75 (translated by Christophe Charle).
2 Pierre Bourdieu, *Manet une révolution symbolique*, coll. Raisons d'agir (Paris: Seuil, 2013).
3 Théodore Duret, *Critique d'avant-garde* (Paris: Charpentier, 1885).
4 Harrison C. White and Cynthia A. White, *La carrière des peintres au XIXe siècle: du système académique au marché des impressionnistes* (Paris: Flammarion, 1991).
5 Théodore Duret, *Les peintres impressionnistes: Claude Monet, Sisley, C. Pissarro, Renoir, Berthe Morisot, avec un dessin de Renoir*, Paris, Librairie parisienne, H. Heymann and J. Perois, May 1878, p. 9. This nominative list was taken out of the version published by Duret in *Critique d'avant-garde*.
6 Anne Distel, *Les Collectionneurs des impressionnistes* (Paris: La Bibliothèque des Arts, 1989).
7 Dominique Lobstein, *Défense et illustration de l'impressionnisme Ernest Hoschedé et son "Brelan de Salons" (1890)* (Dijon: L'Échelle de Jacob, 2008). Géraldine Lefebvre, "Cercles et collections impressionnistes à Rouen: Léon Monet et François Depeaux", in Sylvain Amic (ed.), *François Depeaux: collectionneur des impressionnistes*, exhibition catalogue, Musée des Beaux-Arts, Rouen, 3 April – 7 September 2020 (Paris: In Fine and Réunion des musées métropolitains Rouen Normandie, 2020, pp. 184–96.
8 Ann Dumas, Colta Ives, Susan A. Stein and Gary Tinterow (eds.), *The Private Collection of Edgar Degas. A Summary Catalogue*, exhibition catalogue, The Metropolitan Museum of Art, New York, 1 October 1997 – 11 January 1998 (New York: The Metropolitan Museum of Art, 1997).
9 His partially translated diary has been a very rich source of information: Comte Harry Kessler, *Journal. Regards sur l'art et les artistes contemporains 1889-1937*, 2 vols. (Paris: Éditions de la Maison des sciences de l'homme and INHA, 2017).
10 Chantal Georgel (ed.), *La Jeunesse des musées. Les musées de France au XIXe siècle*, exhibition catalogue, Musée d'Orsay, Paris, 8 February – 7 May 1994 (Paris: RMN, 1994).
11 Pierre Vaisse, *Deux façons d'écrire l'histoire. Le legs Caillebotte* (Paris: INHA and Ophrys, 2014).
12 Anne-Hélène Hoog (ed.), *La Splendeur des Camondo, de Constantinople à Paris (1806-1945)*, exhibition catalogue, Musée d'art et d'histoire du Judaïsme, Paris, 6 November 2009 – 7 March 2010 (Milan-Paris: Skira and Flammarion, 2009).
13 Françoise Cachin and Pierre Rosenberg (eds.), *De Corot aux impressionnistes, donations Moreau-Nélaton*, exhibition catalogue, Grand Palais, Paris, 30 April – 22 July 1991 (Paris: Éditions de la Réunion des musées nationaux, 1991).
14 Marie-Hélène Montout-Richard (ed.), *L'Œil d'un collectionneur: catalogue raisonné de la collection d'Henry Vasnier au musée des Beaux-Arts de Reims* (Paris: Somogy, 2003).
15 Dominique Pety, *Les Goncourt et la collection: de l'objet d'art à l'art d'écrire* (Geneva: Droz, 2003); *Poétique de la collection au XIXe siècle: du document de l'historien au bibelot de l'esthète* (Nanterre: Presses universitaires de Paris Ouest, 2010).
16 Arsène Alexandre, *La Collection Henri Rouart* (Paris: Goupil, 1912), p. 41.
17 Ibid.
18 The Barnes Foundation having kept the original display, we have chosen a work from this collection for our cover, the display being visible on the back cover.
19 Jean Baudrillard, *Le Système des objets. La consommation des signes* (Paris: Denoël and Gontier, 1976). First published 1968.
20 The references are just given as examples of the dynamism of research on the subject and are not intended to be exhaustive.
21 *The Journal of the history of collections*, published by the University of Oxford, covers all the periods: the earliest universal collections and those that came to engage with more specialized subject areas receive equal attention". https://academic.oup.com/jhc/pages/About (accessed 29 July 2021).
22 *Du privé au public. Enjeux et stratégies dans la présentation des collections privées d'art contemporain dans les institutions publiques*, online study day, 13 April 2021, organised by the Université de Grenoble.
23 Call for communication from the Center for Historical Research of the Polish Academy of Sciences in Berlin, *Collection, Modernism and Social Identity*, online symposium planned on 15 and 16 September 2021, http://blog.apahau.org/appel-a-communication-collection-modernism-and-social-identity-online-15-16-sep-21/ (accessed 29 July 2021).
24 *Collections, Displays & The Agency of Objects*, symposium organised at the Keynes Library, The Cambridge Union Society from 20 to 23 September 2017.
25 *Collectionner: acteurs, lieux et valeur(s) (1750-1815)*, online symposium organised by

the Groupe de Recherche en Histoire Moderne (GRHAM) and the Collection conference on 26 and 27 October 2020.
26 *Seminar in the History of Collecting*, organised by the Wallace Collection since 2006 and which works more specifically on the eighteenth and nineteenth centuries in Paris and London.
27 *Les collections et collectionneurs polonais hors de Pologne*, symposium organised by the Société Historique et Littéraire Polonaise in Paris, 1 December 2015; *Collections et collectionneurs d'antiquités en Europe à la Belle Époque (1870-1914)*, Paris, INHA, 7-9 November 2019.
28 *Les Arts décoratifs au musée, instruction, collection et patrimonialisation*, symposium organised by the Université de Haute-Alsace in Mulhouse the 30 and 31 March 2017; round table organised by the INHA for the launch of *Jacques Doucet collectionneur et mécène* on 7 March 2017.
29 *Les collections Rothschild dans les institutions publiques françaises*, research program at the INHA and the symposium organised within the framework of the *Les collections Rothschild: de la sphère privée à la sphère publique* research program, from 4 to 6 December 2018 at the INHA.
30 https://research.frick.org/directory (accessed 29 July 2021).
31 The MO.CO. brings together the Esba (École Supérieure des Beaux-Arts de Montpellier), the Panacée (Centre d'art contemporain) and the Hôtel des collections (a space devoted to exhibiting international contemporary art), https://www.moco.art/fr/pole-de-recherche-sur-les-collections (accessed 29 July 2021).
32 It would be impossible to list all of the scientific events and publications concerned with this relationship as there are so many of them. Among the French ones, we would like to mention the conference Collection https://collection.hypotheses.org/; the Franco-German research program *Art Market and Art Collecting from 1900 to the Present in Germany and France*, supported in 2018-19 by the Forum Kunst und Market/ Centre for Art Market Studies at the Technische Universität Berlin and by the Centre Georg Simmel from the EHESS, in partnership with the Centre Allemand d'Histoire de l'Art Paris and, for England, Pamela M. Fletcher and Anne Helmreich (eds.), *The rise of the modern art market in London, 1850-1939* (Manchester-New York, Manchester University Press, 2011).
33 Caroline Corbeau-Parsons (ed.), *Les Impressionnistes à Londres: artistes français en exil*, exhibition catalogue, Tate Britain, London, 2 November 2017 - 7 May 2018; Petit Palais-Musée des beaux-arts de la Ville de Paris, 20 June - 14 October 2018 (Paris: Paris musées and Petit Palais-Musée des beaux-arts de la Ville de Paris, 2017).
34 In her book, *Nul n'est prophète en son pays? L'internationalisation de la peinture des avant-gardes parisiennes, 1855-1914* (Paris: N. Chaudun, 2009), Béatrice Joyeux-Prunel notably showed the importance of Impressionism abroad in constructing the movement's success in France.
35 Nancy Mathews, Pierre Curie and Flavie Durand-Ruel (eds.), *Mary Cassatt: une impressionniste américaine à Paris*, exhibition catalogue, Musée Jacquemart-André, Paris, 9 March - 23 July 2018 (Brussels: Fonds Mercator, 2018).
36 John Ott, "How New York Stole the Luxury Art Market: Blockbuster Auctions and Bourgeois Identity in Gilded Age America", *Winterthur Portfolio*, vol. 42, no. 2-3, 2008, pp. 133-58. Claire Hendren, *La Patrimonialisation de l'impressionnisme français aux Etats-Unis (1870-1915)*, doctoral thesis in art history, supervised by Ségolène Le Men, Université Paris Nanterre, discussed on 28 May 2019.
37 Alexis Clark and Frances Fowle (eds.), *Globalizing Impressionism* (New Haven: Yale University Press, 2020). The approach developed in this collective work follows on from the symposium held at the Courtauld Institute of Art in 2017, *Writing Impressionism Into and Out of Art History, 1874 to Today*.
38 Norma Broude (ed.), *L'Impressionnisme dans le monde: un mouvement international, 1860-1920* (Paris: Nathan, 1990).
39 *American impressionism a new vision, 1880-1900*, exhibition catalogue, Musée des impressionnismes, Giverny, 23 March - 29 June, 2014; National Galleries of Scotland, Edinburgh, 19 July - 19 October 2014; Museo Thyssen-Bornemisza, 4 November 2014 - 1 February 2015 (New Haven: Yale University Press, 2014); Frances Fowle (ed.), *Impressionism & Scotland*, exhibition catalogue, National Gallery Complex, Edinburgh, 19 July - 12 October 2008: Kelvingrove Art Gallery and Museum, Glasgow, 31 October 2008 - 1 February 2009 (Edinburgh: National Galleries of Scotland, 2008); *Liebermann, Slevogt, Corinth: deutsche Impressionisten aus dem Niedersächsischen Landesmuseum Hannover* (Hamburg: Batig, 1987); Renato Barilli, *Impressionismo italiano*

(Milan: Mazzotta, 2002); William Hauptman and Peter Norgaard Larsen (eds.), *Impressions du Nord: La peinture scandinave, 1800-1915* (Lausanne-Milan: Fondation de l'Hermitage and 5 Continents, 2008); Gotz Czymmek (ed.), *Landschaft im Licht: Impressionistische Malerei in Europa und Nordamerika, 1860-1910*, exhibition catalogue, Wallraf-Richartz-Museum, Köln, 6 April – 1 July 1990 (Köln: Wallraf-Richartz-Museum, 1990); *Deutsche Impressionisten: Liebermann, Corinth, Slevogt*, exhibition catalogue, Museum zu Allerheiligen Schaffhausen, 23 April – 24 July 1955 (Schaffhausen: Buchdruckerei Meier & Cie, 1955).

40 Baetens Jan Dirk and Lyna Dries, *Art Crossing Borders: the Internationalisation of the Art Market in the age of Nation States, 1750–1914* (Boston: Brill, 2019).

41 Jennifer A. Thomson, "Paul Durand-Ruel et l'Amérique", in *Paul Durand-Ruel. Le pari de l'impressionnisme*, exhibition catalogue, Musée du Luxembourg, Paris, 9 October 2014 – 8 February 2015; National Gallery, London, 4 March – 31 May 2015; Philadelphia Museum of Art, Philadelphia, 24 June – 13 September 2015 (Paris: RMN, Musée du Luxembourg and Sénat, 2014), pp. 116–19.

42 This was notably the case with Monet, who after seeming reticent about seeing his works go to the United States, maintained direct relationships with American collectors, as proved notably by his letters with John Singer Sargent, Cornebois auction, lots 301–15, 142–47.

43 Even if the distinction is not always easy to make, the major tours organised by the museums, whether within a promotional framework or due to closures for building works, have not been taken into account in this selection.

44 *La Collection Courtauld: Le parti de l'impressionnisme*, exhibition catalogue, Fondation Louis Vuitton, Paris, 20 February – 17 June 2019 (London-Paris: The Courtauld Gallery and Fondation Louis Vuitton, 2019); Anne Baldassari (ed.), *Icônes de l'art moderne: la collection Chtchoukine*, exhibition catalogue, Fondation Louis Vuitton, Paris, 22 October 2016 – 20 February 2017 (Paris: Gallimard, 2016); *Collection Morozov. Icônes de l'art moderne*, exhibition catalogue, Fondation Louis Vuitton, Paris, 22 September 2021 – 22 February 2022 (Paris: Gallimard and Fondation Louis Vuitton, 2021).

45 Marianne Mathieu and Claire Durand-Ruel Snollaerts (eds.), *Collections privées: un voyage des impressionnistes aux fauves*, exhibition catalogue, Musée Marmottan Monet, Paris, 13 September 2018 – 10 February 2019 (Vanves-Paris: Hazan and Musée Marmottan Monet, 2018); *Les impressionnistes en privé: cent chefs-d'oeuvre de collections particulières*, exhibition catalogue, Musée Marmottan Monet, Paris, 13 February – 6 July 2014 (Paris: Hazan, 2014).

46 Marianne Mathieu and Dominique Lobstein (eds.), *Monet collectionneur*, exhibition catalogue, Musée Marmottan Monet, Paris, 14 September 2017 – 14 January 2018 (Vanves-Paris: Hazan and Musée Marmottan Monet, 2017).

47 Marianne Mathieu (ed.), *Julie Manet: la mémoire impressionniste*, exhibition catalogue, Musée Marmottan Monet, Paris, 19 October 2021 – 20 March 2022 (Vanves-Paris: Hazan and Musée Marmottan Monet, 2021).

48 Marina Ferretti-Bocquillon and Charlotte Hellman (eds.), *Signac collectionneur*, exhibition catalogue, Musée d'Orsay, Paris, 12 October 2021 – 13 February 2022 (Paris: Gallimard, 2021).

IMPRESSIONISM AT HOME: "THE BEST EXHIBITION IS THE ONE THAT TAKES PLACE IN THE *AMATEUR*'S APARTMENT"*

SÉGOLÈNE LE MEN

One of Jean Renoir's childhood memories is a reminder of how important it was for him living every day with his father's paintings on the walls, and he was surprised to find them elsewhere, in the homes of collectors:

> My father's paintings, covering the walls of our apartment, were for me an indispensable part of the decor of my young life. They simply had to be there. When my mother took me to a collector's house, I was shocked to discover the paintings I had seen at home hung in foreign territory. In my father's kingdom, which was also my mother's and Bibon's [Gabrielle], these bouquets, these nudes, these landscapes were as much at home as the door handles, the umbrella stand in the antechamber, the cane chairs from Thonet's and the oil lamp.[1]

Further on, he continues: "I did not look at my father's paintings, but I felt their presence. I knew that if I was deprived of them, it would cause a kind of cataclysm, an earthquake, a flood, a plague of locusts, even the disappearance of my father, my mother and Gabrielle".[2] As recent research and exhibitions have shown, this "presence" of Impressionist painting has left a long-lasting impact on his work as a filmmaker. In this essay, I would like to focus on the life of these object-paintings at home, especially in collectors' homes: compared to the relationship established between museums and visitors, which is mainly of an aesthetic nature, the inhabitants of collectors' homes perceived these pieces of art in a very different way.

Object-paintings at homes are a field of analysis and research in its own right – hard to document because it does not only relate to the history of tastes and art but is also linked to affect, sensibilities, periods of life, gender and family relationships as much as the sociology of collectors and lifestyles

– which also applies to a collector's home. The aforementioned quote by Jean Renoir exemplifies this idea. How do you live with Impressionist paintings, how do you make a collection? How is their "presence" felt? Aside from this complex issue, there are many questions relating to the history of interior decoration,[3] like those revolving around displaying and collecting the pieces: how were Impressionist collections exhibited at home? This subject has been barely explored, despite its importance for material culture and private life, but also for the history of collections – etymologically defined as a group of objects gathered in the same place – not to mention its relevance for the cultural history of looking at works of art, and finally, for the study of Impressionism. It would be premature to put forward a synthesis straight away, and unrealistic to attempt it within the scale of an article. After initially offering a more general overview, I will focus on this question based on two case studies chosen from the period when Impressionism was still an art intended for private collections, connected to the market but also seeking the acknowledgement of museums: the collection of the art dealer Durand-Ruel in 1891 and Moreau-Nélaton's collection which he donated to the Louvre in 1907.

"The Making of a Collection": Preliminary Remarks

In the same way that today we are interested in the "display" of exhibition and museum presentations archived with the help of photography – whether it be the case of temporary exhibitions that have led to the creation of jobs such as scenographer, or of museums that make use of museology – I suggest we look here at the "making of a collection" (*mise en collection*); it can be understood as one of the modalities of displaying and refers to the way in which artworks existed and were presented at home, in a collector's house or apartment. Throughout the Impressionist years and the decades that followed, the principle of displaying was based on conventions which varied depending on the space and which were undergoing a complete transformation both in terms of the way works were hung and visit itineraries arranged. Thus, to understand how collections were formed during this period, it is essential to offer a broader overview of the different modalities of displaying, exploring them both in a diachronic and synchronic context.

The diachronic context: amateur cabinets and paper collections

The history of display has seen some important changes over time which were initially linked to the shift from cabinets of curiosities to art collections. This practice was a royal and princely privilege in court society which

was democratised within bourgeois circles as early as the first half of the nineteenth century, whilst at the time of the French Revolution, royal and Church collections had become national treasures. The multiplication of collections had begun earlier and by the end of the Ancien Régime, both categories existed simultaneously. For instance, the unpublished *Journal* of Madame de Genlis lists, from 1785 to 1791, all of the places – artist studios like David's at the Louvre, aristocratic collections, churches, pre-auction exhibitions – which she visited with her pupils, the children of Orléans, to whom she was "governess", and among whom was the future King Louis-Philippe. Thus, private collections and cabinets – most often of paintings, but sometimes also of "shells" (*coquilles*) or "stones" (*cailloux*) – were accessible to the family of the Duke of Orléans, whose own gallery at the Palais-Royal was quite remarkable.[4]
The pictorial genre of the "amateur cabinet" allows us to understand this sociological change in "collectionism", whereby the aristocratic version of David Téniers the Younger in seventeenth-century Holland contrasts with the bourgeois version of Honoré Daumier in the nineteenth century: on the one hand, Archduke Leopold Wilhelm of Austria, to whom Téniers was the private curator, found himself depicted surrounded by his collections, in an interior covered in paintings, and where there are still certain elements of a cabinet of curiosities, calling on all of the senses. Despite appearances, this was not about depicting a display in a real space, but about constructing a mental space, a memory image (following the traditional mnemotechnics that Francis Yates has analysed in *The Art of Memory*, 1966): this enabled the entire inventory of the collection to be brought together in one single painting[5] and thus gave an empathetic representation of his patron (fig. 1). In 1979, Georges Pérec wrote a head-spinning novel, precisely entitled *Un cabinet d'amateur*,[6] where the author uses an interminable list of catalogues and descriptions, parodying art historians, to endlessly describe an imaginary painting inspired by the genre,[7] devoted to celebrating a splendid collection put up for auction, but which turns out at the very end of the novel to be a pictorial mystification, nothing more than a collection of fake paintings.
On the other hand, shortly after Balzac had introduced the collector character into literature in 1847 in *Le Cousin Pons*,[8] this genre saw an unusual revival in the *Connoisseurs* series, created by Daumier in the early 1860s, at a time when he had been banished from the *Charivari* and was earning his living painting highly accomplished watercolours which Degas, a great collector of Daumier himself, would later define as "articles" intended for "amateurs". Far from being visual inventories of collections, Daumier's *Connoisseurs* belonged to the vein of the physiological genre and sought to reveal a posture, a *habitus*, that of the collector. Sitting comfortably in his

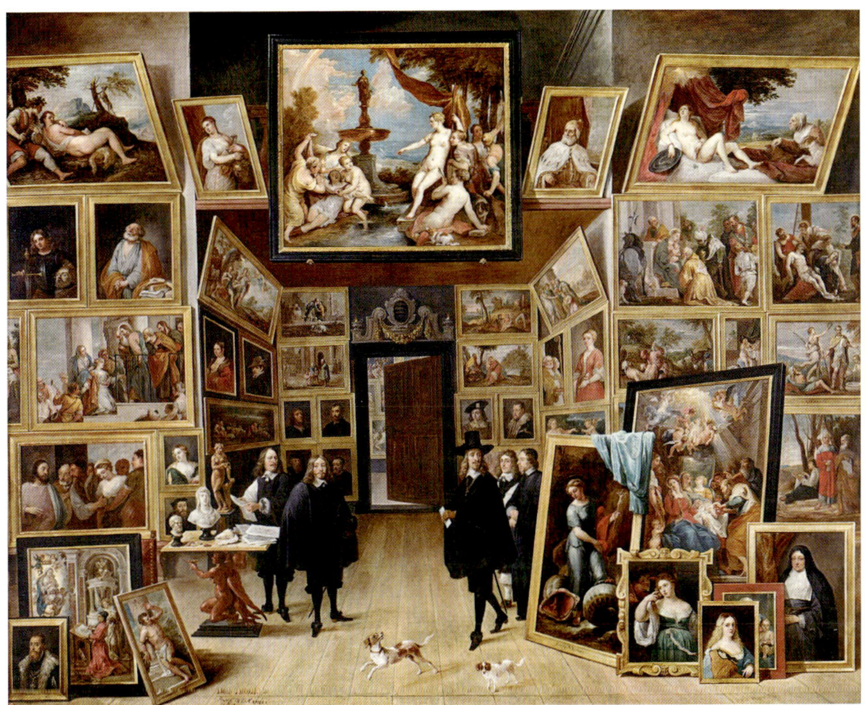

1. David Téniers the Younger, *Archduke Leopold Wilhelm of Austria in His Painting Gallery in Brussels* (*L'Archiduc Léopold-Guillaume dans sa galerie de peinture à Bruxelles*), oil on copper, between 1647 and 1651, 104.8 × 130.4 cm, Museo Nacional del Prado, Madrid, P001813

armchair, the collector revels in the collection surrounding him like a shell, handling a statuette of the Venus de Milo to better signify his visual and tactile pleasure (fig. 2). These watercolours do not show in detail the works exhibited in the background. They are impossible to identify and we only see the arrangement, the scale and the frame, but not the subject nor the style, even though we can sometimes make out the genre (mostly landscapes). Engraved versions of how private collections were displayed led to "paper collections", of which one of the prototypes was the recently studied Düsseldorf Gallery.[9] In court society, they had an ostentatious and demonstrative double function, and the Düsseldorf Gallery, which proposed hanging diagrams as well as engraved reproductions of paintings, used them to promote a model for museographic displays for princely collections, of a gallery naturally lit from above like the one found in the Duke of Leuchtenberg's gallery of engravings in Munich.[10] Téniers the Younger devoted himself to creating such a "paper collection" based on engraved reproductions of art-

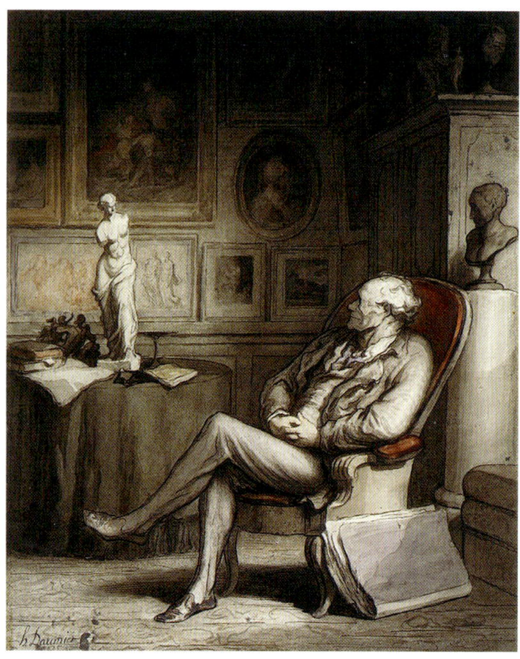

2. Honoré Daumier, *The Amateur* (*L'Amateur*), c. 1860–65, pen and ink, wash, watercolour, lithographic chalk and gouache, signed in ink, on the bottom left, "h. Daumier", The Metropolitan Museum of Art, New York (Jules Dupré Collection, bought at Durand-Ruel's by Louisine Havemeyer)

works, transposing them into a fictive space that, according to Malraux, was like an imaginary museum.[11] In the nineteenth century, paper collections,[12] initially engraved onto copper plates and often etched, multiplied thanks to the different techniques that simultaneously became available, such as lithography, etching and photography: they recorded the works and sometimes showed the modalities of display, by reflecting a change in the paradigm which was marked by a shift from an "edge-to-edge" presentation, inherited from the Salon, towards a more airy form of hanging.

Where possible, it may be pertinent to consider the way Impressionist collections were displayed by using diachronic oppositions, in order to better understand these changes which concern not just the modalities of hanging, but also the sites of presentation, and allow us to realise how Impressionism was included in a longer history of art. Collectors were not the only ones concerned and other actors in the art world were involved: the artists themselves (either in their studios or in the salons and exhibitions they organised) and gallery owners were looking to show their paintings in displays that suggested how they could be installed at home. This was even more so as in a period when those involved in the artworld often played multiple roles at the same time: the role of collector could be combined with several others and could change over time. Painters like Bazille, Degas,[13] Monet[14] or Cassatt – who acted as an intermediary with American collectors, in particular the Havemeyers[15] – and De Nittis, as evoked by Fausto Minervini, were collectors themselves; in turn, some collectors, today increasingly well-known, were also painters: Henri Rouart[16] and Gustave Caillebotte,[17] who were part of the movement, or Étienne Moreau-Nélaton, whom I will come back to later, as well as Fayet, whose case has been studied here by Alexandre d'Andoque.[18] Paul Valéry, for example, described the layout of Degas's home-studio in Rue Victor Massé:

> On the first floor, he had displayed his "museum", made up of several paintings he bought with his own money or obtained through trades. His apartment was on the second floor. On the walls, he had displayed his favourite artworks, his own or by others: a large and very beautiful Corot, some drawings by Ingres, and one special study of a dancer that aroused my jealousy every time without fail.[19]

As for Monet, he had exhibited his paintings in the studio he shared with Bazille early on in his career,[20] and later presented them himself to his visitors, spread out around the different areas of his Giverny house,[21] as he explained to Marcel Tendron.[22] The most beloved part of his collection could be found in his bedroom whilst Japanese prints decorated the dining room, and his own paintings, along with the other works in the collection, were hung throughout the rest of the house.

The synchronic context: graphic, photographic and written representation of collections

The rise of the press made the history of displaying works of art part of media culture, at a time when the private sphere was arousing growing interest and when interior decorating was becoming a hobby, reflected by a new publishing sector: some magazines presented visits to collections in the form of serialised articles, where text and image went hand in hand, or, like *La Gazette des beaux-arts*, offered their readers written reports of major collections according to a model which can also be found in book format, for example in the 1867 *Paris Guide*.[23] These illustrated visits can be compared to the journalistic genre of "visits to-illustrious figures", which had started during the July Monarchy, and gained popularity through a series of articles published with photographs by Dornac (anagram and pseudonym of Paul Cardon), *Nos contemporains chez eux* (from 1889), and Henri Mairet, in particular in the subseries *Une heure chez...*, published by the *Revue illustrée* from 1891 onwards:[24] and so, they were concerned with giving the reader the impression of actually meeting the artist, writer[25] or great man "in slippers", of getting to know them better by entering the studio or home of the person presented through the textual medium, thus paving the way for the development of house-museums, as Elisabeth Emery[26] and Marie-Clémence Régnier have paralleled with writers.[27] Similar reportages have been carried out on collectors, identified as key players in the artworld, and have even led to a section in the magazine edited by the art dealer and publisher of art reproductions, Goupil, *Les Arts, revue mensuelle des Musées, Collections, Expositions* from 1902 to 1920 (excluding 1914 and 1916): a close study from 1902 to 1907 is disappointing because the collector turned out to be less important than the pieces in his collection, and the accent was never placed on Impressionism, even for figures of collectors who were interested in the movement: for instance, two articles focused on the presentation of Jean Dollfus' collections, but they were limited to old masters and stopped at Corot.[28] Nevertheless Anne Distel devoted a chapter of her book on collectors of impressionism to him[29] and Dollfus had figured on the list Duret made of the first patrons (*amateurs*) of the movement: "Messrs. d'Auriac, Étienne Baudry, de Belio [*sic*], Charpentier, Choquet [*sic*], Deudon, Dollfus, Faure, Murer, de Rasty".[30] This broad focus, and omission, says a lot about the reservations that still persisted towards the "new painting" among the readers of the luxury art magazine, although the same cannot be said for the two obituaries of collectors of impressionist art in the *Bulletin de la vie artistique* of the Bernheim-Jeune Gallery.[31] Finally, we can see that out of 24 descriptions read out between 1902 and 1931 at the annual general assembly of the Société des Amis du Louvre, only two of them mentioned collectors-donators of Impressionism: in 1913 *Le Comte Isaac de Camondo*, by Gasteon Migeon, and in 1927 Étienne Moreau-Nélaton, by Raymond Koechlin, its president, himself a collector-donator of decorative arts (Japanese, Chinese, Islamic, mediaeval arts) and Impressionist painting.[32] For many years, collecting Impressionism remained a daring choice, one of personal taste, and the question has to be asked as to how Impressionist works fitted into the rest of a collection, how it found its place in the layout of an interior, how it cohabitated with decorative arts.

The photographs of the interiors of Impressionist collectors have not been published (with a couple of exceptions) and have remained quite rare because they were of a private nature. They have however proven to be an essential source which demands some explanation in order to be fully understood. Although Degas painted the portrait of his friend and patron the manufacturer Henri Rouart on several occasions, it was only through the photographic medium that Rouart was shown at home. He was represented in front of the works in his collection which were hard to identify in the background of a beautiful photo portrait. It remained in the family and was annotated on the back by the model's grandson, Gabriel Rouart who had it in his possession: "photo of my great-grandfather Henri Rouart taken and developed by Degas in 1907 (sic for 1895) at H. Rouart's 24 Rue de Lisbonne

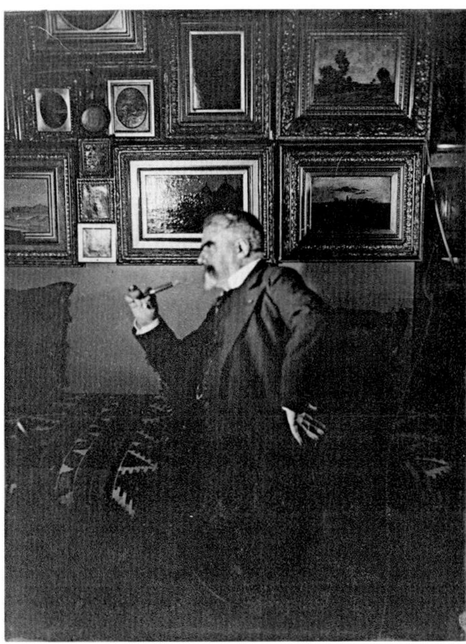

3. Edgar Degas, *Henri Rouart (1833–1912) at Home* (*Henri Rouart [1833–1912] chez lui*), 1895, silver gelatin print from glass negative, enlargement by Tasset, 37.5 × 27.5 cm, Musée d'Orsay, Paris

where my father Olivier Rouart was born" and "on the wall paintings by his friends Corot, Daumier, Degas, Renoir" (fig. 3).

The Impressionism period and the decades that followed affirmed the choice of art collections where painting prevailed, dominated at a time when what Bernard Vouilloux called the "tournant artiste" of literature took place:[33] the publication of *La Maison d'un artiste* by Edmond de Goncourt in 1881[34] was a determining moment in this regard. The writer took his readers on a room by room visit of his house at Auteuil, right down to the famous "attic"; even though the book was not illustrated, a group of photographs was found and completed the history of his house. It preceded *À rebours* by Huysmans in 1884, a manifest for the Decadent movement in which the hero Des Esseintes abandons travel and the outside world, taking refuge in his home, surrounded by some suggestive works of art: the collection is presented in textual form and as Dominique Pety shows, spreads out throughout the novel, becoming literature, according to modalities which shifted from the collection-document to the art collection.[35] This turning point in literary history (which included Georges Lecomte, the man who described Durand-Ruel's collection, and extended as far as Pérec) is also the moment when collectors saw themselves as artists, which was a challenge for many collectors of Impressionism, contemporaries of naturalism and the Decadent movement. Other less literary texts offer just as many, often disseminated clues that tell us a lot about what the collection meant to the collector.

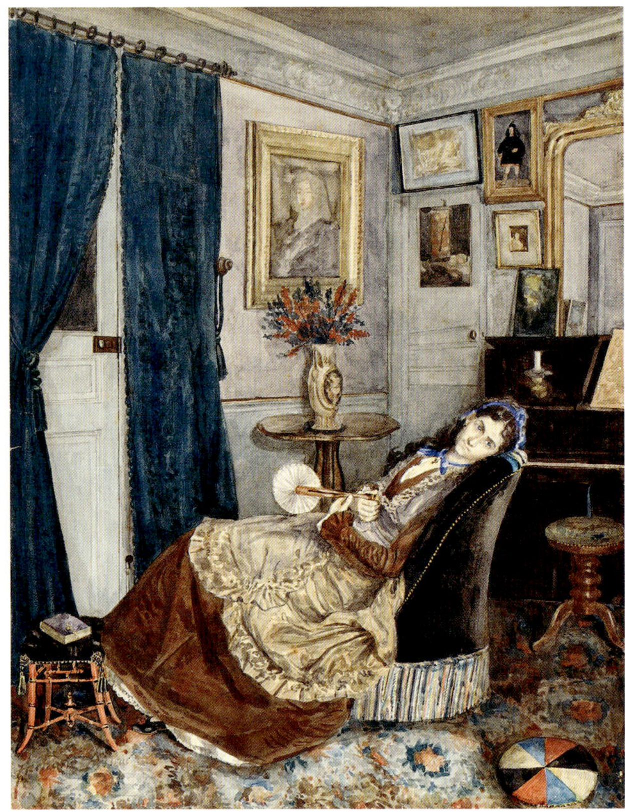

4. Zacharie Astruc, *Parisian Interior* (*Intérieur parisien*), 1874, watercolour, 36 × 28 cm, Musée de l'ancien Evêché, Evreux (shown at the first Impressionist exhibition)

These initial elements have highlighted the types of sources that enabled me to develop the analysis of the subjective signification of collections at home. It is not just about graphic or photographic representations of displays, but also about texts that reported the collector's *parole*, that is speech as an expression of subjectivity, whether it be relayed by someone else or expressed by the individuals themselves, sometimes in a disjointed manner. It would also appear that the making of a collection is a personal undertaking based on the history of private lives. It was intrinsically linked, not just to the history of interior decoration, but also to the history of imaginary museums, to the transformations of media, and finally to the presence or absence of Impressionism in museums.

Impressionism: painting for apartments

By looking to distinguish themselves from the Salon, the Impressionists, who liked to depict their private lives in their paintings, both in small format works or genre scenes, established in 1874 – and afterwards – the principles of display for apartments; these principles were wished for by Degas, among others, as early as 1870, in a letter addressed to the jury of the Salon,[36] in which lighting was important, where the works were spaced out, and not in competition with each other. The Impressionists offered amateurs not just a "new painting" but also a new way of living alongside the paintings in Haussmann's urban Parisian housing. And reciprocally, as the physicist Helmholtz reminded us in his lecture on optics and painting, translated in 1876, painting had to blend with the lighting offered by these contemporary interiors.[37] Nadar's former apartment-studio was chosen by the Impressionists as exhibition space, which exemplifies these principles. There, Nadar had exhibited his private collection of paintings from the Barbizon generation (from Corot to Daumier), surrounded by knick-knacks, thus evoking a kind of "collectionism" similar to Champfleury's. The photographer's apartment was one of the first to have an elevator in Paris, validating the experience of seeing from a height reconstructed in both of Monet's *Boulevard des Capucines*.

> The paintings – wrote the art critic Philippe Burty – were presented much to their advantage; lit more or less like in an ordinary apartment, individually, not too many of them, they were not disadvantaged by their overly loud or drab neighbours.[38]

These modalities of display are conceptualised in the last of six watercolours from the "cadre de figures" by Zacharie Astruc,[39] *Parisian Interior* (*Intérieur parisien*) (fig. 4), where the works of art on the wall are part of the layout "*chez soi*" or in the private "home", *heim* in German,[40] where "the discreet machinery of comfort" is played out.[41] We can see a young woman in an intimate and cosy corner of an apartment, fan in her hand, faced turned toward the spectator, comfortably sitting in a small armchair covered in taupe-coloured velvet, her feet resting on a vaguely Japanese-inspired footstool, with a book nonchalantly left on it. Behind her is a pedestal table with a bouquet in a decorated porcelain vase, and part of a piano with a small frameless painting placed on it, and a gilt moulded mirror reflecting the rest of the room, where we can make out another painting. On the floor, there is a colourful patterned rug with a round cushion resembling a colour wheel, harmonising with the hues of this feminine boudoir with its double doors protected by Prussian blue velvet tenting, pulled back on one side. On the wall, there is a half-length portrait of a woman in a large gilded frame on one side, and on the other, a watercolour and an engraving with Mariette blue and white mounts, black frame, as well as a small, framed painting and another engraving without a frame. This watercolour depicts the wellbeing of the "upper class" homeowner, an amateur in the arts she practices and collects, safe in her home, daydreaming, far from the noise and agitation of the big city.

1892: at Paul Durand-Ruel's home

The great Impressionism art dealer, Paul Durand-Ruel (1831–1922), son and grandson of art dealers whose gallery had moved from Rue Saint-Jacques to Rue des Petits-Champs, then Rue de la Paix and finally Rue Laffitte, embraced this choice of home collections in a rather original manner. He wrote a letter to Monet in 1885, renouncing the idea of exhibitions, too costly and not very profitable:

> Moreover, I believe that the best exhibition is the one that takes place in the *amateur's* apartment. Since I have begun inviting a lot of people to Rue de Rome, it's something of a revelation for most of them who had never seen your paintings look so good.[42]

Located near Saint-Lazare station, on the third floor at number 35, Rue de Rome, the gallerist's own apartment – the one where he lived and, recently widowed, raised his five children – was open to amateurs, in an attempt to convince and charm them, by illustrating an *art de vivre* with the Impressionist collection. As he explained himself on 30 July 1884, the family apartment was also used as a showroom for the gallery, still in Rue Laffitte: "I spent three hours with capitalists whom I was trying to convince and persuade to follow me. I took them to Rue de Rome and there, they feasted on painting. This is where I can obtain the best results".[43] The apartment could be visited on prior request, every afternoon in 1898, then from 2 pm to 4 pm on Tuesdays in 1901, the day the museums were closed.[44] In short, his home "was a precious business tool for Durand-Ruel, who hosted there, invited people to dine, presented works in a living context and thus tried to win over his clients".[45] It was at the end of a meal that Duncan Phillips expressed his desire and obtained at a very high price Renoir's *Luncheon of the Boating Party* (*Le Déjeuner des canotiers*), opposite which he had luncheoned!

The Photographed Apartment

We know what the apartment looked like thanks to some photographs showing the reception rooms, with the small and large drawing room as well as the office, the working area which was open to the clientele, and the dining room, another space for entertaining.[46] In one of the main reception rooms (fig. 5), its doors decorated with panels by Monet, we can see a corner of the room with walls painted in a dark hue; the *Dance in the City* (*Danse à la ville*) by Renoir appears in full light near the door on the wall facing the windows, not far from the slightly smaller *Dancers* (*Danseuses*) by Degas on the other

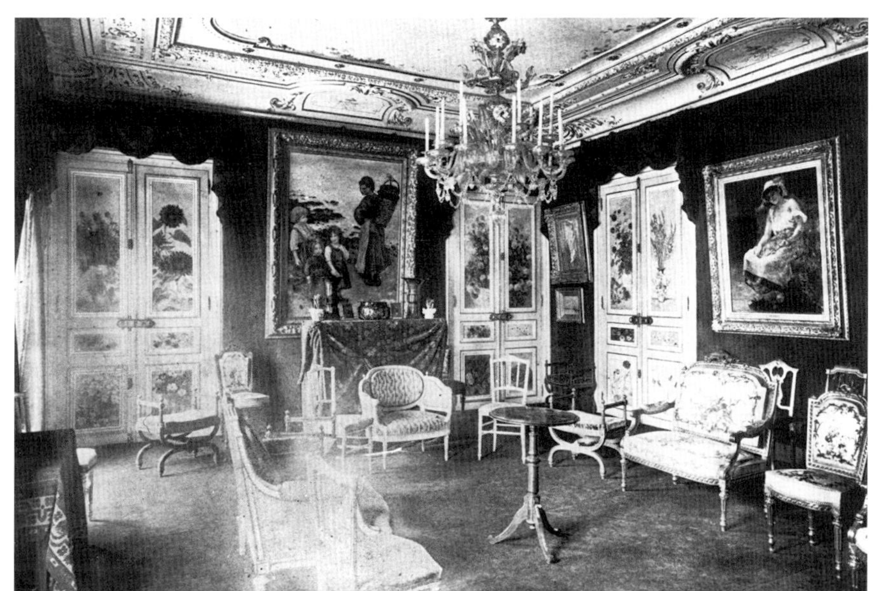

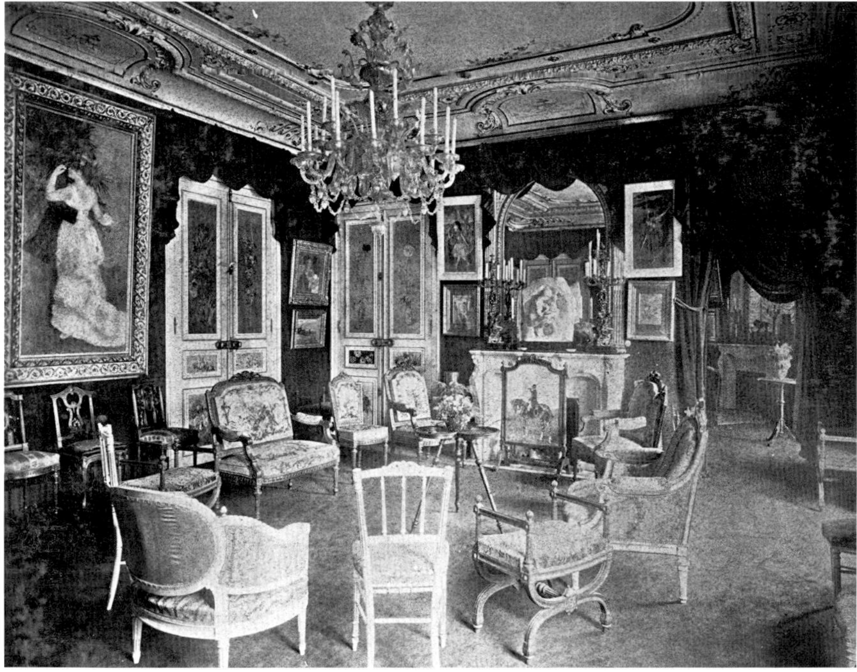

5. Anonymous, two views Paul Durand-Ruel's main drawing room, Paul Durand-Ruel's apartment, 35, Rue de Rome, Paris, c. 1900–10, modern print, Archives Durand-Ruel, Paris

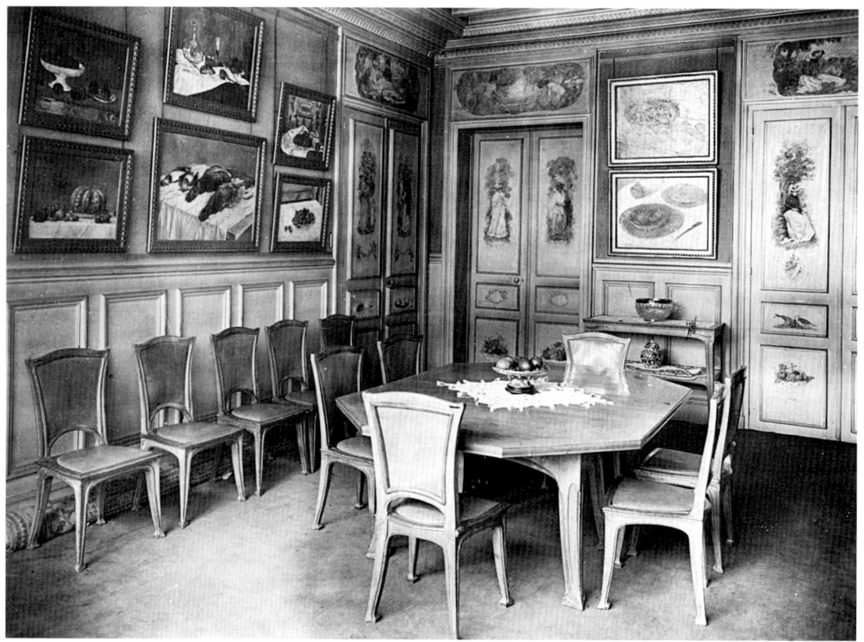

6. *Joseph Durand-Ruel's dining room at Rue de Rome*, photograph, Archives Durand-Ruel (from the *1874 Hommage à Paul Durand-Ruel Cent ans d'impressionnisme* exhibition catalogue, Galerie Durand-Ruel, Paris, 1974, exhibition from 15 January to 15 March 1974)

wall near the fireplace. The paintings are accentuated by rectilinear, gilded frames, in a simpler style for Degas and more ornate for Renoir. The room is decorated with Louis XVI-style (the banquette, placed in front of the double doors, and the armchairs upholstered in Aubusson tapestry, as well as the wingchair and the curule footstool), and Louis XV-style furniture (for the lyre-back chairs placed near the wall). A large Murano glass chandelier hangs from the painted ceiling with its stucco mouldings and *fin-de-siècle* decor. There is an earthenware pot next to the fireplace with a trumeau mirror that reflects the room and makes it appear bigger. Placed on the fireplace are two candelabra with a marble sculpture by Rodin in the middle.[47] The hearth is hidden behind a tapestry fire screen. A vase of flowers is placed on a small pedestal table. The seating – armchairs, banquette and chairs – form a circle, ready to welcome guests, and despite the unity of style create a rather disparate ensemble, giving this solemn drawing room a more homely atmosphere. On the right, a door decorated with tenting opens out to a second drawing room. Impressionism seems at home in this eighteenth-century-style decor, in fashion at the time.[48]

Other photographs of his son and partner Joseph Durand-Ruel's apartment, situated at the same address, shows Impressionism in a more modern setting (fig. 6): we can recognise the Charles Plumet and Tony Selmersheim furniture in the dining room, decorated with magnificent still-lifes by Monet, and the painted decor on the door panels by Albert André, echoing those by Monet in his father's apartment.

The illustrated book as an imaginary museum of an Impressionist art collection

In 1892, Durand-Ruel also made his home known to a public of amateurs in a publication paid for at his own expense. This refined illustrated book written by George Lecomte called *L'art impressionniste, d'après la collection privée de M. Durand-Ruel*,[49] a limited deluxe edition,[50] in which the major paintings were reproduced in etching or drypoint in black ink, sanguine (with variations in the inking) and, in one case, Prussian blue.
This imaginary museum of an art-dealer well-established in both Europe and the United States resulted in an "armchair collection", "collection dans un fauteuil," to follow's Musset's expression, which allowed readers to enjoy a virtual visit from a distance. The paintings were translated into etchings, a medium that perfectly adapted the rapid, fragmented brushstrokes of the Impressionists into tiny etched lines. The subtle inking process was entrusted to Lauzet, a younger painter-engraver, who died soon after the publication of the book; he also designed the ornamentation with floral motifs (head pieces and tail-pieces). The 1892 book, subdivided into chapters decorated with head pieces, ornamented letters, decorative tail-pieces by Lauzet (also the author of the engraved plates) echoed the naturalist decorative theme of the dining room by Monet. Durand-Ruel's book took for granted the victory of the Impressionists and, whilst reworking Goncourt's model of *La Maison d'un artiste* (1881), adapted it to a symbolist vision of Impressionist art. Interspersed between the chapters, or among them, preceding or following the poetic *ekphrasis* of the paintings, the engravings gave the reading rhythm. The writings added a touch of colour and substance to the monochrome engravings: text and images complemented each other and gave the presentation a certain fluidity. Lecomte took the reader on a tour of the apartment: the symbolist narration was punctuated with plates, echoing the hanging of the paintings, thus emphasising the overall effect and general atmosphere unique to Impressionist collections presented at home.
The 1892 book differed from the two previous books published by the gallery on its own collection, *Galerie Durand-Ruel. Specimens les plus brillants de l'école moderne* (1845)[51] and *Galerie Durand-Ruel* (1873).[52] Their func-

tion had been to offer an "imaginary" (and real) museum from the gallerist's stock or works he had been able to sell. Lecomte's *L'art imppressionniste*, added a new objective: to recreate the effect of a complete collection at home through the intermediary of the book-object and literary text, complemented by etched plates, and focusing only on "Impressionist art". Even though the 1873 album was referred to by Lecomte as an antecedent to this one, the "new painting" Durand-Ruel had discovered in London before the invention of the term "Impressionism" was integrated to the history of the French modern school, in a continued entanglement from Romanticism to the École de Barbizon.[53]

Georges Lecomte's interpretation of the collection

With its promotional objective, Lecomte inscribed himself within the "dealer-critic system", with a text offered as "a history of Impressionism". In doing so, he emulated the writings of Duret and Geffroy. Lecomte's history of the movement was based on the collection of the main art dealer who supported the impressionism, in contrary to the Musée du Luxembourg which denied it any value:

> Mr Durand-Ruel has done what the State, disdainful of new art, has been unable to do. For his own pleasure and the charm of his home's interior, with the constant passion of an enlightened amateur, he has brought together paintings which best represent the talent of these painters. He has created the most wonderful museum of contemporary painting that exists in France.[54]

The majority of the book aimed to present the paintings belonging to this "enlightened amateur", which readers discovered through texts and monographic chapters, alternating with chapters describing the rooms in the apartment. This was a way of showing, through this exceptional case, how Impressionist paintings could form a collection, echo each other as a collection, without mentioning the furnishings or the appearance of the apartment (which however are documented in photographs): this was a collection-museum, but without labels, where precise titles were rare and dates were missing.
The study was decorated by the "exquisiteness [of Pissarro's] chromatic symphonies", with its colourful shadows (p. 79), where we can "imagine ourselves in the countryside on intimate, verdant trails, amidst endless fields, among grasses and foliage" (p. 77). This immersion into nature was also rendered through decorative ornamentation: "These natural harmonies sing softly on the wall of the study. It looked like a window opening out onto rus-

tic landscapes ... Mr Pissarro modifies his lines towards ornamentation. His highly descriptive drawing is still so magnificently decorative" (p. 78). Thus, the panel in the collector's house allowed nature and decor, as well as wall and painting, to merge, taking us back to the question of Impressionism as decorative art explored by Marine Kisiel.[55]

The next chapter, "Le petit salon de M. Durand-Ruel – Toiles de MM. Monet, Pissarro, La Femme au chat, de M. Renoir", created a kind of show playing with natural light: when one entered the room, the shift from obscurity to full daylight forced the eye to adjust; when the blinds were lifted, the spectacle of dawn, thematised in *Impression, Sunrise* (*Impression, soleil levant*) was repeated without the room:

> The lowered blinds maintain [the parlour] in a delicate half-light, and already the walls shimmer, glimmer, mysteriously dazzle. The enthusiastic, fresh tones is set alight. It felt like glimpses of radiant colours in the confusion of a dream: like the joy of a dawn attenuated by a subtle mist. But an opening is unveiled and the brightness of daylight spreads freely: suddenly, the invigorating tones burst into life. Twilights set ablaze on radiating seas. Behind the crest of the mountains, the fresh candour of dawn turns to pink ... All of a sudden, the star, for a long time veiled, shines with all its force, no longer blocked by the clouds. This golden shimmering revives the atmosphere of the Salon, warming the daylight. The tones of the painting are exalted in this splendour and, even more, unite in suave harmony.

In this central passage of the book, Lecomte showed how Impressionist painting could live and be transformed according to the "light" in the apartment, resulting in a poetic optical experience. He also adopted the almost cosmic tone of Gustave Geffroy, to whom he dedicated his work, in regards to Monet's haystacks: in the preface to the exhibition catalogue for *Les Meules* held in 1891 at Durand-Ruel's , which was re-printed in 1892 in the first series of *La Vie artistique*, the critic saw Monet as a painter who "constructed pieces of the planet on his paintings",[56] and who was "a great pantheist poet".[57] "A vision is refined and exalted", wrote Geffroy, "in this substance illuminated by embers, the bluish tips of flames, scattered sulphur and phosphorous, which make up the phantasmagoria of the countryside".[58]

The same notion of ensemble dominated in the evocation of the drawing room, where the muse celebrated by Renoir and Degas was the muse Terpsichore, goddess of dance. The chapter "Mr Durand-Ruel's grand drawing room-Decoration by Mr Claude Monet" continued the visit, punctuated with impressions of paintings including the one by Puvis de Chavannes, which proceeded "through syntheses and simplifications" (p. 185) in "distinguished eurythmies" (p. 187), along with those by Pissarro. Lecomte pondered a while

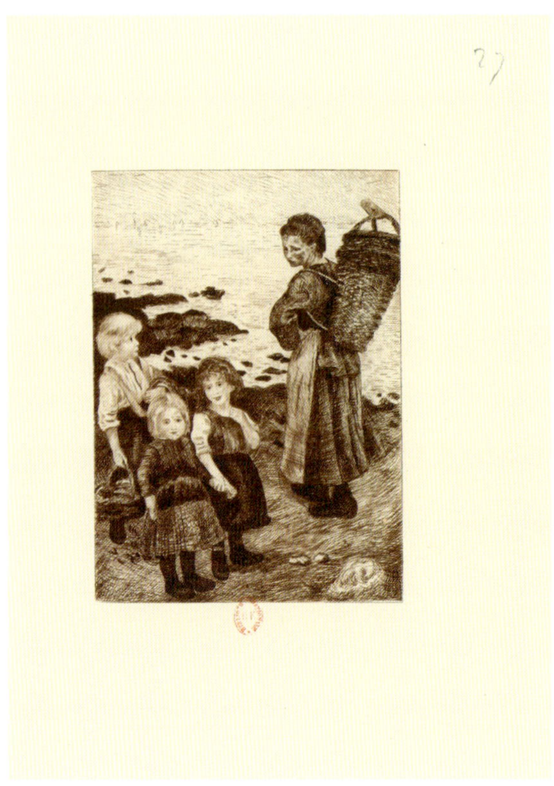

7. Marie-Auguste Lauzet, after Pierre-Auguste Renoir, *Fishermen by the Sea* [*Mussel-Fishers at Berneval*] (*Pêcheurs au bord de la mer* [*Pêcheuses de moules à Berneval, côte normande*]), 1879, oil on canvas, 176.2 × 130.2 cm, The Barnes Foundation, Philadelphia, BF989 (see fig. 21), etched plate, coloured print (sanguine), in Georges Lecomte, *L'art impressionniste, d'après la collection privée de M. Durand-Ruel, avec 36 eaux-fortes, pointes sèches et illustrations dans le texte de A.-M. Lauzet*, Typographie Chamerot et Renouard, Paris, 1892, p. 191 (see fig. 5)

on the main work in the room, etched by Lauzet (fig. 7),[59] *Mussel-Fishers at Berneval* (*Pêcheuses de moules à Berneval*) by Renoir (Barnes Foundation, fig. 21), which can be clearly seen in one of the photographs.[60] He interpreted the door panels and trumeaux painted by Monet – commissioned by Durand-Ruel in 1882, and developed over a long period by the painter who, arriving at Giverny in 1883, took three years to complete them – like a painted, decorative and polychrome "frame" whose flower and fruit motifs perfectly finished the ensemble, in continuity with its symphonic unity.

After the dining room, where Lecomte described at length its major work, *Dinner at Bougival* (*Le Souper à Bougival*) (now known as *Luncheon of the Boating Party*, The Phillips Collection), the visit gathers speed in the following chapters on "diverse other rooms" (p. 208) where painted studies were juxtaposed with graphic arts whilst notations, short or nominal sentences, separated by a full stop and a dash, followed the long *ekphrasei*, resulting in a syncopated rhythm. Such enumerations, so dear to Edmond de Goncourt, reinforced the effect of accumulation through asyndeta and through the use of indefinite articles in the plural form.

Lastly, *Tea* (*Thé*) by Mary Cassatt (today *The Cup of Tea* [*La Tasse de thé*], fig. 8) appeared in the antechamber "on the most brightly lit panel: a lady

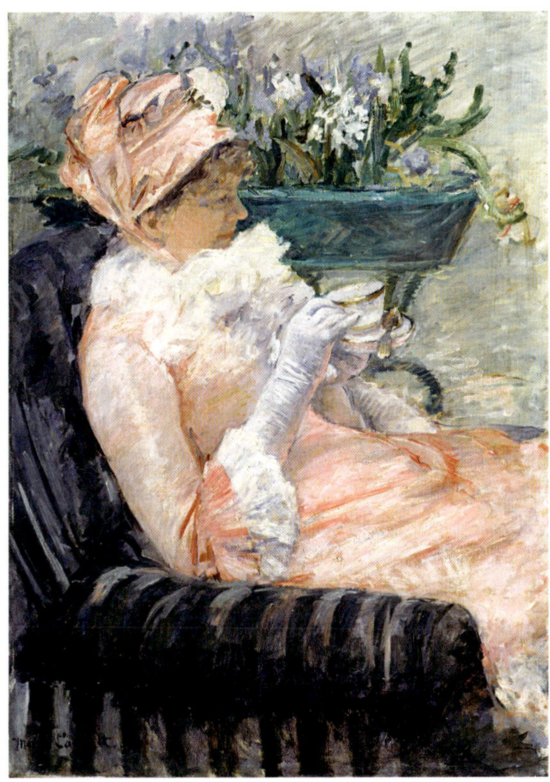

8. Mary Cassatt, *The Cup of Tea* (*La Tasse de thé*), 1880–81, oil on canvas, 92.4 × 65.4 cm, The Metropolitan Museum of Art, New York, 22.16.17, From the Collection of James Stillman, Gift of Dr Ernest G. Stillman, 1922

dressed in pink, sitting nonchalantly in a green armchair, holding a small teacup in her gloved hands. Some irises, hyacinths create a halo around her smiling face" (p. 254). Cassatt had presented this portrait of her sister Lydia, who frequently modelled for her and died prematurely in 1882, at the fourth and sixth Impressionist exhibitions in 1879 and 1881. Huysmans, in his account-promenade from 1881, had admired the mastery of the American woman painter trained by Degas, who rendered Parisian elegance so delicately, highlighting the relationship between the interior and the painting: "in her so Parisian apartments, she sets an atmosphere of feeling content 'at home'; in Paris, she expresses what none of our painters know how to express, that joyful peacefulness, the tranquil warmth of an interior".[61] This painting, *Tea*, comes last in the book and sums up and embodies the art of collecting Impressionism as a means of poeticising the interior, as reflected in Durand-Ruel's private collection according to Lecomte's analysis. The planter of hyacinths placed behind the young woman, these flowers transplanted into this *home*, remind us of one of the decorative constants, so recurrent in paintings, "filled with flowers", as on the doors painted by Monet and the ceiling ornamentation. This motif of cultivated flowers, in bouquets or pots, can also be found in the decorative system of the book itself, in

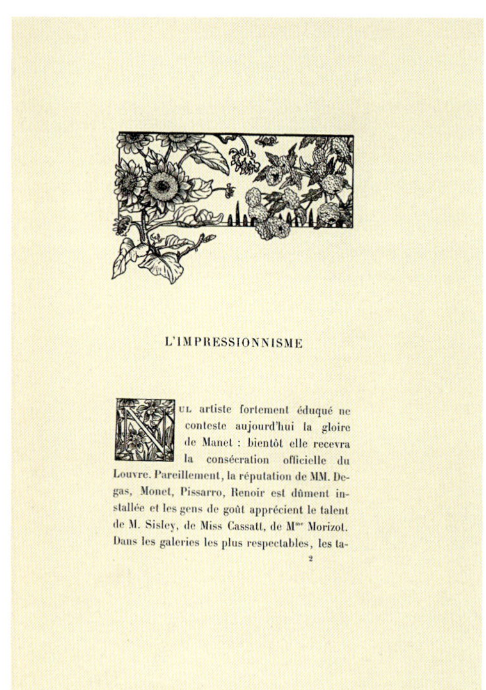

L'IMPRESSIONNISME

NUL artiste fortement éduqué ne conteste aujourd'hui la gloire de Manet : bientôt elle recevra la consécration officielle du Louvre. Pareillement, la réputation de MM. Degas, Monet, Pissarro, Renoir est dûment installée et les gens de goût apprécient le talent de M. Sisley, de Miss Cassatt, de Mme Morizot. Dans les galeries les plus respectables, les ta-

2

9. Marie-Auguste Lauzet, head-piece and ornamented letter "N" in Georges Lecomte, "L'impressionnisme", in *L'art impressionniste, d'après la collection privée de M. Durand-Ruel, avec 36 eaux-fortes, pointes sèches et illustrations dans le texte de A.-M. Lauzet*, Typographie Chamerot et Renouard, Paris, 1892

10. *Comte Isaac de Camondo's Degas drawing room, 82, Avenue des Champs-Elysées*, Paris, anonymous photograph, c. 1910

the head-pieces, ornamented letters and tail-pieces (fig. 9). The naturalistic "magic" of the apartment resided in the way the ensemble of the home collection offered these borders made of paintings that interacted with the interior light, creating a colourful and musical ambiance, whose symphonic harmony emanated from the reunited elements.

The layout of the apartment at Rue de Rome opened up a whole new range of possibilities for collectors. Firstly, the literary collection provided a project similar to an artistic creation which could be read as an analogy of the musical world: the collector was in some ways the composer or conductor. This approach, associating visual art and music, was announced in 1908 by the collector-composer Isaac de Camondo (1851–1911), and echoed by the photograph of the Degas drawing room taken at his home (fig. 10),[62] where the piano takes centre stage: "I have created my collection like one composes an opera",[63] he wrote. Secondly, the collection at the Rue de Rome also appeared as a decor for a French-style *art de vivre*, perfect for promoting the Impressionist movement across the world, and above all in the United States. The choice of the *Tea*, the stylish portrait by Miss Cassatt, who was Louisine Havemeyer's advisor, evokes the "two worlds" from Durand-Ruel's ephemeral advertising magazine launched in 1891, *L'Art dans les deux mondes*,[64] or Henry James's Parisian novels.

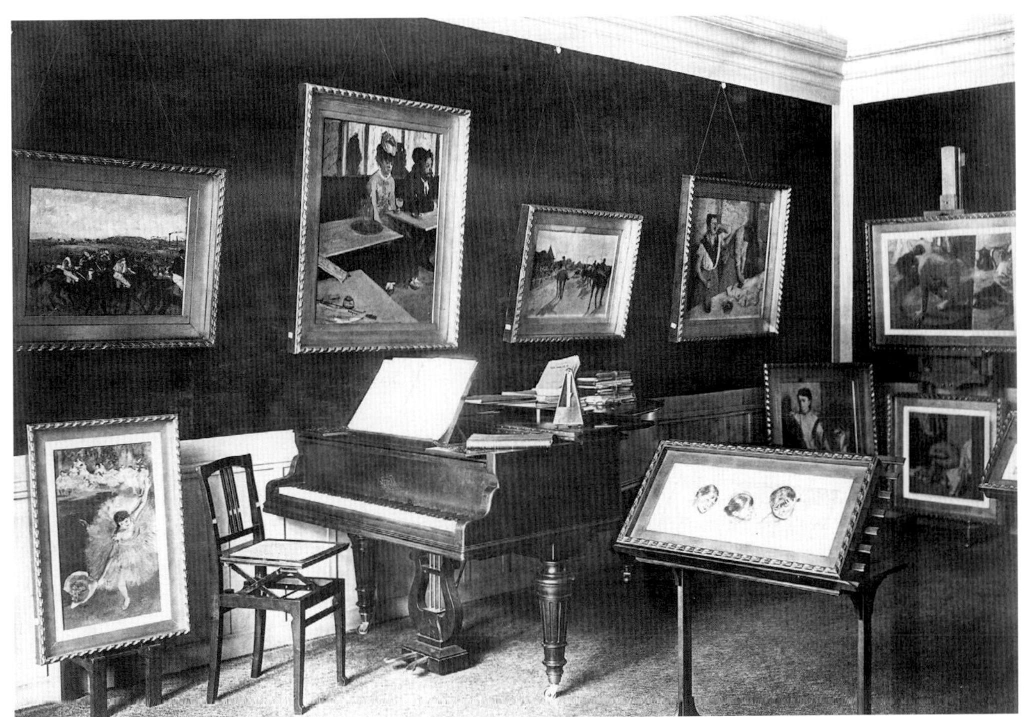

The Collection at Home: The Photographic Album of the Collector Étienne Moreau-Nélaton in 1907

Even though the idea of the collection, strongly rooted in the Impressionist painters, was used as a business model by their famous art dealer, it is clear that it was even more important for the collectors themselves, as we will see with the example of Étienne Moreau-Nélaton (1859–1927), which reveals the effects and significations of collections at home. Indeed, at a time when his prestigious collection was getting ready to leave the walls of his *hôtel particulier* and be donated to the State on 27 January 1906,[65] a group of photographs of his interior were taken, on his request, as a souvenir in January 1907. They were brought together in an album that remained in the family,[66] bound in red with Maroquin leather corners. Written on the back in gold letters was the address of the mansion and the year the photos were taken "73a Faubourg Saint-Honoré, 1907".[67] These photos (which can be compared to those showing the collection of his father, Adolphe Moreau) offer an unrivalled testimony for our research, and despite having been partially published, have not been analysed until now.[68] These photographs – which are paralleled with texts by the collector who was also the family memorialist and an art historian – express on the one hand how the collection was used as a reading of the place of Impressionism in the history of art, and on the other, the personal, complex uses of the collection at home, bringing together decorative and fine arts, as well as its autobiographical and commemorative significance.

Three generations of collectors

Before moving to the album, let us remember that the "Moreau collection", donated in 1907 and then exhibited and catalogued for museum purposes,[69] was built up over three generations of collectors. Even if Étienne's role was determining, this fact appeared to have been an essential factor in developing his vision of the donation which united Romanticism, the École de Barbizon, and Impressionism, also offering a reinterpretation of modern art up to Impressionism. Paul Durand-Ruel – who had inherited a business developed over three generations – found himself in a similar situation, thus confirming that is it important to take into the diachronic aspect of the history of nineteenth-century collections.
A rich stockbroker and passionate amateur, Adolphe Moreau the elder (1800–1859), Étienne's grandfather, remained friends with Delacroix throughout his life, compulsively collecting close to 800 contemporary paintings, from Romanticism to the École de Barbizon (some of which he had reproduced in a collection of lithographs). Adolphe Moreau the younger (1827–1882), Étienne's father, (1827–1882), who was a membre of the Conseil d'Etat and property manager, also had a taste for collecting but was more interested in the decorative arts and furniture: "He had a weakness for ancient-style furniture. He never tired of sculpted wooden buffets and tapestries lurking in second-hand furniture shops. Ceramics were one of his early passions", wrote his son. In *Mémorial de famille*, Etienne Moreau reproduced photographs where we can see two galleries, brightly lit from the ceiling[70] and two *salons*, reminiscent of an antique collector rather than a collector of paintings.[71] These images were taken as a souvenir the day before the move to the faubourg Saint-Honoré, an act documented in the 1907 set of photographs.[72] Adolphe Moreau the younger also had an album of around fifty photos printed using the Rousselon process, published by Goupil in 1871.[73] These pictures of the apartment looked like still-lives laid out in the main gallery; they were a prowess of photographic printing as much as a demonstration of an amateur's taste, based on the arrangement of pieces of art grouped together in a picturesque manner (in the sense of "like a painting"). He was also the author of catalogues raisonnés for Decamps (1869) and Delacroix (1873), the great figures of his own father's collection: as a child, Étienne, his son, saw him at work and thus discovered early the type of documentary art history he would practice later himself.

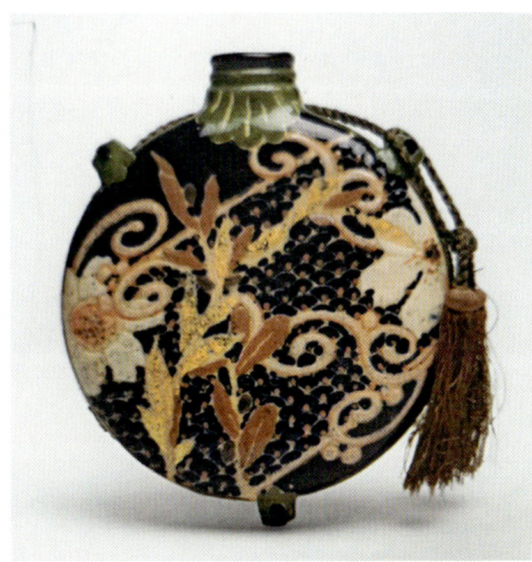

11. Camille Moreau-Nélaton, designer of the ceramics at François Laurin's, ceramicist, or for an unidentified Parisian ceramicist, *Gourd-shaped vase: flowers and scrolls* (*Gourde: fleurs et rinceaux*), 1888, private collection, France (visible in the first plate of the 1907 album, see fig. 12)

His mother, Camille (1840–1897), daughter of an illustrious surgeon, became a painter, encouraged on this path by her husband as soon as they were married. She was also a talented ceramicist, sometimes making pieces with her husband, as well as with Théodore Deck, inspired by their shared collections as well as her own albums of Japanese prints with flowers and birds, which today are recognised as important additions to the history of Japonism and Art Nouveau (fig. 11).[74]

For his part, Étienne Moreau-Nélaton, a student of the École Normale Supérieure and the famous class of 1878 (along with Jean Jaurès, Henri Bergson, Paul Desjardins, and André Mellerio...), had been lucky enough to train under Ernest Lavisse, before being drawn to painting; on Henri Harpignies's advice, he became both a painter and a pastel artist, engraver, lithographer and poster designer. Raised in rue Saint-Georges, he lived with his family and his mother in the *hôtel particulier* in Faubourg Saint-Honoré they had bought in 1880 and where they moved in 1881, a year before the death of his father, reproducing the appearance of the home in rue Saint-Georges where they had lived since 1860: "they endeavoured to recreate the aspect of their old drawing rooms in their new home. They grouped together the same paintings and furniture in the same manner".[75] After a terrible personal tragedy – the death of his mother and his wife Edmée, born Braun, in a fire at the Bazar de la Charité on 4 May 1897 – he became an art historian and collector; he began learning how to make ceramics, like his mother, and belonged to the group *L'Art dans tout*, with whom he exhibited posters and ceramics from 1897 onwards.[76]

The following week, he began acquiring works of art. He was determined to restructure the family collections in view of a donation of paintings to the State and, to collect the funds, he organised a large auction at Georges Petit's in 1900, accompanied by an illustrated sale catalogue.[77] This enabled him to

sort through the collections he had inherited and which he wanted to expand with the Impressionist paintings he loved so much. He rapidly formed his collection, leading to the donation in 1906, exhibited from 1907 at the Musée des Arts Décoratifs – entitled in the catalogue's unsigned preface (probably written by Raymond Koechlin, his longstanding friend), "a centennial in one hundred paintings" – then at the Louvre from 1933, and the Jeu de Paume for the Impressionist works from 1948, before moving to the Musée d'Orsay in 1986. The Corots and the École de Barbizon works have remained until today at the Louvre in their original frames, near the Thomy-Thierry collection.
Moreau-Nélaton, an iconophile passionate about photography, was a huge collector of drawings, albums, artists' sketchbooks, and painters' autographs. He was the first art historian to start a collection, from Delacroix to Manet, of textual documents and photographs which he used in his own books and bequeathed to the State in 1927. Among others, he donated the collection of Dornac's photographs of famous people in their interiors to the Bibliothèque Nationale, a pertinent theme for our discussion here.[78]

Three collections in one: The donation mentioned in the Mémorial

The collection donated to the State was the result of this privileged, yet later dramatic, family history: the *Mémorial de famille* written by Moreau-Nélaton for his children retraced the earlier events and successive moves, interwoven with anecdotes and family memories. Even though he had several photos from the photograph album printed, he did not mention it in the text, with only a discreet and laconic mention of the donation: "1906 / *July*. – Donated my collection of paintings to the State. This donation included pieces from my father's collection kept by myself and those I added myself".[79] This short commentary underscored the crossover of the collections, whilst at once indicated that the 1906 donor, Etienne, had chosen from the initial core which he had added to, so that the collection became a coherent and "personal" body of works, as he emphasised himself. The sole other mention relates to the auction held on 11–15 May 1900 at Petit's, which enabled this selection "of part of the paintings and pieces of art coming from [his] father's collection" and financed the new acquisitions: "I am keeping the major pieces; they make up the core of my personal collection, which is augmented each year with new acquisitions of modern paintings".[80]
There was only one copy of the 1907 photo album of the interior of the *hôtel particulier*, but another contemporary photographic campaign has allowed the majority of the works in the collection to be reproduced, among which the group of paintings from the donation in July 1906. The photographic reproductions of the paintings were conserved in three large albums. It is un-

doubtedly the "imaginary museum", of which a few examples still exist in the hands of the descendants.[81] These albums are mentioned in the footnotes of an article on his friend and collector Moreau-Nélaton by Frédéric Henriet (1826–1918) – painter employed by the department of fine arts, local scholar, and landscape painter from Château-Thierry.[82]

> Mr Moreau-Nélaton has had the works in the donation photographed by a skilled technician, Mr Yvon, with the intention of publishing a complete and detailed catalogue testifying, for the future, to the state of the collection at the time when he donation it to the Musée du Louvre and the importance of this group of works whose reunion was no mere coincidence. This inventory will later act as evidence, whatever happens, and at the same time delight amateurs.[83]

We do not know why, but this project was cut short, probably because other book projects got in the way, including the *Mémorial*. Meanwhile, the paintings from the donation were documented in an official 1907 catalogue, illustrated with reproductions of Yvon's photographs, who became the regular iconographer of Moreau-Nélaton's art history books.

The collection represented in the album

And so, the album has turned out to be an unrivalled but somewhat enigmatic document about the collection, in which the history and writings of the collector enable us to understand the issues at stake. There were eighteen plates, where one could discover the works displayed at home, followed by a final one, as a conclusion, of the father and his two daughters taken from a distance, sitting at a table in the garden. It is the only photo taken outside (that does not show the *hôtel particulier*, built between the courtyard and the garden), at the spot where Moreau-Nélaton himself had made his first attempts at photography: it testifies to the presence of the inhabitants whilst indicating their taste for the open air and nature, right in the heart of Paris. There is nobody in any of the photos of interiors, the place seems deserted, even if the last photo (pl. 18) shows a table laid for five people, indoors, on the second floor: the collector, the governess and the three children.
The excellent quality photos are highly detailed, allowing us to identify the paintings in-situ, whilst at the same time evoking the overall organisation and interior decoration that appears very crowded to us today and which, as we have seen, was inspired by their former home at Rue Saint-Georges. It reminds us of *The Philosophy of Furniture* by Edgar Allan Poe.[84] They recreated the interior "daylight" through a play of light and shade.

The viewer of the photographs perceives the origins of the light, even though the side with the windows opening onto the outside remains the "fourth wall" of the scene and is never photographed. There were probably no works hanging on it due to the backlighting. But looking through the album, it reinforces the effect of the collector's family space as a closed off refuge.[85] The spectator skims over the sections of the walls one after the other, sometimes moving closer, before stepping back to grasp the overall vision of each room. Without captions, commentaries or maps, the layout of the rooms in relation to the others can be understood by looking at the photos grouped together, enabling us to see that there were six spaces in all: four reception rooms – which had previously been his mother's apartments on the first floor and his own on the second – forming the "public" part of the home, and two bedrooms forming the private sphere. The first plates presented the four reception rooms in succession, two on the first floor (pl. 1, 2, 6 and 3, 4, 5) and two on the second (pl. 7, 8, 9 and 10, 11), which were linked by a spiral staircase (pl. 11 and 18), and with double doors protected by hangings, which can sometimes be seen in part (pl. 6) or as a whole (pl. 18). Apart from two of them (pl. 2, a mantelpiece, and pl. 5, a display case with earthenware) which present close-ups of plates 1 and 4, the photos show whole stretches of walls, either from the front, or from the side, presenting the rooms from an angle, which allowed two panels to be shown at once rather than just one. Then came three photographs of the bedrooms: Étienne Moreau-Nélaton's (pl. 10), placed in the middle of the album, and his daughters', with two Louis-Philippe sleigh beds placed end to end (pl. 11) and works of art hanging above them; next, four wide-angle views of the reception rooms (pl. 15 to 18), taken with a greater depth of field: as the most comprehensive images, they were chosen to be printed in the *Mémorial de famille* in 1918, where they appeared with the title "our interior in January 1907",[86] specifying that they were the first and second floor reception rooms.

Paintings by major painters and ceramics by Camille Moreau-Nélaton the amateur

The album starts with a preliminary plate that acts as a frontispiece (fig. 12), because this first drawing room, which had previously been his mother's, shows the patrimonial importance of the donation, whilst revealing the way in which the collection existed in a space full of memories, dispersed around the warm family home symbolised by the central fireplace, in an atmosphere finally destroyed by bereavement.

On both sides of the richly veined marble mantelpiece topped with a big mirror, we can see the second sketch for *The Raft of the Medusa* (*Le Radeau de la Méduse*) by Géricault (1818, 65 × 83 cm), "preliminary work for the ma-

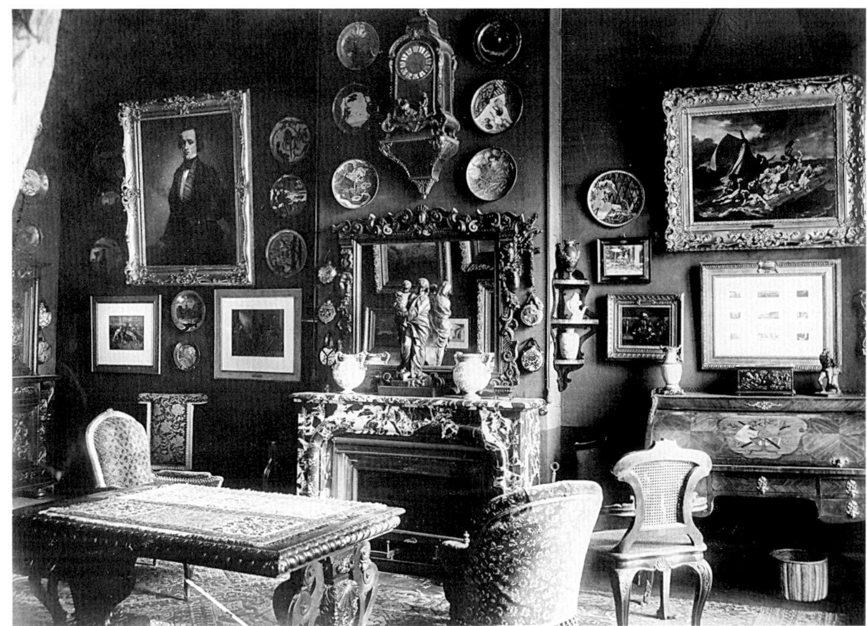

12. Anonymous photograph [Yvon?], main first-floor drawing room, plate 1 in the album *73 a Faubourg Saint-Honoré 1907* containing interior views of Étienne Moreau-Nélaton's private mansion, early 1907

jor painting shown at the 1819 Salon, today at the Louvre",[87] and the portrait by Thomas Couture of Adolphe Moreau the younger (1845, 114 × 88 cm),[88] hung above two drawings by Decamps, *The Wolf* (*Le Loup*) and *Christ at the Courtroom* (*Le Christ au prétoire*). Both paintings were shown at the Centennial exhibition in 1900 and reproduced in the 1907 catalogue. Thus, the path towards the Louvre was mapped out through the reference to Géricault's masterpiece, and tribute paid to the collector's father Adolphe Ferdinand Moreau's son (1827–1882) by his portrait, as well as to his grandfather Adolphe Moreau the elder (1800–1859), himself a collector, who had gathered all of the works appearing in this first photograph.

Next to the Géricault, on the right, a watercolour by Harpignies, Étienne's professor, depicting Camille Moreau-Nélaton painting at her easel in the open air under a parasol (1873, private collection):[89] this placing of the portrait grants his mother the status of an icon, yet a familiar one. It also reveals that working in the open air, often associated with amateur drawing and feminine practices, was also a method used by Harpignies, a landscape art-

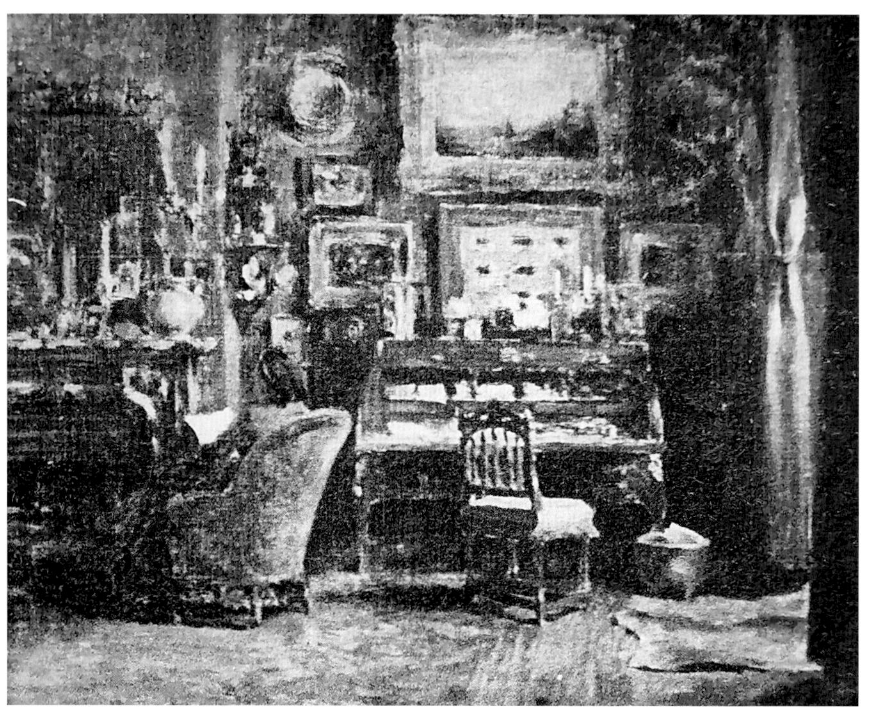

13. Étienne Moreau-Nélaton, *By the Fire* (*Le Coin du feu*), 1887, in Étienne Moreau-Nélaton, *Mémorial de famille*, edited by the author, Paris, 1918, vol. III, fig. 318

ist from the 1830 new school of painting, painting at the time Impressionism emerged. Underneath this watercolour is a small orientalist painting by Delacroix, *Turk Smoking, on a Couch* (*Le Turc fumant, assis sur un divan*, c. 1825), in a beautiful gilded Troubadour-style frame with scrolls and palmettes, where the name of the painter is written in gothic type on a label; on the other side of the desk is another Delacroix, *Woman with White Stockings* (*La Femme aux bas blancs*), which Étienne Moreau-Nélaton had bought in 1904: this homage to the painter reminds us of Delacroix's inaugural status in the history of the family collections, because the grandfather, had befriended him, and because Adolphe, his son, had published the catalogue raisonné of the painter's works in 1873.[90]

This living room takes on an intimate feel, organised into different, cosy areas with armchairs facing the fireplace, the table for reading or studying, and above all on the right a private and feminine space, untouched since the tragic death of Camille (the model of Harpignies's watercolours), who would sit there as we can see in the painting from 1887 by her son, *By the Fire* (*Le*

Coin du feu, 37 × 45 cm) (fig. 13),[91] the view being perfectly reproduced by the photographer, undoubtedly on Étienne's request. Nothing has changed here, apart from the sketch by Géricault replacing a seascape, or the open desk, full of papers, that is now closed, and the woman reading by the fire in the painting that is no longer in the photograph. This absence reminds us of the reason for the donation which was twofold: it was about offering the State an ensemble worthy of the Louvre and a way of working through their family grief with this votive donation.

The presence of Camille was also marked by her work as a ceramicist. In 1899, Étienne Moreau-Nélaton published the catalogue raisonné of her ceramics and paintings (she exhibited at the Salon for many years), which was his first book as an art historian and a tribute to his mother who had recently passed away.[92] The carefully composed mantelpiece is extended by panels devoted to her work in the decorative arts: it is centred around an eighteenth-century Virgin and Child,[93] the Christian figure of the educating mother, which can be seen in front of the mirror with the exuberant frame. Her Japanese-style vases are displayed on both sides (fig. 11),[94] with a crucifix, behind which is slipped a branch of the box wood from Palm Sunday. Higher up, an eighteenth-century cartel clock is surrounded on the wall on either side by three plates by Camille. They are placed in a vertical line, mirroring those arranged around the portrait by Couture. The lay out of this family drawing room by Étienne Moreau-Nélaton – author of the poster for the second exhibition of the *Arts de la femme* organised by the Comité des Dames of the UCAD, where his mother had exhibited some of her works in 1895[95] – marked a significant acknowledgement of her status as a ceramicist, which had begun after she discovered Bracquemond's Rousseau table service at the World Fair in 1867. Despite the success of her showcase at the exhibition in 1878, she remained on the margins of the art market, restricted by her amateur status until her very recent recognition, consecrated by an exhibition in 2020.[96] Plate 1 of the 1907 album, blending private life and the greater history of art through paintings and ceramics, can then be interpreted with the methodology of gender history: she was a woman working in the decorative arts, who was no longer confined to purely ornamental practices and amateur art; but she was recognised as an artist, not just as a housewife, because her work was juxtaposed without any hierarchy with some of the great nineteenth-century painters, at home. Moreover, by highlighting this practice by a woman, the usual divide between fine arts and decorative arts was questioned through the organisation of private collections, and this is confirmed in the other photographs where Camille Moreau-Nélaton's plates and dishes are scattered around the house (pl. 6, 9, 13, 15, 16, 17, 18). On the other hand, works by Étienne Moreau-Nélaton did not appear in any of them. Lastly, photographs, so present in the chronicles of family life referring to the albums, were not displayed either.

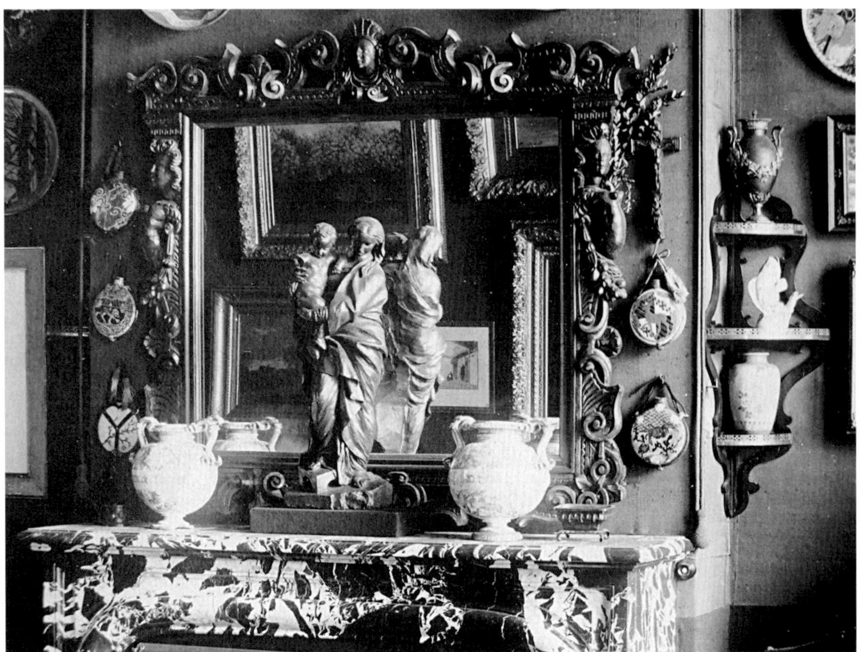

14. Anonymous photograph [Yvon?], fireplace mantel in the main first-floor drawing room, plate 2 in the album *73 bis Faubourg Saint-Honoré 1907* containing interior views of Étienne Moreau-Nélaton's private mansion, early 1907

The significant character of this space which functions as a small domestic altar is highlighted in the second photograph which shows a close-up of it. The mirror above the fireplace reflects other paintings hung on the opposite wall, in a *mise en abyme* effect particularly favoured by the Impressionists and which can be found in the work of both Degas and Manet (pl. 2, fig. 14): we cannot identify them, but, judging by the layout and the frames, they are *Velléda* by Corot and two Monets from the Vétheuil period, which are reproduced in pl. 6 (fig. 15). In this inherited setting, Étienne Moreau-Nélaton shows indirectly how his own collection starts with Delacroix and culminates with Impressionism.

Collections as a visual history of art: Impressionism in perspective, from Corot to Monet

The following two photographs present the second drawing room on the first floor devoted to Delacroix, Decamps and the École de Barbizon, admired and collected by Adolphe the elder (pl. 3, angle view, and 4). As the

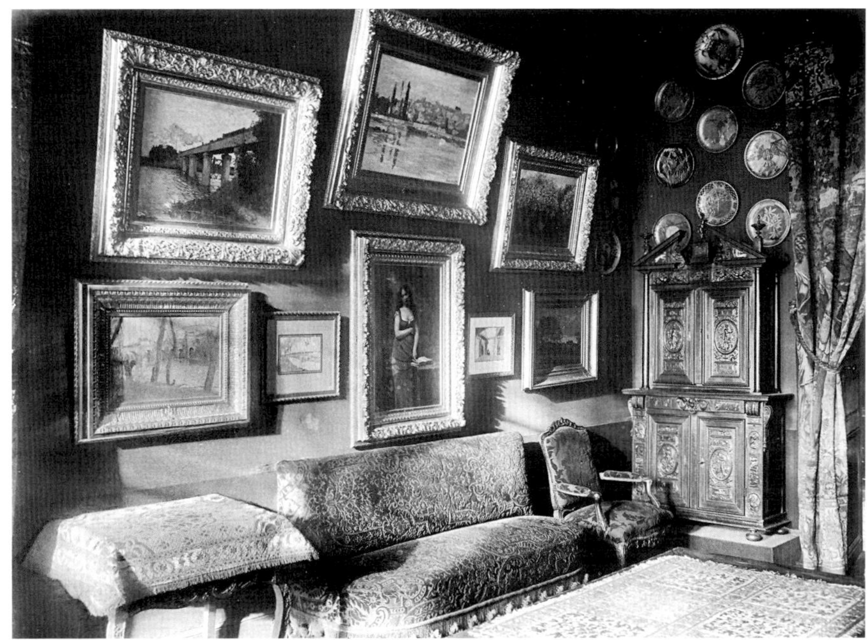

15. Anonymous photograph [Yvon?], main first-floor drawing room, plate 6 in the album *73 bis Faubourg Saint Honoré 1907* containing interior views of Étienne Moreau-Nélaton's private mansion, early 1907

masterpieces testify, they are laid out according to his understanding of the history of nineteenth-century art: in plate 3, on the right-hand wall was Decamps's *Turkish Boys Let Out of School* (*Sortie de l'école turque*), acquired in 1853 at the Decamps auction by Adolphe Moreau the elder.[97] The wall on the left gathered four paintings: at the centre is *The Ford Crossing* (*Le Passage du gué*) by Decamps, whose fluid brushwork and colourful sky is not done justice in the photograph: underneath, are *Entry of the Crusaders in Constantinople* (*Prise de Constantinople par les Croisés*) – the small version from 1852 – and *The Prisoner of Chillon* (*Le Prisonnier de Chillon*), from 1834 (1838 Salon), both by Delacroix, are treated as a pair and are next to *Herd Crossing the Ford* (*Troupeau passant le gué*) from 1852 by Troyon (acquired at the same occasion at the Bonnet auction in February 1852),[98] a painter admired by Monet at the Salon in 1859, and who also inspired Camille Moreau (pl. 3).
Another perspective opens up with plate 6 (fig. 15) which shows in detail a stretch of wall in the first drawing room reflected in the mirror: Monet finally appears in a panel where several masterpieces (*Railroad Bridge, Argenteuil* [*Le Chemin de fer à Argenteuil*], c. 1873[99] – over *The Bridge at*

Mantes [*Pont de Mantes*] by Corot[100] – *Quarries at Saint-Denis* [*Carrières Saint-Denis Vétheuil*], 1872[101] and *Resting under the Lilacs* [*Le Repos sous les lilas*], c. 1873,[102] above *Vachère dans un pré au soleil couchant* by Corot[103]) are grouped around *Velléda*[104] by Corot, a figure in a landscape. The latter is framed by two watercolours: the one on the left could be Jongkind or Daubigny, and the one on the right shows the interior of a Moresque house from Delacroix's trip to Morocco in 1832 (pl. 6, fig. 15). A complete understanding of French nineteenth-century art, analogue to the one supported by Jules Castagnary in the salons brought together in 1892 (who also admired Courbet), is developed in the assemblage of this magnificent panel, similarly to the layout of the drawing room, where Impressionism echoed the École de 1830, and Monet echoed Corot. This artistic connection, revealed in the display at Degas' home described by Valéry, was willingly acknowledged by Monet at the pre-auction exhibition of the jeweller Henri Vever's collection in 1897; here, together with Sisley's and Pissarro's, his works met with those of Corot, Millet and Boudin. He admired Corot as a painter who, according to him, completely surpassed the Impressionists: "Monet", wrote Raymond Koechlin, "had a quick look around the room and, as I went up to him to express my joy at such a beautiful reunion said: 'But then you haven't really looked, there is only one artist here, it's Corot; us, we are nothing next to him! It is the saddest day of my life!'".[105]
For all that, Moreau-Nélaton's display equally shows the divergences in style and visions of the two painters, as highlighted by the superposition of bridges: the one at Argenteuil by Monet (fig. 16), where the railway of modern life flies by, its straight lines dominating the shimmering waters of the river below, whilst the one at Mantes by Corot (fig. 17), with its ancient arches, its orbs visible from afar crossing over the Seine, blends in with the poetic landscape glimpsed through the trees. The paintings are spread out above a long banquette upholstered in velvet, whilst on a section of the side wall is a Renaissance-style two-part sideboard with a flurry of plates hung above it decorated by Camille Moreau.

An autobiography of the collector through paintings, or display as a life story

In the following panel, first drawing room on the second floor (pl. 7, fig. 18), we can see how Étienne Moreau-Nélaton's display reflected this fusion between several generations of artists and collectors. The "making of the collection" brought the works closer together, blending the first half of the nineteenth-century into the second. Moving from left to right, we can first see two paintings by Delacroix, one above the other: the eye is drawn to *Orphan Girl at the Cemetery* (*Orpheline au cimetière*),[106] study for *The Massacre at*

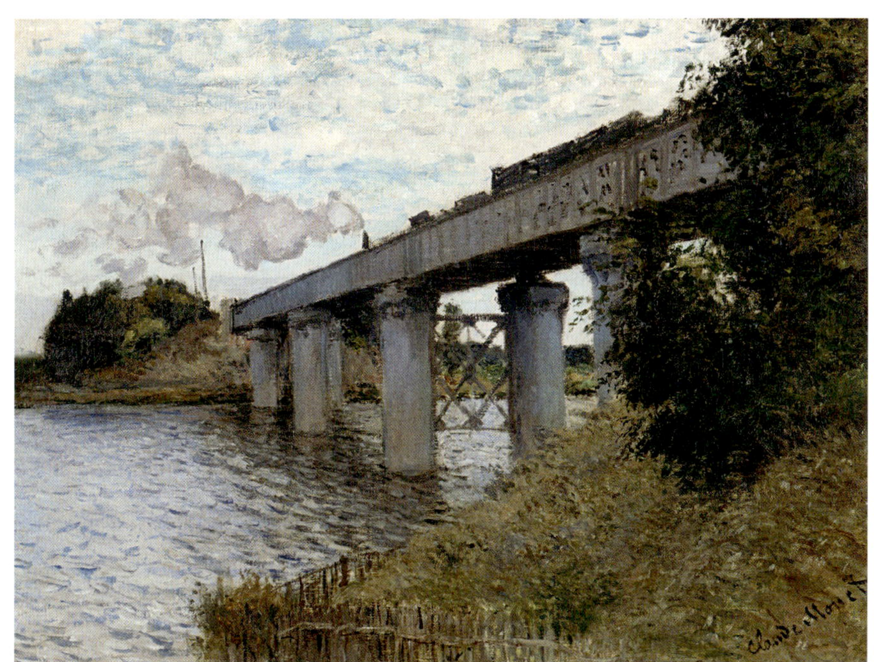

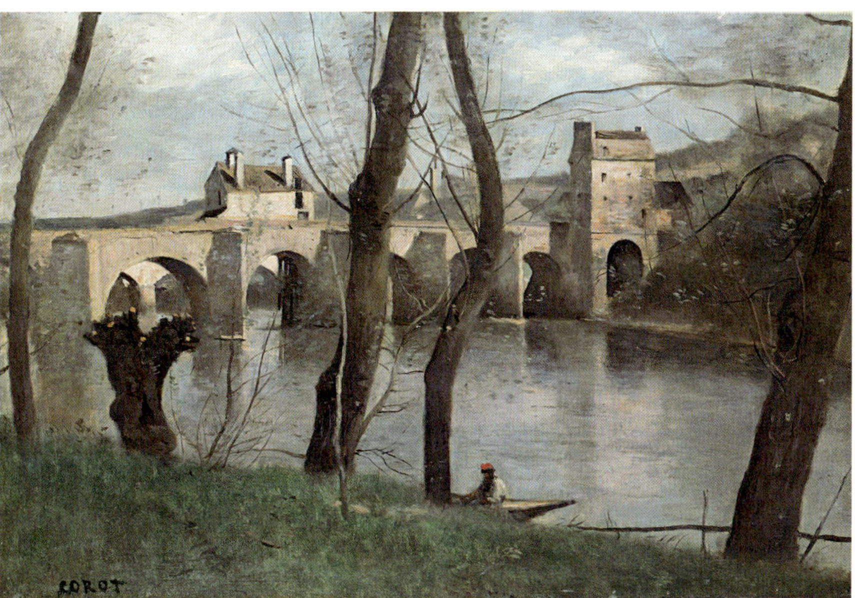

16. Claude Monet, *The Railway Bridge at Argenteuil* (*Le Pont du chemin de fer à Argenteuil*), 1874, oil on canvas, 55 × 72 cm, Musée d'Orsay, Paris, RF 1679, Moreau-Nélaton donation 1906

17. Jean-Baptiste Camille Corot, *The Bridge at Mantes (Le Pont de Mantes)*, c. 1868–70, oil on canvas, 38.5 × 55.5 cm, signed on the bottom left "Corot", Musée du Louvre, Paris, RF 1641, Moreau-Nélaton donation 1906

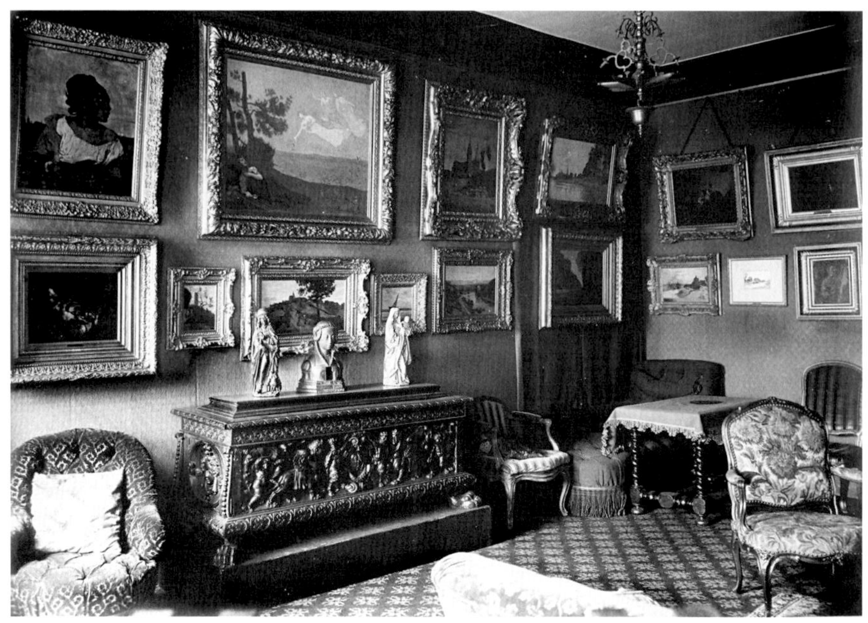

Chios (*Study for Massacres de Scio*, 1824), which his father had described, and *Horse Attacked by Lioness* (*Cheval attaqué par une lionne*),[107] bought by his father on 17 February 1864 at the famous Delacroix auction held after the artist died. The event unveiled the wide array of objects gathered in his house and studio to both collectors and artists, with his furniture and artefacts, from paintings to manuscripts and portfolios of prints and drawings. Then, at the centre of this panel, hanging above a sculpted Renaissance chest, was *The Dream* (*Le Rêve*) by Puvis de Chavannes (1883);[108] at the end of the panel are two works by Monet, one hung above the other: *Zaandam*, painted in Holland in 1871, and *Chailly Road* (*Le Pavé de Chailly*, 1865), with its bridle path running through Fontainebleau Forest, illuminated by a vast sky.[109] On the bottom row is a series of five Corots which form a base for the ensemble: *The Tower at Montléry* (*La Tour de Montléry*), *Saint-André en Morvan*, *Fishing Boat at Low Tide* (*Bateau de pêche à marée basse*),[110] *Chartres Cathedral* (*La Cathédrale de Chartres*), an important addition by Étienne to the collection he had inherited.[111] On the side wall, we can make out two more Corots, *Fishermen's House in Sainte-Adresse* (*Maison de pêcheurs à Sainte-Adresse*) and his *Self-Portrait*[112] (plate 7, fig. 18, and plate 8, which are very similar shots).

The structure of this panel takes on an autobiographical value and can be better understood in light of the confidences the collector made in the *Mémorial*. There, he tells about the origins of his personal artistic tastes, which was a cause of disagreement with his parents during his studies; he became enamoured of painting modern life when he was just a young stu-

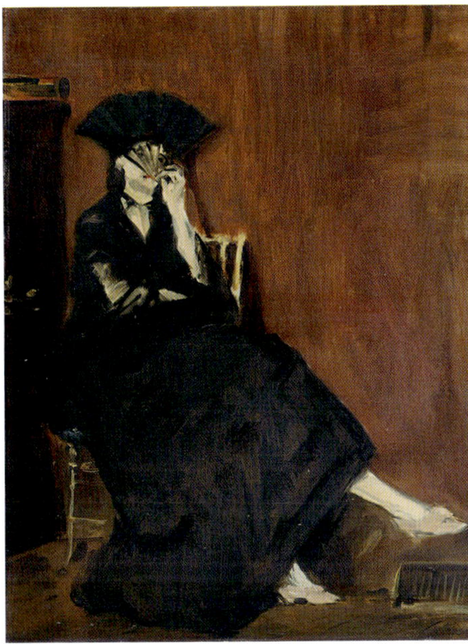

18. Anonymous photograph [Yvon?], second drawing room on the second floor, plate 7 in the album *73 bis Faubourg Saint-Honoré 1907* containing interior views of Étienne Moreau-Nélaton's private mansion, early 1907

19. Édouard Manet, *Berthe Morisot with Fan* (*Berthe Morisot à l'éventail*), 1872, oil on canvas, 60 × 45 cm, Musée d'Orsay, Paris, RF 1671, Moreau-Nélaton donation 1906

dent boarding at the École Normale Supérieure, in Rue d'Ulm (1879–1880 and 1880–1881), and he was attracted just as much to Impressionism as to the art of Puvis de Chavannes:

> The artistic tastes, which I had inherited through family tradition, began to conflict with the vocation I believed I felt for history. On our days out, I rushed to the Louvre or other museums. I never missed an exhibition and, whether it was at *La Vie moderne* [a gallery set up in the building of Charpentier's magazine between 1879–83, where exhibitions of De Nittis and Renoir were held in 1879 then Manet and Monet in 1880, and Sisley in 1881] or in the windows of Durand-Ruel's gallery, the joyfulness of the Impressionist palette delighted me. I crossed swords with my parents on this subject, who were used to a different vision of natural spectacles. Some other innovators found them equally impervious to their talent... At Lerolle's, I admired *The Prodigal Child* (*L'Enfant prodigue*) by Puvis de Chavannes, which had come into his possession after the 1879 salon ... My father ... took pity on me when in 1881, I praised *The Poor Fisherman* (*Pauvre pêcheur*). He mockingly brought me a photograph at the same time as one of a painting from Lerolle's which had pleased me. But me, I pinned the two images on the wall of my room and never tired of looking at the first one.[113]

The photograph pinned to the wall in his student room may be understood as the sign of his future, much later, collection, inseparable from his taste for images and reproductions. Acquired in 1899 from Georges Petit, *The*

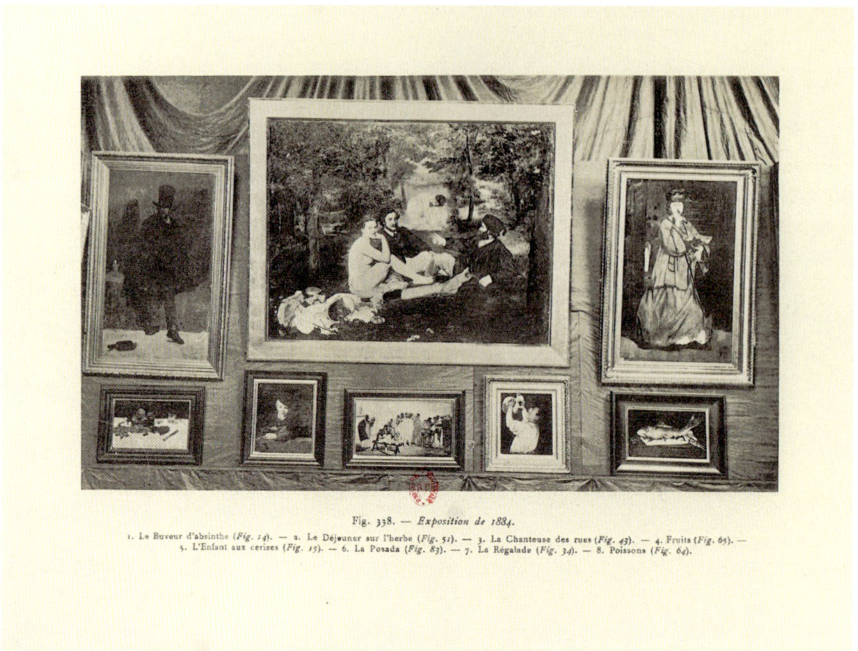

20. *Exposition de 1884. 1. Le Buveur d'absinthe (Fig. 14) - 2. Le Déjeuner sur l'herbe (Fig. 51).- 3. La Chanteuse des rues (Fig. 43).- 4. Fruits (Fig. 63).- 5. L'Enfant aux cerises (Fig. 15).- 6. La Posada (Fig. 83).- 7. La Régalade (Fig. 34). - 8. Poissons (Fig. 64)*, Étienne Moreau-Nélaton, *Manet raconté par lui-même*, Henri Laurens, Paris, 1926, vol. II, fig. 138

Dream by Puvis de Chavannes, which had previously belonged to the Duret collection, after having been sold by Durand-Ruel, had a good pedigree among Impressionist collectors, even if its theme and brushwork, with its soft, broken and flat hues, singled out a style that heralded the Nabis or the École de Pont-Aven, whose art Moreau-Nélaton paid tribute to, notably with his posters.

The autobiographical dimension becomes even more intimate with *Orphan Girl at the Cemetery* (*Orpheline au cimetière*) by Delacroix, which Étienne Moreau-Nélaton acquired in 1904, when this canvas found its place amidst the grieving household, where, now widowed, he raised his three children. Through this series of paintings, a whole life story unfolds, marked by acquisitions and donations, and which was told in the *Mémorial*, about twenty years later: *The Bridge at Argenteuil* (*Le Pont d'Argenteuil*) by Monet was thus the reminder of the first painting his mother had given to him (and which was still in the drawing room which had once been hers). The acquisition of *The Older Sister, Intimacy* (*La Grande Sœur, Intimité*) by Carrière (1889),[114] hanging in the drawing room on the second floor (pl. 10) marked an important rite of passage in his life: his marriage. A week after Camille died, on 29 May 1897, he bought a portrait at an auction of Berthe Morisot by Manet, dressed in black, her face masked by a fan (fig. 19).[115] As a souvenir of the family collections, he gave each of his children a painting, and in 1919 donated to the State, the one he had given his son Dominique, who had died for France in the war. The whole collection progressively became a form of memorial, frozen in time, when it was photographed before the donation to the State. The history of the collection blends both "family romance" (as Lynn Hunt puts it), and national narrative, its private patrimonial value taking on a public, cultural museum value.

From collection to museum: patriotic values at stake

When it entered the public collections, the process of musealisation began; the way it was displayed in the rooms and the catalogue turned out to be very different to how it was hung in the private collection. In the 1907 donation catalogue, the descriptions are normalised, the illustrations presented in separate plates, without showing the frames or the layout of the collector's interior. In it, for instance, is *The Luncheon on the Grass* (*Le Déjeuner sur l'herbe*) by Manet – noticeably absent, with *Hommage à Delacroix* (*Homage to Delacroix*) by Fantin-Latour, from the photographs in the 1907 photo album.[116] Yet in the 1907 catalogue of the donation, a good description of the two paintings is given, as well as a large black and white reproduction.[117] Moreau-Nélaton's books on art history, published afterwards, made little reference to the works in his collection, pointing out that they were in the Louvre Museum, without always indicating the name of the donator. Out of the artists from the "new painting", the only one he talked about as an art historian was Manet. He wrote an initial book, contemporary with the donation, on Manet's prints in 1906,[118] for which he acknowledged "Bracquemond's unlimited kindness" in helping him, assuring that "Degas had been just as helpful". His last book was *Manet raconté par lui-même*, published in 1926,[119] with a conclusion that explored how the painter was viewed in the twentieth century. The tone is extremely vehement, overly criticising the "speculators" – dealers or collectors, to such an extent that he exacerbates nationalistic issues even further: Moreau-Nélaton castigates the way Manet's masterpieces had been taken abroad, mainly to America and Germany, so much so that his donation to the State was presented in retrospect, not just as a means of definitively domiciling a certain number of paintings in France, but also of gaining recognition for Manet, which had begun with the donation of *Olympia* following Monet's subscription, organised in 1884:

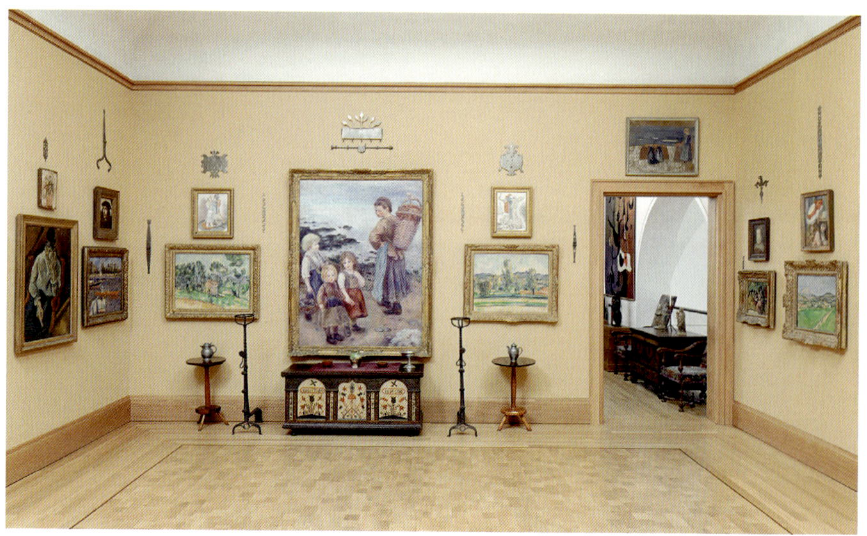

> [In 1906], I took care of getting works of art reunited by myself admitted into the national collections, for which the Pavillon de Marsan would be used as a temporary home, whilst waiting for them to go to the Louvre. Through my act, our great Musée National opened its doors to Manet, his *Luncheon on the Grass* (*Déjeuner sur l'herbe*), his admirable *Bouquet of Peonies* (*Bouquet de pivoines*), one of his paintings of *fruits*, his *Berthe Morisot with a Fan* (*Berthe Morisot jouant avec un éventail*) and his pastel of *Docteur Matern*. This event had one major, and unforeseen consequence. It provoked *Olympia* being moved to the Louvre.[120]

The book concluded with a reminder of the documentary role of photographs stemming from the Durand-Ruel and Druet collections, including Godet's (procured by the widow of the collector Albert Hecht) and Lochard's, to which can be added those taken by his "usual collaborator", Yvon, notably at the home of Berthe Morisot's daughter and son-in-law, Mr and Mrs Ernest Rouart, who "kept a few pieces of the treasure so avidly absorbed by foreign collections". A fascinating document was also published in full as an annex to the book: in it, the 1884 *Manet* exhibition at the École des Beaux-arts is photographed wall after wall, which aimed to inscribe the painter into the republican history of art.[121] The panels were covered with pleated fabric, where the paintings were displayed, in two rows, in a rather crooked way. *Luncheon on the Grass* (*Déjeuner sur l'herbe*) (fig. 20) found its rightful place in the centre – between *The Absinthe Drinker* (*Le Buveur d'absinthe*) and *Street Singer* (*La Chanteuse des rues*) – above a row of smaller works, including, at the bottom left, a still-life with fruits acquired later, around 1902. He was very proud of the fact that his donation of the still-life

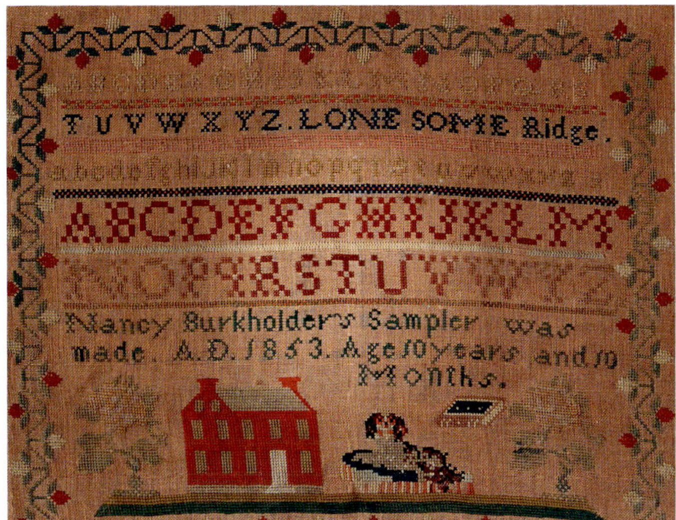

21. The Barnes Foundation, Philadelphia, *Ensemble*, Room 14, East Wall; in the centre, Pierre-Auguste Renoir, *Mussel-Fishers at Berneval* (*Pêcheuses de moules à Berneval, côte normande*), 1879, oil on canvas, 176.2 × 130.2 cm, BF989 (see fig. 7)

22. Nancy Burkholder, *Lonesome Ridge Sampler*, 1853, wool on canvas, from Lonesome Ridge (New Mexico), *Ensemble*, room 8, south wall, The Barnes Foundation, Philadelphia

had enriched the national collections.[122] This annex corroborates the great care the collector took in displaying his works.

Focusing on Impressionist home collections offers an original research angle for studying collecting, more usually concerned with socioeconomic data and the study of art networks. It is founded on the analysis of sources such as stock books, auction catalogues (especially when annotated), letters and testimonies from collectors. During this investigation, this question has proved to be intrinsically linked to Impressionist painting, raised by the different art world "actors" involved: the painters and their initial choices for display; the art dealers – as we have seen with Durand-Ruel – who aimed at building private collections; and the collectors themselves, the proponents of the recognition for Impressionism in public collections. The case of Moreau-Nélaton, which highlights the position of amateurs (collectors and artists) as key players in the artworld of this period, has turned out to be particularly interesting, through the interaction between the rare and precious photographs of the displays, preserved in the 1907 album, and the textual testimonies offered by the writings of the collector himself, both in his family texts and his books on art history. At home, forming a collection enabled collectors to sidestep the institutional choices of the period, according to which works of art had to be organised by school, or in a chronology in which Impressionism was not yet accepted. They could create visual connections between the paintings in the layout of the panels and could break with aesthetic hierarchies, which for instance allowed the ceramics of a woman artist on the margins of the art market to gain recognition and be displayed alongside works by Géricault, Delacroix, Corot or Monet. We can

also see how the semiotics of displaying collections proves not just to be of a personal nature, virtually like a life story, but equally an unstable one, because its meaning was later susceptible to change, when Moreau-Nélaton looked back at his donation from an ultra-nationalist stance. One of the elements shared by the two studies considered here is how several generations were involved in the collections. It is probably less common today, even if a similar situation can be seen in the Senn-Foulds donation to the Musée du Havre (2004), which reflects the aesthetic choices of three successive generations of collectors: the first one collecting Impressionism whilst in the Moreau cases, it was the last member of the family who did so.[123] Finally, throughout the history of the "making of" collections, it would appear that "imaginary museums" are essential documents, as they are compilations of how artworks were displayed and particularly when they are accompanied by written sources.
A further step is made when the private collection is conceived as a museum, or claims to become one, according to a process explored by Anne Higonnet.[124] In the "author museum"[125] at the Barnes Foundation – which was created from a collection that paid tribute to Cézanne and Renoir, among others, alongside works by Matisse – the holder himself organised the display panels into "ensembles" himself (fig. 21), to use his own terms, and continually modified them: the collection of paintings was mixed in with pieces from the ironwork collection, whilst the ceramics displayed on the furniture, and even the fabric of the doilies and the heating outlets, were chosen to harmonise with the art collections. Situated in the Merion district of Philadelphia, the foundation created by the industrialist Albert Barnes interacted with John Dewey's philosophy[126] and was conceived as a museum-school, or a school-museum, sharpening the eye of its visitors and students. Some of the doilies were American alphabet samplers embroidered in cross-stitch, evoking literacy through the coloured threads of embroidery (fig. 22): in this "feminine art" where the material support of the colours is woollen thread, we can find a metaphor for the active apprenticeship of seeing offered by these "ensembles" created by Barnes. Black and white photographs of several of these panels (presented today on the foundation's website, organised as a virtual museum), were brought together in a booklet by Violette de Mazia, *The Display of an Art Collection*, printed as a supplement to the Foundation's magazine *Vistas* (vol. II, no. 2, 1982–83, pp. 107–20).[127] The author, who was then vice-president and director of the education department, offers commentaries based on previous and continuing discussions with the collector: it appears that displaying is part of a system aiming to offer the public an artistic education by training how to look independently at artworks and appreciate the rhythm of the colours, lines, and materials of the panels defined as *wall-pictures*. It relies on the postulate of the pedagogical effects of "the making of collections": here lies a new transatlantic chapter in the history of collecting Impressionism.

* This translation of the original text was revised by Aurélie Petiot, whom the author would like to thank warmly for her time and work.

1 Jean Renoir, *Ma vie et mes films* (Paris: Champs Art, 2005), p. 18. First published 1974 by Flammarion.

2 Ibid., p. 19.

3 Mario Praz, *Histoire de la décoration d'intérieur. Philosophie de l'ameublement* (Paris: Thames & Hudson, 1994). Italian edition 1981.

4 See my study in the soon to be published symposium proceedings, "Le livre, le musée, l'enfant", in Yvanne Rialland (ed.), *La genèse du musée des enfants: De Comenius à Madame de Genlis*.

5 Morse's *La Galerie du Louvre* proceeds in a similar manner: it is a painting in which the main works of the museum are united together, in view of them being promoted on the other side of the Atlantic. Peter J. Brownlee (ed.), *Samuel F.B. Morse's "Gallery of the Louvre" and the Art of Invention* (New Haven, Terra Foundation for American Art-Yale University Press, 2014).

6 Georges Pérec, *Un cabinet d'amateur. Histoire d'un tableau* (Paris: Balland, 1979).

7 The cover of the paperback edition (1990) shows a close-up of one of these paintings.

8 Pierre-Marc de Biasi, "Système et déviances de la collection à l'époque romantique", *Romantisme*, dossier "Déviances" (ed. Marc Eigeldinger), no. 27, 1980, pp. 77–93 (here p. 80).

9 Thomas W. Gaehtgens, Louis Marchesano, *Display & Art history. The Düsseldorf Gallery and its catalogue* (Los Angeles: The Getty Research Institute, 2011).

10 Emilie Malouvier, "Les catalogues de la collection des ducs de Leuchtenberg: rédaction et diffusion de savoirs muséographiques européens", *Musée*, special issue *Musées de Romantisme*, edited by Ségolène Le Men, with Philippe Hamon and Paule Petitier, no. 173, 2016-3, pp. 88–97.

11 André Malraux reproduces the central detail of the painting in the Prado (fig. 1) at the beginning of *Musée imaginaire*, in view of a museum display. André Malraux, "Le Musée imaginaire", in *Les Voix du silence* (Paris: Gallimard, 1951), p. 10.

12 Elisabeth Décultot (ed.), *Musées de papier: L'Antiquité en livres 1600-1800*, exhibition catalogue, Musée du Louvre, Paris, 25 September 2010 – 3 January 2011 (Paris: Louvre Éditions and Gourcoff Gradenigo, 2010).

13 Ann Dumas, Colta Ives, Susan A. Stein and Gary Tinterow (eds.), *The Private Collection of Edgar Degas. A Summary Catalogue*, exhibition catalogue, The Metropolitan Museum of Art, New York, 1 October 1997 – 11 January 1998 (New York: The Metropolitan Museum of Art, 1997).

14 Marianne Mathieu, Dominique Lobstein (eds.), *Monet collectionneur*, exhibition catalogue, Musée Marmottan Monet, Paris, 14 September 2017 – 14 January 2018 (Paris: Hazan and Musée Marmottan Monet, 2017).

15 Frances Weitzenhoffer, *The Havemeyers: Impressionism Comes to America*, New York, 1986; *Splendid Legacy: The Havemeyer Collection*, exhibition catalogue, The Metropolitan Museum of Art, New York, 27 March – 20 June 1993; *La collection Havemeyer: Quand l'Amérique découvrait l'impressionnisme...*, exhibition catalogue, Musée d'Orsay, Paris, 20 October 1997 – 18 January 1998 (Paris: RMN, 1998).

16 Daniel Marchesseau, Françoise Heilbrun et Anne Distel, *Au cœur de l'impressionnisme. La famille Rouart*, exhibition catalogue, Musée de la vie romantique, Paris, 3 February – 13 June 2004 (Paris: Paris Musées, 2004).

17 Gustave Caillebotte's bequest was controversial: Pierre Vaisse, *Deux façons d'écrire l'histoire. Le legs Caillebotte* (Paris: INHA and Editions Ophrys, 2014).

18 Magali Rougeot, *Gustave Fayet (1865-1925), itinéraire d'un artiste collectionneur*, PhD in art history, supervised by Ségolène Le Men, Université Paris Nanterre, and Rodolphe Rapetti, École du Louvre, 2013.

19 Paul Valéry, *Degas Danse Dessin. Illustrations d'Edgar Degas* (Paris: Ambroise Vollard, 1936), p. 25.

20 Frédéric Bazille, *L'atelier de la rue de Furstenberg*, 1865, 80 × 65 cm, Musée Fabre, Montpellier.

21 Ségolène Le Men, "Du salon-atelier à la chambre-collection" and "Trois promenades au jardin de Monet", in *Monet* (Paris: Citadelles & Mazenod, 2010), pp. 370–74 and 374–78.

22 Elder (Marc, pseudonym for Marcel Tendron), *À Giverny, chez Claude Monet* (Paris: Bernheim-Jeune, 1924).

23 W. Bürger (Théophile Thoré, known as), "Les Collections particulières", *Paris guide, par les principaux écrivains et artistes de la France*, Paris, Librairie internationale, A. Lacroix, Verboeckhoven et Cie, Editors, 1867 (ed. Philippe Burty), vol. 1, pp. 536–50. Albert Jacquemart, "Les Collections d'art", *Paris guide* cit., pp. 551–54.

24 Some of the visits were reprinted in Élizabeth Émery, *En toute intimité: Quand la*

presse people de la Belle Époque s'invitait chez les célébrités (Paris: Parigramme, 2015).
25 Olivier Nora, "La Visite au grand écrivain", in Pierre Nora (ed.), *Les Lieux de mémoire*, vol. II: *La Nation *** L'Idéel* (Paris: Quarto Gallimard, 1997), pp. 2131–55 (original ed. 1997).
26 Élizabeth Émery, *Photojournalism and the Origins of the French Writer House Museum (1881-1914): Privacy, Publicity, and Personality* (Farnham–Burlington: Ashgate Press, 2012).
27 Marie-Clémence Régnier, *Vies encloses, demeures écloses. Le grand écrivain français en sa maison-musée (1879-1937)*, thesis in literature, supervised by Florence Naugrette and Françoise Mélonio, Université Paris 4, 2017.
28 Arsène Alexandre, "La Collection de M. Jean Dollfus", *Les Arts*, no. 25, January 1904, pp. 6–16 and no. 26 February 1904, pp. 3–12.
29 Anne Distel, *Les Collectionneurs des impressionnistes. Amateurs et marchands* (Düdingen–Guin–Paris: Trio-Verlag, Franz Stadelmann and La Bibliothèque des Arts, 1989).
30 Théodore Duret, *Les Peintres impressionnistes: Claude Monet, Sisley, C. Pissaro, Renoir, Berthe Morisot avec un dessin de Renoir* (Paris: Librairie parisienne, H. Heymann and J. Perois, May 1878), p. 9. When Duret reprinted the brochure in *Critique d'avant-garde* in 1885, this precious list was omitted.
31 Anonymous [Félix Fénéon?], "Les Disparus – François Depeaux", *Bulletin de la vie artistique*, no. 23, 1 November 1920, p. 639.
32 Marcel Guérin, "Raymond Koechlin et sa collection", *Bulletin des musées de France*, IV, 1932, pp. 66–88.
33 Bernard Vouilloux, *Le Tournant "artiste" de la littérature française – Ecrire la peinture au XIX*[e] *siècle* (Paris: Hermann, 2011).
34 Edmond de Goncourt, *La Maison d'un artiste* (Paris, G. Charpentier, 1881).
35 Dominique Pety, *Poétique de la collection au XIX*[e] *siècle. Du document de l'historien au bibelot de l'esthète* (Nanterre: Presses universitaires de Paris-Ouest, 2010), http://books.openedition.org/pupo/618
36 Edgard Degas, "A Propos du Salon", *Paris-Journal*, 12 April 1870 (Theodore Reff, "Some Unpublished Letters of Degas", *Art Bulletin*, L, 1968, pp. 87–93).
37 Hermann von Helmholtz, *L'Optique et la peinture* (Paris: ENSBA, 1994). "L'Optique et la peinture", symposiums held in Berlin, Dusseldorf and Cologne, *La Revue scientifique de la France et de l'étranger : Revue des cours scientifiques*, second series, sixth year, no. 11, 9 September 1876, pp. 241–55.
38 Philippe Burty, "Exposition de la Société anonyme des artistes", *La République française*, 25 April 1874; Hélène Adhémar and Anthony M. Clark (eds.), *Centenaire de l'Impressionnisme*, exhibition catalogue, Grand Palais, Paris, 21 September – 24 November 1974, Paris, Editions des Musées nationaux, 1974, p. 262.
39 No. 3: "Cadre de figures contenant: / Dames flamandes à leur fenêtre / Scène de Somnambulisme / Enfants flamands dans une serre / Poupées japonaises / Les Présents chinois (Londres) / Intérieur parisien. Aquarelles."
40 The Normandy home of the collector Jean Dollfus, who had moved from Mulhouse after having opted for France in 1870, was called Fleurheim.
41 Manuel Charpy, *Le Théâtre des objets. Espaces privés, culture matérielle et identité bourgeoise. Paris, 1830-1914*, thesis in history, supervised by Jean-Luc Pinol, Université François Rabelais, Tours, 2010, vol. I, p. 187.
42 Underlined by the author. L.A.S. Durand-Ruel to Monet, 25 February 1885, *Archives Claude Monet. Correspondance d'artiste. Collection Monsieur et Madame Cornebois. [de Beriot. Caillebotte. Durand-Ruel. Theodore Duret. Geffroy. Mirbeau. Morisot. Renoir. Rodin. Signac. Sargent. Sisley.]*, auction catalogue Artcurial (Briest – Poulain – F. Tajan), Hôtel Dassault, Paris, 13 December 2006, no. 65.
43 Cited by Caroline Durand-Ruel Godfroy, "Un foyer pour l'impressionnisme", *Paul Durand-Ruel: Le pari de l'impressionnisme. L'objet d'art, Hors-série exposition*, no. 81, 2014, pp. 27–31 (here p. 28).
44 Paul-Louis and Flavie Durand-Ruel, "Paul Durand-Ruel (1831-1922): un portrait", in Sylvie Patry (ed.), *Paul Durand-Ruel: Le pari de l'impressionnisme*, exhibition catalogue, Musée du Luxembourg, Paris, 9 October 2014 – 8 February 2015 (Paris: Editions de la Réunion des musées nationaux – Grand Palais, 2014), pp. 28–45 (here p. 44).
45 Ibid., note XIV, p. 44.
46 Photograph of the dining room, *1874 Hommage à Paul Durand-Ruel Cent ans d'impressionnisme*, exhibition catalogue, Durand-Ruel Gallery, Paris, 15 January – 15 March 1974, n.p. Photographs of Paul Durand-Ruel's apartment, 35, Rue de Rome, Paris, around 1900–10, Archives Durand-Ruel, Paris, *Paul Durand-Ruel* cit., p. 211, figs. 145 and 146, main drawing room; fig. 147, office; fig. 148, Paul Durand-Ruel's small parlour (cats. 105–8).

47 Auguste Rodin, *Jeune mère à la grotte*, 1893, marble, 70.8 × 65.1 × 37 cm, Philadelphia Museum of Art.

48 The Dutch interior decorator Jansen, who moved to Rue Royale in Paris in 1980, became a specialist in the matter right up until the 1900s.

49 Georges Lecomte, *L'Art impressionniste, d'après la collection privée de M. Durand-Ruel, avec 36 eaux-fortes, pointes sèches et illustrations dans le texte de A.-M. Lauzet* (Paris: typography Chamerot and Renouard, 1892).

50 "Fifty copies numbered on the press, thus: Nos. 1 to 25. – Copies on paper from the Manufactures impériales du Japon, with etchings on Japanese vellum; Nos. 26 to 50. – Copies on laid paper, with etchings on Japanese vellum."

51 Published in two volumes with monochrome lithographs printed by Lemercier, introduced with *Salon principal de la galerie Durand-Ruel*, which showed the spacious layout of the gallery at 103, Rue des Petits Champs, where Jean Durand moved in 1839 to offer paintings to rent or buy.

52 *Galerie Durand-Ruel. Recueil d'estampes gravées à l'eau-forte. Préface par Armand Silvestre* (Paris-London-Brussels: Maison Durand-Ruel, 1873), six volumes with 50 plates, or thirty deliveries of which the first was made the 29 November 1873.

53 Armand Silvestre's preface, taken from a text that appeared between 17 August and 28 September 1872, in *La Renaissance littéraire et artistique*, gave a chronological presentation of nineteenth-century artists and their paintings: Delacroix, Huet, Corot, Théodore Rousseau, Millet, then Monet, Pissarro, Sisley and Manet...

54 Lecomte, *op. cit.*, p. 36.

55 Marine Kisiel, *La peinture impressionniste et la décoration* (Paris: Le Passage, 2021).

56 Gustave Geffroy, "Les Meules de Claude Monet, 1er mai 1891", *La Vie artistique*, Paris, Dentu, 1892 (first series), pp. 22–29, here p. **28**. Preface from the exhibition catalogue for the 23 paintings by Mr Claude Monet, at the Durand-Ruel Galleries, from 5 to 30 May 1891.

57 Ibid., p. 29.

58 Ibid., p. 27.

59 Lauzet, *Pêcheurs au bord de la mer*, ibid., p. 191.

60 Exh. 2014, fig. 145. See also Gloria Groom (ed.), *Beyond the Easel: Decorative Painting by Bonnard, Vuillard, Denis, and Roussel, 1890-1930*, exhibition catalogue, The Art Institute, Chicago, 25 February – 16 May 2001; The Metropolitan Museum of Art, New York, 26 June – 9 September 2001 (Chicago: The Art Institute, 2001), p. 10.

61 Joris-Karl Huysmans, "L'exposition des indépendants en 1881", *L'Art moderne*, Paris, Charpentier, 1883.

62 Repr. Anne Hélène Hoog (ed.), *La Splendeur des Camondo: De Constantinople à Paris 1806-1945*, exhibition catalogue, Musée d'art et d'histoire du judaïsme, Paris, 2009–2010 (Paris-Milan: Musée d'art et d'histoire du judaïsme, Skira et Flammarion, 2009), p. 37.

63 Sophie le Tarnec, "J'ai créé ma collection comme on compose un opéra", ibid., pp. 46–70.

64 It is more precisely a reproduction of a drypoint by Mary Cassatt that decorated the "front page" of issue 1, 25 November 1890.

65 Françoise Cachin and Pierre Rosenberg (eds.), *De Corot aux impressionnistes, donations Moreau-Nélaton*, exhibition catalogue, Galeries nationales du Grand Palais, Paris, 30 April – 22 July 1991 (Paris: Réunion des musées nationaux, Bibliothèque nationale, 1991). Abbreviation: MN

66 I would like to thank Xavier de Massary for obtaining the reproductions for me and for helping to prepare this investigation on his grandfather.

67 The layout of the *hôtel particulier* destroyed since is described by Xavier de Massary, who has known the place when he was a child: "It was comprised, garden side (to the south), of six bays on three levels (three floors) and an attic. On each of the levels was a suite of three large rooms, each lit by two windows (facing south, then), leading off a corridor, a staircase and utility rooms on the courtyard side. The bedrooms (or at least the children's) were mostly in the wing that gave onto the courtyard. Etienne Moreau-Nélaton's studio was on the attic floor (with an elevated roof to benefit from a large bay window over the courtyard on the north side), next to the servants' bedrooms. The inner spiral staircase was for private use, the main staircase (courtyard side), at the centre of the stairwell where a lift was later added, for visitors" (email by Xavier de Massary, 7 March 2022).

68 MN, no. 91.

69 *Catalogue de la collection Moreau (tableaux, dessins, aquarelles et pastels) offerte à l'Etat français et exposée au Musée des Arts Décoratifs* (Paris, Imprimerie Frazier-Soye, 1907). Abbreviation: Moreau 1907.

70 Ibid., figs. 276 and 280.

71 Ibid., figs. 277–79.
72 Étienne Moreau-Nélaton, *Mémorial de famille*, Paris, edited by the author, 1918, five volumes including a genealogical table (here volume III, p. 37). Abbreviation: *Mémorial* III.
73 *Meubles et objets d'art des XV-XVI-XVII siècles: 57 planches photoglyptiques Goupil et Cie* (Paris: Goupil & Cie, 1871).
74 Xavier de Massary, "Camille Moreau, une femme peintre et céramiste au XIXe siècle", *Mémoires. Fédération des Sociétés d'histoire et d'archéologie de l'Aisne*, vol. 43, 1998, pp. 147–65. Alexandra Bosc and Xavier de Massary (eds.), *Camille Moreau-Nélaton: Une femme céramiste au temps des impressionnistes*, exhibition catalogue, Musée de la Céramique, Rouen, 3 April – 15 November 2020 (Cinisello Balsamo-Rouen: Silvana Editoriale and Réunion des musées métropolitains, 2020).
75 *Mémorial* III, pp. 37–38.
76 Rossella Froissart Pezone, *L'art dans tout: Les arts décoratifs en France et l'utopie d'un Art nouveau* (Paris: CNRS Éditions, 2005), chap. III.
77 *Catalogue de tableaux modernes, aquarelles, pastels, dessins, objets d'art & d'ameublement de la Renaissance, meubles, tapisseries anciennes provenant de la collection Moreau-Nélaton et dont la vente aura lieu à Paris Galerie Georges Petit, 5, rue de Sèze, les vendredi 11, Samedi 12, Lundi 14 et Mardi 15 Mai 1900 à 2 heures*. Auctioneer, Maître Paul Chevallier, Paris, experts Georges Petit (painting); Mannheim, 7, Rue Saint-Georges, Paris (art objects). 533 lots.
78 *Dornac Photographe. Nos contemporains chez eux*, album of 18 positive albumen or aristotype prints taken from silver bromide negatives, 1887–1917. BNF Est. 4-NA-102.
79 *Mémorial*, III, p. 7.
80 *Mémorial*, III, p. 3. See note 59.
81 According to Xavier de Massary's indications, email, 7 March 2022.
82 Catherine Delvaille-Chevalier, "Frédéric Henriet, Amateur-artiste ou artiste amateur", *Mémoires, Fédération des Sociétés d'histoire et d'archéologie de l'Aisne*, vol. 43, 1998, p. 113–29. Frédéric Henriet was the author of *Paysagiste aux champs Croquis d'après nature* (A. Faure, 1866), who decorated etchings by Corot, Daubigny, Lalanne, etc., gives an account of the traditions of the École de Barbizon landscape painters, and was republished and expanded in 1876 by Lévy.
83 Frédéric Henriet, "Étienne Moreau-Nélaton", *Annales de la Société historique et archéologique de Château-Thierry*, 1906, pp. 63–97 (here pp. 71–72, note 1), pre-original edition of the book by Frédéric Henriet published in the same year as the donation: Étienne Moreau-Nélaton. *Notes intimes, accompagnées d'héliotypies d'après les* œuvres *de l'artiste et d'une pointe sèche inédite* (Paris: H. Laurens, 1907). In response, Moreau-Nélaton published his biography a few years later: *Mon bon ami Henriet : Esquisse biographique avec un portrait et des dessins tirés de ses ouvrages* (Paris: Floury, 1914).
84 Edgar Allan Poe, "La Philosophie de l'ameublement", *Histoires grotesques et sérieuses, Traduction par Charles Baudelaire* (Paris: Michel Lévy brothers, new edition, 1871).
85 The philosopher Gaston Bachelard analysed the metaphors of spaces in the home, including the "gîte", nest or shell from a poetic and psychoanalytic angle. Although he does not mention the collections of paintings, his analyses can serve as a study for creating collections. Gaston Bachelard, *La Poétique de l'espace* (Paris: Les Presses universitaires de France, 1957).
86 *Mémorial*, III, figs. 510 and 511. – *Notre intérieur en janvier 1907. 1er étage*. Figs. 512 and 513. – *Notre intérieur en janvier 1907. 2e étage*.
87 Moreau 1907, no. 39.
88 Moreau 1907, no. 43.
89 *Mémorial*, II, p. 201.
90 Adolphe Moreau, *Eugène Delacroix et son œuvre. Avec des gravures en fac-similé des planches originales les plus rares* (Paris: Librairie des bibliophiles, 1873).
91 *Mémorial*, III, fig. 318. GP. p. 309, fig. 442.
92 Étienne Moreau-Nélaton, *Camille Moreau Peintre et Céramiste 1840–1897* (Paris: H. Floury ed., 1899), two volumes (I: *Céramiques*; II: *Tableaux*). Photographs Yvon. 200 copies printed.
93 Xavier de Massary specifies that it was a terracotta by Augustin Pajou, signed and dated 1764 on the base (private collection).
94 This vase from 1888 was reproduced in *Camille Moreau-Nélaton. Une femme céramiste* cit., p. 52, cat. 47.
95 Étienne Moreau-Nélaton, *Union centrale des arts décoratifs / Les Arts de la femme / 2e exposition / 27 avril – 10 juin / Palais de l'Industrie, Porte VII*, Paris, Impr. lith. Charles Verneau, 1895, lithographic poster in two colours (brown and yellow) on a cream background, done with a brush and crachis, 120 × 74.5 cm.
96 Exh. cat. *Camille Moreau-Nélaton* cit.
97 Moreau 1907, no. 50: "50. SORTIE DE L'ÉCOLE TURQUE. 0.62 × 0.88. – Signed on

the bottom left. This painting is one version of the watercolour on the same subject, shown at the Salon in 1842. It appeared in the auction held by Decamps in 1853, listed as no. 6. – Acquired at this auction by Mr Adolphe Moreau father – 1889 centenary exhibition (no. 249 in the catalogue)".

98 Moreau 1907, no. 31, p. 68.

99 Moreau 1907, no. 90 p. 112.

100 Moreau 1907, no. 40, p. 17. MN, no.73, p. 95.

101 Moreau 1907, no. 93, p. 114.

102 Moreau 1907, no. 96, pp. 116–17.

103 Moreau 1907, no. 29, p. 15 (purchased by Adolphe Moreau father in 1852, it was shown at the *Corot* exhibition at the École des Beaux-Arts in 1875).

104 Moreau 1907, no. 39, p. 17 (purchase 1886). MN, no. 67, pp. 90–91.

105 Raymond Koechlin, "Claude Monet", *Art et Décoration*, vol. 51, février 1927, p. 47. Cited by Michael Pantazzi, "Réalismes", exh. cat. *Camille Corot: Memory between Plein-Air and the Salon*, Madrid, Museo Thyssen-Bornemisza, 7 June – 11 September 2005 (Madrid: Museo Thyssen-Bornemisza, 2005).

106 MN no. 13, p. 55.

107 MN no. 11, p. 54.

108 MN no. 84, p. 106.

109 MN nos. 92 and 87.

110 MN no. 62.

111 MN no. 72.

112 MN nos. 60 and 36.

113 *Mémorial*, vol. IV, p. 29.

114 MN no. 107, pp. 124–25.

115 Édouard Manet, *La Femme à l'éventail*, 1872, Moreau, 1907, no. 71, p. 27. MN, no. 92, p. 104.

116 Xavier de Massary indicates that his grandmother remembered however having played the piano under this painting! Perhaps it was in another property (for example La Tournelle, in Aisne)? Or in another room? There was a piano in the reception room on the second floor, pl. 9 and 17.

117 Moreau, 1907, no. 74, p. 28.

118 Étienne Moreau-Nélaton, *Manet graveur et lithographe* (Paris: Loys Delteil, 1906).

119 Last title in the series "*raconté par lui-même*", begun with *Millet* (1921), continued with *Corot* (1924), *Daubigny* (1925) and *Manet* (1926), published posthumously: *Bonvin* (1927).

120 Étienne Moreau-Nélaton, *Manet raconté par lui-même* (Paris: Henri Laurens, 1926), vol. II, p. 116.

121 Michael Orwicz, "Reinventing Edouard Manet: Rewriting the Face of National Art in the Early Third Republic", *Art Criticism and its Institutions*, edited by Michael Orwicz, Manchester UP, 1994, pp. 122–45.

122 Édouard Manet, *Nature morte: fruits sur une table*, 1864, oil on canvas, 45 × 73.5 cm, 1906 donation (estimation 10,000 francs), Paris, Musée d'Orsay, RF 1670, MN no. 79 p. 101.

123 The donation of Olivier Senn's collection at the end of 2004 (*71 peintures, 5 sculptures et 151 dessins parmi lesquels des oeuvres de Courbet, Boudin, Monet, Pissarro, Renoir, Sisley, Derain, Marquet, Matisse, Bonnard*...) gave rise to an inaugural exhibition in 2005, followed by exhibitions of drawings in 2009 and 2011. Annette Haudiquet and Géraldine Lefebvre (eds.), *De Courbet à Matisse, Donation Senn-Foulds*, exh. cat., Le Havre, Musée Malraux, 13 March – 12 June 2005 (Le Havre–Paris: Musée Malraux and Somogy éditions d'art, 2005); *Henri-Edmond Cross / Ger Van Elk: Un nouveau regard sur la donation Senn-Foulds*, exh. cat., Le Havre, Musée Malraux, 21 February – 26 April 2009; Annette Haudiquet and Géraldine Lefebvre (eds.), *De Delacroix à Marquet. Donation Senn-Foulds. Dessins*, exh. cat., Le Havre, Musée Malraux, 12 March – 22 May 2011 (Le Havre–Paris: Musée Malraux and Somogy éditions d'art, 2011); Annette Haudiquet and Géraldine Lefebvre (eds.), *Le Cercle de l'art moderne. Collectionneurs d'avant-garde au Havre*, exh. cat., Paris, Musée du Luxembourg, 19 September 2012 – 6 January 2013 (Paris: Musée du Luxembourg and RMN-Grand Palais, 2012).

124 Anne Higonnet, *A Museum of One's Own: Private Collecting, Public Gift* (Munich: Periscope Books [Prestel], 2008).

125 Dario Libero Gamboni, *The Museum as Experience – An Email Odyssey through Artists' and Collectors' Museums* (Turnhout: Brepols, 2020). The suggested category of "author's museum" seems pertinent in this case. In this book, chapter 7, "Learning to see", focuses on the Barnes Foundation.

126 John Dewey, *L'Art comme expérience* (Paris: Gallimard, "Folio-essais", 2005). Dominique Chateau, *John Dewey et Albert C. Barnes: Philosophie pragmatique et arts plastiques* (Paris: L'Harmattan, "Ouverture philosophique", 2003).

127 Violette de Mazia, *The Barnes Foundation – The Display of Its Art Collection* (Merion: The Barnes Foundation Press, 1983).

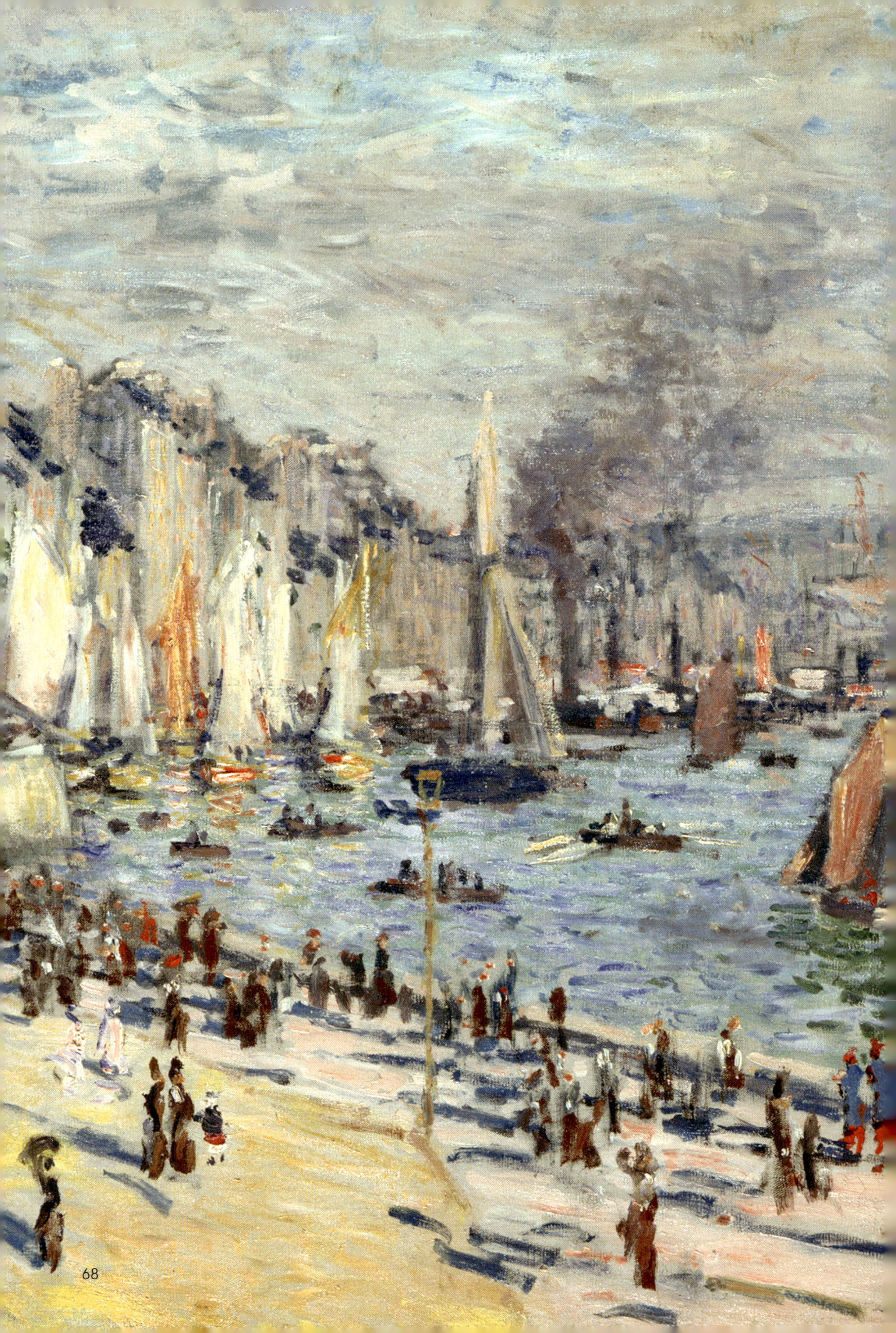

Impressionism Defined by Collections: From the Painter to the Art World

While Impressionism was very much defined by the innovative aesthetics developed by the artists themselves, the movement was actually broader in scope and more complex than just the pictorial aspect. It can also be understood from a social and economic viewpoint and, in this respect, involved a large number of individuals including art dealers, critics and collectors. Only a handful of them supported Impressionism in its early days, but their action was instrumental in the configuration of the movement. The first collectors were often artists themselves, or became close to the artists, sharing an intimate dialogue and playing an important role in the key moments of the movement's creation, particularly in terms of exhibitions and sales.

Impressionism emerged at the turn of the twentieth century, when the art world was being completely redefined. It was not just symptomatic of this evolution, but also actively challenged the aesthetic and institutional academic norms, thus enabling the development of the movement and its actors, and accelerating certain transitions, specifically with regard to exhibitions, which were organised by the artists themselves. By focusing on the role of collectors in shaping the movement, it is the evolution of the art world as a whole and the role each individual plays within it that is ultimately brought to light.

Claude Monet, *Port of Le Havre* (*Vue de l'ancien avant-port du Havre*), 1874, detail, Philadelphia Museum of Art

BUILDING IMPRESSIONIST COLLECTIONS: BETWEEN FRATERNITY AND SALES STRATEGIES

GWENDOLINE CORTHIER-HARDOIN

This study is concerned with analysing how the collections of Impressionist artists were constituted in terms of artistic motivation, the economic and symbolic issues at stake, and social practices. By collection we mean "a group of works temporarily or permanently kept outside of the economic network". According to the definition given by historian Krzysztof Pomian, "the conditions a group of objects must meet to be considered as a collection exclude, on the one hand, exhibitions, which are just moments in the process of the circulation of the production of material goods and, on the other, piles of objects randomly amassed together".[1] This theoretical anchoring allows us to consider various profiles at the core of the Impressionist group: Gustave Caillebotte, Mary Cassatt, Edgar Degas, Paul Gauguin, Berthe Morisot, Giuseppe De Nittis, Camille Pissarro, Auguste Renoir or Henri Rouart among the main ones. These artists were chosen according to two main criteria: their participation in at least one of the Impressionist exhibitions – an exception has been made for Frédéric Bazille and Édouard Manet as their respective collections are firmly rooted within the Impressionist group – and the data we have been able to gather from the primary and secondary sources.[2] Although the status of these artists differs depending on their career path and historiography – Caillebotte and Rouart being considered more as collector artists than artist collectors for example – we have decided to classify them as artist collectors in their own right because of their production, their participation in exhibitions, and the aesthetic and social motivation driving their acquisitions, similarly to artists where there is no ambiguity about their status. Even though the Impressionist artist collectors amassed works throughout their career, for this study we have

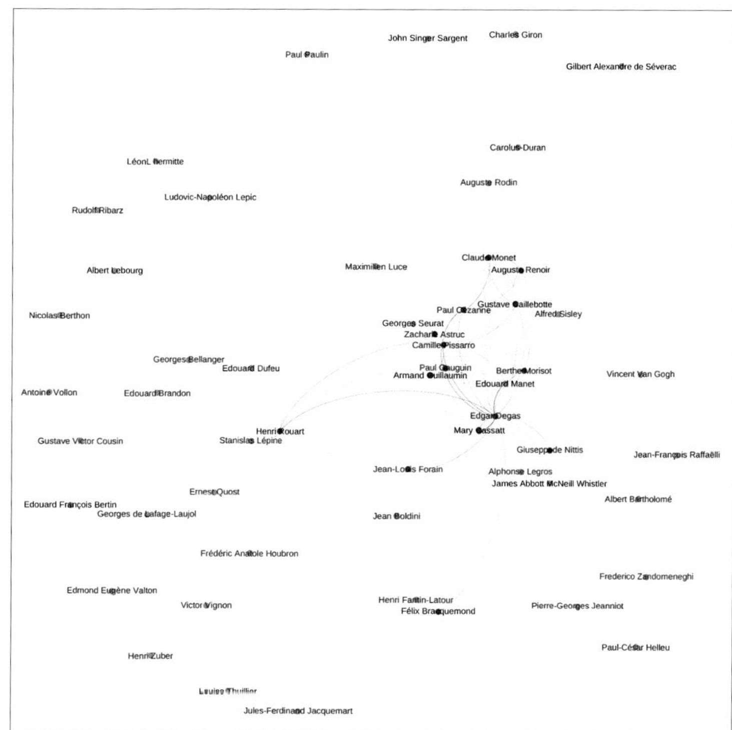

1. Diagram of Impressionist collector artists born between 1830 and 1850, whose collected works were produced between 1860 and 1880. This network contains fifteen collector artists who participated in one of the eight Impressionist exhibitions (blue nodes and links) connected to forty of their collected contemporaries (pink nodes and links) according to the weighted degree. Software: Gephi. Source: Gwendoline Corthier-Hardoin

concentrated on the period from 1867 – the date Bazille bought a work by Monet – to 1884, the year in which the works in Manet's studio went up for sale. A period of around fifteen years, which allows us to see how the Impressionist artists' collections were created according to a self-legitimising solidarity and reaction to the art market.

Creating a Fraternal Network

From 1863 onwards, the "academic" system began to be attacked from all sides.[3] That year, the severity of the Salon judges sparked anger among artists who decided to distance themselves from the academic system.[4] The more innovative artists did not fit in and so grouped together, as much for social reasons as aesthetic ones. They met in cafés where figures like Degas and Manet encouraged them to become more experimental. This was how, during the 1860s, the Groupe des Batignolles took form, made up of artists who had been refused at the Salon, some of them penniless. These moments of sociability contributed to creating a fraternal community, strengthened by the giving, exchanging or buying of works they made in a spirit of support and mutual admiration.

Bazille, for example, was one of the first artists to start collecting work by his colleagues. He bought *Women in the Garden* (*Femmes au jardin*) (1866–67, Musée d'Orsay, Paris) by Monet on credit for 2,500 francs, a painting that had been refused at the Salon in 1867.[5] This expensive acquisition, just several months after the painting was made, was a way for Bazille to help his friends out financially. "His attitude prefigures the type of collectors the new school needed to survive",[6] explains Anne Distel in her major work on Impressionist collectors. Indeed, the avant-garde were not yet attracting collectors and the future Impressionists relied on their colleagues to find amateur enthusiasts. Unlike his colleagues, Bazille, who came from a family of noteworthy protestants from Montpellier, led a comfortable lifestyle. He met Monet and Renoir in Charles Gleyre's studio, and began supporting them materially, morally and financially.

Camaraderie and mutual esteem are the keys to understanding the collections established by these avant-garde artists, in particular because they felt excluded from the traditional art and commercial institutions. They formed what Pierre Bourdieu qualifies as a society of mutual admiration, or in other words a community in which "the 'creator's' total independence was inseparable from their pretensions to not recognising any other recipient for their art than an *alter ego* or, in other words, another 'creator'".[7] Whilst the institutions were not able to accept their innovative productions, those in a position to understand were actually the innovative painters themselves, like Manet.

It was in this context that, in the late 1860s, Morisot donated one of her works to Manet, *The Harbour at Lorient* (*Vue du petit port de Lorient*) (1869, National Gallery of Art, London) which she had just finished. For Morisot, it was an important step. It symbolised not only Manet's recognition of her work but also her acceptance into a group of painters she greatly admired. In the same manner, when a work by Renoir came into Manet's possession around 1870, a portrait of *Frédéric Bazille* (1867, Musée d'Orsay, Paris), it was to show Manet's esteem of his young colleague. Renoir wrote *a posteriori*: "I had even made a portrait of Bazille which was fortunate enough to be noticed by Manet, who did not really appreciate what I was doing ... which leaves us to believe that at least once I have painted something that was not that bad".[8] Manet's watchful eye over his young colleagues comforted them in the new direction they were taking. They saw him as a guiding figure, as Fantin-Latour expressed when he painted *A Studio at Les Batignolles* (*Un atelier aux Batignolles*) (1870, Musée d'Orsay, Paris). In this work, grouped around Manet painting are Renoir, Bazille and Monet, three artists who figured in Manet's own private collection. The latter was also in possession of works by Félix Bracquemond, Fantin-Latour, De Nittis, Pissarro or furthermore Alfred Sisley.[9] These artists testify to the creation of a network around the figure of Manet, on the one hand, and prefigure the circulation of works between innovative painters on the other.

These transactions between Impressionists in fact reflected a close-knit community, driven by friendship, solidarity, but also, as we will see, by strategies of identification and trade. The collections of these painters were mostly made up of works by contemporary artists, but above all Impressionists like themselves. To highlight this, we have recreated the network with the help of Gephi, the major visualisation and exploration software. The resulting diagram allows us to see the connections between the painters when they collected in a completely new way. Nevertheless, this tool must be used with precaution, in so much as the results are the interpretation of the non-exhaustive data we have gathered. As Miriam Kienle reminds us, we must constantly keep in mind that data is never a neutral or natural phenomenon.[10] Our interpretation then is based on the current state of research of our data.

From a methodological viewpoint, the links symbolise how one artist is connected to another. These links move clockwise to signify that individual A collects work by individual B. The artists are represented by nodes. The size of these nodes varies depending on the weighted degree. The weighted degree corresponds to the number of links having a node at its extremity and allows us to determine the most important nodes depending on the intensity of the relationships. Moreover, we have used a colour code to differentiate artist collectors who participated in Impressionist exhibitions (nodes and links in blue) from other artists who didn't take part (pink nodes and links).

A network of 15 artist collectors appears in this diagram (fig. 1): Zacharie Astruc, Félix Bracquemond, Gustave Caillebotte, Mary Cassatt, Paul Cézanne, Edgar Degas, Jean-Louis Forain, Armand Guillaumin, Paul Gauguin, Claude Monet, Berthe Morisot, Camille Pissarro, Auguste Renoir, Henri Rouart and Giuseppe De Nittis. Here, the aim was to show which of their contemporaries they collected (born between 1830 and 1850), in order to highlight the personal relationships they developed.[11] To create this network, we based our research on works produced between the 1860s and the 1880s.[12] The graphic reveals a real community, centred around a "hard Impressionist core" who collected in a reticular manner. The Impressionist circle crystallises the majority of transactions made by this avant-garde in terms of their combined struggles, but also the many social occasions they shared – café, voyages, exhibitions – as well as the aesthetic affinities they developed, allowing them to maintain a united and fraternal community despite their dissensions.

The circulation of the works themselves, reveals some disagreements between the painters. We might think in particular of Degas here, giving back a painting called *Plums* (*Prunes*) that Manet had given to him because of

a supposedly unforgivable gesture made by the latter. Manet had cut up a painting by a Degas stored in his studio on the pretext that his wife was badly painted in it.[13] The work symbolised the fraternal link between the two men, and the restitution of *Plums* was a powerful act that marked an affective rupture. Similarly, after making up with Manet, Degas wanted to retrieve the work in order to symbolically reconstruct their bond.
Finally, this network spotlights the way some artists evolved within more specific networks, like Degas, Monet or Rouart. Thanks to this diagram, the latter appeared to be more of a collector than a collected artist (only Degas seems to have obtained his works). Similarly, Caillebotte was only collected by Monet and Renoir. The visualisation shows the need to understand the artists' collections in relation to the position of each of the painters within the context of modern art, some collecting more than being collected due to the role they had in relation to their colleagues and their respective artistic affinities.

The Impressionists Band Together to Legitimise Their Work

In 1873, Degas, Monet, Renoir, Sisley and Pierre Prins created the Société anonyme coopérative des artistes peintres, sculpteurs et graveurs. The grouping together of these artists is important for understanding the way in which the Impressionists collected. It favoured the circulation of works between these innovative painters not just through mutual esteem but also by financial support. For example, in 1873, Degas bought *Ploughed Fields near Osny* (*Terrains labourés près d'Osny*) by Pissarro for 400 francs at a public sale.[14] A means for Degas to support his penniless friend on the auction market. The same year, Degas received *Study of a Woman* (*Étude de femme*) as a gift from Renoir,[15] a symbolic transaction reflecting this painter's admiration for his elder. These transactions were founded on solidarity within a context of poverty for some and hence the need for helping each other financially. Renoir, who had some major financial difficulties at the start of his career,[16] perfectly summed up what was at stake during these years when he explained in 1918: "It is our shared poverty that unites us and which has also enabled us, having brought us together, to create the Impressionist school. Individually, we would never have had the strength or the courage, nor even the idea. The Impressionist school was founded on our friendship and discussion as well as our misfortune. We quickly had to fight and support each other".[17]
Indeed, the fight, support and friendship favoured the circulation of works among the Impressionists, as reflected for example by a series of

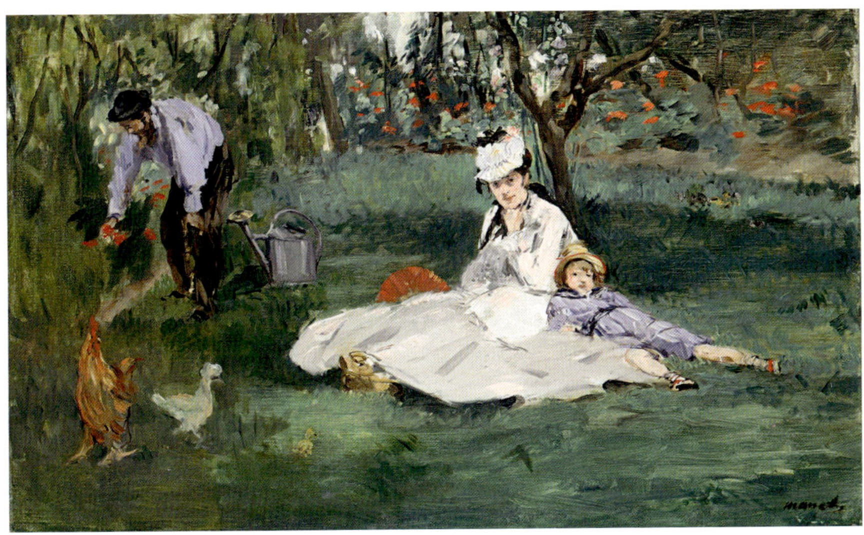

2. Édouard Manet, *The Monet Family in Their Garden* (*La Famille Monet au jardin*), 1874, oil on canvas, 61 × 99.7 cm, The Metropolitan Museum of Art, New York. This work was gifted by Manet to Monet after he made it

transactions that took place between Monet and Manet in the summer of 1874 when they were staying not far from each other. Manet made *The Monet Family in Their Garden* (*La Famille Monet au jardin*) (1874, The Metropolitan Museum of Art, fig. 2) which he offered to Monet. In parallel, Monet painted *Manet at his Easel* (*Manet à son chevalet*) (location unknown), which he then gave to Manet. At the same time, Renoir also came to work with the two artists. He painted *Madame Monet and her Son* (*Madame Monet et son fils*) (1874, National Gallery of Art, Washington, D.C.), given shortly afterwards to his friend Monet.[18] These productions, and in particular the portraits, symbolise both the amicable ties between artists, the esteem they shared for each other, but also a mutual recognition of their respective work.[19] They reflect a social phenomenon known as "gift exchange", whereby an individual is obliged to accept a gift and give one back in return. This is the "triple obligation of giving, receiving and giving back", a social rule highlighted by Marcel Mauss in his *Essai sur le don* in 1925.[20]

These gifts, along with the trades and purchases made through group solidarity, contributed to the process of self-legitimisation of the Impressionist group. A momentum even more visible at the first Impressionist sale on 24 March 1875. The event was initiated by Renoir who rallied the artists in his circle behind his cause and presented his works along with those by Morisot, Monet and Sisley. Research carried out by Merete Bodelsen revealed that among those who supported the Impressionists in the auction room were the Impressionists themselves. Caillebotte probably bought his first Monet there,[21] *A Corner of the Apartment* (*Un coin d'appartement*) (1875, Musée d'Orsay, Paris). Rouart was also one of the main buyers, acquiring Monet's *The Bassin du commerce in the Port of Le Havre* (*Bassin du commerce. Le Havre*) (1874, Musée des Beaux-Arts, Liège) for 200 francs and *Sunrise (Marine)* (*Soleil levant [Marine]*) for 175 francs; Morisot's *Cottage by the Sea* (*Chalet au bord de la mer*) for 230 francs and *Watercolour on the Beach* (*Aquarelle, sur la plage*) for 60 francs.[22] It is possible that Degas bought *Head of a Woman* (*Tête de femme*) by Renoir for 80 francs,[23] although it was probably Rouart who did the bidding.[24]

It was then these artists, who already had comfortable financial means, who created and fuelled the Impressionist market with the aim of aiding their colleagues, because in 1875, the tastes of art enthusiasts were mainly attracted towards artists like Jean-Auguste-Dominique Ingres, Constant Troyon, Ferdinand Roybet, Théodore Rousseau, Jean-François Millet, William Bouguereau or furthermore Eugène Delacroix.[25] Apart from their own colleagues, the Impressionists were still a long way from charming collectors. The purchases made by the Impressionists, boosted by a system of alliance, exemplifies Pierre Bourdieu's notion of a society of mutual admiration and more precisely a cycle of mutual legitimisation resulting from a quest for distinction among individuals who were not in direct competition.[26] The Impressionists may have been in rivalry with their academic homologues, even in a conflictual relationship where realism was concerned, but among themselves the painters showed their solidarity in order to establish their position. And so, the circulation of works within the group participated in a network of legitimisation, particularly evident in regards to the acquisitions of the Italian artist De Nittis or by Caillebotte.

In 1876 for example, De Nittis bought two works by Monet:[27] *White Frost* (*Gelée blanche*) (1875) and *The Museum at Le Havre* (*Le Musée du Havre*) (1873, National Gallery of Art, London). De Nittis had arrived in Paris a few years earlier and had become good friends with Caillebotte, Degas or further still Manet – with whom he exchanged works – and benefitted from comfortable means. His "collectionism" highlights,[28] as with the case of Bazille, a desire to help his colleagues in the greatest financial difficulty at the same time as wanting to reinforce his own assets thanks to the paintings of the artists in his close circle.

As for Caillebotte, the death of his father in 1874 left him with a considerable fortune, sheltering him from the financial difficulties encountered by some of his friends. Probably around the time of the second Impressionist exhibition, on 16 April 1876, Caillebotte bought *Regattas at Argenteuil* (*Régates à Argenteuil*) (c. 1872, Musée d'Orsay, Paris) directly from Monet.[29] In 1877, Caillebotte also acquired two works by Pissarro: *The Harvest* (*La Moisson*) (1876, Musée d'Orsay, Paris) and *Louveciennes*. The same year, Caillebotte came into possession of *The Swing* (*La Balançoire*) by Renoir (1876, Musée d'Orsay, Paris),[30] which he lent for the third Impressionist exhibition. This action, which could be qualified as a purchase with a promotional objective insofar as this work was exhibited after its acquisition, was a recurrent theme in Caillebotte's method of collecting. For example, the same year 1877, he bought *Les Tuileries* by Monet and lent it for the third Impressionist exhibition. For the same event, he also lent some works by Degas he had recently bought: *Women at the Terrace of a Café in the Evening* (*Femmes à la terrasse d'un café le soir*) (1877), *Woman in front of a Café, Evening* (*Femme devant un café, le soir*) (1877) and *The Chorus* (*Choristes*) (1877, Musée d'Orsay, Paris).[31] Even if the public was increasingly growing in number – 8,000 visitors for the third exhibition – and the press praised them more and more, the Impressionists continued, despite everything, to suffer great criticism.[32] Some critics, such as Léon de Lora, called them "eccentric", "incredibly pretentious and loud".[33] And Léon de Lora added: "Nobody has any talent except for them and their friends. They have sworn exclusive mutual admiration and support to each other all the same".[34] On this last point, the critic was not wrong.

In 1878, for example, several painters supported Monet by buying his work. De Nittis acquired *The Turkeys* (*Les Dindons*) (1877, Musée d'Orsay, Paris) by Monet, even though it was mocked when it was first shown at the third Impressionist exhibition. Léon de Lora wrote in particular that "I won't comment on the panel of white turkeys clucking on the garish green grass, as I don't really know what to say".[35] Monet's *Port of Le Havre* (*Vue de l'ancien avant-port du Havre*) (1874, Philadelphia Museum of Art) equally came into De Nittis' possession, similarly to Caillebotte who obtained several works by the same artist that year. On 10 March, Caillebotte bought *The Lunch: Decorative panel* (*Le Déjeuner: panneau décoratif*) (c. 1873, Musée d'Orsay, Paris) from Monet for 600 francs[36] as well as the famous *Gare Saint-Lazare* (1877, Musée d'Orsay, Paris).[37] In addition, during the auction of Ernest Hoschedé's collection in 1878, there was a new recruit in the room, the painter Mary Cassatt from the United States. She acquired two paintings: one by Monet, *The Beach at Trouville* (*La Plage à Trouville*) (1870, private collection) for 200 francs; the other by Morisot, *La Toilette*, for 95 francs.[38] There were multiple reasons for these purchases. For Cassatt, it was about becoming part of a group that would allow her to innovate.[39] For Monet, it was a matter of being helped financially. That year, the artist was still struggling to make a reasonable living from his work and, through their role as collectors, his colleagues provided not just a commercial trampoline, but also moral support.

Still in 1878, Pissarro received the same kind of help from Cassatt. Pissarro was finding it hard to earn enough to support his large family. He wrote to his friend the painter Eugène Murer: "I have been running around the whole of Paris for the last eight days, looking for the kind of man who would buy Impressionist paintings. I am still looking ... I find myself absolutely penniless".[40] But in the summer of 1878 Cassatt supported him financially. Pissarro wrote to Murer in July: "I am probably leaving this evening as I am expecting a visit from Miss Cassatt, who intends to buy some of my paintings".[41] As well as Cassatt's financial and moral support, Pissarro was also aided by Caillebotte who lent him some money: "I am writing to Caillebotte to ask him to do me the same favour; with his 1,000 francs, it's a weight off my mind and I will do my best to hobble along, it's my last hope",[42] Pissarro wrote to Murer in June 1879.

Monet also tried to earn enough to support his family. He was not only discouraged by the lack of success with his works, but also the health of his wife Camille who was very sick. He reluctantly accepted to participate in the fourth Impressionist exhibition in 1879, following which he probably received *Paris Street. Rainy Day* (*Rue de Paris. Temps de pluie*) from Caillebotte as a gift (1877, Musée Marmottan Monet, Paris).[43] As Marianne Mathieu and Dominique Lobstein explain, this gift could have been a means of elegantly ensuring that Monet had a small capital.[44] Indeed, beyond this friendship, mutual esteem and fraternal support, the Impressionist acquisitions were a way of building assets.

Transactions Based on Artistic and Financial Strategies

Without one being incompatible with the other, Impressionist acquisitions oscillated between friendship and strategy. Firstly, an artistic strategy, in order to become part of or consolidate a network; and secondly a financial strategy, by constituting a long-term capital. Gauguin in particular used both these strategies. In 1879, he started his collection of Impressionist works. Aged about thirty, Gauguin was making a comfortable living at that time. After fighting in the war, he became a broker at the Paris stock exchange and led something of a bourgeois life which gave him the means to become a collector. This was how Gauguin acquired works by Pissarro whilst working alongside him during the summer. Their positions in the field of art were however not equal. Pissarro had much more artistic experience than Gauguin, whilst the latter was considered a pupil, but also a patron. And so, he played two roles, one artistic and the other economic. His son Pola recounted *a posteriori*:

> In fact, Gauguin led two lives and began playing for high stakes in both one and the other. On the stock market, with constant good fortune. One year he earned forty thousand francs, so much that he didn't hesitate to satisfy the desire he had had for a long time to invest in some paintings. So he spent fifteen thousand francs in one hit. Guided by his sharp eye, aided by advice from Pissarro and thanks to his useful contacts, he made some good purchases at cheap prices, and established an outstanding collection of paintings by Manet, Renoir, Degas, Sisley, Cézanne, Pissarro and Guillaumin.[45]

Gauguin's involvement at the heart of the Impressionist network – as both an artist and buyer – enabled him to create relationships with the other members of the group such as Mary Cassatt, with whom he exchanged works.[46] Gauguin also exchanged works with Degas, probably between 1880 and 1881.[47] This was a symbolic victory for Gauguin. These trades meant that he had started to be recognised as an artist by his peers. Gauguin obtained the pastel *Dancer Adjusting her Shoe* (*Danseuse ajustant son chausson*) (c. 1879, Ordrupgaard, Copenhagen) by Degas and the latter obtained *On a Chair* (*Sur une chaise*) (private collection) by Gauguin in return. On 6 January 1881, Gauguin bought *By the Seashore* (*Femme au bord de la mer*) (unidentified) from Renoir for 300 francs.[48] Later, it was *Quai Sully* (private collection) by Guillaumin and *Landscape near Pontoise* (*Paysage des environs de Pontoise*) (Ny Carlsberg Glyptotek, Copenhagen) by Pissarro which came into his possession. Some of his new acquisitions figured in the sixth Impressionist exhibition in 1881, alongside works by Pissarro and Guillaumin,[49] a way of valorising his colleagues as well as his own personal collection and hence his assets. This idea is strengthened by the fact that Gauguin's name appeared in the exhibition catalogue which was not the case for all of the collectors.

From the early 1880s onwards, Gauguin also obtained some works by Manet,[50] an artist who became even more sought after when he died in 1883. The sale of Manet's studio work in 1884 enabled the Impressionists to obtain several of his works as souvenirs, but also as a commercial strategy. Morisot, for example, was in the auction room and bought several works, not just for herself, but also for her sister Edma. Morisot wrote to her: "For 620 francs, I obtained the painting of the steamer departing for you ... If you want it, tell me straight away; I'll have it wrapped; otherwise, I'll keep it to sell for a profit ...".[51] A statement that highlights how some

Impressionists acquired pieces with a financial, even speculative aim, by trying to make a profit.
Degas and Caillebotte were also at the auction. Degas bought a study for 40 francs, but also the pair to *Behind the Barricade* (*Derrière la barricade*), for 77 francs.[52] As for Caillebotte, he acquired a study of a race for 200 francs and most importantly *The Balcony* (*Le Balcon*) (1868–69, Musée d'Orsay, Paris) for 3,000 francs.[53] Some artists could not attend and enlisted the art dealer Durand-Ruel to buy works on their behalf. That was how Rouart came to obtain *The Music Lesson* (*La Leçon de musique*) (1870, Museum of Fine Arts, Boston) for 4,400 francs.[54] Monet equally asked the dealer to attend on his behalf and Durand-Ruel bought *Woman in a Fur Coat in Profile* (*Femme à la fourrure de profil*) (c. 1879) for him.[55] Shortly after the sale of his studio works, Pissarro also obtained a work by Manet, *Type espagnol*, from Durand-Ruel for 200 francs.[56]
If so many artists wanted to obtain works by Manet it was because, for a long time, the Impressionists had shared a common pictorial approach with their deceased friend. The art historian Michael Fried has particularly evoked the young painter's modernist interpretation of the flatness of Manet's surfaces.[57] But these shared pictorial experiments were probably not the only reason. The exhibition devoted to Manet at the École des Beaux-Arts in Paris in January 1884 contributed to making the artist famous. From an artistic and financial stance, it was now good taste to obtain works by Manet. During the event, the artists lent works from their own private collections, such as Alfred Stevens,[58] De Nittis,[59] Fantin-Latour,[60] Gauguin,[61] Rouart,[62] Caillebotte[63] or James Tissot.[64] These loans highlight the group's desire to promote their personal collections and simultaneously their capacity to acquire works ahead of public enthusiasm for Manet. The idea was probably to show that the artists themselves had seen Manet's talent before the regular collectors. In addition, the sale of Manet's studio work was a chance to acquire works on a secondary market, outside of Durand-Ruel's circuit. The art historian Robert Jensen talks about a "monopolising" of Manet's work by Durand-Ruel as early as the 1870s, which he bought and sold at high prices.[65] We can consider then that artists looking to buy works by Manet were attempting to obtain works for lower prices at the post-mortem sale, rather than by going through Durand-Ruel. In this way, the artist collectors also positioned themselves as experts, capable of anticipating the changing value of artworks.

Conclusion

Thanks to their status as artists with direct access to contemporary productions, the Impressionists quickly obtained the work of their colleagues, through gifts, exchanges and purchases. These transactions reflect the friendships, mutual admiration, as well as the struggle they shared. In addition, Impressionist artist collectors played a determining role in the spread and valorisation of the movement by lending works by their colleagues to exhibitions, some of which had only recently been made. By adopting a collective and united approach, the Impressionists successfully managed to circulate their works, well before the art enthusiasts, art institutions or sellers began supporting them. In the early 1870s, within a context of rejection, their acquisitions allowed them to legitimise their work. They also contributed to the construction of a market that had excluded them up until then and which they now participated in, sometimes strategically. Looking at the way the Impressionists acquired works has revealed an unknown side to the artists, as buyers, even though they are more often associated with bohemian figures, disinterested in market logic. Of course, these artists were often penniless and obtained works within the framework of their friendships, but their acquisitions were also the result of well-thought-out actions in order to ensure their position and take their stance faced with the market.

1 Krzysztof Pomian, *Collectionneurs, amateurs et curieux. Paris, Venise: XVIe-XVIIIe siècle*, Bibliothèque des Histoires (Paris: Gallimard, 1987), p. 18. Our translation.
2 The works collected by the Impressionists have been taken from post-mortem inventories, exhibition catalogues, auction catalogues and letters for the primary sources, then thanks to historiography for the secondary ones. These sources are mentioned throughout our study. The titles of the works collected are those used in these sources and are accompanied by the date of creation and place of conservation, if this information is available.
3 Harrison and Cynthia White, *La Carrière des peintres au XIXe siècle. Du système académique au marché impressionniste* (Paris: Flammarion, 1991).
4 Gaëtan Picon, *1863: la naissance de la peinture moderne* (Geneva: Albert Skira, 1974).
5 Letter from Claude Monet to Frédéric Bazille, 20 May 1867, cited in Daniel Wildenstein, *Claude Monet*, vol. I (Lausanne–Paris: Bibliothèque des arts, 1974), p. 423, no. 32.
6 Anne Distel, *Les Collectionneurs des impressionnistes: amateurs et marchands* (Paris: Bibliothèque des arts, 1989), pp. 17–18.
7 Pierre Bourdieu, "Le marché des biens symboliques", *L'Année Sociologique* 22, 1971: p. 54.
8 Ambroise Vollard, *En écoutant Cézanne, Degas, Renoir* (Paris: Bernard Grasset, 1938), p. 169.
9 Post-mortem inventory of Édouard Manet, 18 June 1883, National Archives (MC/ET/LXXXIX/1713).
10 Miriam Kienle, "Between Nodes and Edges: Possibilities and Limits of Network Analysis in Art History", *Artl@s Bulletin* 6, no. 3, 2017, online, http://docs.lib.purdue.edu/artlas/vol6/iss3/1
11 The collections of artists such as Manet or Van Gogh do not appear in the network insofar as they did not participate in the Impressionist exhibitions.
12 Undated works have also been included.
13 Vollard, *En écoutant Cézanne*, p. 125.
14 Janine Bailly-Herzberg, *Correspondance de Camille Pissarro, 1865-1885*, vol. I (Paris: Presses universitaires de France, 1980), p. 33.
15 Ann Dumas, *The Private Collection of Edgar Degas* (New York: The Metropolitan Museum of Art and H. N. Abrams, 1997), p. 11.
16 On this subject, see *Renoir Between Bohemia and Bourgeoisie: The Early Years*, Kunstmuseum, Bâle, 1 Apri – 12 August 2012 (Ostfildern: Hatje Cantz Verlad, 2012). Exhibition catalogue.
17 René Gimpel, *Journal d'un collectionneur, marchand de tableaux* (Paris: Calmann-Lévy, 1963), p. 28.
18 Marianne Mathieu, Dominique Lobstein (eds.), *Monet collectionneur*, exh. cat., Paris, Musée Marmottan Monet – Académie des Beaux-Arts, Institut de France, 14 September 2017 – 14 January 2018 (Paris: Hazan, 2017), p. 101–2.
19 Ségolène Le Men, Sylvain Amic, "Le portrait impressionniste, un genre personnel", in Sylvain Amic (ed.), *Scènes de la vie impressionniste*, Musée des Beaux-Arts, Rouen, 16 April – 26 September 2016 (Paris: Éditions de la Réunion des Musées nationaux, 2016), p. 20–47. Exhibition catalogue.
20 Marcel Mauss, *Essai sur le don: forme et raison de l'échange dans les sociétés archaïques*, Quadrige (Paris: Presses universitaires de France, 2007). First published 1925.
21 Another hypothesis is that Monet bought his own work to sell it later to Caillebotte.
22 Merete Bodelsen, "Early Impressionist Sales 1874–94 in the Light of Some Unpublished 'Procès-Verbaux'", *The Burlington Magazine* 110, no. 783, 1968: pp. 335–36.
23 École du Louvre and Musée d'Orsay, *Degas inédit*, conference proceedings, Musée d'Orsay, Paris, 18–21 April 1988, Collection des rencontres (Paris, La Documentation française, 1989), p. 66.
24 Bodelsen, "Early Impressionist Sales", pp. 335–36.
25 See the classification of artists according to the maximum price achieved at the 1875 public auction in Paris, in Léa Saint-Raymond, "Les impressionnistes à contre-courant du marché ? Le musée imaginaire de l'hôtel Drouot (1874-1875)", speech for the symposium *Un portrait intérieur: le musée imaginaire des impressionnistes*, Rouen, Musée des Beaux-Arts, 7–8 September 2016, organised by Paris Nanterre University. See also Pierre Cabanne, *Les Grands Collectionneurs. Vol. I: Du Moyen Âge au XIXe siècle* (Paris: Les Éditions de l'Amateur, 2003).
26 Bourdieu, "Le marché", p. 122.
27 Post-mortem inventory of Giuseppe De Nittis, National Archives, MC/ET/XII/1361. See also Wildenstein, *Claude Monet*, vol. I, pp. 224 and 268.
28 See Fausto Minervini's contribution in this volume about Giuseppe De Nittis's collectionism.

29 Distel, *Les Collectionneurs*, p. 259.
30 See the description of the work on the Musée d'Orsay website, https://www.musee-orsay.fr/en/artworks/la-balancoire-1096 (accessed 18 May 2021).
31 Sophie Monneret, *L'Impressionnisme et son époque: dictionnaire international* (Paris: Robert Laffont, 1987), p. 239. Today this work is called *Bain de mer*.
32 Dominique Lobstein, *Monet* (Paris: Jean-Paul Gisserot, 2002), p. 49.
33 Léon de Lora, "L'exposition des impressionnistes", *Le Gaulois*, 10th year, no. 3094, Tuesday 10 April 1877, pp. 1–2, online, https://gallica.bnf.fr/ark:/12148/bpt6k522313f.item (accessed 10 May 2021).
34 Ibid.
35 De Lora, "L'exposition des impressionnistes".
36 Distel, *Les Collectionneurs*, p. 259.
37 See the description of the work on the Musée d'Orsay website, https://www.musee-orsay.fr/en/artworks/la-gare-saint-lazare-10897 (accessed 18 May 2021).
38 Bodelsen, "Early Impressionist Sales", p. 340.
39 Achille Segard, *Mary Cassatt, un peintre des enfants et des mères* (Paris: Librairie Paul Ollendorf, 1913), pp. 7–8.
40 Letter from Camille Pissarro to Eugène Murer, in Adolphe Tabarant, *Pissarro* (Paris: F. Rieder, 1924), p. 38.
41 Letter from Camille Pissarro to Eugène Murer, c. July 1878, in Bailly-Herzberg, *Correspondance de Camille Pissarro* cit., p. 125, no. 69.
42 Letter from Camille Pissarro to Eugène Murer, June 1879, in ibid., p. 135, no. 78.
43 *Monet collectionneur* cit., p. 128.
44 Ibid.
45 P. Gauguin, *Paul Gauguin, mon père* (Paris: Les Éditions de France, 1938), p. 62.
46 Merete Bodelsen, "Gauguin, the Collector", *The Burlington Magazine* 112, 1970, no. 810, p. 593.
47 Ibid.
48 Ibid., p. 612.
49 Monneret, *op. cit.*, p. 247.
50 Bodelsen, "Gauguin, the Collector" cit., p. 611.
51 Berthe Morisot, *Correspondance de Berthe Morisot avec sa famille et ses amis, Manet, Puvis de Chavannes, Degas, Monet, Renoir et Mallarmé* (Paris: Quatre Chemins-Éditart, 1950), pp. 119–20.
52 Bodelsen, "Early Impressionist Sales" cit., p. 343.
53 Ibid., p. 344.
54 Ibid., p. 342.
55 Letter from Claude Monet to Paul Durand-Ruel, 23 January 1884, in Daniel Wildenstein, *Claude Monet*, vol. II (Lausanne: Paris, Bibliothèque des arts, 1979), p. 232, no. 391.
56 *Monet collectionneur* cit., p. 92.
57 Michael Fried, *Le modernisme de Manet ou Le visage de la peinture dans les années 1860. Esthétiques et origines de la peinture moderne, III* (Paris: Gallimard, 2000), p. 36. See also note 44, p. 294.
58 *Catalogue de l'Exposition des œuvres de Édouard Manet*, École nationale des Beaux-Arts, Paris, January 1884, no. 21. Exhibition catalogue.
59 Ibid., no. 58.
60 Ibid., no. 60.
61 Ibid., no. 54.
62 Ibid., nos. 66 and 71.
63 Ibid., no. 73.
64 Ibid., no. 79.
65 Robert Jensen, *Marketing Modernism in Fin-de-Siècle Europe* (Princeton: Princeton University Press, 1994), p. 82.

THE DE NITTIS, COLLECTORS AND "COLLECTED"

FAUSTO MINERVINI

Within the framework of relationships between collectors and his Impressionist collection, a very unique case is undoubtedly that of Giuseppe De Nittis (1846–1884), an Italian painter who actively belonged to the French avant-gardist group for a short period of time. His experience, in fact, invites us to think about the multiple factors behind the creation of a collection, not just those linked to the owner's aesthetic or artistic tastes, but also the fundamental personal socio-economic aims of a foreign artist and his family settling in Paris. In this respect, as both the first and most important representative of Italian Impressionism in Paris,[1] De Nittis's career was characterised by a clear division between the dynamics of his personal life, which in the 1870s-1880s increasingly led him to mix in official Parisian social and cultural circles, and the way he collected, which, in contrast, reflected the natural inclination and style (very similar to the Impressionists) he already had as a young man in Naples. In order to analyse his activity as a collector, it is essential to start by recreating the key moments in his social ascension. It began in Paris in 1869, when the De Nittis family sojourned at La Jonchère, a small village in the west of France, close to the Parisian cultural elite. In 1867, following his first collaborations with the Maison Goupil, who bought his paintings, the De Nittis family began leading a very comfortable life, marked by the acquisition, between 1870 and 1871, of a first building in Paris on Avenue de l'Impératrice,[2] near to the Bois de Boulogne, elegantly decorated in the fashions of the time. During this period, the Italian artist became close to the Impressionists, not just in terms of his artistic experimentations, but also on a human and social level. In a letter dated April 1873, addressed to Telemaco Signorini – leader of the Tuscan *macchiaioli* – De Nittis revealed that "purely by chance and

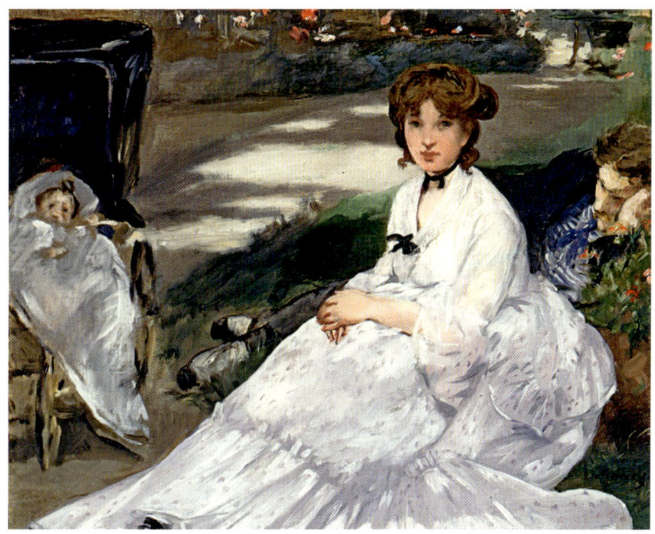

1. Édouard Manet,
In the Garden (Au jardin),
1870, oil on canvas,
44.5 × 54 cm,
Shelburne Museum

quite effortlessly, I got to know people who had already been regularly frequenting each other for the last four years and who shared a certain sympathy",[3] already, then, from the very first meetings of the Impressionist group at Café Guerbois.

When the Franco-Prussian war broke out, the Manet family was invited to the De Nittis's at La Jonchère. A special and increasingly close relationship blossomed between the two painters, based on admiration, affection and a deep reciprocal artistic respect for each other. And this is how the De Nittis acquired Manet's *In the Garden* (*Au jardin*) (1870, Shelburne Museum, fig. 1) for their collection, a work dating from 1870, not depicting the De Nittis family as was thought for a long time – at this time the De Nittis didn't have any children – but Mrs Pontillon and her brother Tiburce Morisot. Around the same period, De Nittis was working at La Grenouillère with Manet and other French artists: painting in open air each with their own style. Even though his drawing was still quite dense – as one can see in *La Grenouillère* (private collection) from 1873 – his brushwork was moving towards a more Impressionist style. Nonetheless, at this same period, De Nittis was still capable of radically moving away from this liberated and non-academic style of painting, making works appreciated by a bourgeois French public which sold very easily. These were scenes of courtly love, with characters often pictured in late-eighteenth-century costumes in the style of Ernest Meissonier (1815–1891) or Mariano Fortuny y Marsal (1838–1874), or anecdotal subjects set in the south of Italy, most of them intended for Adolphe Goupil (1806–1893), the art dealer and editor with whom De Nittis had signed an exclusive contract in 1872.

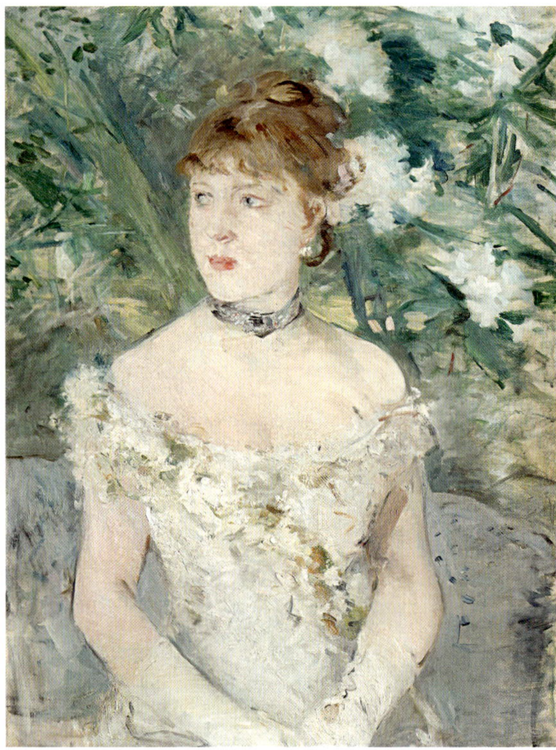

2. Berthe Morisot, *Young Girl in a Ball Gown* (*Jeune femme en toilette de bal*), 1879, oil on canvas, 71 × 54 cm, Musée d'Orsay, Paris

3–4. Contract for the purchase of a building between Giuseppe De Nittis and K. Twinberrow, Lease, 9 May 1879, Los Angeles, Getty Research Institute, Special Collections (860138)

This was an important year for De Nittis. He went back to Naples where he met Gustave Caillebotte (1848–1894), who remained in Southern Italy for several months and became the godfather of little Jacques, the Italian painter's son born on 19 July in Resina.[4] We do not know much about Caillebotte's Neapolitan trip or the relationships he had during this period. Nevertheless, it is certain that, with De Nittis by his side, the same year Caillebotte made *A Road in Naples* (*Une route à Naples*) (private collection) and *Banks of a Canal near Naples* (*Bord d'un canal près de Naples*) (National Gallery of Ireland, Dublin). The great friendship between the two men was vital for the development of the Italian artist's private collection. It was indeed Caillebotte who insistently encouraged him to become more actively involved with the Impressionist initiatives, convincing him to surround himself with paintings by Edgar Degas (1834–1917), Claude Monet (1840–1926), or furthermore Berthe Morisot (1841–1895) (fig. 2). And so De Nittis began to create his own collection which, although modest, highlights his dual position: on the one hand, keen to affirm himself as a talented portraitist of modern high-society life with refined and elegant figurative works, mainly intended for the Salon and, thus, establishing his name in official circles and broadening his network

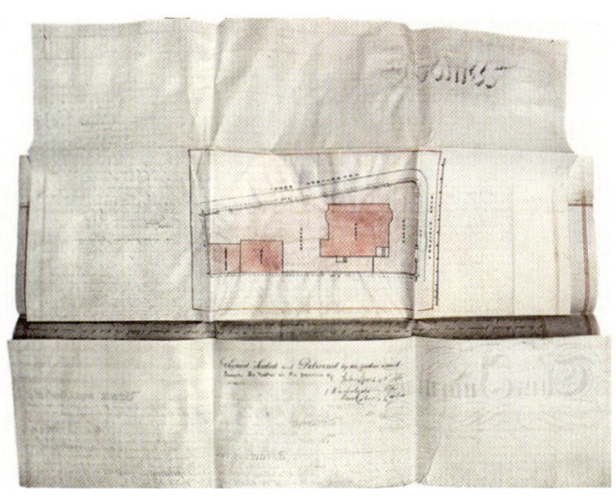

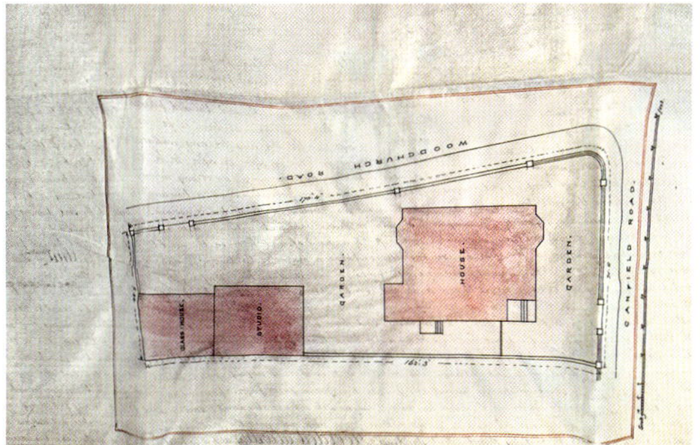

of potential buyers; and, on the other hand, his inclination for collecting Impressionist painting simply to enjoy it in the privacy of his own home. In 1874, Degas invited De Nittis to participate in the first Impressionist exhibition on Boulevard des Capucines. He presented five paintings in a liberated and anti-academic style, including two views of Vesuvius made during his Neapolitan trip in 1872.[5] Two years later, De Nittis ended his contact with Goupil even though he was indebted to him for the sum of around 53,000 francs.[6] However, this debt did not temper the social ambitions of his wife Léontine, who had a rather unhealthy and possessive relationship with their circle of friends, who now regularly frequented their salon, from Edmond de Goncourt to the Daudets, from Dumas the younger to Maupassant and Oscar Wilde, from Jules Claretie to Princess Mathilde Bonaparte. Léontine De Nittis's ambitious nature forced her husband to work relentlessly, allowing them to return to a more stable financial situation and ensure the costs of a such expensive lifestyle, which included buying several "show homes" in the west of Paris and London.[7] In regards to the importance of his work as a painter for the De Nittis family finances, we learn from Léontine's *Journal* that, already as a young married couple, "it was the purchase of a building on Avenue de l'Impératrice – payable over ten years. It required a huge effort because the only capital we had was Peppino's talent".[8] In this sense, it is clear that painting in Impressionist style would not have been enough to meet the needs of their lifestyle. And so, De Nittis's art remained focused on a more commercially viable language and themes and he was never able to abandon the official exhibition art circuits and auctions. Although it is true that, not unlike Léontine, Giuseppe had also tried to impose himself in Parisian artistic and social circles as soon as he arrived in France, but Degas perfectly describes his wife's very specific intentions, underlining her deciding role in managing the painter's strategies: "She most certainly loved her husband, but she had turned him into her business venture".[9]

In 1880, they moved into a new building at 3bis Rue Viète (today Avenue de Villiers),[10] "show homes" in Meissonier style and the umpteenth response to his wife Léontine's desires. It marked the point of no return for the De Nittis's finances, but equally for his relationship with the Impressionists.

> Manet, Degas, Pissarro were regular visitors in this house on Avenue du Bois, where he lived from the start. That was a terrible band: the perfect friends for a single man. They found it hard to adapt to the peaceable habits that led Mrs De Nittis, born in Paris, into an undoubtedly less unruly world. Later Goncourt, Zola and Daudet arrived in the building at Rue Viète. From the old group, only Degas remained a true friend, but so severe![11]

A conversation between De Nittis and his friend the Italian journalist Jacopo Caponi, better-known as Folchetto, sheds some light on this subject:

> You are living happily, content and carefree in your building, which is worth six thousand francs to you. Yet, you are entering a dangerous lair. – But Titine got a good deal: the price of the land has already gone up. – Well, sell it and make a profit. To build a mansion on Avenue de Villiers, bear in mind, you need three hundred thousand francs, and you also need to have three hundred thousand in reserve. Obviously, he didn't take my advice: the mansion was built in Rue Viette [*sic*], where Mrs De Nittis's 'delusions of grandeur' ran riot, welcoming princes and princesses, whilst the old friends abandoned the haunt they loved so much.[12]

Up until now, historiography has rightly acknowledged Léontine De Nittis's fundamental contribution to her husband's career, underlining her role as an inspiring muse, favourite model and constant iconographic source for his production. Her importance is undeniable, whether it's in the Italian painter's taste for elegant scenes with feminine subjects, or above all in the care she took in their relations with the high society Parisian bourgeoisie of the time, an indispensable element in the De Nittis's success. That is why Léontine has been rightly celebrated during the latest exhibitions devoted to De Nittis since 2010,[13] even though today nothing is said about the difficult character of this woman who had such a strong hold over her husband's behaviour and consequently his collectionism and the style of his paintings. One only has to remember, for example, that because of Peppino's difficulties with the French language, reports and letters between the De Nittis family and Adolphe Goupil were almost totally controlled by Léontine, who had become *de facto* the intermediary between them in their everyday business dealings.[14] She was undoubtedly a fundamental resource for her husband, but if up until today we have

only highlighted her determining contribution to De Nittis's painting, no one has ever questioned how more successful his art would have been without her, on all levels.
The Goncourt brothers' *Journal* is one of the most precious resources for an in-depth enquiry into the couple, notably tales of Léontine's frequent attacks of jealousy, elements wrongly neglected by critics. And this is where artistic historiography gets mixed up with gossip:

> Oh! The wife, – and the best! Is that with her nerves, her poor sick mind, she has made the poor man's life hell! Yesterday, the third Thursday of lent, De Nittis came to make some sketches of me for his portrait. The sitting over, there we were on our way to Paris, walking and rambling on as friends do on long promenades. Suddenly, he pulled a letter out of his pocket and said to me: "Read this". Recognising Mrs De Nittis's handwriting, I hesitated, when he made a sign with his eyes that it was imperative to read it. The letter, after several vague complaints about the lack of her husband's assiduity at home, said that because he had told her that if they separated, he would keep Jacques, she announced she was going to kill herself. "Well, my dear, the maid brought in my studio letters like that from my wife half an hour after I came out of her bedroom and without the slightest altercation, the least motif ... Then an hour later, she calmly came and had lunch, and there was nothing wrong." "But can you imagine", he gibbered on, which made it slightly touching and almost childlike, to his dismay, "it's not a life. At the moment, I need peace of mind, I have all kinds of worries... And to think that it's been going on for twelve years and there are days I think I'll shoot myself in the head... Yes, it started as soon as we were married... You haven't the slightest idea the things that come into her head. She might make a scene about something a friend has said about women saying that I enjoy humiliating her. About a purchase that I advise her not to make, she'll tell me: 'Yes, I understand, you make it clear that you married me without a fortune!'"[15]

The long-lasting success of what could be considered as De Nittis's non-Impressionist works were the cause up, until 1884, of much antagonism, notably on behalf of Renoir and Monet, hostile to his taking part at the Salon and, at the same time, jealous of his earnings and brilliant triumphs, in particular the gold medal he won at the World Fair in 1878, followed the same year by the Legion of Honour. These successes also provoked the rage of Degas, who had never hidden that the Italian painter's invitation to the first Impressionist exhibition had served to attract the favours of regulars to the Salon.[16] This dialogue De Nittis had with Adolphe Goupil on his controversial relationships with the Impressionists, towards the end of their collaboration, is of great interest:

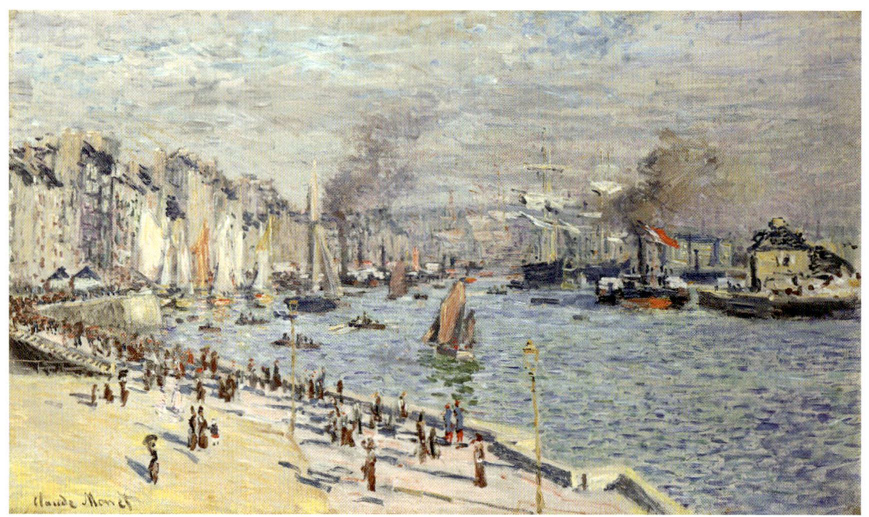

– Name them then, all these famous colleagues? My head high, my lips slightly trembling, I went through the names. He stood up, silently took a sheet of paper out a drawer, read it and said: – Absolutely. They are all there; you have even forgotten a few. – ??? – My dear man, your friends...you can't count on them. Ah! They are kind, your colleagues! I know artists, me. I am here for that. Ah! You were sure about them? They encouraged you? Not a lot, did they? I remained silent. – Do you know what they have done, your friends? – What? – They came as a delegation, with signatures. There was V..., X..., Y..., Z..., the dearest, the most surest in the name of the others. ... In short. Firstly, they demolished your talent as best they could and came to make remonstrances. Yes, yes...Ha! Ha! They came to tell me I was doing a bad thing for France, something antipatriotic by pushing your painting, yours, a foreigner.[17]

Jules Claretie, a friend of De Nittis, a true judge of his pictorial manner and collector of at least four of his works,[18] also commented on this subject:

The painters from the Impressionist school couldn't stand De Nittis, Manet was fairer towards him than his little disciples – I know perfectly well, Nittis used to say, they honour me, when I am not present, with some malice, which is neither very becoming nor very French, because they accept my courteous hospitality. They accuse me of painting like them and of having more supporters than they do. I willingly accept this reproach. It is true that I try and take advantage of all the research of my time, but more than anything, I constantly observe nature which belongs to me, as, I believe, it belongs a bit to everyone.[19]

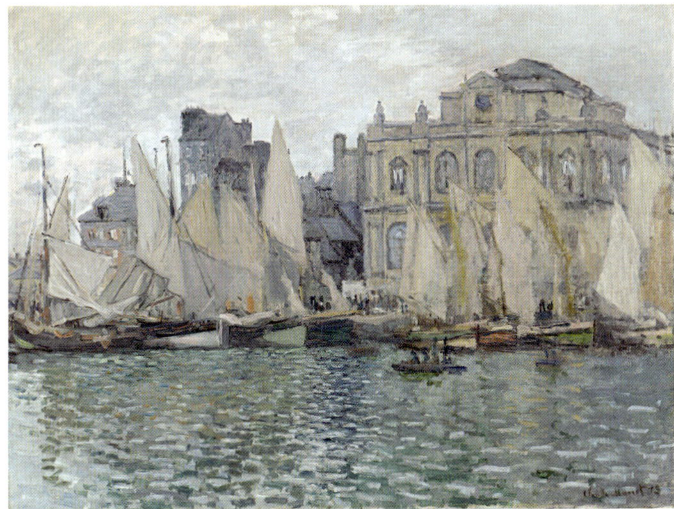

5. Claude Monet, *Port of Le Havre (Vue de l'ancien avant-port du Havre)*, 1874, oil on canvas, 60.3 × 101.9 cm, Philadelphia Museum of Art

6. Claude Monet, *The Museum at Le Havre (Le Musée du Havre)*, 1873, oil on canvas, 75 × 100 cm, The National Gallery, London

It has now been proven that De Nittis welcomed the Impressionist aesthetic principles without any great conviction, or at least his production answered to demands of a commercial nature far removed from the ethics of the French movement. Whilst showing what could be described as a moderate, high society or "sweetened" form of Impressionism, as Vittorio Pica wrote in 1914,[20] it is also true that, in paintings less directly linked to the demands of the market, De Nittis shared the same precepts of observation and translation of reality with the uncompromising French group, as well as a passion for Japanese art and objects. That is how we can affirm that for De Nittis collecting Impressionism meant collecting the things he believed in the most, but to which he couldn't dedicate himself freely and fully. This innate tendency reflected itself notably in his modest but representative collection, which, according to Vittorio Pica, was formed out of convenience, to be everyone's friend, to calm both the elite and the bohemians. On this subject, in *Notes et souvenirs* De Nittis wrote:

> It was affirmed to me from all sides that the Impressionists did not like me very much; that I bought their paintings to win them over; but in vain...and that I suffered for it. My God!...No. I didn't buy the paintings I would have liked because money just slipped through my fingers, like water. But if I did it, it was in all wisdom. The truth is that I bought four absolutely *light-filled and beautiful* paintings, by Mr Claude Monet, on advice from Mr Gustave Caillebotte and two studies by Mrs Berthe Morisot with pretty shades. That is my whole collection.[21]

As we have already pointed out, De Nittis owned *In the Garden* (*Au jardin*) by Manet (1870, Shelburne Museum, fig. 1); *Young Girl in a Ball Gown* (*Jeune femme au bal*) (1879, Musée d'Orsay, Paris, fig. 2) by Morisot, bought at the 1880 Impressionist exhibition and today at the Musée d'Orsay; four works by Monet acquired on advice from Caillebotte, which are *Morning Haze* (*Gelée blanche*), *Port of Le Havre* (*Vue de l'ancien avant-port du Havre*) (1874, Philadelphia Museum of Art, fig. 5), *The Museum at Le Havre* (*Le Musée du Havre*) (1873, The National Gallery, London, fig. 6) and *The Turkeys* (*Les Dindons*) (fig. 7), a painting presented at the third Impressionist exhibition in 1877 and also housed at the Musée d'Orsay. Monet was so attached to this painting that he tried to buy it after the death of the Italian artist, explaining his preoccupation to Théodore Duret about "what will happen to my white turkeys, but I am quite unconcerned because Deudon told me that you now own it".[22] In 1884, the same Duret, replying to Monet that he had indeed become "the owner of your Turkeys", went on to comment on De Nittis's death: "I never thought that this poor Nittis had such little time left. I truly regretted it; with his complex multifaceted character, he was alert, shrewd and truly talented. His house was a hub, which we will sorely miss. After the emptiness caused by Manet's death, it's hard to see another chapter close".[23]

The collection listed by the artist in his *Notes et souvenirs* cannot be considered exhaustive however. No mention is made, for instance, of the works and pastels by Degas, who remained a faithful enthusiast of his friend Peppino's art, as confirmed by the ten paintings appeared in the sale of Degas's collection after his death in 1918: oils and etchings of human subjects, snowy effects and two views of Vesuvius by De Nittis gathered over time by the French artist in his studio.[24] This information shows how, at a specific moment and in parallel to his activities as a collector, the Italian painter's production also caught the attention of some Impressionists, whilst the entry of some of his works into their private collections appears to mark the success of his strategy for getting closer to the group. It is especially true that De Nittis sincerely appreciated Degas's style, as well as that of other colleagues; from a young age, his mind tended naturally towards the free and unconventional observation of nature, in other words the founding principles of Impressionism, whose works decorated the walls of his own house. On this subject, the analysis carried out in 2011 by Manuela Moscatiello of the inventory after De Nittis's death is very interesting, highlighting how the works of his Impressionist colleagues were placed in his studio "to study them perhaps or to have them to hand as cherished objects".[25] The famous chronicle of an evening at the De Nittis's by Diego Martelli (1836–1896) gives us an eloquent insight into the ambiance at the Italian painter's home:

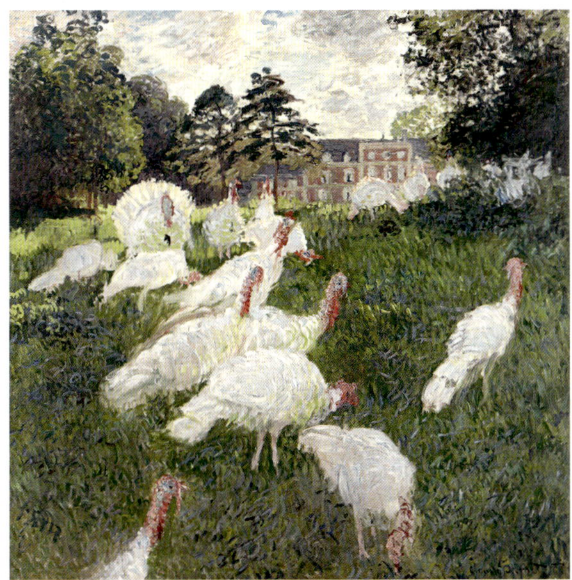

7. Claude Monet, *The Turkeys (Les Dindons)*, 1877, oil on canvas, 174 × 172.5 cm, Musée d'Orsay, Paris

> Knock on the door around five in the afternoon and you'll go into a vestibule where there are sculpted wooden stools and a large Impressionist painting by Monet [*The Turkeys*?]; from this vestibule you enter straight into an elegant Regency salon, where hanging on the walls is an unfinished landscape by Corot, which only partly reveals the secrets of the old master and his complete genius; then an oil painting by Édouard Manet, and a pastel with gouache by Edgar Degas.[26]

One can easily spot the commercial paintings in De Nittis's production, or in other words those constrained to a certain style and those carried out more freely, made for his own pleasure in serene moments, undoubtedly those closest to the Impressionist style. From 1864 to 1881, one of the most regular buyers of this series of works was Jean Dieterle, nephew of Jules, ancestor of the famous family of artists, dealers and collectors active in Paris throughout the nineteenth century. Dieterle was one of De Nittis's most faithful collectors, passionate about the little oil paintings on panels on the theme of Italian nature, with their light and rapid brushwork; works which seemed to fully express his innate attitude as an open-air landscape artist. According to Piero Dini's catalogue, it would seem that Dieterle owned fifty-five paintings,[27] including nine on sale at the *Vente Dieterle* on 18 October 2016, and many others now in the Daxer & Marschall Kunsthandel Collection in Munich. In these smaller pieces, De Nittis reveals his Impressionist vein via a return to the manner of his youth, the years in Resina, made up of rapid touches of light and

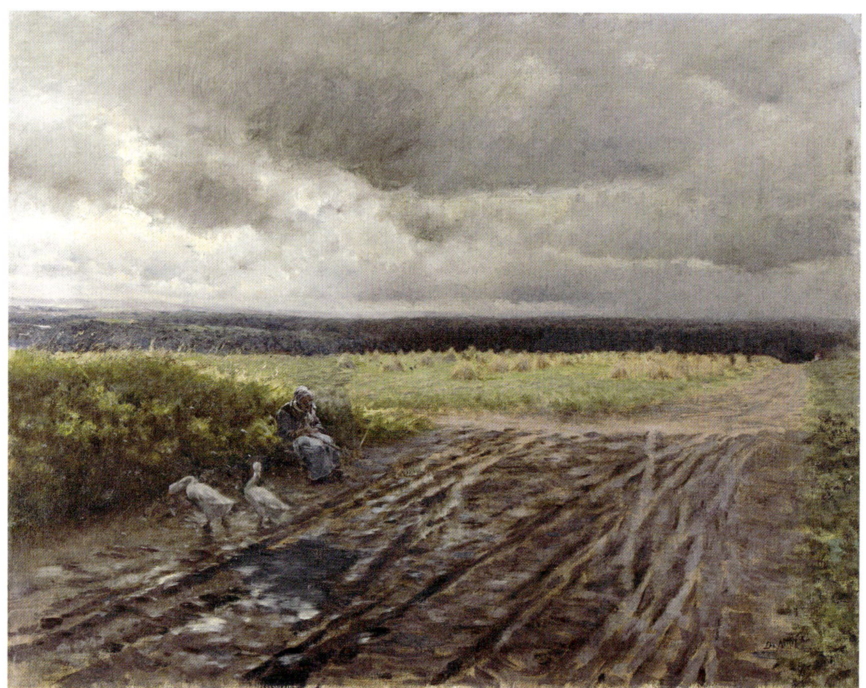

8. Giuseppe De Nittis,
The Geese Keeper
(La Gardeuse d'oies), 1884,
oil on canvas, 65 × 81 cm,
Petit Palais, Musée des
Beaux-Arts de la Ville de Paris

colour, reflecting on the poetic value of nature, looking for the uncapturable moment and the immanent sense of reality, through a formal and chromatic synthesis devoid of any formal research or aesthetic finesse. Among the other famous collectors, one should undoubtedly name Alexandre Dumas the younger (1824–1895), a close friend of the De Nittis family and author of the epitaph on the Italian painter's tomb, the art gallery owner Bernheim, who bought *The Races at Longchamps (II)* (*Les Courses à Longchamps*) (1883–84, private collection) in 1882–83,[28] the famous jeweller Henry Vever (1854–1942), owner of *Old Garden* (*Vieux jardin*) (1883, private collection)[29] from 1883, and furthermore the banker Edmond James de Rothschild (1845–1934), who enriched his collection with *The Geese Keeper* (*La Gardeuse d'oies*)[30] from 1884 (fig. 8), today at the Petit Palais in Paris. In addition is the dealer and friend from London, Kaye Knowles, a character who is still little-known today and whose collection, sold after his death, included thirteen urban London scenes by De Nittis.[31]

De Nittis's Impressionist collectionism offers in some ways a clue to his attempt at getting closer to a group of personalities with whom he had in common a certain observation of reality and cultivate a fruitful dialogue, made up of shared ideas and works, some of which were hung in his own home, for all to see. With this in mind then, his collection appears to express a spontaneous initiative based on well-defined aesthetic and methodological motivations, simultaneously linked to his desire for recognition and acceptance by the Impressionist group on a pictorial level. Consequently, this invites us to question where De Nittis's real artistic inclination lay during his Parisian period, in his artistic repertoire noticeably influenced by external factors, or in his collectionism, free and exempt from any form of conditioning. Undoubtedly, for him, collecting Impressionism meant surrounding himself with a poetic and sincere vision of nature and a pictorial manner which, despite his vast fashionable production, he himself continued to practice relentlessly until he died, and which instantly took him back to his youth in Naples. This radical duality between his art and his behaviour as a collector made him something of a "transformist" on the Parisian art scene in the second half of the nineteenth century, an artist who knew how to adapt his language to meet the demands of the market without abandoning his pictorial credo.

1 With this term we are referring generally to Giuseppe De Nittis, Giovanni Boldini (1842–1931) and Federico Zandomeneghi (1841–1917), who settled permanently in Paris in the late 1860s, each for different reasons, and who are today considered the three main representatives of the Italian Impressionist school. On this subject, see also M. Lagrange, *Les Peintres italiens en quête d'identité, Paris, 1855-1909* (Paris: CTHS-INHA, 2010); F. Dini (ed.), *Boldini e gli italiani a Parigi. Tra realtà e impressione*, exhibition catalogue, Chiostro del Bramante, Rome, 14 November 2009 – 14 March 2010 (Cinisello Balsamo: Silvana Editoriale, 2009); M. Ferretti Bocquillon, "De Nittis, Boldini e Zandomeneghi a Parigi (1867-1917)", in A. Dumas (ed.), *Degas e gli italiani a Parigi*, exhibition catalogue, Palazzo dei Diamanti, Ferrara, 14 September – 16 November 2003 (Ferrara: Ferrara Arte, 2003), pp. 113–46.

2 *Notes et souvenirs du peintre Joseph De Nittis* (Paris: Librairies-Imprimeries Réunies, 1895), pp. 57–58: "In 1870, I bought a small town house Avenue de l'Impératrice, on advice from James Tissot ... I hesitated a lot, because it meant committing for the future. The house was to be paid back over ten years, with interest as rent. Since I didn't have the capital, it was a big venture and my wife ... didn't think it was a good idea ... The friend who accompanied me took me aside. – It's not the right time to buy a house. The war... it's too uncertain. We are not ready... I had a ringing in my ears. My mind was made up. – Bah! I have faith in France's good fortune. I bought the house. And I signed the agreement to sell". By looking closely at this fundamental text, we should nonetheless be very cautious and take into account that it is a diary written a long time after De Nittis's death by his wife Léontine, who used his notes freely to reinstate her reputation and her husband's. We can notice this in certain parts and reflections in *Notes et souvenir*, which are identical to the letters addressed by Léontine to Edmond de Goncourt, published by M. Moscatiello, "Léontine e Giuseppe De Nittis: lettere inedite a Edmond de Goncourt e a Jules Jacquemart", *Saggi e memorie di storia dell'arte*, vol. 32, 2008, pp. 269–301.

3 Paris, 7 April 1873, Lamberto Vitali Archive, Milan. See A. Cecioni, *Scritti e ricordi*, edited by G. Uzielli (Florence: Tipografia Domenicana, 1905), p. 391, cit. in P. Dini, G. L. Marini, *De Nittis. La vita, i documenti, le opere dipinte*, vol. I (Turin: Allemandi, 1991), pp. 290–91.

4 Former name of the town of Herculaneum.

5 Société anonyme coopérative des artistes peintres, sculpteurs et graveurs, etc., *Première Exposition 1874, 35, boulevard des Capucines. Catalogue*, Paris, Alcan-Levy printers, 1874, n. 116-117.

6 Letter from Goupil & Cie to Giuseppe De Nittis, Paris, 19 June 1874, in M. Pittaluga, E. Piceni, *De Nittis* (Milan: Bramante, 1963), pp. 335–36.

7 It is dated 9 May 1879 the purchase of a property situated between Woodchurch Road and Canfield Road in London, comprised of the main building, two gardens, a studio and a conservatory, for the sum of almost 211.000 francs. The Getty Research Institute in Los Angeles owns the lease contract between De Nittis and K. Twinberrow, with the planimetry of the site (*Lease, 1879 May 9*, Special Collections, 860138) (fig. 3–4).

8 Léontine De Nittis's *Journal*, in P. Dini, G. L. Marini, *op. cit.*, vol. I, p. 364. On this subject, see also note 2.

9 Letter from Edgar Degas to Ludovic Halévy, Mésnil Hubert, by Gacé (Orne), [September 1884], in M. Guérin (ed.), *Lettres de Degas* (Paris: B. Grasset, 1931), p. 66, cit. in M. Pittaluga, E. Piceni, *op. cit.*, p. 371.

10 *Notes et souvenirs* cit., p. 216.

11 P. Fresnay, "L'Atelier de J. De Nittis", *Le Progrès de Lille*, cit. in P. Dini, G. L. Marini, *op. cit.*, vol. I, pp. 111–12, note 80.

12 J. Caponi, *Ricordi di Folchetto* (Turin: Società tipografico-editrice nazionale, 1908), pp. 404–7.

13 G. Chazal, D. Morel, E. Angiuli (eds.), *Giuseppe De Nittis. La modernité élégante*, exhibition catalogue, Petit Palais – Musée des Beaux-Arts, Paris, 21 October 2010 – 16 January 2011; Palazzo del Governatore, Parma, 6 February – 8 May 2011 (Paris: Paris Musées, 2010); E. Mazzocca, E. Angiuli (eds.), *De Nittis*, exhibition catalogue, Palazzo Zabarella, Padua, 16 January – 26 May 2013 (Venice: Marsilio, 2013); M. L. Pacelli, B. Guidi, H. Pinet (eds.), *De Nittis e la rivoluzione dello sguardo*, exhibition catalogue, Palazzo dei Diamanti, Ferrara, 1 December 2019 – 13 April 2020 (Ferrara: Fondazione Ferrara Arte, 2019).

14 See M. Pittaluga, E. Piceni, *op. cit.*, pp. 316–36; to better understand his wife's role in the private correspondence of the De Nittis family, see also M. Moscatiello, *op. cit.*

15 E. and J. de Goncourt, *Journal. Mémoires de la vie littéraire*, vol. XII (Monaco: Les éditions de l'Imprimerie nationale de Monaco, 1956 [1881]), pp. 108–9.

16 "For the first Impressionist exhibition, Degas asked me to send him a major work." He added: "As you're showing at the Salon, the ill-informed won't be able to say that we are the exhibition for the Refusés." (*Notes et souvenirs* cit., p. 237).

17 Ibid., pp. 107–8.

18 *Road from Tavoliere* (Rue du Tavoliere), 1872, oil on canvas, 35 × 45 cm (P. Dini, G. L. Marini, *op. cit.*, vol. II, p. 389, n. 349); *Madame Claretie*, dedicated to Jules Claretie, 1875, oil on panel, 41 × 26 cm (ibid., p. 399, n. 573); *The Forum in Pompeii* (Le forum de Pompéi), 1876, oil on canvas, 80.5 × 57.3 cm (ibid., p. 400, n. 599); *Flowers* (Fleurs), 1882, pastel on paper, 735 × 540 mm (ibid., p. 414, n. 894).

19 *L'Indépendance belge*, 16 May 1886, cit. in P. Dini, G. L. Marini, *op. cit.*, vol. I, p. 152, note 111.

20 V. Pica, *Giuseppe De Nittis. L'uomo e l'artista* (Milan: Alfieri & Lacroix, 1914), *passim*; P. Dini, G. L. Marini, *op. cit.*, vol. I, p. 167.

21 *Notes et souvenirs* cit., p. 236.

22 D. Wildenstein, *Claude Monet, biographie et catalogue raisonné*, vol. II (Paris-Lausanne: La Bibliothèque des Arts, 1974–79), pp. 256–57. On the relationship Monet-De Nittis, see F. Minervini, "Attorno a una lettera di Claude Monet a Giuseppe De Nittis: un confronto artistico possibile?", in *MDCCC 1800*, vol. 7, 2018, pp. 37–52.

23 Letter from Théodore Duret to Claude Monet, 16 June 1884, private collection, Artcurial sales catalogue, *Archives Claude Monet. Correspondance d'artiste. Collection Monsieur et Madame Cornebois*, Paris, 13 December 2006, n. 89.

24 A. Dumas, C. Ives, S. A. Stein, G. Tinterow (eds.), *The Private Collection of Edgar Degas. A Summary Catalogue*, exhibition catalogue, The Metropolitan Museum of Art, New York, 1 October 1997 – 11 January 1998 (New York: The Metropolitan Museum of Art, 1997), p. 104, n. 909–18.

25 M. Moscatiello, *Le Japonisme de Giuseppe De Nittis: un peintre italien en France à la fin du XIXe siècle* (Berne: Peter Lang, 2011), p. 137.

26 D. Martelli, *Scritti d'arte*, edited by G. Boschetto (Florence: Sansoni, 1952), pp. 126–28.

27 These include: *The Lady in Black* (La Dame en noir), 1878, oil on panel, 35 × 25 cm (P. Dini, G. L. Marini, *op. cit.*, vol. II, p. 406, n. 721; Rossini auction house, sale catalogue *Collection Dieterle*, Paris, 18 October 2016, p. 35, n. 48), private collection; *The Rowing Boat* (La Barque), 1866, oil on panel, 9 × 17.5 cm (P. Dini, G. L. Marini, *op. cit.*, vol. II, p. 379, n. 120; *Collection Dieterle* 2016, p. 36, n. 49), Daxer & Marschall Kunsthandel Collection, Munich; *The Road from Naples to Brindisi* (La Route de Naples à Brindisi), 1872, oil on panel, 9 × 17.5 cm (P. Dini, G. L. Marini, *op. cit.*, vol. II, p. 386, n. 298; *Collection Dieterle* 2016, p. 36, n. 50), Daxer & Marschall Kunsthandel Collection, Munich; *Swans on the Lake* (Cygnes sur l'étang), 1874, oil on panel, 25 × 35 cm (P. Dini, G. L. Marini, *op. cit.*, vol. II, p. 395, II, n. 499; *Collection Dieterle* 2016, p. 37, n. 51), private collection; *Beach with Boat* (Plage et bateau), 1866, oil on panel, 9 × 17.5 cm (P. Dini, G. L. Marini, *op. cit.*, vol. II, p. 379, n. 116; *Collection Dieterle* 2016, p. 38, n. 52), Daxer & Marschall Kunsthandel Collection, Munich; *Sunny Street* (Rue ensoleillée), 1873, oil on panel, 9 × 14 cm (P. Dini, G. L. Marini, *op. cit.*, vol. II, p. 393, n. 455; *Collection Dieterle* 2016, p. 38, n. 53), private collection; *Vesuvius* (Le Vésuve), 1872, oil on panel, 18 × 31.5 cm (P. Dini, G. L. Marini, *op. cit.*, vol. II, p. 392, n. 427; *Collection Dieterle* 2016, p. 39, n. 54), former Daxer & Marschall Kunsthandel Collection, Munich, today private collection Italy; *Silhouette of a Parisian Woman* (Silhouette de parisienne), watercolour, 215 × 125 mm (*Collection Dieterle* 2016, p. 40, n. 55), private coll.; *Port in the Evening* (Port le soir), 1866, oil on panel, 9 × 17.5 cm (P. Dini, G. L. Marini, *op. cit.*, vol. II, p. 379, n. 121; *Collection Dieterle* 2016, p. 40, n. 56), Daxer & Marschall Kunsthandel Collection, Munich; *Woman with a Blue Hat* (Femme au bonnet bleu), watercolour, 240 × 160 mm (*Collection Dieterle* 2016, p. 41, n. 57), private collection; *Elegant Lady and Couple* (Élégante et couple), watercolour, 240 × 180 mm (*Collection Dieterle* 2016, p. 42, n. 58), private collection; *Porch in the Sunshine* (Porche au soleil), 1864, oil on panel, 9 × 17.5 cm (P. Dini, G. L. Marini, *op. cit.*, vol. II, p. 375, n. 11; *Collection Dieterle* 2016, p. 42, n. 59), Daxer & Marschall Kunsthandel Collection, Munich.

28 Oil on canvas, 100 × 120 cm (P. Dini, G. L. Marini, *op. cit.*, vol. II, p. 415, n. 925).

29 Oil on canvas, 47 × 65 cm (ibid., p. 416, n. 935).

30 Oil on canvas, 65 × 81 cm (ibid., p. 419, n. 990).

31 *Catalogue of the Highly Important Collection of Modern Pictures and Water-Colour Drawings of Kaye Knowles*, auction catalogue, Christie, Manson & Woods, London, 14 May 1887, pp. 19–21, n. 134–46.

GUSTAVE FAYET'S IMPRESSIONIST COLLECTION

ALEXANDRE D'ANDOQUE

On 23 October 1900, Gustave Fayet visited the Exposition centennale de l'art français (1800–1889) organised for the World Fair. He contemplated works by Degas, Monet, Pissarro, Renoir, Sisley and, that same evening, wrote to his wife: "I have just spent the day with Jean de Gonet at the Grand Palais. There was a wonderful collection of paintings. The Impressionists beat everything else…".[1] Continuing his stay in Paris, three days later he visited Rue Lafitte with George-Daniel de Monfreid, a fellow painter and Gauguin's confident. They spent "the morning looking at Cézannes at Vollard's"[2] and, struck by *Self-Portrait in a White Cap* (*Autoportrait au bonnet blanc*),[3] he paid 5,000 francs to the art dealer,[4] who sent the painting to Béziers where it became part of a collection Fayet had started a year earlier.

Gustave Fayet was born in Béziers on 20 May 1865 and was the only heir in a line of shipowners and vineyard owners who, thanks to the Canal du Midi, had constituted a very large fortune over three generations. An entrepreneur at heart and a talented businessman, he was also a painter, ceramicist and, towards the end of his life, illustrator and interior designer.[5] Although recent retrospectives[6] have focused on telling us more about Fayet the artist, he remains nevertheless better-known in the history of art for his collection.[7] A collection which owed its notoriety to numerous works by Gauguin and Redon, today hung in some major museums. However Fayet, who began his collection by buying a group of forty paintings from Armand Cabrol, a collector from Languedoc, was first and foremost a collector of Impressionist works and in particular Degas, Cézanne, Renoir, to which we might also add Toulouse-Lautrec. In parallel, he enjoyed collecting works by Gauguin, bringing together a unique ensemble of paintings, drawings, engravings, ceramics and wooden sculptures, and by Van Gogh, testifying to his early taste for the avant-gardes. He equally became very fond of Redon's "black" works, later enriching his collection with some of the finest pastels and oils by the master of Symbolism. After settling in Paris around 1905, he discovered a new generation of artists, Bonnard, Vuillard, Denis, Matisse, Derain, Marquet, Maillol, who in turn became part of his collection, although they didn't remain so for long. Out of all of these works, it was the Gauguins, presented at the Autumn Salon of 1906 and the Redons, shown at a retrospective in 1926 at the Musée des Arts Décoratifs, which forged Fayet's reputation. His Impressionist collection had neither the scale nor the notoriety of those belonging to the great second-generation collectors such as Isaac de Camondo (1851–1911), François Depeaux (1853–1920), Antonin Personnaz (1854–1936), Auguste Pellerin (1853–1929), Georges Viau (1855–1939), Olivier Sainsère (1852–1923) or Charles Pacquement (1871–1950), and hence has never been the subject of any in-depth studies up until recently. Roseline Bacou uncovered several elements at the end of her life during a symposium organised at Fontfroide Abbey in 2008 for the centenary of Gustave and Madeleine Fayet's acquisition of the property.[8] In her thesis, Magali Rougeot[9] was more interested in the artist than the collector and did not have access to all of the sources. Exploiting the sources conserved in the private collections of Fayet's descendants, and in particular Gustave Fayet's notebooks, the collection file, Maurice Fabre's correspondence with Gustave Fayet, the letters exchanged between Gustave Fayet and his wife, and Roseline Bacou's archives, has enabled us to present the history of this Impressionist collection, constituted mainly between 1900 and 1905 and comprising around fifty works.

Beyond the list of works acquired by Fayet, reconstructing the history of this collection and notably the Impressionist part has enabled us to put Fayet's role into perspective within the artistic landscape of his time. The collection is above all the work of a representative of the grand provincial bourgeoisie in the South of France, certainly an artist accepted at the Salon, but who didn't belong to the Parisian network of collectors. Fayet also exemplifies the relationships between Paris and the provinces at the turn of the twentieth century. The manner in which the collection was constituted, by purchasing an initial lot of forty works, then through exchanges and successive resales in order to acquire works of the highest quality, makes a particularly interesting case study for understanding the whys and wherefores of building such a collection. Lastly, Fayet is interesting in terms of the part he played in promoting modern art. Whilst creating his own collection, he first invested his time in organising an annual fine arts fair in Béziers and tried to bring avant-garde works into the public collections at the Musée des Beaux-Arts in his hometown, where he was curator for several years. But tired of the lack of interest from the local town councillors and elite, he ended up settling in Paris where he opened his gallery to visitors one afternoon a week.

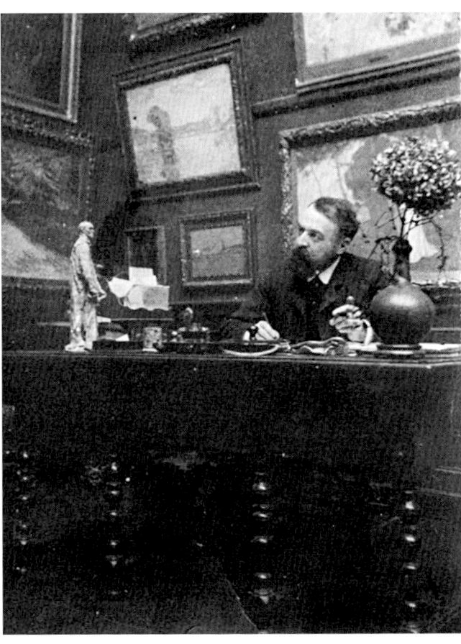

1. *Gustave Fayet at his desk, Hôtel Fayet, 7 Rue du Capus, Béziers*, anonymous photograph, c. 1902-4, private collection

How Gustave Fayet Came to Acquire Armand Cabrol's Collection

1899 and 1900 marked an important turning point for Fayet. On 19 January 1899, Gabriel Fayet, Gustave's father, died leaving his only heir all of his vineyards. And so, Fayet found himself "at the head of one of the most important land assets and property holdings in Béziers, made up by a progressive concentration and passed down according to a particularly well-advised strategy" (fig. 1).[10] At the end of the same year, on 18 December, Gustave Fayet acquired forty paintings, pastels and drawings belonging to Armand Cabrol for 20,000 francs. Among this ensemble were works by Degas, Monet, Pissarro, Renoir and Sisley alongside others by Carrière, Fantin-Latour, Manet or Monticelli.

A poet, collector and winemaker, Armand Cabrol was an interesting figure who seems to have been completely overlooked by art history. Born on 21 January 1861 near Béziers, he managed the family vineyard whilst at the same time devoting himself to poetry. In the 1880s, his work was published in *Parnasse* and at around the same time he created some rather short-lived magazines. In 1882, he had his first success with the publication of *Chants du pauvre*, prefaced by the journalist Henri Deloncle, then in 1894 with a poetry collection called *Grisailles*, judged by Gustave Geffroy to be "touchingly melancholic". On his short trips to Paris he mixed in artistic circles, supplying them with "white Picpoul wine known as *Impressionnists*".[11] He boasted about "conquering the most high-profile celebrities in the artistic and literary world"[12] with whom he traded paintings in return for wine.

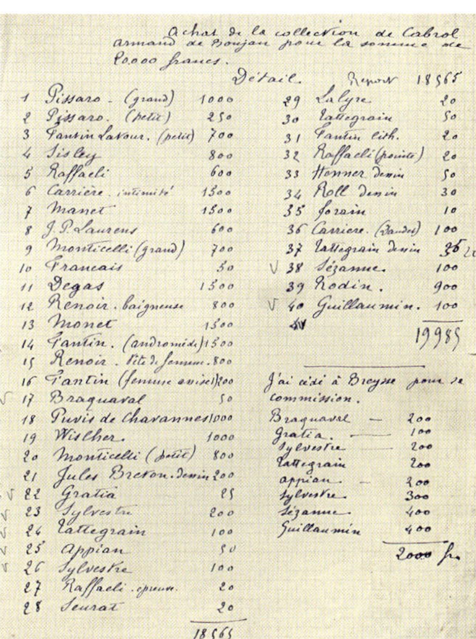
Achat de la collection de Cabrol
Armand de Boujan pour la somme de
20.000 francs.

Détail. Report 18565

1 Pissaro - (grand) 1000
2 Pissaro. (petit) 250
3 Fantin Latour. (petit) 700
4 Sisley 800
5 Raffaeli 600
6 Carrière. intimité 1500
7 Manet 1500
8 J. P. Laurens 600
9 Monticelli (grand) 700
10 Francais 50
11 Degas 1500
12 Renoir. baigneuse 800
13 Monet 1500
14 Fantin. (andromède) 1500
15 Renoir. tête de femme. 800
16 Fantin (femme assise) 200
17 Braquaval 50
18 Puvis de Chavannes 1000
19 Wislher. 1000
20 Monticelli (petit) 800
21 Jules Breton. dessin 200
22 Gratia 25
23 Sylvestre 200
24 Lattegrain 100
25 Appian 50
26 Sylvestre 100
27 Raffaeli. épreuve. 20
28 Seurat 20
18565

29 Lalyre 20
30 Lattegrain 50
31 Fantin lith. 20
32 Raffaeli (pointe) 20
33 Henner dessin 50
34 Roll dessin 30
35 Forain 10
36 Carrière. [illegible] 100
37 Lattegrain dessin 35 20
38 Sézanne. 100
39 Rodin. 900
40 Guillaumin. 100
19985

J'ai cédé à Breysse pour sa commission.
Braquaval — 200
Gratia. — 100
Sylvestre — 200
Lattegrain 200
Appian — 200
Sylvestre 300
Sézanne 400
Guillaumin 400
2000 fr.

2. List of works in the Armand Cabrol collection bought by Gustave Fayet, Archives Fayet

This was notably the case with Carrière who gave him a sketch of a mother and child in 1894. They maintained a correspondence "full of admiration and friendship"[13] for slightly over ten years. He also took advantage of these stays to buy works by Renoir, Puvis de Chavannes, Pissarro or Whistler at Sagot's, Durand-Ruel's or Bernheim-Jeune's.[14] In late 1899, probably in need of money, Cabrol sold his 41-piece collection to Gustave Fayet. Breysse, an art dealer trading at 11 Rue Lafitte, initially estimated it to be worth slightly over 30,000 francs. A shrewd negotiator, Fayet ended up getting it for 20,000 francs, after Cabrol had taken back his *Motherhood* (*Maternité*) by Carrière – "the only painting I have left",[15] he wrote to the artist on 30 December 1899. Fayet left Breysse eight paintings "for his commission" worth a total of 2000 francs and hence found himself in possession of 32 works: 19 oils, pastels or watercolours by Pissarro, Fantin-Latour, Sisley, Raffaëlli, Carrière, Guillaumin, Manet, Laurens, Degas, Renoir, Monet, Puvis de Chavannes and Whistler, as well as some drawings and lithographs and a terracotta sculpture by Rodin (fig. 2).

Although we have a list of the works, only a few pieces have been identified and some research still remains to be carried out. But, just by the names of the artists alone, this collection appears to reflect certain late-nineteenth-century tastes in Paris with well-established and famous painters such as Carrière, Monet, Degas or Renoir, even if they remained less well-known and less valuable than the academic artists showing at the Salon. On the other hand, it is very unusual to find a collection of this kind in a village near Béziers, which had at the time just over 1000 inhabitants, denoting both

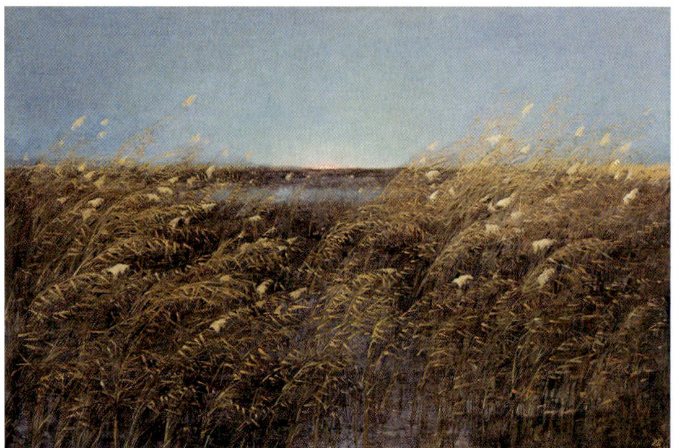

3. Gustave Fayet, *Moon Rising over the Lake at Vendres (Lever de lune sur l'étang de Vendres)*, 1896, oil on canvas, 92 × 142 cm, private collection

Cabrol's undeniable taste and real proximity with the Parisian artistic circles. Cabrol, whose correspondence with Carrière does not say much about this sale, perhaps quietly consoled himself for having sold his collection to Fayet, whom he introduced to the painter as "a rich art enthusiast from Béziers, painter-landscape artist in his day, who has good taste and with whom I was happy to share similar ideas, because he loved your painting".[16]

These works joined the collection created by the Fayets, which included works we can discover in the pages of Fayet's notebooks and which testify to the artistic leanings of a certain provincial bourgeoisie. Also hanging on the walls of Hôtel Fayet were representatives of academic art like Thomas Couture and Jean-Noël Sylvestre from Béziers, painters from the Ecole de Barbizon including Ziem, César de Cock, Alfred de Knyff, Diaz and Brendel, Impressionist paintings by Guillaumin, the naturalists, notably Vaysson, Guignard, Cottet, symbolists including Aman-Jean, Carrière and Moreau or local painters such as Gagliardini or Monticelli, an artist dear to his father, Gabriel Fayet, whom he had met during a stay in Béziers.[17] Also hanging alongside the collection at the mansion were works by the Fayets themselves, those painted by Gabriel, the father, Léon, the uncle and Gustave, who was taught by the others. In the early 1890s, Gustave began to make a name for himself with his motifs and viewpoints; he worked on the light with atmospheric changes and lightened his palette. His works were presented at the regional salons and were recompensed; then in 1896 he was accepted at the Salon des Artistes Français. The following year he showed a surprising *Moon Rising over the Lake at Vendres (Lever de lune sur l'étang de Vendres)*,[18] where the only thing depicted was "the flexible gorse springing out of the waters, bending and foaming in the darkness, whilst in the centre on the horizon, you can just make out the glimmer of the moonlight. A unique work for its layout, colourful palette, poetic intensity",[19] wrote Roseline Bacou in an unpublished text (fig. 3).

In December 1899, the purchase of the Cabrol collection was a very sound investment for Fayet, who, although he didn't obtain any masterpieces, was taking no risk in acquiring these paintings. He now owned works by some indisputable artists which any good collector would be proud to own. And whilst some of the works were not to his taste, he could put them on the market or use them as currency for future transactions with art dealers in Rue Lafitte.

The First Negotiations with Dealers in Rue Lafitte

Before becoming a great collector whose name remained firmly associated to Gauguin, Fayet got to know the workings of the art market with the help of Maurice Fabre, who knew and mastered these codes and practices well. Like Gustave Fayet, Maurice Fabre (1861–1939) was a former pupil of the Sorèze Dominicans. A trained lawyer and vineyard owner in the Corbières, Fabre moved to Paris in the middle of the 1880s and collaborated on a new literary and artistic magazine, *Le Passant*. He was one of the first to buy Redon's "Black paintings", wrote regularly to him between 1888 and 1915 and met other painters and writers in his studio. Over the years, he created a collection that brought together works by Cézanne, Redon, Gauguin, Van Gogh, but he had limited financial means. Speaking of him Gauguin said "he's an admirer, but a *platonic* one I believe".[20] He got rid of some of his collection in 1902 and 1911 at public auctions in Paris.
With a long experience of the capital, his daily visits to art dealers and his friendships with artists, Fabre was something of a mentor for Fayet, who trusted his judgement. In the early 1900s, he admired Cézanne, considering him to be "the strongest, simplest, most solid, healthiest painter in our troubled times";[21] he thought Van Gogh and Gauguin were "greater artists than Monet!",[22] and wanted to discover Redon, for whom he had "an admiration which has grown over the last twelve years".[23] But Fabre was also interested in the younger generation. "Today, Vollard opens an exhibition of the young Spanish painter Picasso", he wrote to Fayet in June 1901. "If he doesn't lose himself in facility and virtuosity, he could come to something = he has character."[24]
In March 1900, Fayet made his first trip to Paris, where he met up with Fabre who took him to Rue Lafitte, and together they visited Redon's studio. Then, in Béziers, he held the yearly exhibition of the Société des Beaux-Arts which revealed a clear concern for innovation by hosting "elite artists"[25] with no link to the region like Carrière, Rodin, Degas, Henri Martin, Gauguin or Matisse. On 27 April, during the exhibition, the town council of Béziers nominated Gustave Fayet, up until then deputy curator, curator of the Musée de Béziers, taking over from Charles Labor who had died a few

weeks earlier. And so, he became part of the circle of artists – but also provincial curators. With his new status, in June, he met once again with Fabre in Paris, armed with a list of the names and addresses of artists such as Rodin, Carrière, Bartholomé, Delaherche, Willette, Henri Martin or dealers he wanted to visit to ask for donations to the museum or loans for the forthcoming exhibition of the Société des Beaux-Arts, of which he was still vice-president. After these two stays, during which Fayet discovered some studios and galleries but bought nothing, he was back in Paris as soon as the grape harvests were over and covered the pages of his notebooks with numerous "combinations" of how he could use the Cabrol collection (as well as other works he owned), as currency with art dealers to redirect his collection towards more sound investments.

He did his first deal on 24 September at Bernheim-Jeune's,[26] where he initially acquired a painting by Guillaumin, *The Hamlet of Peschadoire in the Sunlight* (*Le Hameau de Peschadoire au soleil*)[27] (fig. 4), worth 4,200 francs in exchange for four paintings: *The Road at Damont* (*La Route de Damont*) by Armand Guillaumin, *The Haystack* (*La Meule*) by Victor Vignon, *Sheep Drinking* (*Moutons à l'abreuvoir*) by Albert Brendel, *Back to Pasture* (*Retour du pâturage*) by Paul Vaysson and 1,150 francs.[28] He then purchased a work by Manet, the *Head of a Woman* (*Tête de femme*),[29] which had come from the Pellerin collection for 11,100 francs and his first pastel by Degas, *La Toilette*,[30] which was a female nude brushing her hair, with a red slipper at her feet, for the sum of 5,900 francs. He gave the art dealer 3,000 francs and eleven paintings for these two works, six from the Cabrol collection, *Andromedas* (*Andromède*) by Fantin-Latour, a drawing by Forain, *Head of a Woman* (*Tête de femme*) by Degas, *Motherhood* (*Maternité*) by Carrière, a landscape by Français, *Head of a Cardinal* (*Tête de Cardinal*) by Jean-Paul Laurens, plus five from the Fayet collection, *The Path* (*Le Chemin*) by Guillaumin, *View of the South of France* (*Vue du Midi*) by Gagliardini, a sketch by Willette, *The Presentation* by Ziem and a work by César de Cock. "How these trades amuse me!!!",[31] he wrote to his wife, Madeleine.

By buying these three works for a total of 21,500 francs, the equivalent of the price of the Cabrol collection, Fayet immediately revealed his ambitions by choosing modernity over more recognised artists, whose works were circulating on the market and thus limiting the risks.

He stayed once again in Paris the following month and visited the World Fair at the Grand Palais with his cousin Jean de Gonet where, he said, "there is a marvellous collection of paintings. The Impressionists beat everything else". And he added: "What a shame that the compagnies don't give us an income!!! It would be money well invested".[32] He also went round the galleries, admired a view of London by Monet and a Renoir at Bernheim-Jeune's and thought up ideas for new exchanges which he wrote down in his notebook.

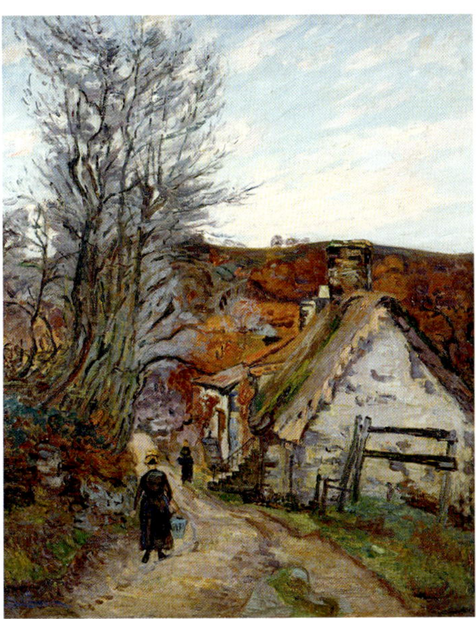

4. Armand Guillaumin, *The Hamlet of Peschadoire in the Sunlight* (*Le Hameau de Peschadoire au soleil*), c. 1895, oil on canvas, 81 × 65 cm, Musée des Beaux-arts, Rennes, on loan from the Musée du Louvre

On 26 October, Fayet went to Rue Lafitte with Monfreid and spent "the morning looking at Cézannes at Vollard's".[33] The latter had become the artist's appointed dealer after having organised his first solo exhibition in 1895, which was a revelation, followed by two others in 1898 and 1899 and after having bought part of his studio collection. Fayet was in absolute awe in front of *Self-Portrait in a White Cap* (*Autoportrait au bonnet blanc*).[34] But, before making his mind up, he wanted Fabre's opinion, who answered from his home in Gasparets on 5 November: "I can't visualise the Cézanne portrait you are talking about; he did his own portrait so often; and I have indeed seen some very beautiful self-portraits as well as some of his wife too".[35] On his return from Paris, Fabre also visited Vollard's and judged the portrait to be "magnificent" before adding: "Strength and delicatesse, gravity and force, inner life and material creation, it's all there".[36] The painting was acquired for the sum of 4,500 francs. Fayet left a one-thousand-franc deposit with Vollard[37] then the rest was taken by Maurice Fabre[38] who "added *In Parallel* (*Parallèlement*) and a small Bonnard, a view of Paris, exquisite to see for its spirit and facture".[39] It was the first Cézanne in the collection and Fayet, proud of his purchase, informed Monfreid: "Do you know that Bernheim is organising an exhibition for Cézanne on 15 January! If the Bernheim's join Vollard in raising the prices, adieu the Cézannes. We'll have to content ourselves with seeing them at Camondo's and Cie. Fortunately I have one of his most beautiful works".[40]

Fayet did not just choose Impressionist works; on 24 October, he bought his first two works by Gauguin at Monfreid's, *Crimson-Flowered Breasts* (*Les*

Seins aux fleurs rouges),[41] today housed at the Met in New York and *Three Tahitians* (*Les Trois Tahitiens*),[42] which is in Edinburgh. These two works by the artist, which would make the Fayet collection famous, made their entrance at the same time as those by Guillaumin, Degas, Cézanne and just before the first purchases of Van Gogh and Toulouse-Lautrec. This testifies to the collector's taste for the avant-gardes as well as the Impressionists.
In February 1901, Fayet returned to Paris and, as soon as he arrived, he went straight to Vollard's, where he acquired two new works by Cézanne, *The Great Pine* (*Le Grand Pin*),[43] a "large stone pine on the edge of a wood, standing out against the blue sky",[44] as well as a watercolour still life described in the collection file as "fruit and a teapot on a table",[45] with the dimensions "H 0.24; W 0.36", which correspond to *Pot of Ginger and Fruits on a Table* (*Pot de gingembre et fruits sur une table*).[46] He agreed on another still life with the dealer, *Still Life with Compotier* (*Compotier, assiette et pommes*),[47] which he paid for in March. He also bought a drawing by Degas from Bernheim-Jeune[48] representing, according to what is written in the files, "a woman sitting drying her feet" – still unidentified and which Fayet called *After the Bath* (*Après le bain*). He wrote daily to his wife. "My stay in Paris is delightful", he wrote on 8 February. "We have not left each other's side with Fabre, who is the sweetest boy on the planet. Tomorrow we are going with Odilon Redon to the Lamoureux concert ... I have bought a beautiful bronze by Rodin in the most exceptional conditions,[49] a landscape by Cézanne and a Gauguin.[50] All of this at unimaginable prices."[51]
But all of these purchases were not to his wife's taste who criticised his spending. Fayet replied to his wife from his stance as a businessman: "I have just received the most dreadful letter! A spendthrift! Money waster, etc. ... I am just as invested in buying my paintings as I am in selling my wine? I believe that currently it is a better investment to buy Cézanne, Gauguin, Degas than annuities. I have had a generous offer for the portrait by Cézanne. If this painting didn't make me so happy, I would sell it straightaway to prove to you that we can make money with painting. And the Cabrol deal! Do you know that the Pissarros and Monets are selling for 10,000 francs to 20,000 francs? Bernheim would give me 4,000 francs for the Fantin-Latour I still have; I bought it for 800 francs".[52]
His wife's criticism did not stop Fayet's enthusiasm, who just before going back to the South, acquired *Madame Chocquet Reading* (*Madame Chocquet lisant*)[53] by Renoir from Durand-Ruel, a painting from the Victor Chocquet collection which had been split up a few months earlier. The painting, made in 1876 and shown the same year at the second Impressionist exhibition, represented "framed by a window, [Madame Chocquet] sitting in profile on the left and ... wearing a pale, ample bathrobe. She is holding a book. On the window ledge, some flowers".[54] Then, on the train back to Béziers, he drew

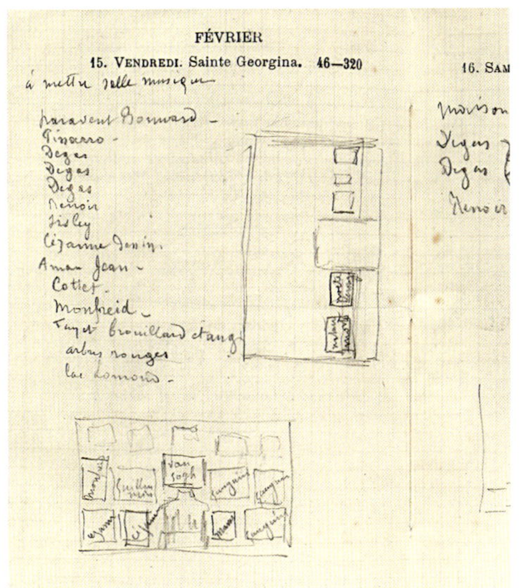
FÉVRIER
15. VENDREDI. Sainte Georgina. 46—320
16. SAM

5. Gustave Fayet, notebook, 15 February 1901, Archives Fayet

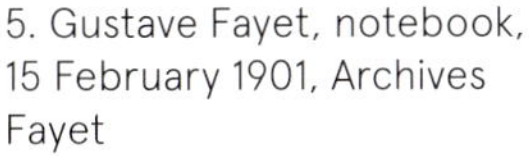

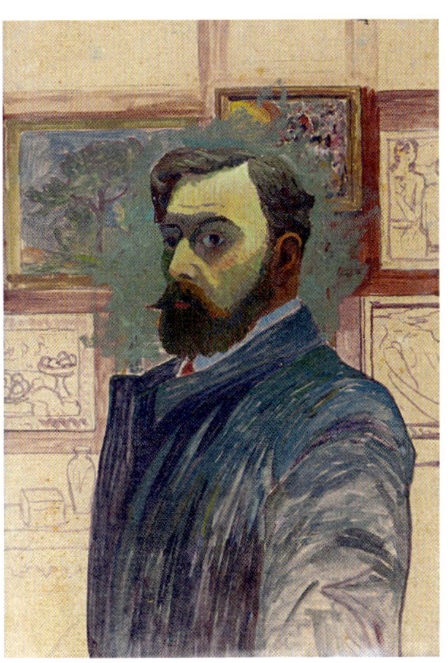

6. Gustave Fayet, *Self-Portrait* (*Autoportrait*), 1901–2, gouache on paper, 73 × 50 cm, private collection

how he would hang them in the music room, mixing his latest acquisitions with older pieces and his own work, and recapitulated the purchases he had made at Vollard's, Durand-Ruel's and Bernheim-Jeune's (fig. 5).

On 9 March 1901, he sent 3,500 francs to Vollard from the South of France for the still life[55] which he presented at the exhibition he was organising with the Beaux-Arts Society in Béziers. It was only later, that it became clear that it had had an impact that went far beyond regional boundaries.
Besides Cézanne's *Still Life with Compotier* (no. 17), Fayet lent *Reading* (*La Lecture*) by Renoir (no. 110a), as well as *The Earth, Large Model* (*La Terre, grand modèle*) by Rodin (no. 170) and *The Flageolet Player on the Cliff* (*Joueur de Flageolet sur la Falaise*) by Gauguin (no. 51), whilst showing six of his own works. Progressively, throughout the spring of 1901, the artist seemed to disappear behind the collector and this is confirmed in the only self-portrait we have of Fayet where he depicts himself, not painting, but in the gallery of the family residence in Rue du Capus in Béziers, in front of his collection. We can recognise the two Cézannes, *The Great Pine* (*Le Grand Pin*) and *Still Life with Compotier*, *The Arena at Arles* (*Les Arènes d'Arles*)[56] by Van Gogh, *Three Tahitians* (*Les Trois Tahitiens*) by Gauguin (fig. 6).
Collector, director of the museum and exhibition organiser, along with the close circle around him, Fabre and Monfreid, Fayet had the ambition of

being ahead of the times in terms of taste. Here is what he wrote to Redon, thanking him for the paintings he had sent for the exhibition:

> Béziers is really a small town, but there are some extraordinary things happening here. Firstly, we are opening an exhibition to the public where there are works by Cézanne, Degas, Redon, Renoir, Pissarro, Gauguin, Rodin, Albert André, Valtat, Maurice Denis, and de Monfreid.
> Throughout the winter we would play music by Beethoven, Bach, C. Franck, Chausson, etc. etc. for the public.
> Sometimes we are booed by the public. But nothing will stop us and we will continue, unperturbed, our work for aesthetic innovation.[57]

So here in this letter, we can see what motivated Fayet, "spreading all forms of modernity"[58] even if it shocked people. He followed the advice of his friend Fabre, who in November 1900, when Fayet started collecting, wrote to him: "When you have a collection that all your visitors find slanderous, then you can be proud, but only then".[59]

Degas, Cézanne, Renoir

In the seven months from September 1900 to March 1901, Fayet acquired a Guillaumin, two Degas, three oil paintings and a watercolour by Cézanne as well as a Renoir. In the months and year that followed, he would strengthen the place of these artists in his collection (with the exception of Guillaumin), alongside works by Gauguin, Van Gogh or Toulouse-Lautrec.
In all, Fayet had twelve or thirteen Degas. Not being one of those collectors who talked a lot about his collection, there is nothing in the correspondence that explains this passion for bathers or dancers. We can however imagine that Fayet was undoubtedly sensitive to the quality of the drawing which, as Fabre wrote in the preface to the catalogue for the exhibition in Béziers, was "accurate and sharp to capture the most daring and natural movements"[60]. Occupied with the Société des Beaux-Arts, Fayet could not be present for the sale of father Gaugain's collection from 6 to 8 May 1901, but won bids on two pastels of dancers that brilliantly immortalised the life of the "petits rats" at the Opéra de Paris, *Dancer Adjusting the Shoulder Strap of her Bodice* (*Danseuse rajustant ses épaulettes*)[61] and *Seated Dancer in a Pink Tutu, Sleeping* (*Danseuse assise, en jupe rose, endormie*),[62] for 3,000 francs and 1,900 francs respectively, excluding costs. Fabre wrote the next day: "Yesterday at the father Gaugain sale. Great astonishment when I saw that you had won the bid for Degas. They are delightful and you didn't pay too much for them. You even got the best deal of the auction".[63]

Fayet still had works he wanted to get rid of and he made a list of them in his notebook.[64] In December 1901, during another trip to Paris, he traded these works in order to acquire four extra Degas. At Bernheim-Jeune's he chose two pastels. The first one, *Woman, Warming Up* (*Femme se chauffant*)[65] belonged to Chtchoukine but remains unidentified. He obtained it in exchange for a Fantin-Latour from the Cabrol collection, *Woman Sitting* (*Femme assise*), estimated at 3,000 francs, and a landscape by Roll, "a sad plain",[66] estimated at 500 francs, to which he added 2,000 francs. The second pastel was *The Splinter* (*L'Epine*)[67] representing "a naked young girl on a bed, holding her right foot in her hands. On the right a table, a lamp",[68] which we know about from photos of the Fayet collection taken by Druet in 1905 or 1906 and an auction at Christie's in 2007.[69] This pastel had been offered to Fayet in the spring for 12,000 francs. He obtained it for 9,200 francs in December and gave the art dealer 2,000 francs and two paintings, *The Hamlet of Peschadoire* (*Le Hameau de Peschadoire*) by Guillaumin, which he offered at a value of 4,200 francs, the price he had paid a year earlier, and a landscape with snowy effect by Pissarro, from the Cabrol collection, for 3,000 francs, although it had been valued at 1,000 francs in 1899. By getting rid of these two canvases, Fayet followed Fabre's advice who was riled up "against this madness for Sisley, Guillaumin, Pissarro...".[70] On 9 December 1901, Hessel confirmed the transaction and announced the speedy expedition of the two pastels.[71] In response to the argument he had had earlier in the year, he announced to his wife: "I've finally got rid of the Fantin-Latour for 3,000. There is nothing more to say."[72]

Two days after this purchase, Fayet wrote to Durand-Ruel and offered "5,000 for two other pastels by Degas, *Woman Drying her Neck* (*Femme se frottant le cou*)[73] and *Bather Stepping into a Tub* (*Femme entrant dans sa baignoire*)".[74] Durand-Ruel replied the next day specifying the provenance of the two pastels "I bought 5182 *Woman Drying her Neck* (*Femme se frottant le cou*) at the Sisley sale on 2 May 1899 for the sum of 2,885 francs; 5043 was bought from Mr Tavernier on 24 February for 2,000 francs" and accepted to sell them for 5,500 francs justifying this by saying: "The two pastels cost me 4,885 francs ... You see that it's not a brilliant deal and I have barely made any interest on the money I paid" (fig. 7).[75]

When stopping by at Durand-Ruel's several weeks later, Fabre learned that Fayet had "accepted the offer for the two Degas", and commented on this purchase: "You won't regret it: that's ten Degas?"[76] But Fayet didn't stop there and bought another pastel of a group of three dancers at the Strauss auction in May 1902,[77] lot no. 75, from the Blot collection. Two other pastels figured in the file for the collection but have not yet been identified: a *Woman Washing* (*Femme à la toilette*) "naked, her legs on the fireplace with her maid combing her hair", wrote Fayet, and *Two Dancers* (*Deux danseuses*) as well as a sketch of some dancers.

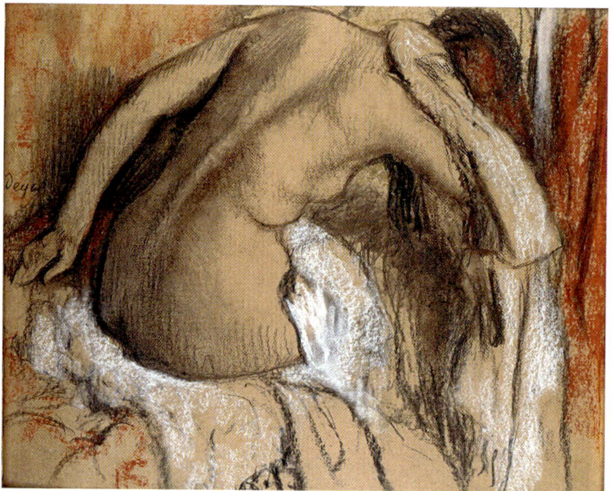

7. Edgar Degas, *After the Bath* (*Après le bain*), c. 1888, pastel and fusain, 50 × 60 cm, Musée d'Art Moderne André Malraux, Le Havre, Senn-Foulds Collection

And so, over two years, through exchanges or purchases at auction, Fayet established a beautiful collection of pastels by Degas, some of them coming from prestigious collections such as Tavernier, Blot, father Gaugain or Sisley. But he only kept these works for a few years and used them in turn for trades or to be sold in auction houses. In October 1902, Fayet announced to Fabre his intention of trading some canvases against some very major paintings. At Durand-Ruel's, he proposed *Intimacy* (*Intimité*)[78] by Courbet, *Farmyard* (*Cour de ferme*)[79] by Monet from the former Cabrol collection, *Nude Kneeling Seen from behind* (*Femme nue à genoux de dos*)[80] by Toulouse-Lautrec and an unidentified study by Degas against another Monet, *Rocks at Belle-Île* (*Rochers à Belle-Île*),[81] from the Shchukin collection, one of the most beautiful studies made after the *The Pyramids at Port-Coton* (*Pyramides de Port-Coton*), and *Two Peasants Resting* (*Deux paysannes assises*)[82] by Pissarro, representing two peasants chatting under some trees in Pontoise. They were two major Impressionist artists who were under-represented in the Fayet collection. Then, over the following years, Fayet exchanged the Degas for other works. *La Toilette* was traded for *Interior* (*Intérieur*)[83] by Vuillard. He swapped two other Degas in 1908 for *Trees at the Jas de Bouffan* (*Bosquet au Jas de Bouffan*)[84] by Cézanne. Some were sold to Druet or Moline and ended up with other collectors, like *Dancer Adjusting the Shoulder Strap of her Bodice* (*Danseuse rajustant ses épaulettes*), bought by Maurice Masson. Others still were sold at auction like *Woman Drying her Neck* (*Femme se frottant le cou*) by Degas bought by Olivier Senn on 16 May 1908 in a sale of modern paintings (no. 50) which included many works by Gauguin, Van Gogh, Matisse, Monticelli, Signac from the Fayet collection and today housed at the Musée d'Art Moderne André Malraux in Le Havre.

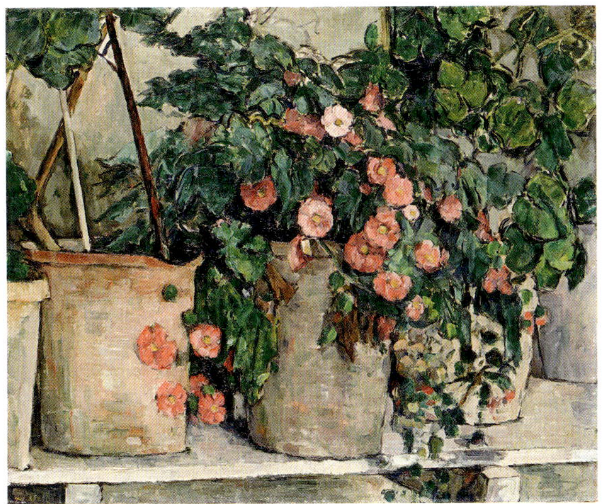

8. Paul Cézanne,
The Begonias (*Les Bégonias*),
1875–76, oil on canvas,
46 × 54 cm,
private collection

Fayet already possessed a self-portrait, a still life and a landscape by Cézanne, but he was no longer the "enigmatic, solitary and nomadic painter"[85] he had been at the debuts of Impressionism. His painting sold thanks to Vollard's efforts and the major auction houses, his work increased in value and the young generation, immortalised by Maurice Denis in his *Homage to Cézanne* (*Hommage à Cézanne*), proclaimed to be his followers. Fayet strengthened Cézanne's place in his collection. In early 1902, just before the sale of some of his collection at Bernheim-Jeune's,[86] Fabre offered to sell him two paintings by Cézanne. The first, *The Begonias* (*Les Bégonias*),[87] depicted four terracotta pots with begonias on a wooden shelf (fig. 8). Sold again in 1910, it belonged to Charles Pacquement and then to Sacha Guitry, before being bought by Paul Rosenberg. The second painting, *La Toilette*,[88] a work inspired by Delacroix's *Rising* (*Lever*), was of a female nude set in a Baroque decor, her arms raised above her head arranging her hair. Today it is housed at the Barnes Foundation. Fayet paid his friend 4,000 francs for these two works.
Then, Fayet left for Paris with his wife and George-Daniel de Monfreid, who kept a day-to-day record of the trip in his notebook. Together, they were preparing the next exhibition of the Société des Beaux-Arts in Béziers devoted to Monticelli and so were seeking loans from Hessel and Vollard. Fayet was thinking of exchanging a Cézanne but, perhaps frightened of his wife's reaction, this plan was never put into action. On the other hand, along with Monfreid he took his wife to discover the galleries in Rue Lafitte and showed her the private collections of Durand-Ruel, Rue de Rome, Isaac de Camondo, Rue Gluck, Emile Schuffenecker, Rue Paturle, and Dr Viau, Boulevard Haussmann, as if to convince her of the wisdom of his choices. As Monfreid reported in a letter to Gauguin: "In February, I spent a few days in Paris. I

met up with Fayet, who at the moment is completely taken with Cézanne. That of course changes nothing of his admiration for you".[89]
Fayet's collection was enriched with several other works by Cézanne over the following years. In 1903, he exchanged with Vollard one of three paintings Gauguin had managed to send to Fayet from his Tahitian retreat just before he died, for a new watercolour of the entrance to a garden in a country house.[90] After Emile Schuffenecker's divorce, Fayet received several offers from her brother Amédée including one for *The Sea at L'Estaque* (*La Baie de l'Estaque*),[91] representing a bay caught between some greyish-blue rocky cliffs dotted with bouquets of pines and a few houses on the water's edge lost in dense vegetation. He had admired this painting at Emile Schuffenecker's and bought it for 5,000 francs. The following year, on 4 March 1904, at Vollard's, who had become his main supplier since he had started his collection, he bought one of the numerous representations of bathers, *Six Bathers* (*Six baigneuses*) for 3,000 francs.[92] Finally, in 1908, several years later, at Bernheim-Jeune's, he exchanged two Degas for *Trees at the Jas de Bouffan* (*Bosquet au Jas de Bouffan*),[93] estimated at 2,000 francs. The file mentions a small painting, *Female Nude Reclining* (*Femme nue couchée*),[94] date of purchase unknown, which was bought by Bernheim-Jeune in 1909, who offered it to Auguste Pellerin, a great collector of Cézanne.
We know that for Fabre, Cézanne's works were "things we never get tired of".[95] Fayet, who had nonetheless acquired some beautiful pieces, was less categorical, much to Fabre's dismay who questioned his friend: "Would you have such doubts about Cézanne's paintings, poor soul!",[96] and ended up driving him into a corner: "You rediscovered Cézanne with Jas Bouffan. When will you rediscover Cézanne in his own work? You know we have an old quarrel to settle on that subject".[97]
In truth, Fayet's taste was gradually evolving. Since he had settled in Paris in February 1905, he had become firm friends with Odilon Redon who, Fayet admitted, "quickly made me understand things I hadn't really seen before. He nurtured in me the notion of spirituality".[98] In his *Souvenirs sur Odilon Redon*, Fayet cited the artist who told him: "Pissarro is wrong. Painting is not about an apple on the edge of a table",[99] and added: "The arrival of these spiritual works in my collection has forced me to part with some of my realist works."[100] In 1906, Fayet still imagined the possibility that, if Druet bought the Manet from him, he could "buy himself two beautiful Cézannes from Vollard".[101] But two years later, on 10 January 1908, he sold *Self-Portrait* (*Autoportrait*) for 10,000 francs to Druet who sold it to Hugo von Tschudi, director of the Nationalgalerie in Berlin, who took the painting to Munich where it is still on show today. The most astonishing sale took place on 2 June 1910, the day Fayet sold, through Druet, his seven Cézannes to Charles Pacquement for the sum of 100,000 francs. Redon wrote about this sale

that "Fayet has just sold his Cézannes for a hundred thousand francs. Our changing market is still reeling from the affair. A round figure for just seven paintings, several of which are not the best works".[102]

The sale of the Cézannes testifies to the evolution of the collector's taste but was not just about buying other works or supporting new talent. In fact, in January 1908, Fayet bought Fontfroide abbey and, by selling works from his collection, he hoped to make a profit to restore the building. Already, shortly after he purchased the abbey, Fayet who was in contact with Druet for the sale of some of the Gauguins, wrote to his wife: "To sell we have to make a large profit which I put between 90,000 and one hundred thousand francs ... If this deal happened we could arrange our living room with a few Cézannes, some beautiful ornaments; and it would look less like a museum. And with the profit, we could not only pay for Fontfroide, but the finishing touches such as statues, vases, etc., etc."[103]

Fabre, who had encouraged him to buy the Cézannes, shared his admiration for Renoir's painting with Fayet, writing in the preface to the catalogue for the 1901 exhibition in Béziers that it was "a sight for sore eyes. Its grace and charm make all our senses rejoice. The artist seems to be telling us that there is only one joy in life: the joy of painting".[104] Two years after *Madame Chocquet Reading* (*Madame Chocquet lisant*) came into his collection, on 12 June 1903, Fayet bought *Place de la Trinité,*[105] from Lucien Moline, one of the most beautiful views of Paris in the 1870s which had once belonged to Georges de Bellio. The dealer let him have it "for the sum of two thousand five hundred francs in cash and a pastel by Aman-Jean".[106] Then, several weeks later, he bought *Couple Reading* (*Couple lisant*)[107] from him, a work dated 1877 representing Edmond Renoir, the artist's brother, and Margot Legrand, his favourite model, leaning over an open book. Finally, at the end of the year, he swapped a Raffaëlli with Cabrol, who had started collecting again with Fayet's money, for "a small but exquisite, old Renoir",[108] *Woman with a Parasol* (*Jeune Femme à l'ombrelle*)[109] he had acquired at the Blot sale in May 1900. Before parting with it, Cabrol had called in Durand-Ruel to get Renoir to sign the painting.[110] While Fayet continued to passionately look for works by Gauguin to have a representative collection and took an interest in the young Fauves, he bought two more Renoirs from Bernheim-Jeune. On 7 April 1905, Fayet traded *Rocks at Belle-Île* (*Rochers à Belle-Île*) by Monet for *Young Girl with a Swan* (*La Jeune Fille au cygne*) or *Apparition*,[111] from the Tavernier collection, which was of a young girl, facing us, against a backdrop of Japanese tenting. Then, on 24 May 1906, Fayet bought his last Renoir, *Young Woman Standing in the Fields* (*Jeune femme debout dans les champs*)[112] for 12,450 francs, a sum he settled thanks to having sold *Head of a Woman* (*Tête de femme*) by Manet a few days earlier, some flowers by Vuillard and a scaled-down bronze of Rodin's *The Kiss* (*Baiser*) to Bernheim Jeune.[113]

Unlike the works by Degas and Cézanne, Fayet kept his six Renoirs, which with the exception of Monet's *Young Girl with a Swan* (*La Jeune Fille au cygne*) from 1886, were all works from the artist's Impressionist period. These works were initially hung at 51 Rue de Bellechase, in his wife's bedroom and boudoir, then at Château d'Igny still in the bedroom of his wife who appreciated the distinction and subtility of these works. Three years after Fayet's death, five of these paintings, along with those by Gauguin, Van Gogh and Bonnard, were among the 34 paintings sold by his heirs to Paul Rosenberg for a total sum of 5.4 million francs; a sale which marked the dispersion of the Fayet collection.

The Impressionists were not the main focus of the Fayet collection, but his acquisitions of works by Degas, Cézanne, Renoir, Monet or Pissarro enabled Fayet to become familiar with the world and practices of art dealers, to spend long days talking about painting, listening to their advice about creating his collection, going to the auction rooms, understanding how the prices of artworks were fixed and making a name for himself, even a reputation in the small world of the art market.

Unfortunately, Fayet did not keep these works, sometimes selling them for a huge profit like the Cézannes, but sometimes at a loss. In 1906, he confessed to his wife, "... visit at the Bernheims who have just opened a new gallery in Rue Duphot opposite the Trois quartiers? Claude Monet exhibition. I feel nothing in front of these paintings and am increasingly disappointed".[114]

In fact, Fayet focused his activity on Gauguin and Redon whilst at the same time taking an interest in a new generation of artists which included Matisse, Derain, Vuillard, Bonnard, Signac, Denis. He went from being a follower of these painters to becoming a discoverer, defender, commissioner, protector and friend of these artists. A status which reflected his ambitions far better.

1 Letter from Gustave Fayet to Madeleine Fayet, Paris, 23 October 1900, AF.

2 George-Daniel de Monfreid, notebook, 26 October 1900, private archive, microfilm available at the Musée d'Orsay archives library.

3 Paul Cézanne, *Self-Portrait in a White Cap* (Autoportrait au bonnet blanc), 1875–77, oil on canvas, 55.5 × 46.2 cm, Bayerische Staatsgemäldesammlungen, Munich (Venturi 284).

4 Received by Vollard on 21 and 26 November 1900, AF.

5 Dario Gamboni et al., *Gustave Fayet. L'œil souverain* (Paris: Éditions du Regard, 2015).

6 *Gustave Fayet. Un artiste en sa demeure*, Musée Fayet, Béziers, 2015; *Gustave Fayet. Paysages rêvés*, Musée des Beaux-Arts – Hôtel Fayet, Béziers, 2016; *Gustave Fayet. "Vous, peintre..."*, Musée Terrus, Elne, 2006.

7 Jean-Gabriel Goulinat, "Les collections Gustave Fayet", *L'Amour de l'Art* 4, Paris, April 1925; Roseline Bacou, *Odilon Redon* (Geneva: Pierre Cailler, 1956); Roseline Bacou, "Paul Gauguin et Gustave Fayet", in *Gauguin*, conference proceedings, Musée d'Orsay, Paris, 11–13 January 1989, French archives, 1991. Marie-Pierre Salé, "Redon et ses collectionneurs", in exh. cat. *Odilon Redon. Prince du rêve*, National Galleries, Grand Palais, Paris, 23 March – 20 June 2011 (Paris, RMN Grand Palais and Musée d'Orsay, 2011), pp. 43–53.

8 Roseline Bacou, "Gustave Fayet collectionneur", in *Cahiers de l'association française* *pour la protection des archives privées*, II, 2008, pp. 49–66.

9 Magali Rougeot, *Gustave Fayet, itinéraire d'un artiste collectionneur*, thesis in art history, Université Paris X Nanterre and École du Louvre, 2013. The thesis is available online at https://bdr.parisnanterre.fr/theses/internet/2013PA100218.pdf

10 Natacha Abriat et al., *Gustave Fayet. Châteaux, vignobles et mécénat en Languedoc* (Lyon: Éditions Lieux-Dits, 2013), p. 20.

11 Armand Cabrol, "Viticulture littéraire", *L'Art moderne*, 31 May 1903, p. 198.

12 Ibid.

13 Guillaume Labussière, "Eugène Carrière – Armand Cabrol. Correspondance (1894–1906)", *Le Journal du musée Eugène Carrière* 4, 2016, pp. 15–37.

14 Puvis de Chavanne, *Head of a Woman* (Tête de femme), bought for 1,000 francs from Durand-Ruel on 13 October 1898; Renoir, *Bather* (Baigneuse), bought for 1,400 francs from Durand-Ruel on 17 October 1898; two paintings by Whistler bought on 12 August 1899 from Bernheim for 3,000 francs and 2,500 francs respectively.

15 Letter from Armand Cabrol to Eugène Carrière, [30 December 1899], BCMN Ms425 (02); Labussière, "Eugène Carrière – Armand Cabrol. Correspondance".

16 Letter from Armand Cabrol to Eugène Carrière, November 1898, in ibid.

17 "Foreword", in *Catalogue des peintures, pastels, aquarelles, dessins objets d'art, lithographies, etc.*, Béziers, 1902.

18 Gustave Fayet, *Moon Rising over the Lake at Vendres* (Lever de lune sur l'étang de Vendres), 1896, oil on canvas, 92 × 142 cm, private collection.

19 Roseline Bacou, *Gustave Fayet*, unpublished manuscript, AF.

20 Letter from Paul Gauguin to George-Daniel de Monfreid, August 1901, in *Lettres de Gauguin à Daniel de Monfreid* (Paris: Georges Falaize, 1950), p. 182.

21 Letter from Maurice Fabre to Gustave Fayet, [Paris], 18 November 1900, AF.

22 Letter from Maurice Fabre to Gustave Fayet, [Paris], [December 1900], AF.

23 Ibid.

24 Letter from Maurice Fabre to Gustave Fayet, Paris, 25 June 1901, AF.

25 Letter from Armand Cabrol to Eugène Carrière, [Boujan-sur-Libron, 30 December 1899], in ibid.

26 Gustave Fayet, notebook, 23 September 1900, AF; letter from Joseph Bernheim, 24 September, AF.

27 Armand Guillaumin, *The Hamlet of Peschadoire in the Sunlight* (Le Hameau de Peschadoire au soleil), c. 1895, oil on canvas, 81 × 65 cm, Musée des Beaux-Arts, Rennes, on loan from the Musée du Louvre.

28 Letter from Joseph Bernheim to Gustave Fayet, Paris, 24 September 1900, AF.

29 Édouard Manet, *Head of a Woman* (Tête de femme), 1870, oil on canvas, 56 × 46 cm, Rudolf Staechelin Collection, Basel, Beyeler Foundation (Rouart-Wildenstein 156).

30 Edgar Degas, *Woman Combing her Hair* (Femme se coiffant), *La Coiffure*, *La Toilette*, 1887–90, pastel, 57 × 45 cm, private collection (Lemoisne 935).

31 Letter from Gustave Fayet to Madeleine Fayet, [Paris], n.d., AF.

32 Letter from Gustave Fayet to Madeleine Fayet, Paris, 23 October 1900, AF.

33 Monfreid, notebook, 26 October 1900.

34 Paul Cézanne, *Self-Portrait in a White Cap* (Autoportrait au bonnet blanc), 1875–77, oil on canvas, 55.5 × 46.2 cm, Bayerische Staatsgemäldesammlungen, Munich (Venturi 284).

35 Letter from Maurice Fabre to Gustave Fayet, Gasparets, 5 November 1900, AF.

36 Letter from Maurice Fabre to Gustave Fayet, [Paris], 18 November 1900, AF.

37 Receipt from Vollard, 21 November 1900, AF.

38 Receipt from Vollard, 26 November 1900, AF; day to day register of receipts and payments ms 421 (4.9), p. 53, transaction date 22 November 1900.

39 Letter from Fabre to Gustave Fayet, [Paris], [November 1900], AF.

40 Letter from Gustave Fayet to George-Daniel de Monfreid, Béziers, 22 December 1900, ms 5272, Musée du Prieuré Archives, Saint-Germain-en-Laye.

41 Paul Gauguin, *Crimson-Flowered Breasts* (Les Seins aux fleurs rouges), 1899, oil on canvas, 94 × 72.4 cm, The Metropolitan Museum of Art, New York (Wildenstein 583).

42 Paul Gauguin, *The Three Tahitians* (Les Trois Tahitiens), 1898, oil on canvas, 73 × 94 cm, Scottish National Gallery, Edinburgh (Wildenstein 573).

43 Paul Cézanne, *The Great Pine* (Le Grand Pin), 1896, oil on canvas, 85 × 92 cm, Museu de Arte, São Paulo (Venturi 669).

44 Gustave Fayet collection file, AF.

45 Ibid.

46 Paul Cézanne, *Pot of Ginger and Fruits on a Table* (Pot de gingembre et fruits sur une table), 1888–90, pencil and watercolour on paper, 24 × 36 cm, location unknown (FWN 1943, Rewald 289, Venturi 1134).

47 Paul Cézanne, *Still Life with Compotier* (Compotier, assiette et pommes), 1879–82, oil on canvas, 43.5 × 54 cm, Ny Carlsberg Glyptotek, Copenhagen (Venturi 342).
48 Edgar Degas, *After the Bath, Seated Woman Drying Her Feet* (Après le bain, Femme assise s'essuyant les pieds) (Bernheim register no. 9114; inventory entry Fayet no. 37), unidentified.
49 Auguste Rodin, *The Earth, Large Model* (La Terre, grand modèle), before 1896, bronze 1899, 47 × 106 × 37 cm, Musée Rodin, Paris.
50 Paul Gauguin, *The Flageolet Player on the Cliff* (Joueur de Flageolet sur la Falaise), 1889, oil on canvas, 73 × 92 cm, Indianapolis Museum of Art, Indianapolis (Wildenstein 361).
51 Letter from Gustave Fayet to Madeleine Fayet, Paris, 8 February 1901, AF.
52 Ibid.
53 Pierre-Auguste Renoir, *Madame Chocquet Reading* (Madame Chocquet lisant), 1876, oil on canvas, 65 × 54 cm, former Mrs Harris Jonas collection, location unknown (Daulte 174).
54 Gustave Fayet, collection file, AF.
55 Paul Cézanne, *Still Life with Compotier* (Compotier, assiette et pommes), 1879–82 (Venturi 342).
56 Vincent van Gogh, *The Arena at Arles* (Les Arènes d'Arles), oil on canvas, 73 × 92 cm, 1888, Museum of Modern Art, Moscow (La Faille 548).
57 Letter from Gustave Fayet to Odilon Redon, Béziers, 27 April [1901], in *Lettres à Odilon Redon* (Paris: J. Corti, 1960), pp. 289–90.
58 Alexandre d'Andoque and Pierre Pinchon, "Un cercle wagnérien en 1913; Burgsthal, Fayet, Strohl et Redon", in Cécile Leblanc and Danièle Pistone (eds.), *Le Wagnérisme dans tous ses états, 1913–2013* (Paris: Presses Sorbonne nouvelle, 2016), p. 86.
59 Letter from Maurice Fabre to Gustave Fayet, s.l., 18 November 1900, AF.
60 Maurice Fabre, "Préface", in *Catalogue des peintures, pastels, aquarelles, dessins, sculptures, céramiques, objets d'art, lithographies, etc.*, Béziers, 1901.
61 Edgar Degas, *Dancer Adjusting the Shoulder Strap of her Bodice* (Danseuse rajustant ses *épaulettes*), 1896–99, pastel, 44 × 35 cm, private collection (Lemoisne 1273).
62 Edgar Degas, *Seated Dancer in a Pink Tutu, Sleeping* (Danseuse assise, en jupe rose, endormie), 1895–98, pastel, 35 × 25 cm, location unknown (Lemoisne 1203).
63 Letter from Maurice Fabre to Gustave Fayet, Paris, 7 May 1901, AF.
64 Gustave Fayet, notebook, 29 November 1901, AF.
65 Edgar Degas, *Woman, Warming Up* (Femme se chauffant), pastel, unidentified (Bernheim-Jeune no. 9127).
66 Letter from Gustave Fayet to Madeleine Fayet, [Paris, December 1901], AF.
67 Edgar Degas, *The Splinter* (L'Épine), 1883–85, pastel and charcoal, 28 × 38 cm, private collection (Lemoisne 1089).
68 Gustave Fayet, collection file, AF.
69 Christie's, Impressionist and modern sale, London, 6 February 2007, lot 8.
70 Letter from Maurice Fabre to Gustave Fayet, Paris, 7 May 1901, AF.
71 Letter from Jos Hessel to Gustave Fayet, Paris, 9 December 1901, AF.
72 Letter from Gustave Fayet to Magdeleine Fayet, [Paris, 1901], AF.
73 Edgar Degas, *After the Bath* (Après le bain), c. 1888, pastel and charcoal, 50 × 60 cm, Musée d'art moderne André Malraux, Le Havre.
74 Edgar Degas, *Bather Stepping into a Tub* (Femme entrant dans sa baignoire), c. 1889, pastel, 31 × 48 cm, location unknown, Lemoisne 1309; Gustave Fayet, notebook, 14 December 1901, AF.
75 Letter from Paul Durand-Ruel to Gustave Fayet, 12 December 1901, AF.
76 Letter from Maurice Fabre to Gustave Fayet, [Paris], 28 January 1902, AF.
77 Edgar Degas, *Three Dancers* (Trois danseuses), pastel and charcoal on grey paper, 47 × 51 cm, private collection (MS-1468).
78 Gustave Courbet, *Intimacy* (Intimité), 1860, oil on canvas, 61 × 50 cm (F 272), despoiled, location unknown.
79 Claude Monet, *Farmyard* (Cour de ferme), 1878, oil on canvas, 61 × 50 cm, location unknown (Wildenstein 494).
80 Henri de Toulouse-Lautrec, *Nude Kneeling Seen from Behind* (Femme nue à genoux de dos), 1896, oil on cardboard, 52 × 40 cm, Paris, Musée d'Orsay (Dortu P614).
81 Claude Monet, *Rocks at Belle-Île* (Rochers à Belle-Île) or *The Pyramids at Port-Coton, Belle-Île-en-Mer* (Les Pyramides à Port-Coton, Belle-Île-en-Mer), 1886, oil on canvas, 60 × 73 cm, Ny Carlsberg Glyptotek, Copenhagen (Wildenstein 1086).
82 Camille Pissarro, *Peasants in the Wood* (Paysannes au bois), 1881, oil on canvas, 55.5 × 46 cm, private collection (catalogue raisonné no. 652).
83 Édouard Vuillard, *Interior* (Intérieur) or *Ker-Xavier Roussel Sitting in Front of a Window and Annette Standing in Front of an Indian Voile Curtain* (Ker-Xavier Roussel assis devant la fenêtre et Annette debout devant une portière en voile des Indes), 1903, oil on card,

58 × 54 cm, Albright Knox Gallery, Buffalo, NY (Cogeval 138).

84 Paul Cézanne, *Trees at the Jas de Bouffan* (Bosquet au Jas de Bouffan), 1875–76, oil on canvas, 54 × 73 cm, Portland Museum of Art, Portland, ME (Venturi 161).

85 Georges Lecomte, "Cézanne", in *Catalogue de tableaux, aquarelles, pastels et dessins composant la collection de M. E. Blot*, Hôtel Drouot, 9 and 10 May 1900.

86 ale of modern paintings, watercolours, pastels and drawings, Hôtel Drouot, 10 March 1902. Cabrol, who had started collecting again, sold a few pieces and Fayet reinforced the sale with some remaining pieces from Cabrol Manet's former collection: Manet's *The Fisherman* (Le Pêcheur) (no. 35), Pissarro's *Promenade on the Water's Edge* (Promenade au bord de l'eau) (no. 40), and perhaps a pastel by Renoir, *Women Dressed in City Clothes* (Femme en costume de ville) (no. 73).

87 Paul Cézanne, *The Begonias* (Les Bégonias), 1875–76, oil on canvas, 46 × 54 cm, private collection (Venturi 198).

88 Paul Cézanne, *La Toilette*, 1885–90, oil on canvas, 32 × 24 cm, Barnes Foundation, Philadelphia (Venturi 254).

89 Letter from George-Daniel de Monfreid to Paul Gauguin, Saint-Clément, 10 April 1902; *Lettres de Gauguin à Daniel de Monfreid, précédées d'un hommage à Gauguin par Victor Segalen*, edition established an annotated by Mrs Joly-Segalen, Paris, Georges Falaize, 1950, 251 pp., "Notes", p. 225–26.

90 Paul Cézanne, *Entrance to a Garden* (Entrée de jardin I), 1872–77, graphite and watercolour on laid paper, 46 × 30 cm, The Metropolitan Museum of Art, New York (Venturi 842).

91 Paul Cézanne, *The Sea at L'Estaque* (La Baie de l'Estaque), 1879–83, oil, 60.3 × 74.3 cm, Philadelphia Museum of Art, Philadelphia (Venturi 489).

92 Paul Cézanne, *Six Bathers* (Six baigneuses) or *The Undines* (Les Ondines), 1887, oil on canvas, 33 × 44, private collection, Geneva (Venturi 538).

93 Paul Cézanne, *Trees at the Jas de Bouffan* (Bosquet au Jas de Bouffan), 1875–76 (Venturi 161).

94 Paul Cézanne, *Female Nude Reclining* (Femme nue couchée), 1875–77, oil on canvas, 8.5 × 13 cm, Jasper Johns Foundation (Venturi 279).

95 Letter from Maurice Fabre to Gustave Fayet, December 1900, AF.

96 Letter from Maurice Fabre to Gustave Fayet, 10 June 1901, AF.

97 Letter from Maurice Fabre to Gustave Fayet, Bagnères, 23 July 1903.

98 Gustave Fayet, "Souvenirs sur Odilon Redon", *Critique, Art, Philosophie. Bulletin mensuel d'art et de littérature*, May–June 1924.

99 Ibid.

100 Ibid.

101 Letter from Gustave Fayet to Madeleine Fayet, 9 March 1906, AF.

102 Letter from Odilon Redon to Gabriel Frizeau, 11 June 1910, in Moueix, vol. I, 1969, p. 209, cited by Magali Rougeot, p. 99.

103 Letter from Gustave Fayet to Madeleine Fayet, [1908], AF.

104 *Catalogue des peintures, pastels, aquarelles*... cit.

105 Pierre Renoir, *Place de la Trinité*, 1875, oil on canvas, 51.5 × 62.8 cm, private collection, Los Angeles (Daulte 185).

106 Lucien Moline, received 12 June 1903, AF.

107 Pierre Renoir, *Couple Reading* (Couple lisant), 1877, oil on canvas, 32 × 24 cm, private collection (Daulte 237).

108 Letter from Gustave Fayet to George-Daniel de Monfreid, 2 November 1903, Musée du Prieuré, Saint-Germain-en-Laye, ms 5276.

109 Pierre Renoir, *Woman with a Parasol* (Jeune Femme à l'ombrelle), 1872, oil on canvas, 25.5 × 19 cm, private collection (Daulte 79).

110 Letter from Durand-Ruel to Armand Cabrol, 16 July 1903, AF. "Following my letter on 11 July, I am writing to inform you that I managed to make Mr Renoir agree to sign his initials on the small painting *Woman with a Parasol* dating from 1865–66. I did everything I could to get the artist to consent to signing which he does not usually do for paintings that left his studio such a long time ago."

111 Pierre Renoir, *Young Girl with a Swan* (La Jeune Fille au cygne) or *Apparition*, 1886, oil on canvas, 76 × 62 cm, location unknown (Daulte 495).

112 Pierre Renoir, *Young Woman Standing in the Fields* (Jeune femme debout dans les champs), 1874, oil on canvas, 71 × 43 cm, private collection, New York (Daulte 109).

113 Gustave Fayet, notebook, 10 May 1906, AF.

114 Letter from Gustave Fayet to Madeleine, s.l., 1906, AF.

AN IMPRESSIONIST DOCUMENT: THE FIRST VERSION OF THE EXHIBITION CATALOGUE OF THE SOCIÉTÉ ANONYME DES ARTISTES PEINTRES, SCULPTEURS, GRAVEURS ETC... PARIS, 1874[1]

ANNE DISTEL

The history and context of the first exhibition held by the Société anonyme des artistes peintres, sculpteurs, graveurs etc... in 1874 or, more simply put, the first Impressionist exhibition, are well known thanks to the work of John Rewald[2] and Paul Tucker,[3] completed by a compilation of contemporary reviews published by Ruth Berson.[4] Both Tucker and Berson reproduced the exhibition catalogue printed by Alcan-Lévy, 61 Rue Lafayette, Paris and thus widely accessible.

However, a booklet printed in Paris by Edmond Baume, 109 Rue de Lafayette which, as we will see, was the first version of the exhibition catalogue, seems to have been overlooked.

First noticed by Claude Roger-Marx, who specified that it came from Philippe Burty's archives (1830–1890),[5] one of the first critics to follow and support the project from the start, this slim booklet with a blue cover might have disappeared for good had it not been for the active and kind cooperation of Claude Roger-Marx's daughter, Mrs Paulette Asselain, who donated it to the Musée d'Orsay in 1989. It was then deposited at the Bibliothèque centrale des musées nationaux, and later transferred to the INHA library.[6] Its integral reproduction for this article allows us to appreciate its interest, as well as to accompany it with a few additional remarks.

A Legally Binding Document

As explained in a handwritten note on page 1 – "Catalogue of prices announced by the members at the board meeting" – signed by the board's secretary, Alfred Meyer (1852–1904),[7] an enameller and exhibitor, this doc-

ument is above all a mandate from member artists to sell their works as agreed in the society statutes; the society was entitled to 10% of any sales made. We will come back to the prices later. The society's official looking stamp appears on each page. Some artists signed it, others did not, which at least indicates a certain administrative flexibility. In some cases (besides works lent by amateurs), the absence of prices might be explained by the absence of the work in the exhibition or the fact that the exhibitor did not want to sell it. An additional note dated 23 April (thus after the exhibition opening on the 15th) from Léontine De Nittis, the wife and very active agent of the painter, who was staying in London at the time, has been added to replace his signature (see transcription).
The works were classified in alphabetical order according to the name of the exhibitor, with an inversion for the letter R, an order which was respected, probably so as not to have to redo the numbering system in the later Alcan-Lévy edition. The main reason for us to consider the INHA annotated version printed by Baume, as earlier than the one by Alcan-Lévy, is its poor quality: it would seem that it is indeed a document compiled hurriedly to be ready in time for the opening and annexed with the society's documents; the large number of errors and typos (the title page, for example, reads "boulevart", gives opening hours that were later changed, indicates the price of 50 centimes, implicitly the price of the catalogue, but does not specify the admission price) is proof of this; in the case of Pissarro, Meyer or Auguste de Molins, the need to complete the titles of the works by hand (for numbers 91 bis, 94 bis, 139, 140), is another. Finally, work no. 142, by Renoir, entitled *L'Avant-scène*, in the Baume version, unexplainably became *La Loge* (*The Theatre Box*), but several critics cite the first title which proves that the Baume catalogue had circulated and was used during at least the first two weeks of the exhibition.[8]

A Concern for Elegance

When comparing the two versions, the most striking difference is how much the Alcan-Lévy catalogue has gained in elegance and clarity. Not only have the errors been rectified, but the overall aspect is much clearer, with a real attempt at improving font, especially for the artists' names. Abandoning the idea of one artist on each page, the booklet also has fewer pages. Who, among the associates, might have encouraged this choice? Perhaps Degas or Pissarro, so sensitive to such details? Making allusion to the unpublished (and late) memories of Edmond Renoir, the painter's younger brother, John Rewald recounted that Edmond "was in charge of printing the catalogue" but we do not know the exact source, nor any other testimony that confirms it. Another likely lead, Durand-Ruel: the graphic design of the title page of the 1873 album, *Galerie Durand-Ruel. Recueil d'estampes*, features indeed an identical italic type.[9] But if Alcan-Lévy also printed the group's second exhibition catalogue in 1876, the presentation was very different from the first one, and also differs from those printed by others for the following exhibition catalogues.

The Price of the Works

Clearly, the price of the artworks quoted is the most interesting part of this document.

The most expensive painting, worth 5,000 francs, was no. 103, Monet's *The Luncheon* (*Déjeuner*), the masterpiece from the museum in Frankfurt, whilst *Impression, Sunrise* (*Impression, soleil levant*), now at the Musée Marmottan, was quoted at 1,000 francs. Astruc (a group of watercolours), Bracquemond (but the work was not for sale), Colin, De Nittis, Auguste Ottin (a marble), Pissarro, Renoir and Rouart announced prices of 2,000 francs and higher, but the majority of the prices were around 200 or 300 francs. Without going into detail, the highest prices corresponded to the average price of similar size works by artists exhibited at the Salon, including Millet, Courbet or even Manet,[10] and of course excluding stars like Meissonier, Gérôme or Bonnat which cost nearer to 50,000 francs. On this subject, let us not forget that Giuseppe De Nittis also exhibited at the 1874 Salon;[11] the relatively high prices given by his wife are relative to those he practised with his dealer, Goupil.[12]

However, what interests us here are specifically the works of the "real" Impressionists.

To touch on the question of the equivalence of prices in 1874 and today, we suggest that, rather than the financial indexes of economists, you bear in mind the cost, according to the accounts of a collector friend of Degas, Albert Hecht (1842–1889), of luxury objects, such as a pearl necklace, more than 4,000 francs, an Indian cashmere, 2,400 francs or a velvet dress, 500 francs; on the other hand, a rolling pin cost just 4 francs and a set of saucepans slightly more than 400 francs.[13]

First case, Cézanne, the eternal "refusé" at the Salon and known as such: 200 francs, the price of a Béliard or a Latouche, *The Hanged Man's House* (*La Maison du Pendu*) (Musée d'Orsay, Paris) was acquired by Count Armand Doria,[14] who sold it to Victor Chocquet: both belonged to the small world of the group's first collectors; whilst the prices of Cézanne's work promoted by the art dealer Ambroise Vollard were quickly rising, it was bought by the Count de Camondo for 6,510 francs at the Chocquet auc-

tion in 1899. It was probably one of the first works sold by the artist who did not have a dealer other than his paint supplier, the legendary Père Tanguy, and there were no references at public auction. Prices for his friend Guillaumin were not very much high either.
By exhibiting works declared already to be belonging to collectors in the catalogue, Degas promoted his status as a recognised artist who had no desperate need for immediate gain; his participation in the exhibition was essentially a confirmation of his independence. Moreover, no. 54, *The Dance Examination* (*Examen de danse au theatre*), a commission from the baritone Jean-Baptiste Faure, not mentioned in the press, was probably not exhibited.[15] This may also reveal a cautious attitude aiming to avoid the stigma of not selling. However, eight hundred francs for a "drawing" described as a "study", might seem expensive. But his art dealer, Paul Durand-Ruel, asked for these relatively high prices, certainly superior to those of his colleagues, because he could count on clients like Faure or Ernest Hoschedé who were already willing to pay this much. No. 63, *At the Races in the Countryside* (*Aux courses, en province*) (Museum of Fine Arts, Boston), a work bought from the artist by Durand-Ruel in 1872 for 1,000 francs, was acquired by Faure in 1873 for 1300 francs.[16] As for Hoschedé, he had acquired a work entitled *The False Start* (*Courses au Bois de Boulogne [Le Faux Départ]*) (Yale University Art Gallery) from Durand-Ruel for 2,400 francs, on 25 April 1873; and rather foolishly he later sold it at the Hôtel Drouot, on 13 January 1874, for 1,100 francs.[17]
Let us now look at Monet. Apart from *The Luncheon* (*Déjeuner*), a large, not so recent painting from 1868 that was difficult to sell, the other average-size works were quoted within a high price range, justified by previous sales, like the 1,000 francs paid in February 1873 by the musician Charles Wilfrid de Bériot for *The Garden of the Infanta* (*Jardin de l'Infante*) (Allen Memorial Art Museum, Oberlin College, Oberlin, Ohio).[18] At this time, Durand-Ruel paid the artist between 300 and 500 francs for some similar works, which he intended to sell at double the price, although this did not happen for years... At Hoschedé's sale on 13 January 1874, the Monets "made" between 400 and 550 francs,[19] confirming this minimum price. However, we have no precise records for no. 95, *Poppies* (*Coquelicots*), now at the Musée d'Orsay, no. 96, *Fishing Boats Leaving the Port of Le Havre* (*Le Havre; bateaux de pêche sortant du port*) and no. 97, *Boulevard des Capucines* (moreover, for the last two, their identification is uncertain) to corroborate the prices mentioned in the catalogue. On the other hand, no. 98, *Impression*, deserves a special mention.
It is stated that it was "sold by the company"; however, Monet's account books note amongst the "paintings sold/1874": "May impression 800/to M. Hoschedé by Durand".[20] This again implicates the dealer, of whom Ho-

schedé was the client, in the company's affairs. The difference between the price received by Monet and the one displayed might include the modest commissions for the intermediaries if the buyer actually paid the price displayed.

The prices of Berthe Morisot's works were less than one thousand francs. But, once again, these prices were similar to those charged by Durand-Ruel, whom she knew as early as 1871 thanks to Édouard Manet. Indeed, the art dealer had exhibited *The Cradle* (*Le Berceau*) in London in 1873, setting the price at 1,500 francs even though he had bought *View of Paris from the Trocadero* (*Vue de Paris des hauteurs du Trocadéro*) (Santa Barbara, Santa Barbara Museum of Art) for 500 francs and sold it to Hoschedé for 750 francs.[21]

The high prices of Pissarro's works can be justified, too. Once again, the prices established by Durand-Ruel were used as a reference: *The Hill of Hermitage, Pontoise* (*Les Côteaux de l'Hermitage, Pontoise*) (Solomon R. Guggenheim Museum, Thannhauser Collection, New York), for example, was bought by the art dealer from the artist on 23 March 1873 for 2,250 francs and sold the same day to Faure with a small profit of 250 francs.[22] At the Hoschedé auction on 13 January 1874, already mentioned, *Factories and Dam on the Oise* (*Fabriques et barrage sur l'Oise*) was sold for 950 francs, almost 1,000 francs with costs, to the broker Hagerman, acting on behalf of Durand-Ruel.[23]

Sisley's prices were also set in accordance to those practiced by Durand-Ruel and the prices attained at the Hoschedé auction in 1874, already mentioned. It should be noted that in the catalogue he was the only artist to have an established link with Durand-Ruel, who had lent some of his works. The only other dealer mentioned in the catalogue was Pierre-Firmin Martin – Père Martin – with whom Béliard and Cals were domiciled, and who, on a smaller scale, was one of the group's regular dealers. On the other hand, Louis Latouche, who exhibited the group's work in his art supplies shop (where those who were refused at the Salon gathered), appears here, solely as a painter, whilst also showing at the Salon.

Finally, Renoir, although he had a business relationship with Durand-Ruel since 1872, rarely dealt with him in this period.[24] Three thousand francs for *Dancer* (*Danseuse*) (National Gallery of Art, Washington) was clearly too much to ask, since this painting was only sold by Durand-Ruel to Charles Deudon in 1878 for 3,000 francs![25] However, the exhibition proved to be of some use because, as the catalogue states, Renoir sold a painting to Hartmann, the music publisher, who then probably commissioned (the opposite is also possible) a full-length portrait of his wife (Musée d'Orsay, Paris).

In short, the prices announced in the catalogue reflect the prices that Durand-Ruel practiced with his clients and reveal the work the for-

ward-thinking art dealer had accomplished since 1870. But they were not very realistic and so the exhibition was not an immediate commercial success. Moreover, Théodore Duret wrote shortly after to Pissarro, on 2 June 1874: "Finally, you have managed to attract a public of tasteful and selected amateurs but who are not rich amateurs willing to pay high prices. In this small world you will find buyers willing to pay 2, 4 and 6 hundred francs. Before managing to regularly sell for 1,500 and 2 thousand, I think you'll have to wait a few more years".[26]
With the catastrophic public sale of March 1875 organised by the artists (as well as the one in 1877), along with Hoschedé's bankruptcy in June 1878, the future took its toll on the artists and their dealer, crushing their hopes: *Impression* by Monet plummeted to 210 francs at the 1878 sale; acquired by Georges de Bellio, it was never sold again before entering the Musée Marmottan Monet. It was not until 1880 that prices gradually returned to the level of 1874.

Letter from Léontine De Nittis probably to Alfred Meyer, 23 April 1874

23 April 74
Sir
I am going to give you some rough prices for my husband's paintings.
Study of Vesuvius with horses in the brooms 2,000
Moon rising over Vesuvius 1200 Study of sun-bathed road 1,500
Large study of black lava 4,500
If you were unable to show it, please let me know and I will take it back.
Kindest regards
Line de Nittis

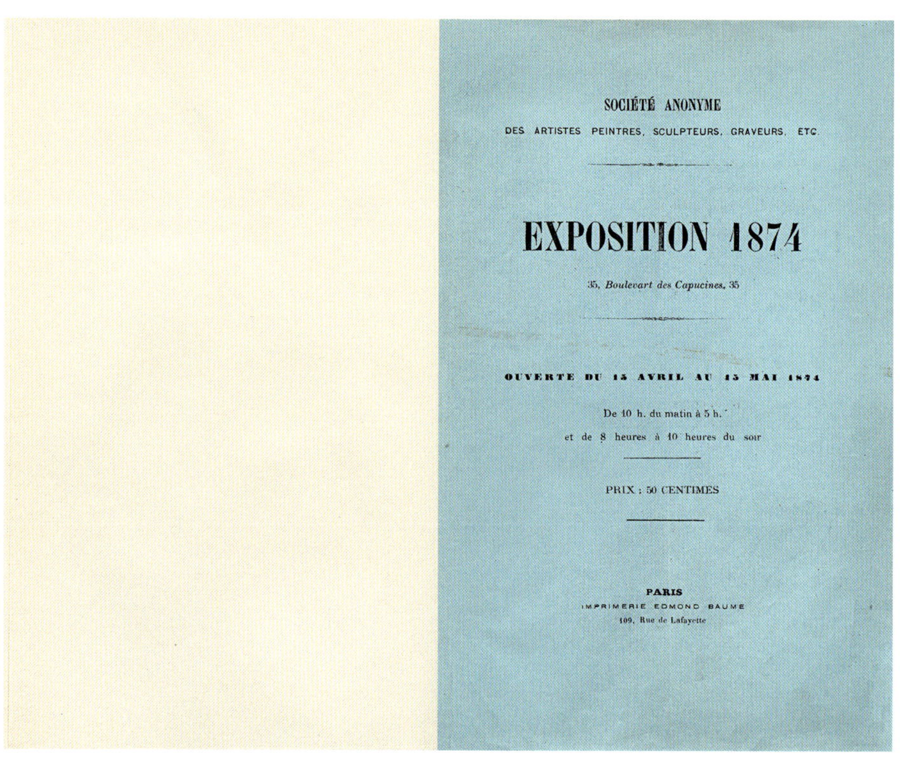

SOCIÉTÉ ANONYME

DES ARTISTES PEINTRES, SCULPTEURS, GRAVEURS, ETC.

EXPOSITION 1874

35, *Boulevart des Capucines*, 35

OUVERTE DU 15 AVRIL AU 15 MAI 1874

De 10 h. du matin à 5 h.

et de 8 heures à 10 heures du soir

PRIX : 50 CENTIMES

PARIS

IMPRIMERIE EDMOND BAUME

109, Rue de Lafayette

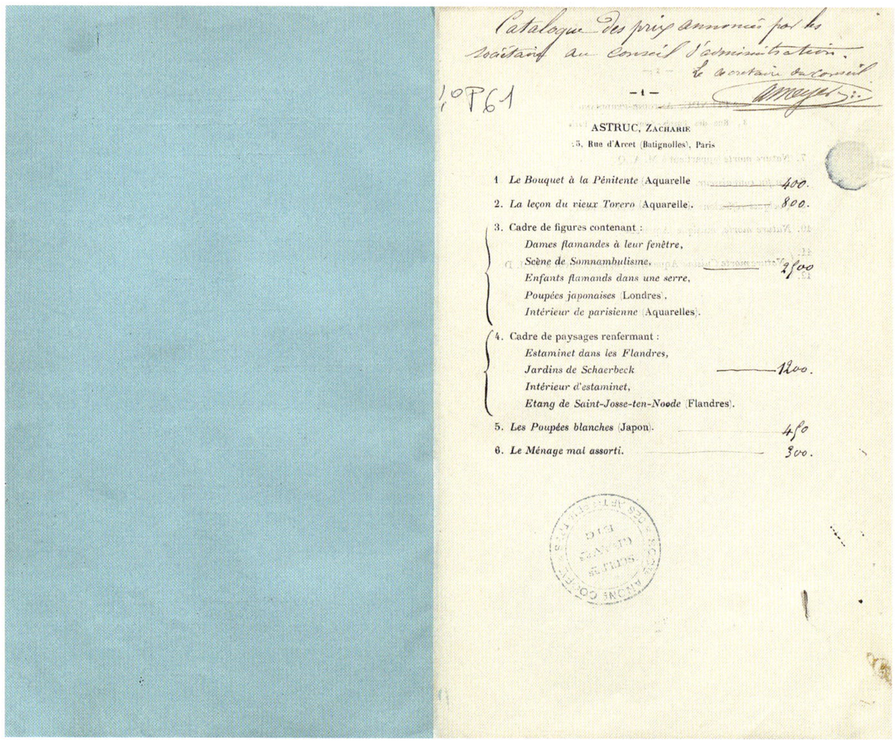

Catalogue des prix annoncés par les sociétaires au Conseil d'administration.
Le secrétaire du conseil

— 1 —

ASTRUC, Zacharie

5, Rue d'Arcet (Batignolles), Paris

1. *Le Bouquet à la Pénitente* (Aquarelle) — 400.
2. *La leçon du vieux Torero* (Aquarelle). — 800.
3. Cadre de figures contenant :
   Dames flamandes à leur fenêtre,
   Scène de Somnambulisme,
   Enfants flamands dans une serre,
   Poupées japonaises (Londres),
   Intérieur de parisienne (Aquarelles). — 2500
4. Cadre de paysages renfermant :
   Estaminet dans les Flandres,
   Jardins de Schaerbeck
   Intérieur d'estaminet,
   Etang de Saint-Josse-ten-Noode (Flandres). — 1200.
5. *Les Poupées blanches* (Japon). — 450
6. *Le Ménage mal assorti.* — 300.

126 185

— 2 —

ATTENDU, Antoine-Ferdinand

3, Rue des Fossés-Saint-Jacques, Paris

7. *Nature morte* (appartient à M. A. Q.)
8. *Un fin connaisseur.* — 200
9. *Quelques réflexions* (au XIIIe arrondissement). — 150
10. *Nature morte, musique* (Aquarelle). — 25.
11. } *Nature morte Cuisine* (Aquarelles), appartiennent à M. J. D.
12. }

— 3 —

BELIARD, E.

Chez M. Martin, Marchand de tableaux, rue Laffitte.

13. *Le fort de la Halle* (appartient à M. D...)
14. *Saules.* — 200
15. *Rue de l'Hermitage à Pontoise.* — 200.
16. *Vallée d'Auvers.*

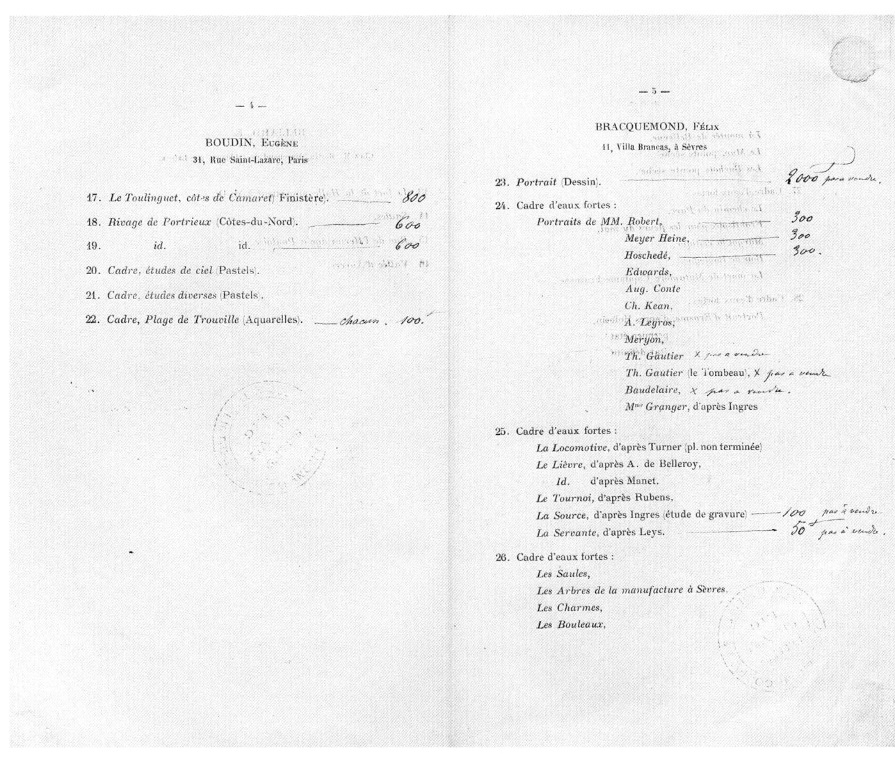

— 4 —

BOUDIN, Eugène

31, Rue Saint-Lazare, Paris

17. *Le Toulinguet, côtes de Camaret* (Finistère). — 800
18. *Rivage de Portrieux* (Côtes-du-Nord). — 600
19. id. id. — 600
20. *Cadre, études de ciel* (Pastels).
21. *Cadre, études diverses* (Pastels).
22. *Cadre, Plage de Trouville* (Aquarelles). — chacun. 100.

— 5 —

BRACQUEMOND, Félix

11, Villa Brancas, à Sèvres

23. *Portrait* (Dessin). — 2000 pas à vendre.
24. Cadre d'eaux fortes :
    Portraits de MM. Robert, — 300
    Meyer Heine, — 300
    Hoschedé, — 300.
    Edwards,
    Aug. Conte
    Ch. Kean,
    A. Legros,
    Meryon,
    Th. Gautier × pas à vendre
    Th. Gautier (le Tombeau), × pas à vendre
    Baudelaire, × pas à vendre.
    Mme Granger, d'après Ingres
25. Cadre d'eaux fortes :
    La Locomotive, d'après Turner (pl. non terminée)
    Le Lièvre, d'après A. de Belleroy,
    Id. d'après Manet,
    Le Tournoi, d'après Rubens,
    La Source, d'après Ingres (étude de gravure) — 100 pas à vendre.
    La Servante, d'après Leys. — 50 pas à vendre.
26. Cadre d'eaux fortes :
    Les Saules,
    Les Arbres de la manufacture à Sèvres,
    Les Charmes,
    Les Bouleaux,

— 6 —

La montée de Bellevue,
Le Mur, (pointe sèche),
Les Bachots (pointe sèche).

27. Cadre d'eaux fortes :
Le chemin du Parc,
Frontispice pour les fleurs du mal, × pas a vendre
Margot la critique,
Bois de Boulogne,
La mort de Matamore (Capitaine Fracasse). × pas a vendre

28. Cadre d'eaux fortes :
Portrait d'Erasme, d'après Holbein,
premier état ———— 500 pas a vendre
état définitif ———— 50

— 7 —

BRANDON, Edouard
77, Rue d'Amsterdam, à Paris

29. *Première lecture de la Loi.* ———— 1500

30. *Portrait de M. A. Z.* (Dessin).

31. *Aquarelles.*

32. *Exposition du corps de Ste-Brigitte à Rome,* en 1392 (carton fusain).

32 *(bis). Le maitre d'école*

— 8 —

BUREAU, Pierre-Isidore
59, Rue de Turenne, Paris

33. *Le Clocher de Jouy-le-Comte.* ———— 500

34. *Près de l'étang de Jouy-le-Comte.* ———— 300

35. *Bords de l'Oise* (Isle-Adam), Clair-de-Lune. ———— 250

35 *(bis). Clair de lune* ———— 200

— 9 —

CALS, Adolphe-Félix
Chez M. Martin, Rue Laffite, 52, Paris

36. *Portrait de Mme Ed. G.*

37. *Le bon père Pêcheur à Honfleur,* appartient à M. M...

38. *Vieux Pêcheur,* appartient à M. R...

39. *Paysage,* appartient à M. H...

40. *Bonne Femme tricotant.*

41. *Fileuse.*

CEZANNE, Paul
120, Rue de Vaugirard, Paris

42. *La Maison du Pendu*, à Auvers-sur-Oise. 200 f

43. *Une moderne Olympia* (esquisse), appartient à M. le Dr Gachet

44. Etude : *Paysage à Auvers*. 100 f

— 11 —

COLIN, Gustave
14, Rue Fontaine, Paris

45. *Haurra-Maria.* 2200

46. *La maison du Charpentier.* 1600

47. *L'Etang aux poules d'eau.* 1500

48. *Marchande de poissons de Fontarabie* (Espagne). 2500

49. *Entrée du port de Pasages* (Espagne). 2400

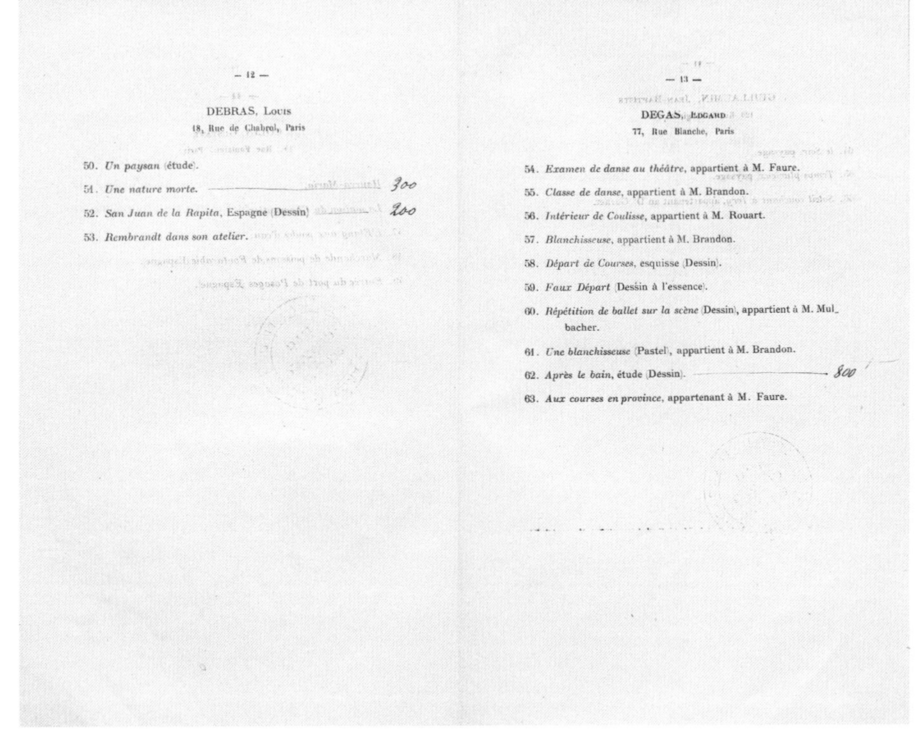

— 12 —

DEBRAS, Louis
18, Rue de Chabrol, Paris

50. *Un paysan* (étude).

51. *Une nature morte.* 300

52. *San Juan de la Rapita*, Espagne (Dessin) 200

53. *Rembrandt dans son atelier.*

— 13 —

DEGAS, Edgard
77, Rue Blanche, Paris

54. *Examen de danse au théâtre*, appartient à M. Faure.

55. *Classe de danse*, appartient à M. Brandon.

56. *Intérieur de Coulisse*, appartient à M. Rouart.

57. *Blanchisseuse*, appartient à M. Brandon.

58. *Départ de Courses*, esquisse (Dessin).

59. *Faux Départ* (Dessin à l'essence).

60. *Répétition de ballet sur la scène* (Dessin), appartient à M. Mulbacher.

61. *Une blanchisseuse* (Pastel), appartient à M. Brandon.

62. *Après le bain*, étude (Dessin). 800

63. *Aux courses en province*, appartenant à M. Faure.

— 14 —

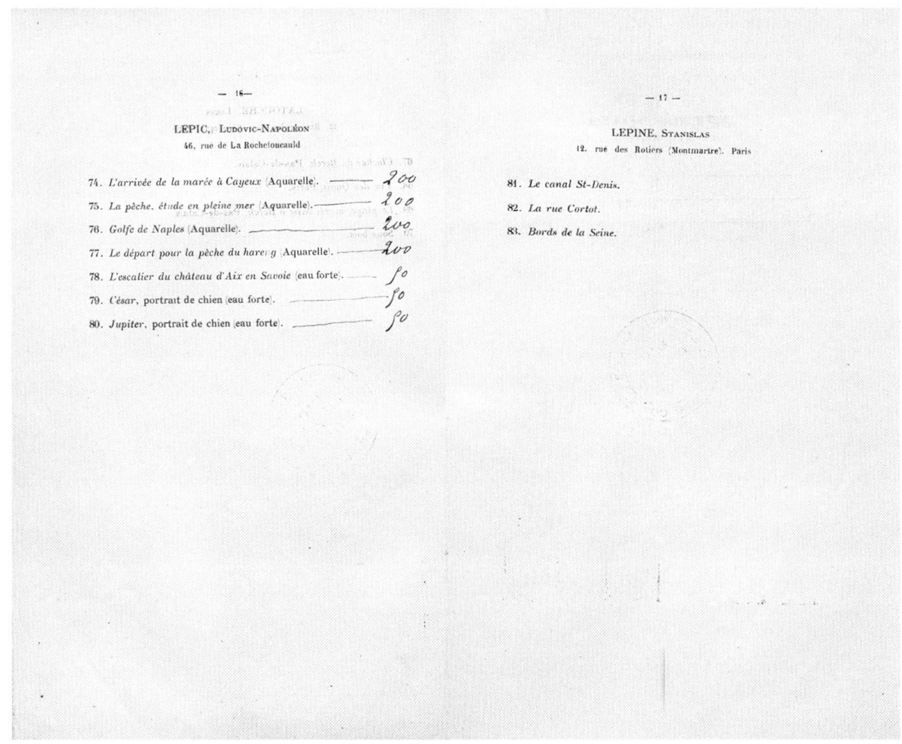

GUILLAUMIN, Jean-Baptiste

120, Rue de Vaugirard, Pari

64. *le Soir*, paysage. 300

65. *Temps pluvieux*, paysage. 350

66. *Soleil couchant à Ivry*, appartenant au Dr Gachet.

— 15 —

LATOUCHE, Louis

12, Rue de La Tour d'Auvergne, Paris

67. *Clocher de Berck.* Pas-de-Calais. 200

68. *Vue des Quais*, Paris. 350

69. *La plage, marée basse à Berck*, Pas-de-Calais. 250 Vendu p. la société.

70. *Sous bois.* 500.

— 16 —

LEPIC, Ludovic-Napoléon

46, rue de La Rochefoucauld

74. *L'arrivée de la marée à Cayeux* (Aquarelle). 200

75. *La pêche, étude en pleine mer* (Aquarelle). 200

76. *Golfe de Naples* (Aquarelle). 200

77. *Le départ pour la pêche du hareng* (Aquarelle). 200

78. *L'escalier du château d'Aix en Savoie* (eau forte). 50

79. *César*, portrait de chien (eau forte). 50

80. *Jupiter*, portrait de chien (eau forte). 50

— 17 —

LEPINE, Stanislas

12. rue des Rotiers (Montmartre). Paris

81. *Le canal St-Denis.*

82. *La rue Cortot.*

83. *Bords de la Seine.*

— 18 —

LEVERT, Jean-Baptiste-Léopold

chez M. H. Rouart, rue de Lisbonne, 34

84. *Bords de l'Essonne.* ——— 250

85. *Le moulin de Touviaux.* ——— 250

86. *Près d'Anvers.* (Deux sur le même numéro.) — 150

— 19 —

MEYER, Alfred

57, rue de Dunkerque, Paris.

87. *Estienne Marcel*, prévôt des marchands (email). ——— 1000

88. *Dona Maria Pacheco*, épouse de Don Juan de Padilla, chef de l'insurrection, qui avait pris le nom de sainte ligue des communes sous Charles Quint (email). ——— 1000

« Loin de s'abandonner à la douleur, lorsque son « époux fut conduit à l'échafaud, elle ne songea « qu'à la vengeance. Elle soutint avec un rare cou- « rage le siége de Tolède, et remporta plusieurs « avantages sur les troupes royales ; mais trahie « par le clergé qui persuada au peuple qu'elle était « sorcière, elle se retira dans la citadelle, où elle « se défendit encore longtemps. Enfin, elle s'échappa « déguisée, et se retira en Portugal, où elle mourut « en 1522. »

89. *Le Firmament*, d'après Emile Lévy (email). ——— 600

90. figure d'après Raphaël (email). } appartiennent à Mr E. Waddington.

91. — id. — (email).

Idylle. dessin non catalogué. — 100

reconnu conforme à la déclaration.

A. Meyer

— 20 —

DE MOLINS, Auguste

chez M. Marchand, 15, rue Neuve-des-Petits-Champs, à Paris

et 7, route du Calvaire, à St-Cloud

92. *The Comming Storn.* ——— 1200

93. *Rendez-vous de chasse.* Deux même titre esquisse 600.

94. *Relai de chiens.* grande esquisse. ——— 800.

94 rendez vous de chasse. ——— 1200

Aug de Molins

— 21 —

MONET (Claude)

à Argenteuil (Seine-et-Oise).

95. *Coquelicots.* ——— 1500

96. *Le Havre ;* bateaux de pêche sortant du port. — 2000

97. *Boulevard des Capucines.* ——— 1500.

98. *Impression*, soleil levant. ——— 1000. vendu par la société.

99. *Deux croquis* (Pastel).

100. *Deux croquis* (Pastel)

101. *Deux croquis* (Pastel).

102. *Un croquis* (Pastel).

103. *Déjeuner.* ——— 5000

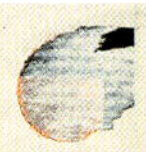

— 22 —

Mademoiselle MORISOT, Berthe

7, rue Guichard, Passy.

104. *Le berceau.* ———— 800

105. *La lecture.* ———— 800

106. *Cache-Cache*, appartient à M. Manet.

107. *Marine.* ———— 100

108. *Portrait de Mlle M. T.* (Pastel).

109. *Un village* (Pastel). ———— 500

110. *Sur la Falaise* (Aquarelle). ———— 100

111. *Dans le bois* (Aquarelle). ———— 100

112. (Aquarelle). ———— 100

— 23 —

MULOT DURIVAGE

13, rue Neuve-le-Berry, au Havre (Seine-Inférieure)

113. *Barques à plomb.* ———— 300

114. *La Rampe.* ———— 400

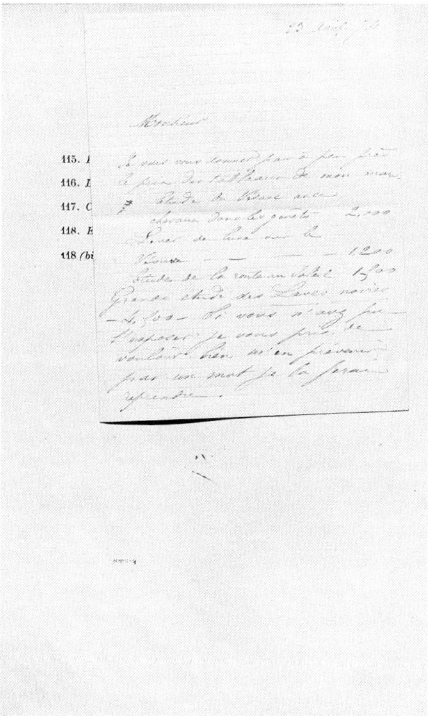

Monsieur

Je viens vous donner par à peu près le prix des tableaux de mon mari

Etude du Vésuve avec chevaux dans le genet — 2.000

Lever de lune sur le Vésuve — 1200

Etude de la route en Italie 1500

Grande étude des Laves noires — 4.500 — Si vous n'avez pu l'exposer je vous prie de vouloir bien m'en prévenir par un mot je la ferai reprendre

avec bien cordiale salutation

Léo de Nittis

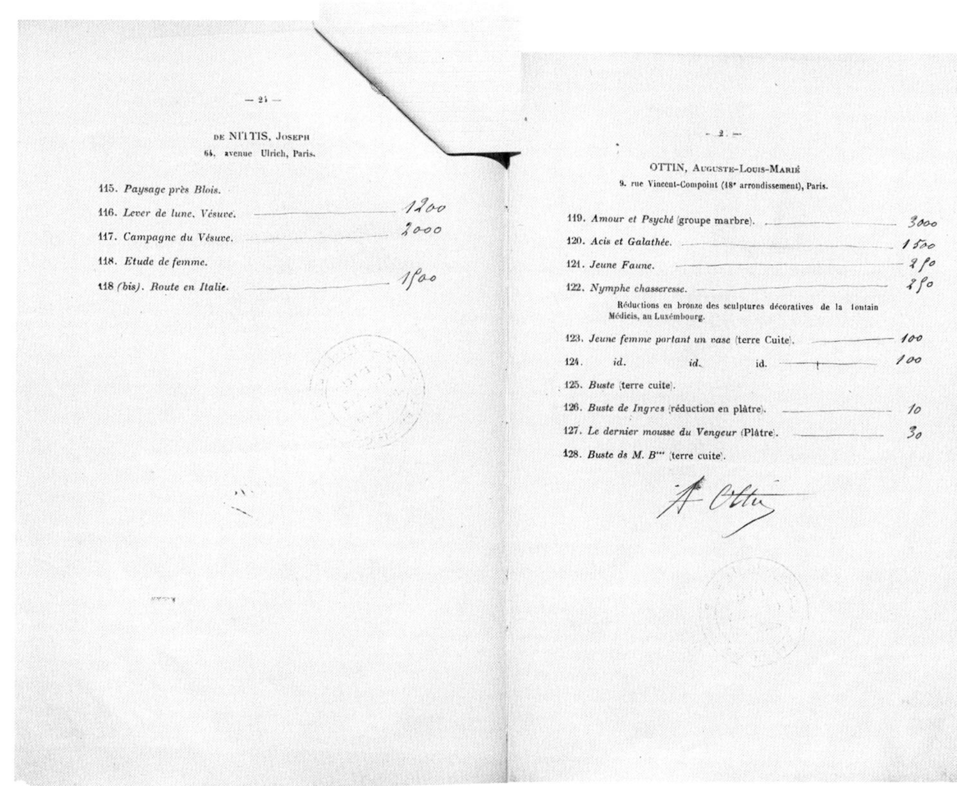

— 24 —

DE NITTIS, Joseph

64, avenue Ulrich, Paris.

115. *Paysage près Blois.*

116. *Lever de lune. Vésuve.* — 1200

117. *Campagne du Vésuve.* — 2000

118. *Etude de femme.*

118 *(bis). Route en Italie.* — 1500

— 2 —

OTTIN, Auguste-Louis-Marie

9, rue Vincent-Compoint (18e arrondissement), Paris.

119. *Amour et Psyché* (groupe marbre). — 3000

120. *Acis et Galathée.* — 1500

121. *Jeune Faune.* — 250

122. *Nymphe chasseresse.* — 250

Réductions en bronze des sculptures décoratives de la fontain Médicis, au Luxembourg.

123. *Jeune femme portant un vase* (terre Cuite). — 100

124. id. id. id. — 100

125. *Buste* (terre cuite).

126. *Buste de Ingres* (réduction en plâtre). — 10

127. *Le dernier mousse du Vengeur* (Plâtre). — 30

128. *Buste de M. B**** (terre cuite).

A. Ottin

— 26 —

OTTIN, Léon-Auguste
2, rue Bervic (18e Arrondissement), Paris

129. *Après la messe à la campagne.* — 500
130. *Au château* (Sannois). — 350
131. *La butte Montmartre*, versant sud. — 200
132. *La fête chez Thérèse*, projet de rideau de théâtre (Aquarelle).
133. *Une bergerie sans moutons* (Lithographie).
134. *At home*
135. *Mariette* (tête d'étude). — 200

L. Ottin

— 27 —

PISSARRO, Camille
26, rue de l'Hermitage, à Pontoise (Seine-et-Oise)

136. *Le verger.* — 1000
137. *Gelée blanche.* — 2500
138. *Les chataigners à Osny.* — 1500
139. Jardin de la ville de Pontoise. — 1500
140. Matinée au mois de Juin. — 2500

C. Pissarro

— 28 —

RENOIR, Pierre-Auguste
35, rue St-Georges

141. *Danseuse.* — 3000
142. *L'avant-scène* — 2500
143. *Parisienne.* — 3500
144. *Moissonneurs.* — 1000 vendu par la société à Mr Martinez
145. *Fleurs.*
146. *Croquis* (Pastel). — n'a pas été envoyé à l'Exposition.
147. *Tête de femme.*

— 29 —

ROUART, Stanislas-Henri
34, rue de Lisbonne

148. *Ferme bretonne.* — 2200
149. *Levée d'étang.* — 1200
150. *Vue de Meulan*, appartient à M. J.-D.
151. *Village.* — 600
152. *Forêt.* — 300
153. *Route bretonne.*
154. *Ferme bretonne* (Aquarelle).
155. *Maisons Béarnaises* (Aquarelle).
156. *id.* *id.*
157. *Eau forte.*
158. *id.*

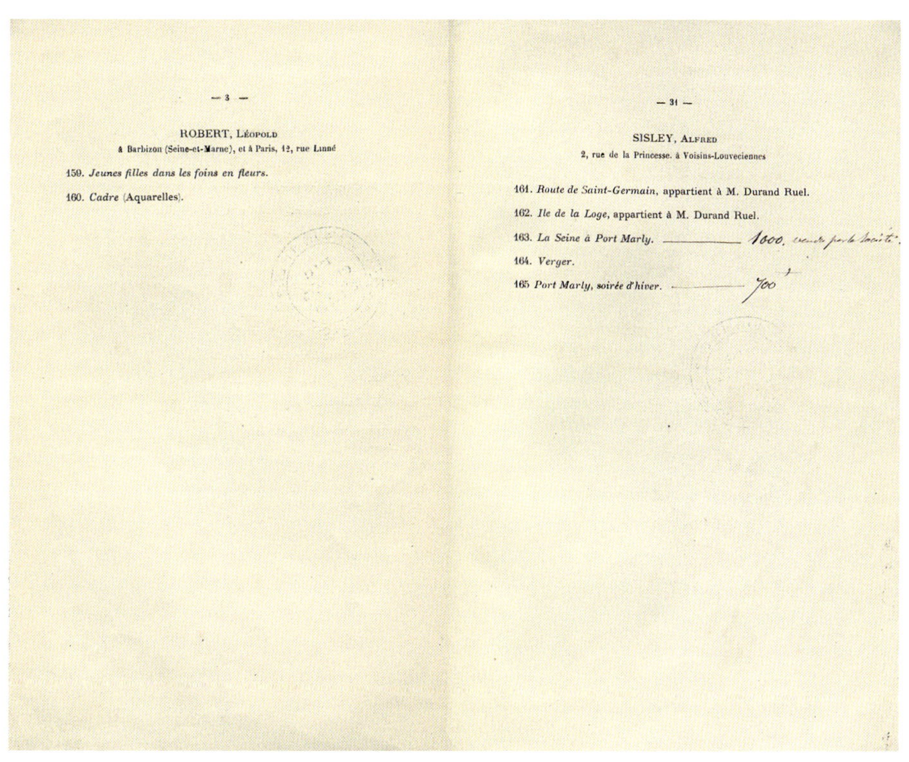

— 3 —

ROBERT, Léopold

à Barbizon (Seine-et-Marne), et à Paris, 12, rue Linné

159. *Jeunes filles dans les foins en fleurs.*

160. *Cadre* (Aquarelles).

— 31 —

SISLEY, Alfred

2, rue de la Princesse. à Voisins-Louveciennes

161. *Route de Saint-Germain*, appartient à M. Durand Ruel.

162. *Ile de la Loge*, appartient à M. Durand Ruel.

163. *La Seine à Port Marly.* ———— 1000. vendu par la Société.

164. *Verger.*

165 *Port Marly, soirée d'hiver.* ———— 700

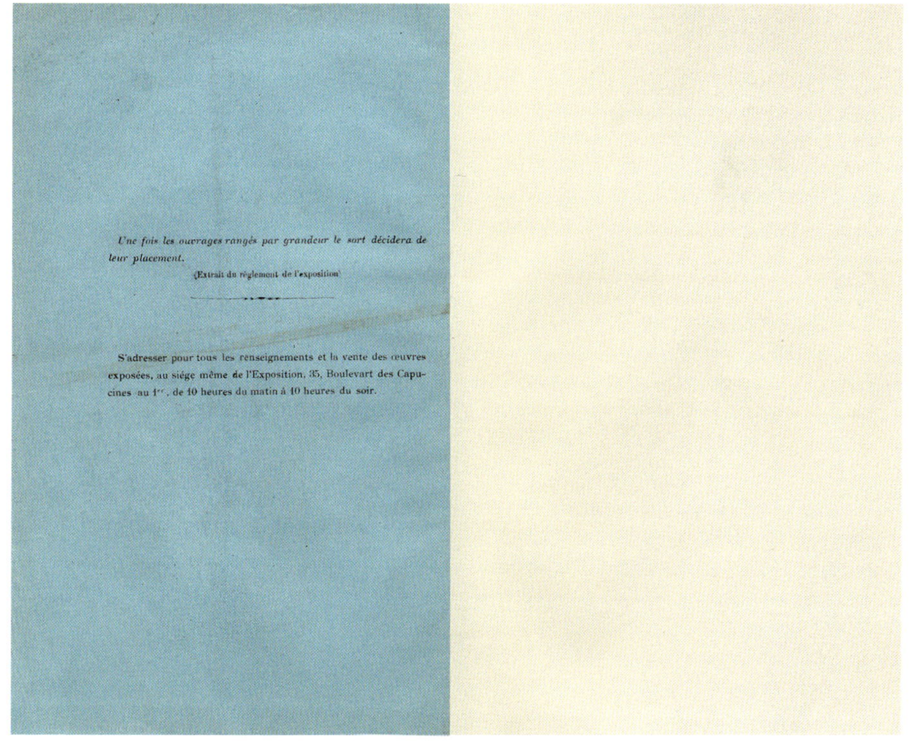

Une fois les ouvrages rangés par grandeur le sort décidera de leur placement.

(Extrait du règlement de l'exposition)

S'adresser pour tous les renseignements et la vente des œuvres exposées, au siége même de l'Exposition, 35, Boulevart des Capucines (au 1er), de 10 heures du matin à 10 heures du soir.

1 I would like to dedicate this article to the memory of Mrs René Asselain, born Paulette Roger-Marx (1913–1994), daughter of Claude Roger-Marx (1888–1977), writer and art critic, and granddaughter of Roger-Marx (1859–1913), inspector of fine arts, who favoured the Impressionists; not only did she, on my request, take the time to look for this catalogue in the family library, but she also donated it to the Musée d'Orsay, in addition to the other precious donations made by her father and herself. I would also like to thank Ségolène Le Men and Félicie Faizand de Maupeou for allowing me to return to an old subject revived at the symposium in 2020.

2 John Rewald, *Histoire de l'Impressionnisme*, Paris, 1955, pp. 358–64, with documents from Camille Pissarro's archives. We might also add the legal publication of the dissolution of the society, signed by Renoir, Bureau and Sisley, which was only registered on 23 April 1875 (Archives de Paris, D31 U3 356).

3 Paul Tucker, "The First Impressionist Exhibition in Context", in Charles S. Moffett (ed.), *The New Painting, Impressionism 1874-1886*, exhibition catalogue, National Gallery of Art, Washington; Fine Arts Museums of San Francisco, 1986, pp. 93–117, with bibliography.

4 Ruth Berson, *The New Painting: Impressionism 1874-1886*, 2 vols., Fine Arts Museums of San Francisco, 1996. For more on this subject, see also Ed Lilley, "A rediscovered English review of the 1874 Impressionist exhibition", *The Burlington Magazine*, CLIV, no. 1317, December 2012, pp. 843–45.

5 Claude Roger-Marx, "En marge de la première exposition du groupe dit impressionniste", in *Hommage à Paul Durand-Ruel. Cent ans d'impressionnisme*, exhibition catalogue, Galerie Durand-Ruel, Paris, 15 January – 15 March 1974. The information was reproduced literally by Hélène Adhémar, "L'exposition de 1874 chez Nadar", in *Centenaire de l'impressionnisme*, exhibition catalogue, Galeries nationales du Grand-Palais, Paris; The Metropolitan Museum, New York, 1974–75, p. 224, cited by Tucker, *op. cit.*, p. 116, note 76. For the 1974 exhibition, Charles Durand-Ruel had the Alcan-Lévy (Éditions STEFF, Paris) version reprinted in a thousand copies.

6 Measuring 26 cm high and with 31 pages, it is classified Res P0061 at the INHA.

7 The three little dots in his signature probably point to his affiliation with freemasonry. We can see from his letters to Camille Pissarro, which we have been able to access from the archives (*Archives de Camille Pissarro*, auction, Paris, Hôtel Drouot, 21 November 1975, no. 82), that Meyer was heavily involved with the constitution of the society, even preparing new statutes in October-November 1874 with Henri Rouart. He was also linked to Dr Gachet, one of the lenders. We might think then that as a historian, Burty kept the document after the society was permanently dissolved.

8 The articles (see Berson, *op. cit.*, note 4) by Drumont, Prouvaire, Gantès, Burty in *La République française*, "Le Père siffleur", published before 26 April, cite *L'Avant-scène* even though articles published afterwards (Carjat, Castagnary) mention *La Loge*; the article by C. de Malte (Villiers de l'Isle Adam) in *Paris à l'eau-forte*, from 19 April, cites *La Loge de théâtre* but seems to have used titles to suit itself and two more detailed articles by Montifaud and Chesneau, dated early May, still use *L'Avant-scène*, but might have taken longer to be published.

9 Title page republished in Claire Durand-Ruel-Snollaerts, Joachim Pissarro, *Pissarro: Critical Catalogue of Paintings*, 3 vols. (Milan–Paris: Skira and Wildenstein Institute, 2005), vol. I, p. 16.

10 The Durand-Ruel gallery stockbook for 1872 printed on the flyleaf of the *Paul Durand-Ruel: Le pari de l'impressionnisme*, exhibition catalogue, Musée du Luxembourg, Paris; National Gallery, London; Philadelphia Museum of Art, Philadelphia, 2014–15, gave an idea of the price he paid the artists (Manet, Millet, Degas, etc.) the optimistic prices asked were frequently reduced in the case of (rare) quick sales.

11 Astruc, Boudin, Bureau, Colin, Debras, Latouche, Lepic, Lépine and Meyer were also accepted at the 1874 Salon which opened in May.

12 See the Getty Institute online archives (book 7) for the years 1872–74. On the other hand, the art dealer often made a large profit. It would appear that the more important painting De Nittis exhibited at the Salon in 1874, *How Cold!!* (Fait-il froid!!) (no. 1395), was bought for the exceptional price of 7500 francs from the artist and sold for 10,000 francs to M. C. Blair. The more modest prices for work at the Nadar's exhibition might suggest that the painter had sent a "Salon painting" to the Salon, more to Goupil's taste, reserving his less academic works for the independent exhibition, landscapes or sketches to be sold directly to art enthusiasts. At this time, the painter also distanced himself from Goupil, getting out of his contract (P. Dini and G. L. Marini, *De Nittis: La vita, i documenti, le opere dipinte*, Turin, 1990, vol. I, pp. 154–61).

13 Anne Distel, "Albert Hecht, collectionneur (1842-1889)", *Bulletin de la Société de l'Histoire de l'Art français*, 1981 [1983], p. 273, note 13.

14 It has often been mentioned that the work was sold for 300 francs, but the annotation in the catalogue seems pertinent.

15 Gary Tinterow and Anne M. P. Morton, "Degas aux expositions impressionnistes", in *Degas inédit*, Paris, Documentation française, 1989, p. 289.

16 See *Degas*, exhibition catalogue, Galeries nationales du Grand-Palais, Paris; Musée des Beaux-arts du Canada, Ottawa; The Metropolitan Museum of Art, New York, 1988–1989 (Paris: RMN, 1988), no. 95.

17 Henri Loyrette, *Degas* (Paris: Fayard, 1990), p. 208. Henri Rouart, who acquired the painting, a friend of the artist and member of the group, perhaps "pushed up" the auction price.

18 Anne Distel, "À la conquête du public, Monet et ses premiers amateurs (1864-1874)", in Géraldine Lefèvre (ed.), *Monet, les années décisives au Havre*, Paris, 2016 p. 220.

19 Merete Bodelsen, "Early Impressionist Sales 1874–94 in the light of some unpublished procès-verbaux",*Burlington Magazine*, CX, 783 (June 1958) p. 332.

20 Paris, Musée Marmottan Monet (Michel Monet bequest, 1966); this page was republished in Anne Distel, "À la conquête du public", *op. cit.*, p. 223.

21 Hughes Wilhelm, "Biographie de Berthe Morisot", in *Berthe Morisot (1841-1895)*, exhibition catalogue, Palais des Beaux-Arts, Lille; Fondation Pierre Gianadda, Martigny, 2002, p. 95.

22 Durand-Ruel-Snollaerts, Pissarro, *op. cit.*, vol. I, p. 16.

23 Bodelsen, *art. cit.*, p. 332; Durand-Ruel-Snollaerts, Pissarro, *op. cit.*, vol. II, no. 249 (these authors have not retained the certainly surprising mention that the painting had been bought by the dealer for Pissarro himself quoted_by Anne Distel, "Some Pissarro Collectors in 1874", in Christopher Lloyd (ed.), *Studies on Camille Pissarro*, London-New York, 1986, p. 66).

24 On 16 March 1872, Durand-Ruel acquired *View of Paris, Pont des Arts* (Vue de Paris, Pont des Arts) (probably the large painting from the Norton Simon Foundation, Pasadena) from Renoir for 200 francs, hoping to sell it for 500 francs and on 23 May, a still life, *Peonies and Poppies* (Pivoines et coquelicots), for 300 francs (probably Mannheim, Kunsthalle), hoping to sell it for 600 francs. But we do not know the circumstances of their resale. Another painting was bought from the painter on 30 December 1873 for 300 francs; no purchases noted in 1874–75 (Archives Durand-Ruel, Paris).

25 Anne Distel, "Charles Deudon (1832–1914), collectionneur", *La Revue de l'art*, no. 86(1989), p. 59; the painting appears to have been bought for 500 francs before 1876, date when it was recorded as no. 544 (Archives Durand-Ruel, Paris).

26 Fondation Custodia, Institut néerlandais, Paris.

RELATIVE INDEPENDENCE: THE DETERMINING ROLE OF COLLECTORS AT THE FOURTH "IMPRESSIONIST" EXHIBITION IN 1879

CATHERINE MÉNEUX

As Ronald Pickvance wrote, historians have barely even noticed the 4th "Impressionist" exhibition.[1] Nonetheless, it makes an interesting case study for exploring the place and role of collectors in 1879, as almost 37% of the works belonged to various owners,[2] differentiating it from the eight other "Impressionist" exhibitions for the high number of works on loan mentioned in the catalogue. Out of the fourteen artists listed,[3] it was mainly Edgar Degas, Jean-Louis Forain, Claude Monet and Camille Pissarro who asked collectors to add to the works they sent in. Their names or initials appeared in the catalogue and among the thirty or so people identified, there were some well-known personalities such as Georges de Bellio, Théodore Duret, Ernest May and Eugène Murer, as well as other artist-collectors like Gustave Caillebotte, Paul Gauguin and Henri Rouart.[4]

Whilst this unusual configuration can be explained by the difficulties some artists had in painting works at this time, it begs the question as to the real motivation of Degas, Forain, Monet and Pissarro when they asked collectors to participate in the group exhibition. In fact, in these specific cases, most of their entries were not for sale and other factors were behind their presenting large groups of works, sometimes with a retrospective aim. It seems essential then to highlight the relationships these artists had with a heterogeneous group of collectors who enabled them to exist on the artistic scene and create a new market. These collectors were scarcely talked about in the press and are only visible by reading between the lines. But there are many questions that need to be answered: were they linked to each other? How crucial was their support to the 1879 exhibition? Did their participation in the exhibition as lenders result in a desire to buy and lead them to start collecting works from artists that they hadn't collected before? Analysing their careers and the specificity of the 4th exhibition will allow us to answer these questions and revalorise the role collectors and the public played in the late 1870s. Consequently, we will not adopt a monographic and diachronic approach, but rather a synchronic and systemic one that focuses specifically on the 4th painting exhibition held between 10 April and 10 May 1879, and an ecosystem, understood here as a community of artists and collectors brought together by a shared project and acting in an inter-dependent manner.

Collectors, Painters and Entrepreneurs

In 1879, two famous names stand out from the rest: Gustave Caillebotte and Henri Rouart; not only did they agree to lend some of their major works but they also played a determining role in the organisation of the exhibition and figured as painters. They are the only ones to have this triple status. In his account of the exhibition, Bertall (pseudonym of Charles d'Arnoux), did not hesitate to point this out when referring to Caillebotte:

> Whilst Mr Manet gave everything he had to the crusade for art camp, it was Mr Caillebotte who firmly steered this boat which, without him, may have gone adrift.
> The independents have absolute faith in him. If we are to believe the truly official sources, Mr Caillebotte, a charming and well-bred young man, is at the head of an income of around hundred thousand francs: enough to ensure his total and enduring independence.
> Whilst Mr Caillebotte is devoted enough to the cause to pay a high price out of his own pocket to promote the school of which he has become the revered leader, he is also committed on a personal level. He has no less than thirty-five magnificently-framed paintings, which affirm most energetically his temperament and convictions.[5]

After his mother died in 1878, Caillebotte became a millionaire when he was only thirty years old. His career is well-documented: invited by Renoir and Rouart to take part in the 2nd painting exhibition, from 1876 on, he supported Monet and Pissarro by buying their works. Following the death of his elder brother, he wrote up a will that instructed his paintings to be left to the State when they entered the Musée du Luxembourg then the Louvre. In 1879, not content with exhibiting twenty-five paint-

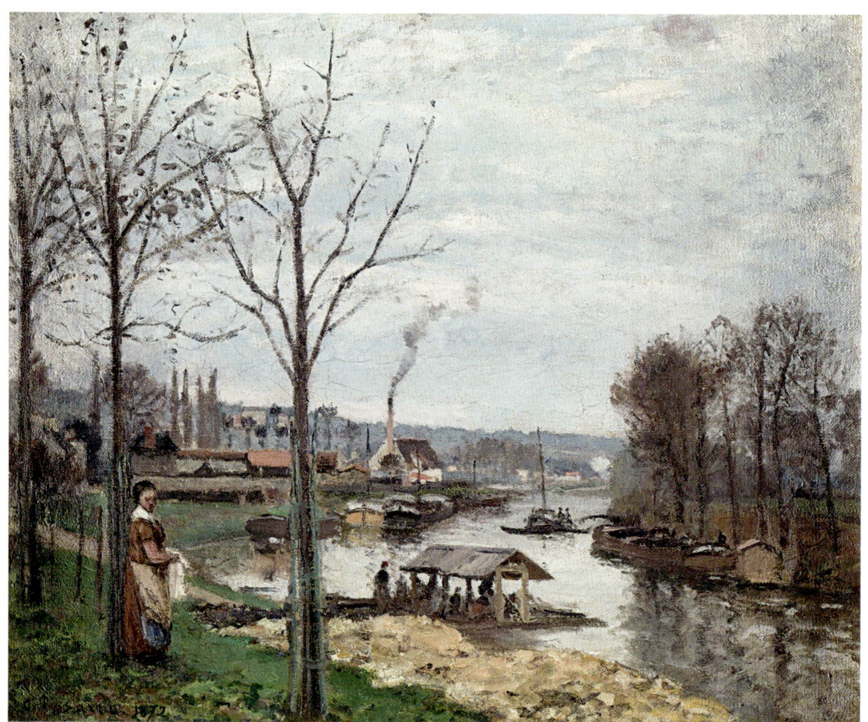

ings and drawings, he also drew from his own collection to enrich Monet and Pissarro's entries by lending nine works,[6] mainly landscapes. The two works by Monet were painted at Vétheuil and were recent purchases; the six paintings by Pissarro were fairly representative of his production during the 1870s (fig. 1) and we should also mention a fan designed by the artist especially for the exhibition.

In many respects, Henri Rouart (fig. 2) played a similar kind of role. Together with his old friend Degas, he co-organised the exhibition, lending works from his collection and presenting his own paintings and drawings. It was Rouart who negotiated the rental of an apartment at 28, Rue de l'Opéra for the exhibition and, similarly to Caillebotte, continued investing in its organisation.[7] On the other hand, their careers and tastes were very different. Rouart began collecting in the 1860s by frequenting Martin's boutique and the Hôtel Drouot. Through his connections with Victor Tillot, a close friend of Millet in Barbizon, he became interested in the "1830 School" and also became one of the greatest collectors of Corot, whilst in parallel buying works by Delacroix, Millet, Daumier, Jongkind and Lépine. A founding member of the Société des Artistes Peintres, Sculpteurs, Graveurs & Lithographes in December 1873, Rouart's support was essential for the cause of independent exhibitions. He put his managerial experience and

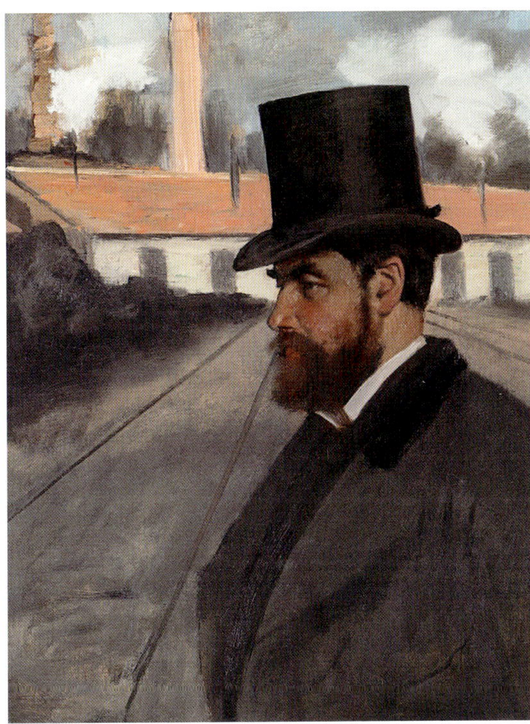

1. Camille Pissarro, *The Seine at Port Marly, the Wash House* (*La Seine à Port-Marly, le lavoir*), 1872, oil on canvas, 46.5 × 50 cm, Musée d'Orsay, Paris

2. Edgar Degas, *Henri Rouart in front of His Factory* (*Henri Rouart devant son usine*), c. 1875, oil on canvas, 66 × 50 cm, Carnegie Museum of Art

capital at the service of artists. Similarly to Count Armand Doria, he too loved Adolphe Cals's dark and sensitive painting, lending perhaps three works by the artist for the 1879 exhibition.[8] Henri Rouart supported his good friend Degas by acquiring, for example, *The Rehearsal* (*La Répétition*), which he lent in 1879;[9] we should add that his wife is mentioned for a fan on the same ballet theme equally by the artist.[10] Rouart's name is also perhaps behind the initial "R." associated with a *Head of a Young Girl* (*Tête de jeune fille*) by Mary Cassatt,[11] and he might be the person who lent a still life with fruits and flowers by Monet,[12] dating from the late 1860s.

His profile as a collector differs from Caillebotte, who saw buying Impressionist works as a militant act. Rouart was more an amateurs committed to his painter friends. Not only did he have an unfailing friendship with Degas, but he also knew Pissarro, Monet and Renoir very well. Like Caillebotte, however, Rouart is representative of an industrial and liberal bourgeoisie in favour of self-management rather than artists being dependent on the State and a network of art dealers. Caillebotte's father had made a fortune thanks to a military equipment supply business; as for Rouart, he created his own company and rapidly became the number one specialist in metal tubing in France. Both of them believed in free enterprise, far from the formatted and limited system of the Salon organised by the State.

Existing Individually Thanks to Collectors

In order to understand the extent of their implication, it is essential to look at the context of the 4th exhibition, which for the first time, was held independently. It was by no means the same experience as in 1877 when posters advertised an "Exhibition of Impressionist Painters", and it was Degas who more or less imposed a different banner, that of "independent artists". This 4th painting exhibition was organised in a particularly morose context and carried the hopes of a group of artists who were in the throes of disbanding. In 1877, the 3rd exhibition did not generate the expected purchases and, on the market, sales of "Impressionist" works ended in failure. After the 1878 Universal Exposition, which was disappointing for the fine arts, Impressionism remained nonetheless more than ever worth defending and, for Caillebotte, they embodied the next generation of French painting at a time when the "great masters" were dead and the École de 1830 was becoming historicised. In other words, Caillebotte wanted to use the exhibition to make Impressionism part of history through exhibitions and then museum patronage. But, for those with liberal ideas, the independent group exhibition was the only solution for showing their works and possibly selling them, at a time when they did not have the support of art dealers. Reading through the letters, it was above all Caillebotte, Degas, Pissarro and Rouart who organised the 4th exhibition, which took place just before the opening of the Salon.[13] Nevertheless, they struggled to find participants because the catalogue only mentions fourteen, to which we should add Gauguin, who was called in late in the day to show a sculpture; a dozen or so works by Ludovic Piette were also presented posthumously. In fact, the unity of the group was crumbling; in 1879, Renoir returned to the Salon with the help of Georges Charpentier and his wife, and Sisley dreamt of doing the same. The choices made then for this 4th exhibition reveal a growing tension between individual aspirations and the need for a collective dynamic. Diego Martelli touched on this when he explained to one of his Italian painter friends the artists' decision to juxtapose large well-defined monographic groups of works:

> This year, thanks to Degas, they have innovated by moving away from the narrow character of painting in a certain style to the broader question of everyone painting in their own style, outside of the protective sphere of official favouritism. Hence, those who exhibit with the independents have to give up the Salon.[14]

The support of collectors was essential in creating these monographic groups. In contrast to the two works in each technique authorised by the

Salon, here they were concerned with showing the public the full range of an artist's work. The examples of Monet and Pissarro are particularly representative of this new exhibition practice which was more like a showcase for promoting a new way of painting than a space for actually selling. In fact, if we are to believe the catalogue, Monet and Pissarro exhibited 29 and 38 works respectively and, out of those, 80% of Monet's and 60% of Pissarro's were on loan.[15] Discouraged and besieged with doubt, Monet only agreed to take part after friendly persuasion from Caillebotte. He sent him a list of works belonging to collectors and, living in Vétheuil at the time, didn't even visit the exhibition himself. It was Caillebotte who took charge of tracking down the works and convincing their owners to lend them for the exhibition.[16] Monet and Pissarro heavily relied on collectors for their participation as painters in the exhibition and two of them played a particularly important role: Georges de Bellio and Eugène Murer.

Originally from Bucharest, Georges de Bellio settled in Paris shortly after 1850. His family fortune allowed him to live comfortably and although he had studied medicine he did not have to work for a living. Similarly to Rouart, he started collecting in the 1860s, with a particular interest in seventeenth-century Dutch painting, the French eighteenth-century masters as well as Delacroix. In 1874, he acquired his first Monet at the Hoschedé's sale and became a compulsive collector of the artist's work. And so, between 1876 and 1881, he acquired fifty-eight works by Monet, some of which he sold later.[17] He also admired Pissarro, Berthe Morisot, Renoir and Sisley. During the 1879 exhibition, Georges de Bellio generously lent no less than six paintings by Monet.[18] Among these works, there were some which would later become hugely famous such as *Impression, Sunrise* (*Impression, soleil levant*) and *La Rue Montorgueil* (fig. 3), as well as some snow-covered landscapes and the brighter canvases from 1878. Moreover, it was through the intermediary of Bellio that Schlesinger acquired *The Church at Vétheuil* (*Église de Vétheuil*) from Monet in December 1878, a work equally lent for the exhibition.[19]

Hyacinthe Eugène Meunier, alias Eugène Murer, had a completely different profile. In contrast to Bellio, he didn't belong to the wealthy bourgeoisie. His portrait, executed in pastel by Pissarro and exhibited in 1879 (fig. 4), perfectly sums up these differences: Pissarro captured Murer working at his pastry oven in the half-light of his shop at 95 Boulevard Voltaire. A far cry from the western neighbourhoods of the capital where Caillebotte and Rouart lived, Eugène Murer came from a different background, an artisan-merchant from the 11th arrondissement. A childhood friend of Guillaumin, he met Cézanne, Sisley, Renoir, Pissarro and Monet in the early 1870s and amassed the best part of his collection between

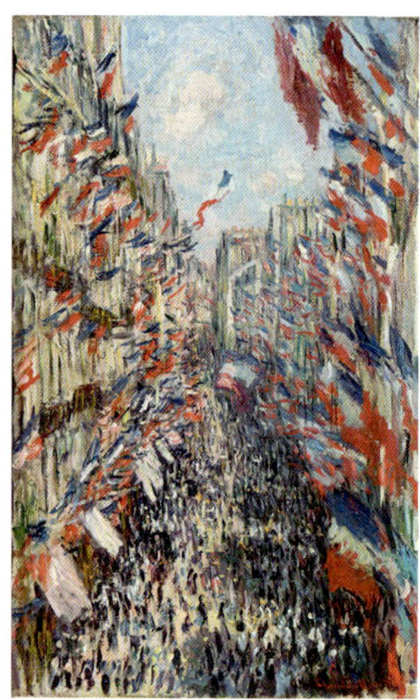

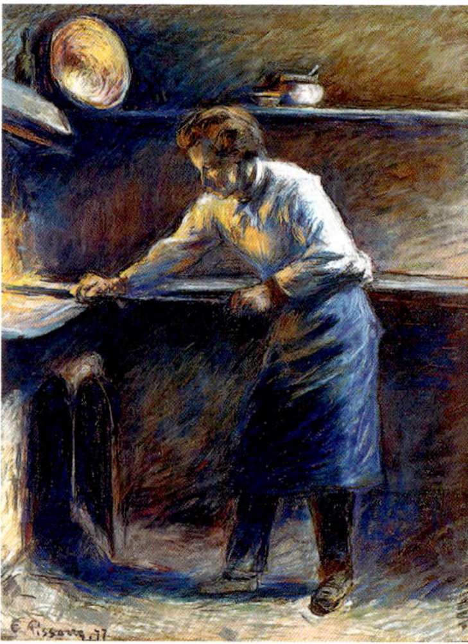

3. Claude Monet, *The Rue Montorgueil in Paris, Celebration of 30 June* (*La Rue Montorgueil, fête du 30 juin*), 1878, oil on canvas, 80 × 50.5 cm, Musée d'Orsay, Paris

4. Camille Pissarro, *The Baker* (*Le Pâtissier*), 1877, pastel on paper, 65 × 48 cm, localisation unknown

5. Camille Pissarro, *Pea Harvest, Fan* (*Cueillette de petits pois, éventail*), gouache on silk, 16.5 × 52.1 cm, The Metropolitan Museum of Art, New York

1877 and 1880. At the 1879 exhibition, he lent six works by Pissarro and a painting by Monet.[20] Murer then was one of the major lenders of Pissarro's work which included landscapes of the area around Pontoise. As for the work by Monet, it was a view of Lavacourt that the artist had sold a few months earlier.[21]

In fact, around 1878–79, Murer and Bellio acquired a number of works and these purchases reflected their humble origins. Murer was one of the rare buyers of works by Monet and Pissarro whose prices barely ever went higher than 200 francs, even less when they were smaller canvases.[22] Similarly, Georges de Bellio bought works by Monet at prices that oscillated between 60 and 400 francs.[23] The other major lenders also acquired their works for small sums and were friends with the two painters. Théodore Duret and his cousin Etienne Baudry lent four works by Monet. Baudry, a militant republican and friend of Castagnary and Courbet acquired *The Blue House* (*La Maison bleue*) by Monet[24] at Hoschedé's first sale in 1874. As for Théodore Duret, he too had strong republican convictions, and although he was not always in favour of the independent exhibitions, as a critic he had defended Monet since the 1860s.[25] Emmanuel Chabrier moved more or less in the same circles. Friends with Zola and Alphonse Daudet, this admirer of Wagner was good friends with Monet as he was present at the birth of the painter's second son in the spring of 1878 alongside Édouard Manet. Under this name, he lent *Banks of the Seine* (*Bords de Seine*), acquired in 1878, bearing in mind that he also owned *La Rue Saint-Denis* as Monet had sold it to him for 200 francs the same year.[26] Caillebotte equally borrowed some of Monet's old works from more distant celebrities, such as Eugène Lecadre, the painter's cousin, and Victor Frat, who lived

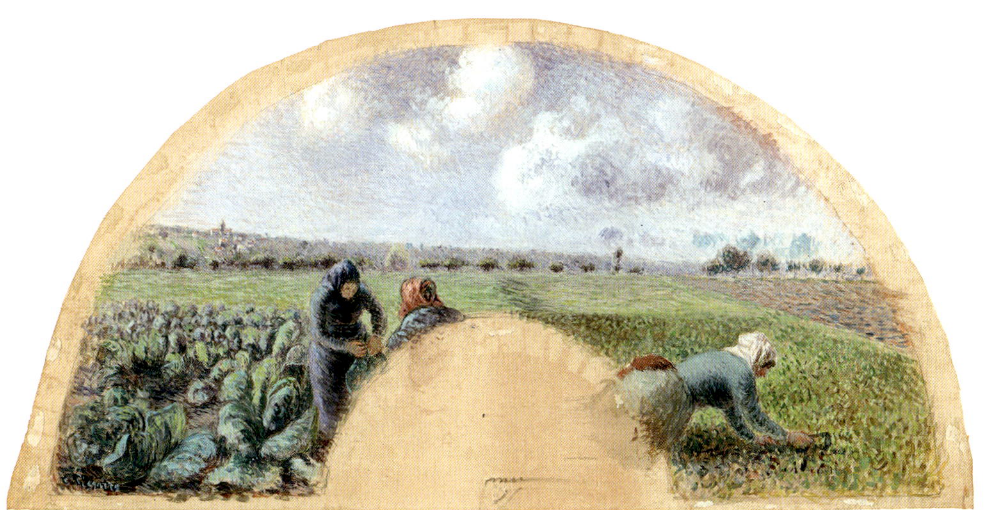

in Montpellier,[27] before becoming one of the biggest collectors of Gustave Moreau's oeuvre, Charles Hayem had acquired some Impressionist paintings by Monet such as *The Coal Workers* (*Les Charbonniers*), bought from one of the Hecht brothers around 1879.[28] Finally, Monet directed Caillebotte towards Ernest Duez and Antoine Guillemet, painters he had known for a long time and who lent works from the early 1870s.[29]

To add to the works he had already submitted, Pissarro called upon the little-known artists Paul Gauguin and Mary Cassatt, who were both collectors and participants in the exhibition. The former was still only considered an amateur painter who worked at the Stock Exchange and collected Impressionist works, including two recent landscapes by Pissarro and a fan.[30] At this time, he was not yet Pissarro's student and the two men became close friends shortly after. As for Mary Cassatt, it was her first participation at the independent exhibition. In parallel, she was creating her own personal collection and advising American amateur art enthusiasts, a role which progressively developed over the following years. This other status was only vaguely mentioned at the 1879 exhibition in regards to the fan by Pissarro (fig. 5) which she lent for the occasion.[31]

Ultimately, very few works by Monet and Pissarro were for sale and the works they sent in differed from the choices they had made for previous exhibitions. Pissarro chose highly-finished[32] works, mainly painted over the last two years, as well as four pastels, and he also designed a dozen fans for the occasion. As for Monet, he entrusted Caillebotte with organising a kind of mini-retrospective with paintings dating from the late 1860s to 1879.[33] These two monographic ensembles were the complete opposite of the Salon system, where Renoir had had huge success with his grand

Portrait of Mme Charpentier and her Children (*Portrait de Mme Charpentier et de ses enfants*), commissioned a year earlier by the publisher.[34] In this competitive context, the different strategies opposed each other by the intermediary of the collectors.

A Collector-Public System

The organisers' bet paid off, as more than 15,000 people visited the 1879 exhibition,[35] each generally paying the one franc entrance fee and potentially buying the catalogue, which cost fifty centimes. Moreover, Armand Silvestre wrote that one "of the prominent features of this exhibition was that the public had clearly become accustomed to this summary translation of exterior things and was no longer astonished, as with the first ones".[36] At the end of the exhibition, the profit of around 7,000 francs was divided among the participants.[37] This profit was mainly the result of a high attendance and not the sale of artworks. And so, in 1879 the organisers were aiming for an alliance between artists and collectors in order to make Impressionist art known to a wider public. During the 4th exhibition, there were only a few loans from art dealers, and just Hector Brame and Paul Durand-Ruel figure among the names mentioned in the catalogue.[38] At this time, the latter had stopped buying Impressionist works, falling back on safer investments. He only went back to his acquisitions in 1880 when he had more capital and the artists had conquered a more developed network of collectors and had a stronger presence on the market.[39] Furthermore, in his brochure *Les Peintres impressionnistes*, published in 1878, Duret did not mention art dealers and, to highlight the development of the small "clan" who favoured Impressionists, he successively evoked the critics, "then literary men like Alphonse Daudet, d'Hervilly, Zola [and] finally collectors".[40]

In this "collector-public" system, criticism had the double function of mediation and mediatisation which enabled to make the exhibition a real event and potentially legitimise the art it showed to the public. In his account, Jules Claretie, perfectly sums up the issues at stake:

> On the contrary, the 'independent artists' who have just opened their fourth annual exhibition Avenue de l'Opéra, know the advantages of making some noise. They are of the opinion – reflecting their excellent understanding of modernity – that silence is the cruellest of enemies for artists and they don't mind one bit overdoing it somewhat to grab people's attention. The fact is that at this current time, the *Impressionists* have their public, their clientele and their school.[41]

And so, the organisers were above all concerned with increased mediatisation and frequentation as a source of revenue rather than selling a large number of works. Their exhibition might appear like a demonstration of forces from artists who progressively conquered a small part of the market in full swing with a network that still remained highly endogamic.

A Collectionist Ecosystem?

But was this really an ecosystem in the sense of a group of artists in which each one contributed to creating value that benefitted the others? Or, to put it another way, did the collective dimension of the exhibition establish a shared network of collectors susceptible to benefit each artist? To answer this question, we need to examine the case of Degas and Forain, and start by acknowledging the fact that they did not use the same network of collectors at all. In fact, Degas sold at higher prices than the others and those who lent his works were not called Georges de Bellio[42] or Eugène Murer but had names such as Coquelin Cadet, Ernest May, Henri Rouart, Camille Groult, Hermann de Clermont or Ludovic Halévy. In short, celebrities who had greater financial means than the others, for example the banker Ernest May who lent a pastel by Caillebotte,[43] two works by Degas and a water colour by Forain.[44] May had been interested in the Impressionists since the mid-1870s because he had acquired a painting by Monet in 1875 and became friends with the artists shortly after; at the 1879 exhibition, he proved himself to be a collector of Degas with two works on the theme of dancers (fig. 6), one of which was shown but not in the catalogue.[45] As usual, Degas did not exhibit all of the works announced, and it is most likely that *Portraits at the Stock Exchange* (*Portraits à la bourse*), which figured Ernest May,[46] was not shown in 1879.
He solicited some of his other collectors like Camille Groult,[47] who owned the large Grands Moulins de Paris, Coquelin the Younger, the talented and famous member of the Comédie-Française, Hermann de Clermont, a businessman,[48] and his brother Auguste, who was a painter.[49] According to the latter's family, Degas had borrowed some money from the Clermont brothers when he was faced with family debts and paid them back by giving them some of his works.[50] The loans from the two brothers were then within a context of financial difficulty and a certain solidarity. As for Coquelin the Younger, he lent *Washerwomen Carrying Laundry* (*Blanchisseuses portant du linge*) by Degas[51] and a watercolour by Forain.[52] His presence was even more noticeable as according to a journalist from the *Soir*, he figured in the exhibition as the model for a portrait:

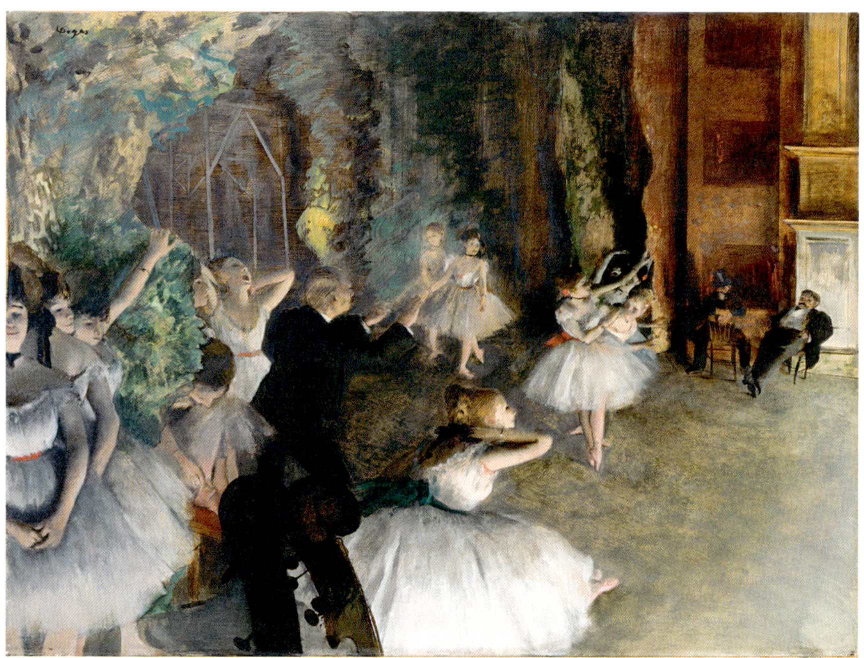

6. Edgar Degas,
The Rehearsal of the Ballet Onstage (*Répétition d'un ballet sur la scène*),
c. 1874, pastel over pen and ink drawing on paper mounted on canvas,
53.3 × 74.4 cm,
The Metropolitan Museum of Art, New York

> We should point out portraits by Mr Degas; by the same artist, washerwomen carrying laundry in town (a sketch in essence) the booklet says, belonging to Mr Coquelin the younger!! The latter is involved in Impressionism: not only does he possess some paintings, but two Impressionists have painted his portrait: Mr Degas and Mr Forain.[53]

And so, the actor's fame spilled over onto the artists and it is undeniable that Degas got more media attention than the others; Philippe Burty pointed out that "the amateur elite" "fought over" his pastels.[54] More generally speaking, Degas had envisaged sending in more portraits than before; to charm potential buyers, he also showed a group of fans and it was at his instigation that Pissarro and Forain equally presented this kind of decorative work, susceptible of pleasing a feminine clientele. Similarly, he favoured pastels on paper or canvas, like Caillebotte and Pissarro. And

so, this exhibition, made possible thanks to collectors and intended for them, had an influence on the creation of the artworks themselves.[55]
The pieces Forain sent in were wholly representative of this new strategy: his twenty-six works listed in the catalogue (mainly watercolours) were mostly not for sale because twenty-two of them belonged to various different owners.[56] They were linked to other networks such as the naturalist writers; among the lenders were names such as the novelists Léon Hennique and Joris-Karl Huysmans (who both made their debuts in Zola's circle), as well as the publisher Georges Charpentier or Alphonse Daudet. Forain had met Huysmans in 1876 and their early years of friendship resulted in the engraved frontispiece for the French edition of the writer's first novel, *Marthe, histoire d'une fille* (1879).
Degas and Forain both used collectionist networks that differed slightly from those of Monet and Pissarro.[57] Degas asserted himself as a kind of artist entrepreneur who already demanded high prices and whose works were hardly accessible to the majority of art enthusiasts. The first to have one of his paintings in a public collection, he sold *The Cotton Exchange, New Orleans* (*Portraits dans un bureau de coton*) to the Musée de Pau for 2,000 francs in 1878. These underlying economic factors resulted in a certain disparity between the artists and undermined the bucolic unity advertised in the catalogue. Consequently, the collective dimension of the exhibition did not systematically lead to a shared network of collectors susceptible of benefitting each artist.
In the end, the 1879 exhibition appears to have been a very specific moment that might be considered as a caesura. Indeed, reading between the lines enables us to analyse the reconfiguration of the Impressionist collecting network at this time because neither Ernest Hoschedé, nor Jean-Baptiste Faure are mentioned in the catalogue. Moreover, Georges de Bellio and Eugène Murer stopped buying shortly afterwards as the artists were progressively able to demand higher prices.[58] In the background, a female collector appeared who would become very famous, Louisine Elder, Havemeyer's future wife, who bought Pissarro's fan, *Pea Harvest* (*Cueillette de petits pois*), on loan from Mary Cassatt. In addition, the latter used the money from the exhibition to buy a painting by Monet and a fan by Degas.[59] In fact, the fans were in part as successful as hoped for and Albert Hecht acquired one of them for 300 francs.[60]
The young Jacques Doucet, who had lent a watercolour by Forain in 1879, bought a fan by Pissarro, shown in 1880.[61] As for Ernest May, he continued supporting Degas and his circle over the following years as reflected by his purchase of *The Dance Examination* (*Examen de danse*),[62] exhibited in 1880 and his support for the project for *Le Jour et la Nuit* magazine, launched by Degas following the 1879 exhibition.[63] Charles Haviland, who

was friends with the Bracquemond and Degas, also lent a pastel by the artist for the 5th exhibition.[64]

By enlisting the help of collectors in the organisation of this independent exhibition, the artists were above all looking for recognition from the public for their individual styles of painting. This relatively common strategy did not however mask the specific positions of Degas and Forain, as well as Monet's marginal position, who returned to the Salon in 1880. But in 1879, the unabashed desire for independence carried with it above all liberal ideas which opposed the State's control over artists through the Salons and, although the latter were not yet dependant on art dealers, they were for this very specific and transitional moment.

1 Ronald Pickvance, "Contemporary Popularity and Posthumous Neglect", in Charles S. Moffett (ed.), *The New Painting, Impressionism 1874-1886*, exhibition catalogue, National Gallery of Art, Washington; The Fine Arts Museums of San Francisco, 1986, pp. 243–65.

2 The catalogue for the 4th exhibition indicates that 90 out of the 246 works listed were on loan. This figure is only an indication as some of the works were not shown in the end and others were shown even though they don't appear in the catalogues.

3 Marie Bracquemond, Félix Bracquemond, Gustave Caillebotte, Adolphe-Félix Cals, Mary Cassatt, Edgar Degas, Louis Forain, Albert Lebourg, Claude Monet, Camille Pissarro, Henri Rouart, Henry Somm, Charles Tillot, Federico Zandomeneghi.

4 Most of these collectors were studied by Anne Distel in *Les Collectionneurs des impressionnistes: amateurs et marchands* (Paris: Bibliothèque des arts, 1989).

5 Bertall [Charles d'Arnoux], "Expositions des Indépendants, Ex-Impressionnistes, demain intentionnistes", *L'Artiste*, 1 June 1879, pp. 396–98.

6 Exhibition catalogue 1879 (catalogue of the 4th painting exhibition, Paris, 1879), nos. 143, 144 (Monet), 181, 182, 183, 184, 185, 186, 192 (Pissarro). For the identification of these works, see Berson, pp. 115–18 (Ruth Berson [ed.], *The New Painting: Impressionism 1874-1886. Documentation* [San Francisco-Seattle: Fine Arts Museums of San Francisco and University of Washington Press, 1996], vol. II); W. 490, 506 (Daniel Wildenstein, *Monet ou le Triomphe de l'Impressionnisme*, 4 vols. [Cologne-Paris: Taschen and Wildenstein Institute, 1996]); D-R. S. P. 489, 449, 494, 564, 399, 229 (Claire Durand-Ruel-Snollaerts, Joachim Pissarro, *Pissarro: Critical Catalogue of Paintings*, 3 vols. [Milan-Paris: Skira and Wildensetin Institute, 2005]).

7 Degas wrote to Caillebotte: "Telegram from Rouart this morning – Orléans station, deal done with Dupont 3200. Wait for my return. Rouart." (Letter from Edgar Degas to Gustave Caillebotte, Sunday, [Paris, March 1879], private collection, in *Letters of Edgar Degas*, bilingual edition, edited and annotated by Theodore Reff [New York: The Wildenstein Plattner Institute, 2020], vol. 1, pp. 244–45); Theodore Reff specifies in a note: Dreyfus Dupont owned a building at 28, Avenue de l'Opéra.

8 1879 exhibtion catalogue, nos. 38, 39. Ruth Berson suggests that the note "belongs to M. R." refers to Henri Rouart (Berson, p. 108).

9 Edgar Degas, *La Répétition*, New York, The Frick Collection (exhibition catalogue 1879, no. 66).

10 1879 exhibition catalogue, no. 79.

11 1879 exhibition catalogue, no. 50. The work isn't identified.

12 1879 exhibition catalogue, no. 142; W. 139. Identification suggested by Berson, p. 114. The work was not mentioned by the press in 1879; it does not figure in the sale of Henri Rouart's estate, held in 1912–13. Wildenstein puts forward the hypothesis that it was bought from Monet by H. Rouart in December 1878.

13 Pickvance, *op. cit.*, pp. 246–50.

14 Letter from Diego Martelli to Cecco Francesco Gioli, Paris, 52, Rue de Douai, [late March – early April 1879], in *Diego Martelli: Les impressionnistes et l'art moderne*, texts compiled and annotated by Francesca Errico (Paris: Éditions Vilo, 1979), p. 39.

15 Out of the 29 works by Monet listed in the catalogue, 23 of them are mentioned as loans, to which must be added *The Rue Saint Denis, Celebrations of 30 June 1878* (La Rue Saint-Denis, fête du 30 juin 1878), which belonged at that time to Emmanuel Chabrier. It is however unclear whether all the works listed were shown and other works seem to have been hung during the exhibition. In a letter, Caillebotte mentions "Durand-Ruel's dahlias", which seem to have been shown but not in the catalogue (perhaps *The Artist's Garden at Argenteuil* [Le Jardin de Monet à Argenteuil], 1873, National Gallery of Art, Washington. Letter from Gustave Caillebotte to Claude Monet, Wednesday evening [9 April 1879], in sale *Archives Claude Monet*, Cornebois Collection, Paris, Artcurial, 13 December 2006, no. 17). In another letter, Caillebotte writes: "Luquet's painting (the last one) arrived and is on an easel" (Letter from Gustave Caillebotte to Claude Monet, Thursday evening, [10 April 1879], in Marie Berhaut, *Gustave Caillebotte. Catalogue raisonné des peintures et pastels* [Paris: Wildenstein Institute, 1994], no. 17, pp. 274–75). This work is unidentified. On 1 May, Caillebotte wrote again to Monet: "I have just received your two paintings – both torn, was it you? Anyway, I have sent them to be fixed up. Tomorrow they will be in the Exhibition. I have nearly sold the bigger one, to Miss Cassatt." (Letter from Gustave Caillebotte to Claude Monet, place unknown, 1 May 1879, in Berhaut, *op. cit.*, no. 19, p. 275). Out of the 38 works by Pissarro listed in the catalogue, 23 of them are mentioned as loans.

16 Letter from Gustave Caillebotte to Claude Monet, place unknown, undated [mid-March 1879], in Berhaut, *op. cit.*, no. 15, p. 274.

17 Marianne Delafond, "Georges de Bellio. 'Le plus Parisien des Parisiens'", in *À l'apogée de l'impressionnisme: la collection Georges de Bellio*, exhibition catatalogue, Musée Marmottan Monet, Paris, 10 October 2007 – 3 February 2008, Lausanne, 2007, p. 22.

18 Exh. cat. 1879, nos. 145, 146, 152, 164, 165, 166; Berson, p. 115-116; W. 469, 263, 468, 362; Delafond, *op. cit.*, p. 28. *Sunset* (Coucher de soleil) (exh. cat. 1879, no. 164), unidentified neither by Wildenstein, nor by Mr Delafond.

19 Exh. cat. 1879, no. 156; W. 474.

20 Exh. cat. 1879, nos. 162 (Monet), 174, 175, 176, 177, 187, 203 (Pissarro); Berson, pp. 117–19; D-R. S. P. 442, 507, 535, 578. *The Poplars (Summer Morning)* (Les Peupliers [Matinée d'été]) (no. 177), unidentified neither by Berson, nor by Durand-Ruel-Snollaerts, Pissarro.

21 Exh. cat. 1879, no. 162; W. 496.

22 See the correspondance between Pissarro and Murer, in *Correspondance de Camille Pissarro*, edited by Janine Bailly-Herzberg, vol. 1: 1865-1885 (Paris: Éditions du Valhermeil, 2003).

23 Delafond, *op. cit.*, pp. 22, 64.

24 1879 exhibition cat., n° 138; W. 184.

25 Th. Duret lent three works by Monet (1879 exhibition cat., n° 139, 140, 141; W. 457, 528). The work entitled "Seascape (1875 (n° 140) was identified by Pickvance and Berson as *The Green Wave* (*La Vague verte*), New York, The Metropolitan Museum of Art.

26 Exh. cat. 1879, nos. 153, 154; W. 456, 470.

27 Exh. cat. 1879, nos. 157, 155; W. 95, 68.

28 Exh. cat. 1879, no. 158; W. 364. This work was not mentioned in the press 1879, nor in the correspondence between Caillebotte and Monet.

29 Exh. cat. 1879, nos. 147, 163; W. 154; Berson, p. 116.

30 Exh. cat. 1879, nos. 178, 179, 189. See Merete Bodelsen, "Gauguin, the Collector", *The Burlington Magazine*, September 1970, pp. 588–615, nos. 34, 43; D-R. S. P. 579, 574; Camille Jacob Pissarro, *Eventail. L'Hiver, retour de la foire*, Paris, Musée Marmottan Monet.

31 Pissarro's fan entitled *Picking Peas* (no. 200) is mentioned as belonging to "Miss C...". According to the Metropolitan Museum of Art's notice, it was the fan housed at the museum and which was perhaps acquired around 1879 by Mary Cassatt, then Louisine Elder, future Mrs Havemeyer. The Metropolitan Museum of Art, online, https://www.metmuseum.org/art/collection/search/437315 (accessed 18 March 2021). Berson, p. 119, identified another fan conserved in a private collection in 1996.

32 Pissarro wrote to Caillebotte: "Let's do some good paintings, not just show sketches, let's be very hard on our paintings, it is better, don't you think? Because the public disapproves of even the most beautiful sketches, it's a pretext." (Letter from Camille Pissarro to Gustave Caillebotte, [around March 1878], in Berhaut, *op. cit.*, no. 11, p. 274).

33 Félicie Faizand de Maupeou, *Claude Monet et l'exposition: une stratégie de carrière à l'avènement du marché de l'art* (Mont-Saint-Aignan, Presses universitaires de Rouen and du Havre, 2018), p. 96.

34 Auguste Renoir, *Portrait of Mme Charpentier and her Children* (Portrait de Mme Charpentier et de ses enfants), The Metropolitan Museum of Art, New York.

35 Caillebotte wrote to Monet: "We have had 15,400 and some entries. In short, it's progress. I am sorry that you couldn't follow it more closely. But we did a lot for the painters, for the public, despite the ill will of the press." (Letter from Gustave Caillebotte to Claude Monet, Tuesday evening, [13 May 1879], in Berhaut, *op. cit.*, no. 20, p. 275).

36 Armand Silvestre, "Les Expositions. Des Indépendants", *L'Estafette*, 16 April 1879, p. 3.

37 "17,000 people will pay 1 franc entry. The costs will not be more than 10,000 francs. We will discuss how to use the remaining 7,000 francs." (Achille Segard, *Mary Cassatt. Un peintre des enfants et des mères* [Paris: Paul Ollendorf, 1913], p. 23, note 1).

38 H. Brame lent two works by Degas (Exh. cat. 1879, nos. 72, 77); Durand-Ruel lent two works by Monet (exh. cat. 1879, nos. 159, 160).

39 Sylvie Patry (ed.), *Paul Durand-Ruel: Le pari de l'impressionnisme*, exhibition catalogue (Paris: RMN – Grand Palais, 2014).

40 Théodore Duret, *Les Peintres impressionnistes. Claude Monet, Sisley, C. Pissarro, Renoir, Berthe Morisot* (Paris: H. Heymann and J. Peyrois, 1878), pp. 8–9.

41 Jules Claretie, "Le Mouvement parisien. Les *Impressionnistes* et les *aquarellistes*", *L'Indépendance belge*, 20 April 1879, p. 1.

42 We should specify that Georges de Bellio acquired a work by Degas, undoubtedly around 1876: *A Woman Ironing* (Repasseuse), c. 1873, The Norton Simon Foundation, Pasadena. Norton Simon Museum, online, https://www.nortonsimon.org/art/detail/M.1979.05.P (accessed 18 March 2021).

43 Gustave Caillebotte, *Vallée de l'Yerres*, private collection (exh. cat. 1879, no. 28).
44 Exh. cat. 1879, no. 90 (*Around the Folies-Bergère* [Pourtour des Folies-Bergère]). The work has not been identified.
45 Edgar Degas, *The Dance Class* (Leçon de danse), Shelburne Museum (not in the catalogue). This work was identified by Berson, p. 112.
46 Edgar Degas, *Portraits at the Stock Exchange* (Portraits à la bourse), Musée d'Orsay Paris (Gary Tinterow and Anne M. P. Norton, "Degas aux expositions "impressionnistes"", in *Degas inédit* [Paris: La Documentation Française, 1989], p. 317).
47 C. Groult lent Degas's *Café singer* (Chanteuse de café), The Fogg Art Museum, Cambridge, Havard Art Museums (exh. cat. 1879, no. 70).
48 H. de Clermont lent Degas's *Dancers in the Wings* (Danseuses derrière le portant), Norton Simon Museum, Pasadena. Not listed in the catalogue, the work was identified by Tatsuya Saito, "La quatrième exposition impressionniste en caricature. De nouvelles identifications d'œuvres", *Revue de l'art*, nos. 189, 2015-3, pp. 24–25.
49 Edgar Degas, *Dancer in her Dressing Room* (Loge de danseuse), Sammlung Oskar Reinhart, Winterthur (exh. cat. 1879, no. 71). In the catalogue, the work is mentioned as belonging to "Mrs A. de C.", referring to Mrs Auguste de Clermont.
50 Marylin R. Brown, "A entrepreneur in spite of himself: Edgar Degas and the market", in *The Culture of the Market. Historical Essays* (New York: Cambridge University Press, 1994), p. 282.
51 Edgar Degas, *Washerwomen carrying Laundry* (Blanchisseuses portant du linge), private collection (exh. cat. 1879, no. 64).
52 *Ham Actor in Mourning* (Cabotin en demi-deuil), watercolour (exh. cat. 1879, no. 99). For more on this work, see Tatsuya Saito, "La quatrième exposition impressionniste", *op. cit.*, p. 26.
53 N. S., "Exposition des impressionnistes", *Le Soir*, 12 April 1879, p. 1. These portraits by Degas and Forain have not been identified. The portrait of Coquelin by Degas is not listed in the 4th exhibition catalogue whilst Forain's is catalogued as no. 83, *Portrait de M. Coquelin the Younger, in the Sphinx* (Portrait de M. Coquelin Cadet, dans le Sphinx), watercolour. There were no portraits by Degas and Forain in the sale of Coquelin the younger's estate which took place in Paris at the Hôtel Drouot on 26 May 1909. As the columnist from the *Soir* was the only person to evoke a possible portrait of Coquelin by Degas, the verity of his comment is doubtful.
54 Ph. B. [Philippe Burty], "L'Exposition des artistes indépendants", *La République française*, 16 April 1879, p. 3.
55 In 1878, Pissarro wrote to Caillebotte: "Let's do some good paintings, not just show sketches, let's be very hard on our paintings, it is better, don't you think? Because the public disapproves of even the most beautiful sketches, it's a pretext." (Letter from Camille Pissarro to Gustave Caillebotte, Pontoise, Saturday, n.d. [late March 1878], in Berhaut, *op. cit.*, no. 11, p. 274).
56 One of the Hecht brothers had notably lent four watercolours by Forain two of which were identified: no. 94, *Protector in the Wings* (Le Protecteur dans les coulisses) (Berson, p. 113); no. 88, *Actress in her Dressing Room* (Loge d'actrice) (Tatsuya Saito, "La quatrième exposition impressionniste", *op. cit.*, pp. 26–27).
57 For more on the collectors of Monet's work at this time, see Félicie Faizand de Maupeou, *Claude Monet et l'exposition*, *op. cit.*, pp. 119–22.
58 Anne Distel, *Les Collectionneurs des impressionnistes*, *op. cit.*, pp. 115 et 212.
59 Edgar Degas, *Dancers* (Danseuses), fan, The Metropolitan Museum of Art, New York. Monet's work was *Spring* (Printemps) (Walters Art Gallery, Baltimore), which means that it was presented at the 1879 exhibition in May (see note 15).
60 Edgar Degas, *The Ballet* (Le Ballet), fan, Kuboso Memorial Museum of Art, Izumi (Anne Distel, "Albert Hecht collector (1842-1889)", *op. cit.*, p. 277).
61 Camille Pissarro, *The Railway Bridge, Pontoise* (Le Pont du chemin de fer, Pontoise), private collection (catalogue for the 5th painting exhibition, Paris, 1880, no. 138).
62 Edgar Degas, *The Dance Examination* (Examen de danse), The Denver Art Museum (exh. cat. 1880, no. 40).
63 On this project and the works sold during the exhibition, see Ronald Pickvance, "Contemporary Popularity", *op. cit.*, p. 261.
64 Edgar Degas, *La Loge*, The Museum of Fine Arts, Houston (exh. cat. 1880, no. 38).

IMPRESSIONISM IN COLLECTOR DIRECTORIES, IN FRANCE AND ABROAD (1878–1937)

LÉA SAINT-RAYMOND

Collections have a performative dimension. It is not just about possessing a relatively large group of more or less homogeneous objects to be called a collector. On the contrary, it is by saying we "collect" something that enables us to enter into the field of collections, even if the fruit of our collecting is meagre or virtual.[1] Although contemporary or posthumous bibliographies consider them as such, owning a large number of the same type of objects does not make the owner a "collector" per se. Intention comes before action.

To understand "collectors" of Impressionist art, then, it is essential to look at the historical sources that tell us something about their ambitions. Ris-Paquot and Campbell's artistic directories meet this condition and therefore underpin this chapter.[2] Founded in 1879 by painter and ceramics historian Oscar Ris-Paquot, followed later by Ernest Renard between 1893 and 1904 and taken over, between 1911 and 1937, by Francis Campbell, these directories provide a list of collectors both in France and abroad, classified by department, then by town.[3] This inventory had the advantage of being declarative, meaning that collectors had to make themselves known in order to appear in the directory. Registrations had to be written and the listing was entirely free. Each individual gave their first and last names, profession, if applicable, and their medals, address and, above all stated exactly what they collected. Hence, three collectors in Sedan, in the Ardennes, put their names down for the 1882 directory: Dumoustier, who collected curiosities, Pastor Goulden, who collected furniture, bronzes and curiosities, and H. Daire, who declared having a "beautiful collection of old paintings".[4]

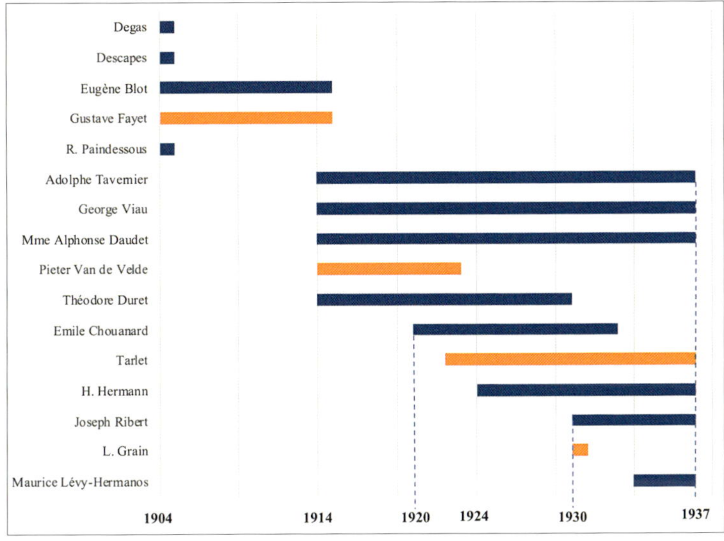

1. Presence of self-declared collectors of "Impressionist" paintings in the Ris-Paquot and Campbell directories, residing in Paris (in blue) and in other French towns (in orange)

But what can we learn from these artistic directories about collectors of Impressionism in France and abroad? Do the lists correspond to the guardian figures identified by Anne Distel in her fundamental analysis,[5] or are they somewhat of a surprise in terms of the relevant bibliography? An exhaustive examination of the directories between 1878 and 1937 has allowed us to make a list of connoisseurs of Impressionist painting and to study their specificity within the social space of self-declared collectors. However, this list has its limits inherent in the collector directories themselves.

Impressionist Collectors

Although contemporary with the development of Impressionism, the movement was only first mentioned in the directories in 1904. Apart from Gustave Arosa, no other enthusiasts identified in the bibliography figured in the 1879 volume, nor in the 1882 one. What is more, Arosa hardly even bothered to describe his collection which makes specifying his preferences rather difficult. Impressionism only began appearing in the Ris-Paquot directories from the time the movement was endorsed and institutionalised in the early twentieth century. Hence, the 1904 edition counts five self-declared collectors of Impressionist painting (fig. 1): Eugène Blot, Edgar Degas, a certain Descapes, and R. Paindessous, living in Paris, and Gustave Fayet, residing in Béziers. Only the latter and Eugène Blot remained in the following editions up until 1914.

New collectors started to appear in this edition (fig. 1): Adolphe Tavernier, George Viau and Mrs Alphonse Daudet – all three remained faithful to the directory up until the last volume in 1937 – Théodore Duret – was listed until 1929 – and Pieter van de Velde from Le Havre, between 1914 and 1922. The following issue, in 1920, saw the appearance of Émile Chouanard among collectors of Impressionist works, then, from 1922, Tarlet, an advocate from Montpellier and, two years later, the Parisian H. Hermann. In 1930, Joseph Ribert declared collecting paintings from the "Lyon Impressionist School" and a certain L. Grain, from Rouen, "Impressionist paintings". Finally, in 1935, Maurice Lévy-Hermanos stopped calling himself a "buyer of beautiful paintings and drawings by nineteenth-century masters (School of 1830 and Impressionist and contemporary masters)", removing the term "buyer" and presenting himself as a just collector of this category up until 1937.
This recension astonishingly testifies to the low number of declared collectors of Impressionist works: in 1904, there were five out of 1331 residing in Metropolitan France and in 1925, seven out of 3834. There were no foreign collectors in this category. However, the directories' international connections were very limited at the time they were taken over by Campbell: the 1911, 1912 and 1914 issues had no international section at all and in 1925, only 25 individuals living abroad figured in the directory. Women were also noticeably absent from this list. Only the poetess and journalist Julia Daudet (1844-1940), wife and collaborator of Alphonse Daudet, declared herself as a collector of Impressionist paintings. This under representation went hand in hand with a structural effect, because female collectors remained a minority in the directories, representing just 4% of the effectives in 1904 and 7% in 1925.
The self-declared collectors of Impressionism can be divided into three broad groups. The first was made up of those known in the bibliography and who were promoters of Impressionism. Among these supporters were Edgar Degas (1834–1917), both an artistic colleague and collector; the journalist and critic Théodore Duret (1838–1927), defender from the outset, friend and historiographer of the movement,[6] but also well-known amateurs like the founder Eugène Blot (1857–1938), who documented the history of his collection,[7] the dental surgeon[8] George Viau (1855–1939), the fencer and man of letters Adolphe Tavernier (1853–1945) and Gustave Fayet (1865–1925), painter and curator of the Musée de Béziers.[9] The second group brings together self-declared collectors of Impressionism, little-known to the bibliography but identifiable thanks to documents of the time: Émile Chouanard, who made a donation of André Metthey's ceramics to the town of Paris,[10] Julia Daudet, already mentioned, R. Paindessous, main publicity agent for Indicateurs-Chaix,[11] Joseph Ribert –

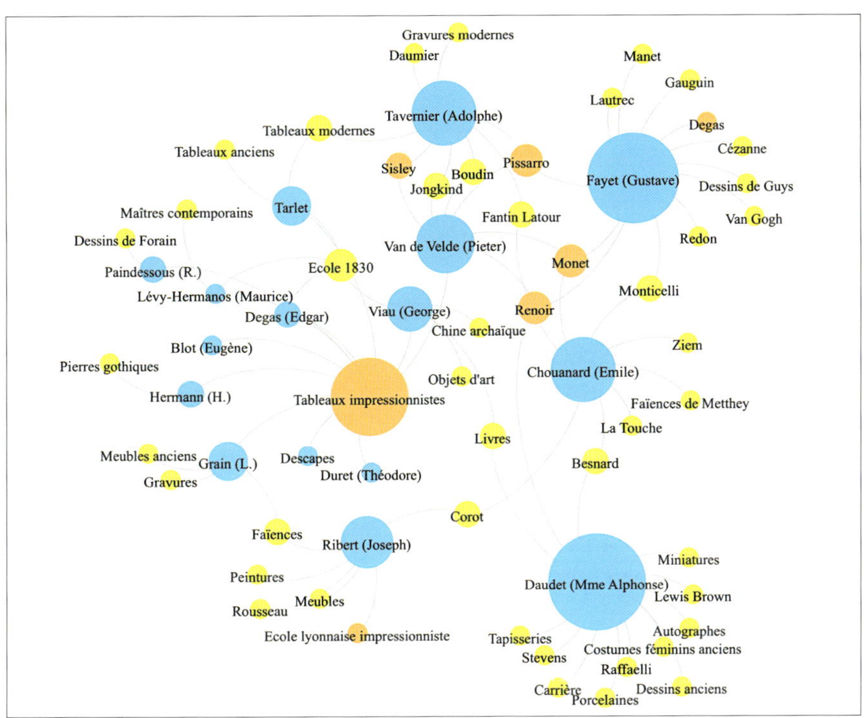

2. Network of collectors of Impressionist works between 1904 and 1937 (in blue), according to the categories they declared collecting (in yellow and orange)

insurance director and finance inspector[12] – Tarlet, advocate, president of the Hérault Société artistique and member of the Board at the Musée Fabre in Montpellier, or furthermore a Le Havre businessman originally from Amsterdam,[13] Pieter van de Velde,[14] and Maurice Lévy-Hermanos, associate of the art gallery owner Marcel Bernheim[15] deported from Drancy in 1943.[16] Finally, L. Grain and H. Hermann make up the last group of unidentified collectors.

A Preferential System for Impressionism

Apart from Descapes, Eugène Blot and Théodore Duret, who declared collecting solely Impressionist paintings, the others noted diverse interests (fig. 2). This graphic enables us to recreate the "system of objects" collected, or to paraphrase Jean Baudrillard,[17] i.e. what enthusiasts of

Impressionist works collected at the same time as the latter. By comparing this network with the results of Parisian public sales at the same period,[18] it is possible to highlight a certain homological relationship between the preferences of these collectors and the success encountered by certain categories of works on public sale. Indeed, self-declared collectors of Impressionist paintings also mentioned works from the School of 1830 or so-called "modern" paintings. After the Great War, the works of the old masters were sold at much higher prices and in parallel, appeared in the preferences of art enthusiasts in the directories: H. Hermann declared collecting "gothic stones", Tarlet "ancient paintings", and Mrs Alphonse Daudet "ancient drawings". Similarly, ancient Chinese ceramics dethroned Japanese objects in the early twentieth century,[19] echoing George Viau's taste for "(archaic Chinese) art objects".
The connoisseurs of Impressionist paintings identified in the directories declared a preference then for safe investments on the market at a time when the movement had been endorsed. But even so, were their profiles similar to the other self-declared collectors in the directories? In order to compare their systems of objects with those of their colleagues, two surveys were carried out in 1904 and 1925: we have transcribed the whole of the directories for these two years in order to be able to study them quantitatively. Computational analysis of the profiles has allowed us to distinguish military men, ecclesiastics, teachers and women, whose preferences stand out for these two years.[20] More than the other socio-professional categories, military men collected militaria, ecclesiastics and teachers collected documents relating to local history, prehistoric objects and naturalia, and the women were more drawn to collections of tapestries and fabrics than the men. And so, Julia Daudet fitted into this category whilst standing out from the other Impressionist collectors with the mention of tapestries and "ancient female costumes", she showed nonetheless great similarities with her female colleagues listed in the directories.
One aspect, however, distinguishes this small group of collectors from all of the others who appear in the directories: their relative indifference to bibliophilia. In fact, in 1904 similarly to 1925, books were by far, the category the most frequently mentioned by collectors.[21] In contrast, only George Viau and Julia Daudet declared themselves to be bibliophiles, the latter also adding autographs to her specialties. Nonetheless, this information should be taken with some caution as the directories have extensive limitations: enthusiasts of Impressionist art perfectly highlight the bias of the Ris-Paquot and Campbell directories.

A Representative Source of Collections?

This source reveals all the inconveniencies of its main quality: it is based on self-declaration. As it was imperative for the entries to be short, it is very difficult to measure the economic and emotional investment the different collectors put into their collections. Or, to put it another way, the form of the directories led to a levelling out of those cited. Hence, George Viau and Tarlet figured as two collectors of "Impressionist paintings", without any distinction, even though the former's collection was much bigger than the latter's. Similarly, the directories said very little about the extent of this activity. For example, in the 1904 directory, nothing distinguished Théodore Duret, an ardent defender of Impressionism,[22] and Descapes, who wanted to remain more anonymous.[23]

The briefness of the entries was also a source of imprecision about the content of the collections. Many recognised collectors of Impressionist works were only able to mention a more general specialty in the directories, like "paintings" or "modern paintings". And so, in 1914, Jean-Baptiste Faure declared collecting "modern paintings" just like Auguste Pellerin. Similarly, in 1914 Tarlet called himself a connoisseur of "ancient and modern paintings" then, in 1922, he modified his entry to "ancient and modern paintings, 1830 School, Impressionists": does this addition mean that Tarlet started his Impressionist collection in 1922 or that this group of works was implicitly included in his "modern paintings" in 1914? The directories alone do not tell us this. Similar doubts can be cast on Maurice Lévy-Hermanos, who was registered between 1922 and 1929 as a collector of "ancient and modern paintings, eighteenth-century engravings". Inversely, should a certain Heugel who, in 1922, declared collecting "paintings and art objects of all periods and styles" be included in the list of connoisseurs of Impressionism?

Whilst the directories of collectors are vague due to the shortness of the entries, they require even greater methodological caution – here, once again thanks to the example of Maurice Gangnat, Impressionism, allows us to reveal another bias. We know that Gangnat collected works by Pierre-Auguste Renoir as he had bought a consequential group of paintings by the artist at auction in 1925.[24] Yet, in the directories from the 1920s, Maurice Gangnat declared himself uniquely as a bibliophile, completely omitting any mention of the paintings. Did he consider Renoir's paintings to be simply a decorative pleasure and the books as his only centre of interest as a collector? Only his personal archives could give us access to his inner thinking.

This example has led us to corroborate our sources and cross-reference the collector directories with the minutes of sales at public auctions for

Behrendt	Paul Durand-Ruel	Rigaux
Bernheim Jeune	Foinard	Lucien Sauphar
Mme Besnard	Charles Guasco	Sechbach
Eugène Blot	Guillaume Ibos	Schoengen
Boussod & Valadon	Ch. Malcoud	Jules Strauss
Auguste Breysse	J. Mancini	Ivan Stchoukine [sic]
Isaac de Camondo	Lucien Moline	Stumpf
Gaston Camentron	Octave Mirbeau	**Adolphe Tavernier**
Choppy	Nuchlbacher	**Dr George Viau**
Dantan	Revillon	Ambroise Vollard

3. Buyers of Impressionist works at public sale in 1900

Prince Aga Khan	Fiquet	Marczel de Nemes
Allard	Fougeirol	Melet
Barbier	Fukushima	Mietschaninoff
Bendeur	Gangnat	W. Muller
Georges Bernheim	Gaumont	Oppenheimer
Marcel Bernheim	Goldet	Payet
Bignon	Goldschmidt	Georges Petit
Eugène Blot	Paul Guillaume	Mme Pierre Lantz
Brenner	Sasha Guitry	Pigard
André Breton	Haine	Porget
Cellier	Mme Halphen	Oskar Reinhart
D'Heucqueville	Hansen	Renier
Darmetal	Baron Heckren	Jane Renouardt
Davis	Helft	Mme Reville
De Noailles	Hessel	Rigaudias
Desportes	Hodebert	Sauphar
Dru	E. Jonas	Savoir
Druet	Alphonse Kann	Jules Strauss
Durand-Ruel	Kapferer	G. Tanner
Esmon	Knoedler	Vollard
Mme Ephrussi	A. Lapp	Wolff
Escoffier	Lotiron	

4. Buyers of Impressionist works at public sale in 1925

example. These documents, available for Parisian auctions, gives us access to the names – and sometimes addresses – of the successful bidders.[25] And so, it is possible to compare the directories with, for example, the record of buyers of Impressionist paintings in 1900 (fig. 3) and in 1925 (fig. 4). Although some more committed collectors commented their acquisitions – Eugène Blot, Adolphe Tavernier, George Viau – the other self-declared enthusiasts of Impressionism were glaringly absent from the auction rooms. Perhaps they preferred the more private network of art galleries or simply buying directly from the artists themselves – when they were still alive. Public auctions were an openly male environment and so female collectors may have preferred this alternative means of acquiring works, like Julia Daudet – moreover, when Renoir painted her portrait in 1876 (fig. 5) it was in the privacy of her own home, during a period when the painter was staying with her.[26]

And so, buyers of Impressionist works at public auctions were not always those who claimed to be collectors of Impressionist paintings in the directories. Sasha Guitry, for example, acquired Renoir's *Apples* (*Pommes*) at the Gangnat sale in 1925 but called himself a bibliophile in the directory of the same year. Two categories of amateurs are completely ignored

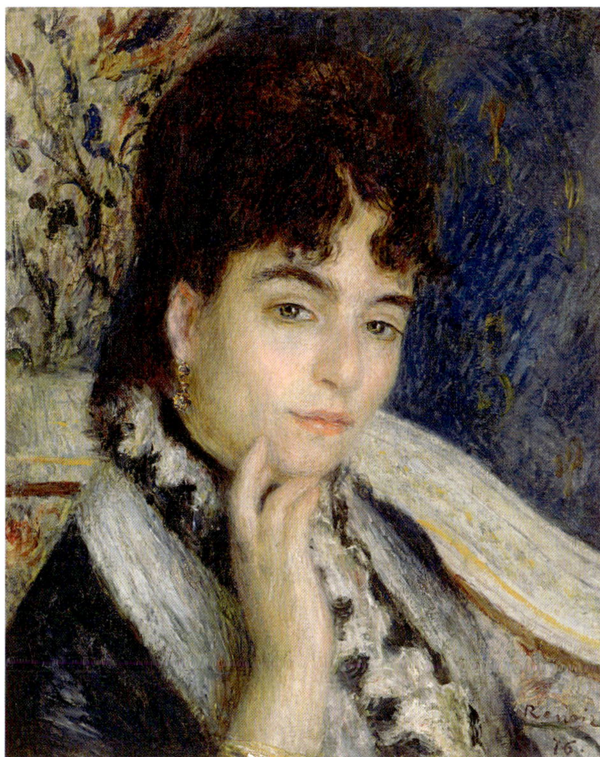

5. Pierre-Auguste Renoir (1841–1919), *Madame Alphonse Daudet*, 1876, oil on canvas, 46 × 38 cm, Musée d'Orsay, Paris, MNR 201

by the directories. On the one hand, the bankers Isaac de Camondo, Jules Strauss, Lucien Sauphar and Alphonse Kann – who was dispossessed of his collection during the Occupation, similarly to Jules Strauss – made major acquisitions of Impressionist works in 1900 and/or 1925 (figs. 3–4) without ever declaring to be collectors in the directories. The shortfall is even more noticeable with international connoisseurs. In 1925, the minutes testify to a strong internationalisation of buyers of Impressionist works (fig. 4): Prince Aga Khan and Oskar Reinhart living in Switzerland, Fukushima was Japanese; Marczel de Nemes, Hungarian, and Wolff lived in London. Favouring French collectors, the directories completely ignored this international market.

Does the bias presented by the collector directories mean that we should completely ignore this source? All historical documents should be analysed by taking into account their inherent blind spots and limitations: no source is "objective" or perfect, and the collector directories are no exception. Used with a quantitative approach that "horizantalises" the data, this ensemble has the advantage of distancing preferences from their typology and their evolution, and is also very useful for spotting certain collectors who would have otherwise gone unnoticed, and who merit more in-depth monographic research, like Julia Daudet, Joseph Ribert, H. Hermann or R. Paindessous.

The directories also highlight certain geographical areas that have not been researched as much as the capitals of the art market like Paris, London or New York, and focus more on collectors living in France, such as Tarlet, from Montpellier, or Pieter van de Velde, living in Le Havre. They are the keystone in the DatArt research project which will be developed within the framework of the Digital Humanities Observatory at the ENS-PSL, in order to better understand the regional functioning of the art world.[27]

1 See the example of Alexandre Berthier, Prince of Wagram's "virtual" collection: Léa Saint-Raymond and Hadrien Viraben, "The Virtual Collection of Alexandre Berthier, Prince of Wagram", *Nineteenth-Century Art Worldwide* 19, no. 2, 2020, https://dx.doi.org/10.29411/ncaw.2020.19.2.4

2 Paul Lacroix's directories, published between 1860 and 1862, were the first examples, but the lists of collectors were not self-declarative, unlike Ris-Paquot's directories.

3 Léa Saint-Raymond, "Vers une histoire élargie des collections ? Les annuaires artistiques des collectionneurs au prisme des humanités numériques", *Histoire de l'art*, no. 87, 2021, pp. 1–12.

4 Oscar Ris-Paquot, *Annuaire artistique des collectionneurs* (Paris: Raphaël Simon, 1882–83), p. 107.

5 Anne Distel, *Les Collectionneurs des impressionnistes: amateurs et marchands* (Paris: La Bibliothèque des Arts, 1989).

6 Théodore Duret, *Histoire des peintres impressionnistes: Pissarro, Claude Monet, Sisley, Renoir, Berthe Morisot, Cézanne, Guillaumin* (Paris: H. Floury, 1906).

7 Eugène Blot, *Histoire d'une collection de tableaux modernes, cinquante ans de peinture (de 1882 à 1932)* (Paris: Éditions d'art, 1934).

8 See Christian Theuveny and Claude Petit-Castelli, *George Viau, un amateur éclairé. 50 ans de collection d'un ami des impressionnistes*, 2 vols. (Paris: Ecila, 2018 and 2020).

9 See Alexandre d'Andoque's chapter on this collector.

10 https://www.parismuseescollections.paris.fr/fr/recherche/type/oeuvre/donateur/chouanard-emile-jules-295066 (accessed 4 April 2021).

11 *Almanach Didot-Bottin du commerce*, 1904, p. 584.

12 *Combat*, 9 December 1944, p. 1.

13 https://museeduluxembourg.fr/fr/collection/objet/la-seine-au-point-du-jour

14 See Géraldine Lefebvre, *Le Cercle de l'Art moderne au Havre* (Paris: Somogy, 2012).

15 *Les Échos*, 14 December 1936, p. 2.

16 https://fr.findagrave.com/memorial/31916918/maurice-levy_hermanos, https://issuu.com/hesiod/docs/r_pertoire_des_biens_spoli_s_en_france_pendant_la_/21

17 Jean Baudrillard, *Le système des objets* (Paris: Gallimard, 2014). First edition 1969.

18 Léa Saint-Raymond, À la conquête du marché de l'art: le Pari(s) des enchères (Paris: Classiques Garnier, 2021).

19 Léa Saint-Raymond, "Les collectionneurs d'art asiatique à Paris (1858-1939): une analyse socio-économique", in Marie Laureillard and Cléa Patin (eds.), À la croisée des collections entre Asie et Occident, du *XIXe siècle à nos jours* (Paris: Hémisphères, 2019), pp. 229–47.

20 Léa Saint-Raymond, "Vers une histoire élargie des collections? Les annuaires artistiques des collectionneurs au prisme des humanités numériques", *art. cit*.

21 Léa Saint-Raymond, "Vers une histoire élargie des collections? Les annuaires artistiques des collectionneurs au prisme des humanités numériques", *art. cit.*, p. 4.

22 See Shinegi Inaga, *Théodore Duret (1838-1927): du journaliste politique à l'historien d'art japonisant: contribution à l'étude de critique artistique dans la deuxième moitié du XIXe et au début du XXe siècle*, unpublished doctoral thesis supervised by Anne-Marie Christin, Université Paris Diderot-Paris 7, 1989.

23 As we can see from the anonymous sale of his collection in 1901: *Collection de Monsieur X****, Hôtel Drouot, 15 April 1901, auctioneer: Mr Paul Chevallier, experts: MM. Bernheim Jeune.

24 *Catalogue des tableaux composant la collection Maurice Gangnat, 160 tableaux par Renoir, œuvres importantes de Paul Cézanne, tableaux par E. Vuillard*, Paris, 25 and 26 June 1925, auctioneer: Mr Lair-Dubreuil, expert: Jos Hessel.

25 Léa Saint-Raymond, À la conquête du marché de l'art: le Pari(s) des enchères, *op. cit*.

26 https://www.musee-orsay.fr/fr/collections/catalogue-des-oeuvres/notice.html?nnumid=1131 (accessed 4 April 2021).

27 See Léa Saint-Raymond *et al.*, "Toulouse, the glorious Athens of the South? Computational analysis of the Salons des Artistes Méridionaux (1907-1939)", *Preprints*, 2021, https://www.preprints.org/manuscript/202104.0525/v1 (accessed 30 April 2021).

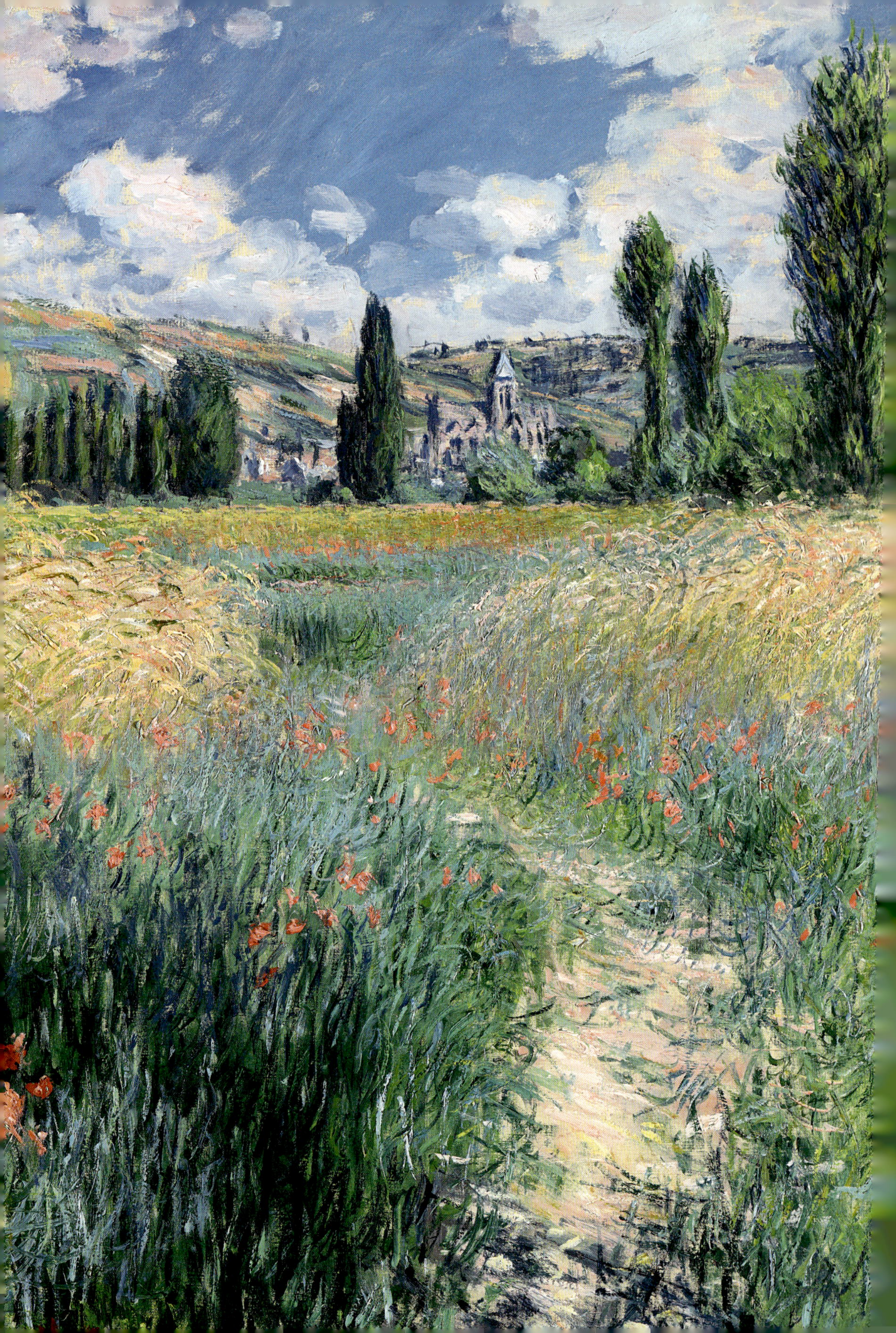

The Spread of Impressionism through Collections: From One Continent to Another

In the second half of the nineteenth century and the first decades of the twentieth century, Paris was the capital of art worldwide. It was the place where artists came to train and where collectors discovered the latest trends in the art market. Although initially marginal, international support for Impressionism played an essential role, not just in relation to the artists, by representing new and immediate prospects, but also in a much broader sense, opening up new markets for the movement as a whole. The international spread of Impressionism took place over a long period of time and in a differentiated manner. Besides the individual tastes of each collector, shared interests for specific artists or genres became apparent in various regions or countries.

And from the first collectors who collaborated with painters to those who today follow an equally buoyant market, the way they bought works and collected them tells a lot about the evolution of the Impressionist movement as a whole. Very early on, Impressionism spread beyond the frontiers of its birthplace thanks to collectors who participated in forging a common taste for these paintings by following their own personal inclinations.

Claude Monet, *Path on the Island of Saint Martin, Vétheuil* (*Sentier sur l'île de Saint-Martin, Vétheuil*), 1881, detail, Philadelphia Museum of Art, gift of John C. Haas and Chara C. Haas, 2011

FRENCH IMPRESSIONISM IN SWITZERLAND: A LOOK BACK

LUKAS GLOOR

The story surrounding the discovery of French Impressionism in the various European countries and in the United States has been the subject of a number of publications and exhibitions over the past forty years, and it is now almost as well-known as the heroic story of the beginnings of the movement itself, which John Rewald described in two volumes published by the Museum of Modern Art in New York in 1946 and 1956. The author of these lines recently explained how, since 1980, aside from the appreciation of art, the analysis of the mechanisms that control the reception of art was increasingly pushed to the fore, and how, alongside the story of the great artists, a different narrative has emerged regarding the great museum curators, critics, collectors and dealers who ensured that art history unfolded in such a way that the public, as exhibition and museum visitors, as art connoisseurs and amateurs, has become accustomed to perceiving it.[1] Instead of retelling this well-known tale from beginning to end, the aim here is to approach it in reverse, that is, to follow it from the present back into the past, as opposed to the usual chronological vision of history.

The Ongoing Interest in French Impressionism Beyond the Turn of the Millennium

Although the reception of French Impressionism in Switzerland began over 110 years ago, its consequences are still apparent today. The continuing success of three exhibiting institutions immediately proves how widespread interest in Impressionism and the history of modern painting that it initiated still is in Switzerland: the Fondation Beyeler in Riehen, near Basel, the Fondation Pierre Gianadda in Martigny and the Fondation de l'Hermitage in Lausanne. All three institutions came into being as a result of private initiative which shows that their programmes meet the expectations of a public that also rewards what is on show financially. The Gianadda and Hermitage foundations in the French-speaking part of the country were established in 1976 and 1977. The creation of the Fondation Beyeler, inaugurated in 1997, was based on the collection that the Basel art dealer Ernst Beyeler had gradually managed to move from storage into his own property. But, from the very beginning, the foundation also owed its appeal primarily to the modern art exhibitions which made the establishment one of the best-known museums internationally in a very short space of time.

All three establishments shared a focus on classical modernism in how their works were put together, as had been commonplace in Switzerland for decades. It began with French Impressionism and Post-Impressionism, followed by the succession of -isms that had defined the avant-garde since 1900. Consequently, when it began exhibiting in 1984, the Fondation de l'Hermitage presented an overview of *L'impressionnisme dans les collections romandes* [Impressionism in the Collections of French-Speaking Switzerland], and in the following year it held a second exhibition entitled *De Cézanne à Picasso dans les collections romandes* [From Cézanne to Picasso in the Collections of French-Speaking Switzerland]. Unlike in the early twentieth century, when the reception of French Impressionism was largely limited to German-speaking Switzerland, the art collections of French-speaking Switzerland were now in keeping with international standards, not least thanks to many foreign collectors who lived on the shores of Lake Geneva. At the Fondation Gianadda in 1981, Picasso began the series of exhibitions of modern artists since Impressionism that followed one another in Martigny over the next few decades – with its high point in 2000 when Vincent van Gogh attracted more than half a million visitors to Valais. Unlike the two French-speaking Swiss establishments which did not have their own collection, the Fondation Beyeler was able to use the collection donated by its founder to obtain high-quality loans from leading establishments around the world. The initial exhibitions in Renzo Piano's new building focused on Wassily Kandinsky, Jasper Johns and Roy Lichtenstein, and had a close relationship with Ernst Beyeler's own collection. Beyeler's selection tells the story of modern art from early abstraction in the various centres of Europe before the First World War to the period after the Second World War when the heart of the action shifted from Europe to the United States. In 1999, the exhibition *Paul Cézanne and Modernism* was a reminder that Beyeler's collection – as in the Museum of Modern Art (MoMA) in New York – also began with the French Post-Impressionists and gave a special place to Claude Monet's *Water Lilies* triptych (fig. 1).[2]

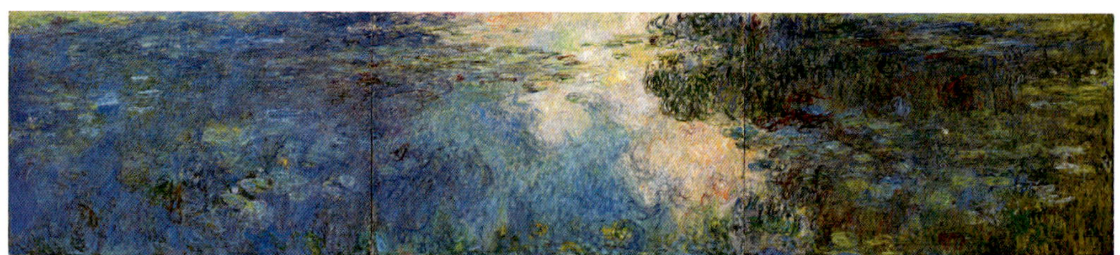

Already in 1986, the Kunstmuseum Basel had organised the largest ever exhibition of Claude Monet's *Water Lilies*. Although the museum itself did not own a painting from the cycle on which the artist had worked constantly in his final years in his garden and studio in Giverny, the catalogue could still point to the close connection between Monet's *Water Lilies* and works by the Abstract Expressionists from New York, four of which had been on display in the Basel museum since 1958.[3] That was the time when Monet's "decorations" were given the status of works of fine art rather than decorative art at the MoMA in New York and, at the same time, a tour starting at the Basel Kunsthalle placed contemporary art from the United States on an equal footing with European creative output for the first time. Hand in hand with this paradigm shift, New York replaced Paris as the capital of art for the following decades and, naturally, this also had an effect on the reception of French Impressionism in Switzerland. This was particularly striking in Geneva where the Musée du Petit Palais closed its doors in 1998 after thirty years of showing the works that the industrialist Oscar Ghez had collected to provide a comprehensive overview of different periods of the "École de Paris".[4] Having this collection had prompted Ghez to open a museum in 1968 to show these works, but now, in a changed art world, they no longer attracted enough visitors to keep the operation of the museum going.

After 1945: with French Impressionism towards International Recognition

The 1964 Exposition Nationale Suisse in Lausanne clearly showed how ubiquitous French Modernism with its roots in Impressionism was in Switzerland in the 1960s (fig. 2): of the 357 works from Swiss private collections on display, 300 were of French origin. It made sense therefore to repeat this show in a more concentrated form three years later in Paris.[5] In 1960, the Foundation E. G. Bührle Collection opened a museum in a residential district of Zurich that fitted in perfectly with the preference for French art that was then prevalent in Switzerland. The museum made an important

part of the works acquired by the arms manufacturer Emil Bührle between 1936 and his death in 1956 accessible to the public. With his collection, Bührle pursued his aim of providing an overview of French Impressionist and Post-Impressionist painting with examples from the leading representatives of this movement (fig. 3). Over time, Bührle also supplemented this key area with important collections of old masters and the Parisian avant-garde after 1900, thus giving Impressionism its place within the continuity of European art history. Bührle, who had emigrated from Germany to Switzerland in 1924 and built up one of the largest Swiss industrial groups in Oerlikon in Zurich, saw in the French Impressionist paintings a connection to his new home which granted him citizenship in 1937. Bührle had first seen Impressionist works as a student in Berlin before the First World War, works which the director of the Nationalgalerie, Hugo von Tschudi, had bought in the face of much opposition, and he now realised that the love for this art was also widespread in Switzerland. As a member of the board of the Zürcher Kunstgesellschaft, Bührle made a major contribution to the development of the Kunsthaus Zürich museum to which he donated an exhibition hall. He twice gifted works of art that he saw in connection with the donated building: in 1949, when he bought a cast of Rodin's *Gates of Hell* for the Kunsthaus, and in 1952, when he acquired two *Water Lilies* by Claude Monet, thus becoming the second buyer ever to show an interest in the "decorations" that had been stored unnoticed in Giverny since the artist's death.[6] The close links between Bührle's collection and the acquisition policy of the Kunsthaus Zürich became apparent in 1955, when the Kunsthaus managed to buy the large-format painting *Rochefort's Escape* by Édouard Manet.
During the first phase of his collection, because of the Second World War, Emil Bührle bought almost exclusively from the Swiss art trade. It was only

1. Claude Monet, *Water Lily Pond* (*Bassin aux nymphéas*), 1917–20, Fondation Beyeler, Riehen/Basel

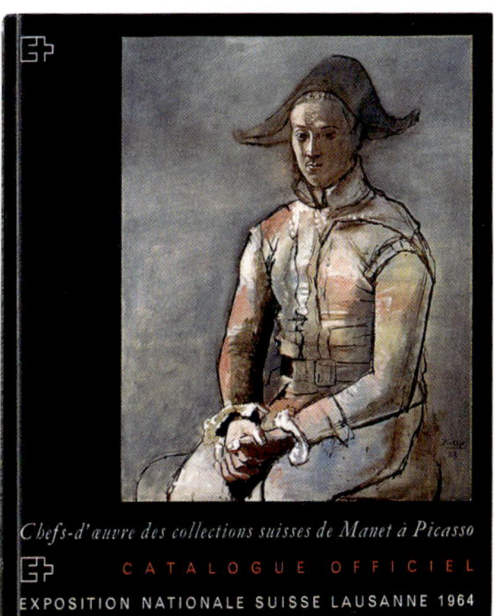

2. Catalogue of the Exposition nationale suisse de Lausanne, 1964

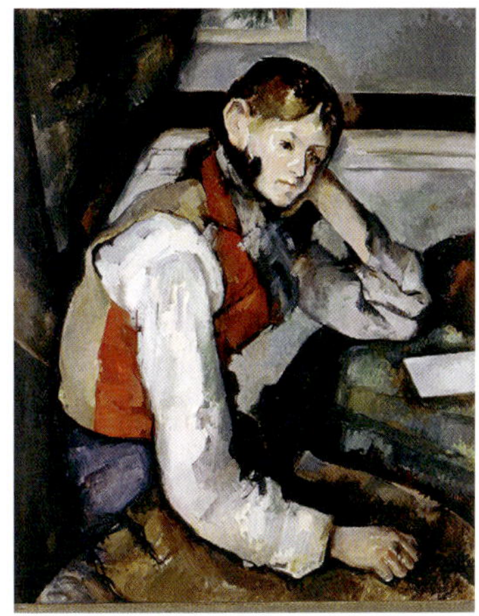

3. Paul Cézanne, *Boy in a Red Vest* (*Le Garçon au gilet rouge*), 1888–90, Emil Bührle Collection, permanent loan at Kunsthaus Zürich

during the second phase that he became a driving force in the transatlantic art market, acquiring over 400 works from dealers in Paris, London and New York between 1951 and 1956. When, in October 1941, during a business trip to occupied Paris, Bührle visited the Galerie Wildenstein, then run by Roger Dequoy, and acquired five paintings there, he followed an initiative taken by Charles Montag who, immediately before war broke out, had tried to introduce Georges Wildenstein to Bührle in Zurich. Originally from Winterthur, Montag had settled in Paris just after the turn of the century and had gone from painter to art dealer there.[7]

The Interwar Years: French Impressionism Shaping Identities

In 1938, Montag had made an appearance as the organiser of an exhibition that also highlighted his own achievements of the previous thirty years. In the Galerie Wildenstein, masterpieces of nineteenth-century French painting from Swiss collections were presented to the Parisian public, and most of the loans came from the circle of collectors advised by Montag. The best represented artists were Paul Cézanne and Auguste Renoir. This reflected the widespread view of Impressionism at the time which regarded Renoir as the conservative and Cézanne as the revolutionary, a judgment first made by the German art critic Julius Meier-Graefe. Impressionist landscape painting somewhat faded into the background, while many examples of its predecessors Camille Corot, Eugène Delacroix and Gustave Courbet could be seen. In the catalogue, Hedy Hahnloser, the wife of the Winterthur ophthalmologist Arthur Hahnloser described the Impressionist works she had bought with her husband and brother-in-law Emil Hahnloser to give an art-historical context to the many Nabis paintings in her collection.[8]

Three important Swiss collections were missing in Paris: those of Rudolf Staechelin and Karl Im Obersteg in Basel and that of Oskar Reinhart in Winterthur. Staechelin did not belong to the circle of Montag's collectors any more than Karl Im Obersteg did.[9] Oskar Reinhart was missing because he did not lend paintings as a matter of principle. Since 1924, Reinhart, whose family run a large import company in Winterthur, had devoted himself entirely to building up an art collection for which he had a magnificent gallery built beside his villa "Am Römerholz" (fig. 4).[10] There he demonstrated that nineteenth-century French art could hold its own against the old masters of European art history. In Reinhart's collection, therefore, Corot, Delacroix and Courbet were given a prominent place as forerunners, while Impressionism itself was mainly represented with works by Cézanne and Renoir. In addition, paintings by Rubens, Poussin, Lorrain, Chardin and oth-

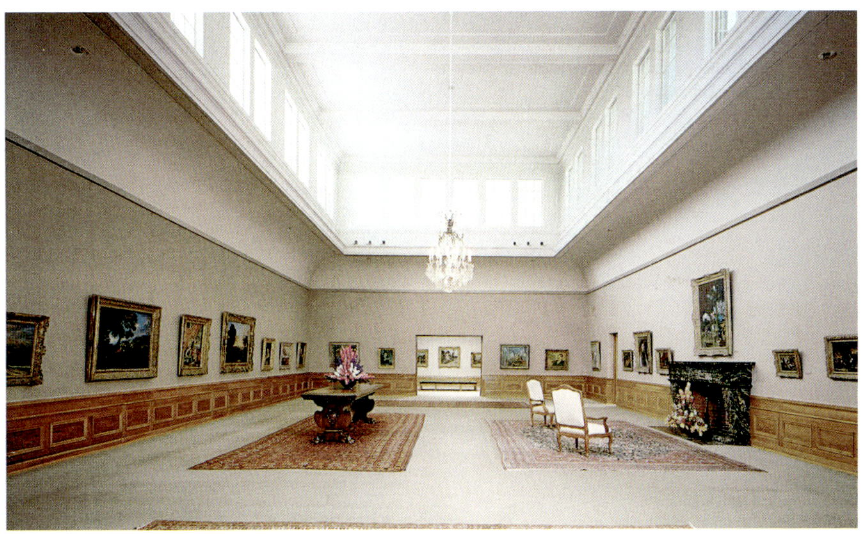

4. Oskar Reinhart Collection, "Am Römerholz" gallery, Winterthur, c. 1990

ers offered a view of the relationship between old and new masters. Oskar Reinhart left his villa "Am Römerholz" and its art collection to the Swiss Confederation which opened the house and gallery to the public as a museum in 1970. Together with the Emil Bührle Collection, which has been deposited as a long-term loan at the Kunsthaus Zürich since autumn 2021, and the Fondation Beyeler, the Reinhart Collection is part of the group of three major private twentieth-century Swiss art collections, each created a generation apart, all of which – with shifts in emphasis specific to the generation – have their roots in French art of the previous century.

The completely undisputed supremacy of French painting in Switzerland in the interwar years also influenced domestic artistic creation. The death of Ferdinand Hodler in 1918 allowed a new generation of Swiss painters to break away from its role model and explore different directions. Great hope rested on Alexandre Blanchet from Geneva who was inspired by Cézanne,[11] while Maurice Barraud gave Swiss painting a French flavour of Mediterranean serenity for decades to come (fig. 5). Galleries like that of Tony Aktuaryus in Zurich represented these artists and supplemented what they had to offer whenever the opportunity arose with works by French Impressionists. Typical of this juxtaposition was the collection built up from 1934 by the chemist Arthur Stoll who lived near Basel and on Lake Geneva.[12] Stoll's most extensively featured artist was Ferdinand Hodler. His collection also included artists from both German and French-speaking regions

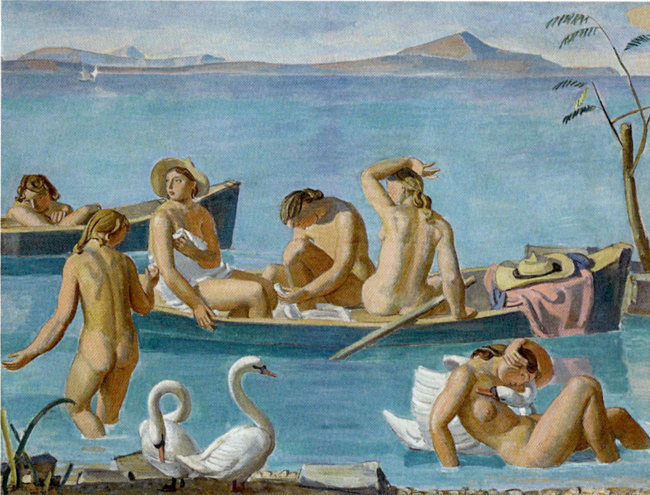

5. Maurice Barraud, *Bathers (Baigneuses)*, c. 1945, Kunstmuseum Solothurn, purchased in 1955

6. Barthélemy Menn, *View of Lake Geneva from Coinsins (Blick von Coinsins auf den Genfersee)*, after 1865, Kunst Museum Winterthur / Reinhart am Stadtgarten

of Switzerland and positioned them in the European tradition with landscapes from Camille Corot to Maurice Vlaminck. Thus, a historical tension lived on in Arthur Stoll's collection that had determined the reception of Swiss Impressionism from the very beginning: the contrast between the short-lived success that the "Swiss School" around Ferdinand Hodler had experienced in the Secessions of German-speaking countries in Europe until the First World War and the international reputation that French art gained at the same time and which proved to be more long-lasting.
An inspiration for Arthur Stoll's collection was Oskar Reinhart who, in 1927, shortly after the opening of his "Am Römerholz" gallery, had turned his attention towards a second collection. Initially it focused on nineteenth-century German and Swiss art and was regarded by the collector as a separate entity, which is why it was not shown in the "Am Römerholz" gallery, but in a converted schoolhouse provided by the local authorities in Winterthur. The nineteenth-century Swiss part of the collection consisted largely of painters from French-speaking Switzerland (fig. 6) and thus indirectly reflected the decisive turn towards nineteenth-century French art that Switzerland had made in the preceding years.[13]

The Turning Point of the First World War: French Impressionism Gains Ground in German-Speaking Switzerland

There were also political reasons for this. The German defeat in the First World War triggered a profound crisis for the culturally-oriented middle-class in the German-speaking part of the country since their tradi-

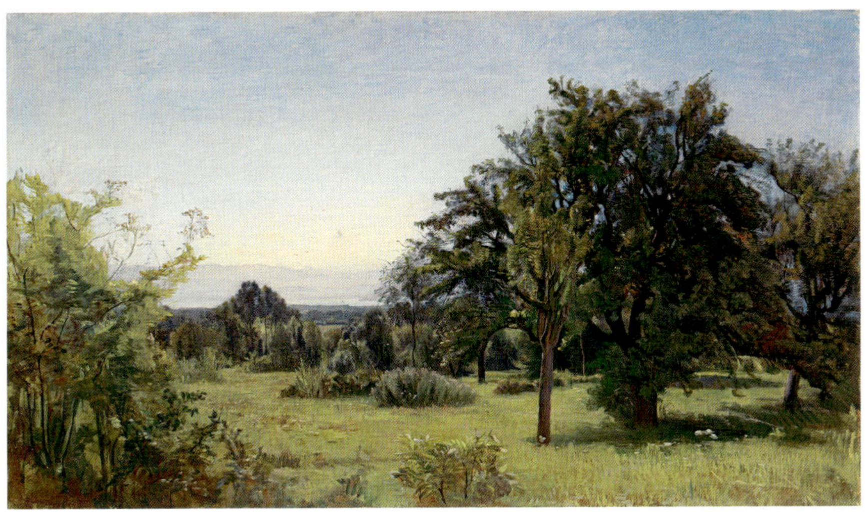

tional and natural identification with the cultural life of their large neighbour was suddenly no longer viable. A commitment to modern French art offered a way out. It was therefore no coincidence that there was a real boom in French art in German-speaking Switzerland even during the last years of the war. It was actively encouraged to some extent by French war propaganda which recognised that exhibitions with French Impressionist paintings resonated strongly in Switzerland. Charles Montag took on the role of "Ambassadeur de l'art français" and ensured that an overview of Impressionism and Post-Impressionism was shown at the Kunsthaus Zürich in 1917 featuring 362 paintings. The exhibits in the younger artists' section were selected by the board of the Paris Salon d'automne, while the works of the older artists – again focusing on Cézanne and Renoir – came from leading Parisian collectors and galleries such as Ambroise Vollard, Durand-Ruel and Bernheim-Jeune.[14] This gallery had been particularly attached to Switzerland ever since Paul Vallotton, the brother of the painter Félix Vallotton, opened a branch in Lausanne. Although the takeover of the Tanner art dealership in Zurich by Bernheim-Jeune ended soon afterwards, it also demonstrated how Switzerland was suddenly discovered by Paris as a very promising market during the war years.[15] Even the new Swiss ambassador to the United States, Hans Sulzer, sent to Washington in 1917, used French Impressionist paintings to show his host country that Switzerland shared the cultural values of the Entente. Works by Monet, Pissarro, Renoir and Sisley that were discreet loans from Galerie Durand-Ruel adorned the embassy of Switzerland that had a reputation in the United States – not entirely without cause – for being politically and economically firmly on the side of the German Empire.[16]

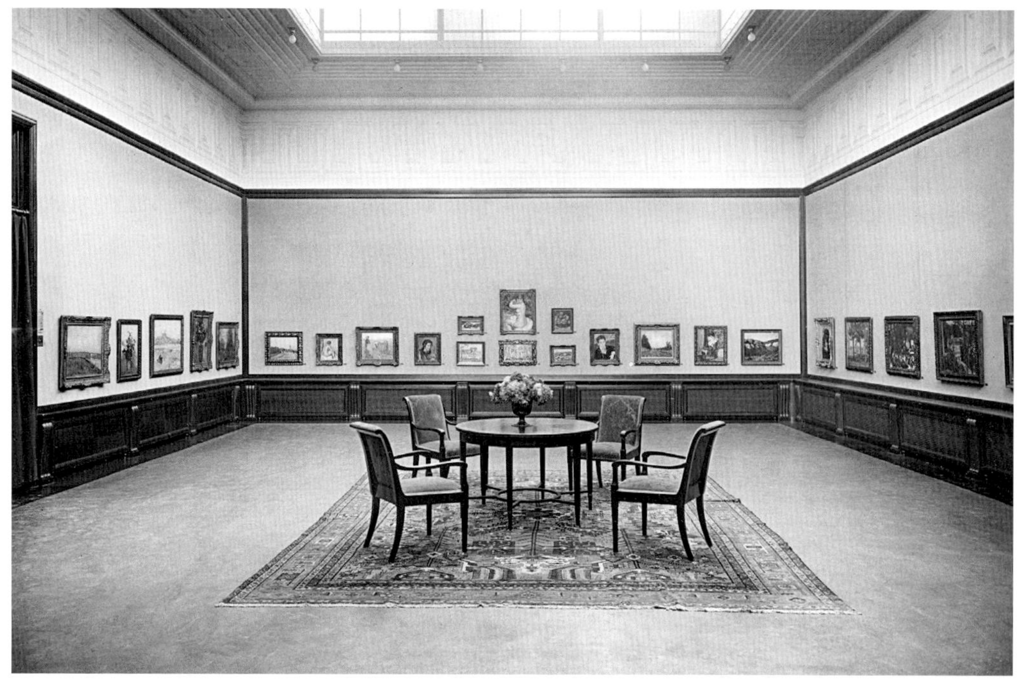

7. *Französische Malerei* (*French Painting*) exhibition at the Kunst Museum Winterthur, 1916

Hans Sulzer, co-owner and manager of the largest engineering works in Winterthur, was not an art collector himself. He owed his knowledge of modern French painting to his membership of the board of the Winterthur Kunstverein, and along the way he gained insight into the processes which made Winterthur the centre for promoting French art in Switzerland at that time. In 1916, a new art museum was inaugurated in the city, and its second show already indicated the direction that the museum would be taking in the coming decades. Supported by Charles Montag, who forged the link with the Parisian trade, the President of the Kunstverein, Richard Bühler, organised a comprehensive exhibition of modern French art which opened in the autumn of 1916 (fig. 7).[17] The art dealer Ambroise Vollard travelled from Paris to entertain the Winterthur public with a "causerie" and, at the end of the exhibition, Richard Bühler was able to transfer a considerable amount made from sales to the lenders. Thanks to its resounding success, the exhibition lived long in public memory as the occasion on which the reception of French Impressionism in Switzerland began. However, a quarter of the works on display in the Winterthur Museum already came from Swiss collections, most of which dated back to the time before the war.

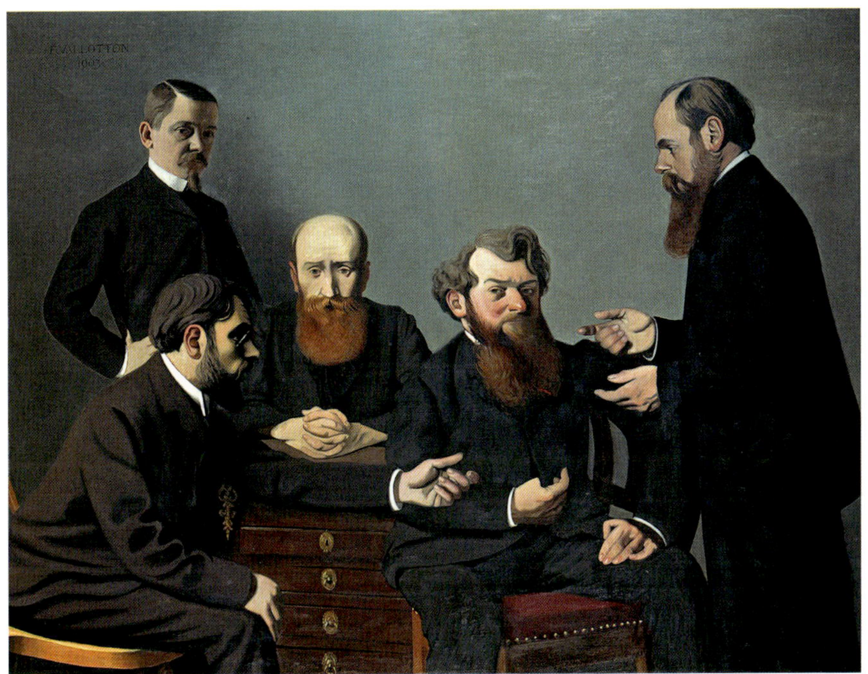

8. Félix Vallotton,
The Five Painters (The Nabis)
(*Les cinq peintres [Les Nabis]*), 1902–3,
Kunst Museum Winterthur

Before the First World War: Collections in Winterthur and the Zurich Exhibition of 1908

Richard Bühler's own collection was also part of it.[18] He owed his encounter with contemporary French art to his cousin Hedy, Arthur Hahnloser's wife. In Paris, through Charles Montag, they both met Félix Vallotton, for whose paintings they were constantly looking for buyers in Switzerland. At the same time, Bühler became acquainted with Pierre Bonnard and Édouard Vuillard who, like Vallotton, belonged to the Nabis group (fig. 8): younger painters who saw themselves as successors to the Impressionists, but who developed their own forms of expression.[19] While Arthur and Hedy Hahnloser extended their contacts on regular trips to Paris and convinced friends and family members – such as Richard Bühler – to buy paintings produced by the Nabis, Charles Montag accompanied other acquaintances from Winterthur on their first steps into the relevant art market in Paris. "Yesterday, we 'worked' at Durand-Ruel and Vollart [*sic*] and are well on the way to being brought to reason", wrote Georg Reinhart, Oskar Reinhart's older brother, to Charles Montag around 1910, and the house he built at

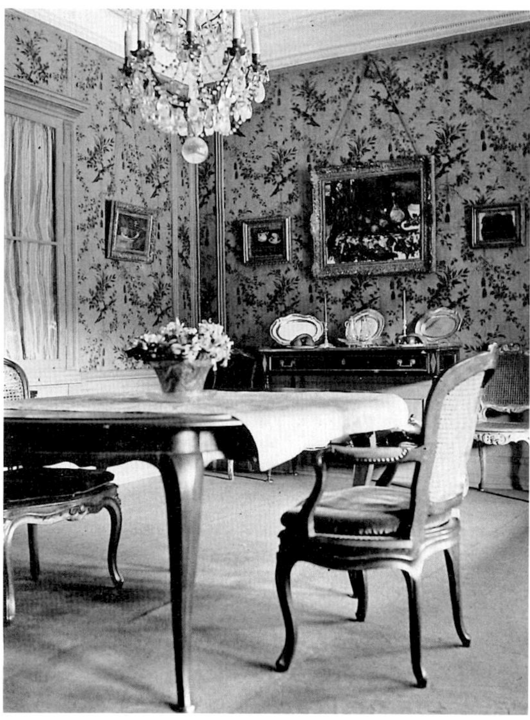

9. Paul Cézanne, *Peaches, Carafe and Figure* (*Pêches, carafe et personnage*), c. 1900, in the dining room at Villa "Langmatt", Baden, c. 1924

the time soon took in a group of important works by well-known Impressionists.[20] However, Georg Reinhart's example shows in particular how collectors in German-speaking Switzerland first encountered French Impressionism in Germany before their interest led them directly to Paris. In art magazines and on their travels, they witnessed how Impressionism gained a foothold in German museums after Hugo von Tschudi began showing the first paintings of the movement in the Nationalgalerie in Berlin from 1896. "Tschudi set a precedent for German gallery directors", Georg Reinhart wrote in 1911, upon his return from a trip to Germany. The following year, his brother Oskar saw the French Impressionist paintings of the "Tschudi donation" at the Neue Pinakothek in Munich, so named to honour the memory of the recently deceased museum director.[21]

Even before Reinhart, Montag had accompanied the industrialist Sidney Brown from Baden to the relevant galleries in Paris. Brown's wife Jenny was Hans Sulzer's sister, which is why the couple was closely associated with the Winterthur circle. Sidney and Jenny Brown had a large art gallery added to their Langmatt Villa after it had been completed in 1901, but at the time they tended to look more towards Munich than Paris. However, the large-format compositions by Munich Secession painters soon made room for other works. In November 1908, the Brown-Sulzer couple bought Paul Cézanne's *Peaches, Carafe and Figure* (*Pêches, carafe et personnage*) (fig. 9) from Ambroise Vollard in Paris, and in doing so brought the first French Impressionist painting to Switzerland. Others followed, not just up until the outbreak of the First World War, but also on regular trips to Paris made by the couple during the war.[22]

The fact that the time was ripe for a thorough examination of French Impressionism was demonstrated when, at the same time as the purchase of Cézanne's painting in Paris – but entirely unrelated to it – the first exhibition of the movement's painters took place at the Künstlerhaus Zürich (the predecessor of the Kunsthaus Zürich which opened shortly afterwards). The event was a novelty in that for the first time it selected contemporary art not from a national-geographical perspective, but for reasons to do with art history, and presented it to the public. While there had already been exhibitions of French art in the major cities of German-speaking Switzerland with a random selection determined by what the participating art dealers had to offer (although much less frequently than those of German art), the Zurich Impressionist exhibition was the result of a specific wish to show to the public an art movement that was seen as exemplary. In this case, too, the road to Paris initially passed through Germany. When the secretary of the Zürcher Kunstgesellschaft sought help from painter Ottilie Roederstein, who grew up in Zurich, lived in Frankfurt and had returned home from a longer stay in Paris with some paintings by French colleagues, she soon realised that an exhibition of her collection was not enough. She established contact with the German art dealer Wilhelm Uhde, who lived in Paris and who managed to gain the support of specialised Parisian galleries. This was not easy because Switzerland was not yet regarded as a place where interest in modern French art was to be expected. The Zurich exhibition did indeed not end up as a success in terms of sales, but it did attract a great deal of attention for the art on display. The art critic Julius Meier-Graefe travelled from Berlin to familiarise the Zurich public with the essential features of his *History of the Development of Modern Art*. The book had been published in 1904 and had identified French Impressionism as a turning point in the recent history of painting – the starting point for a modernism in the visual arts that broke with the historicism of the nineteenth century and only picked out things from the past that were related to Impressionism.[23]

This view of recent art history fell on even more fertile ground in Switzerland because there was far less art by the old masters than elsewhere in Europe. A decisive commitment to modernism thus characterised artistic life in the country for long periods of the twentieth century and went on to shape private and public collections, the art trade, art criticism, as well as university teaching. Camille Pissarro's landscape painting (fig. 10), which was acquired in 1912 at the request of some Basel artists from an exhibition

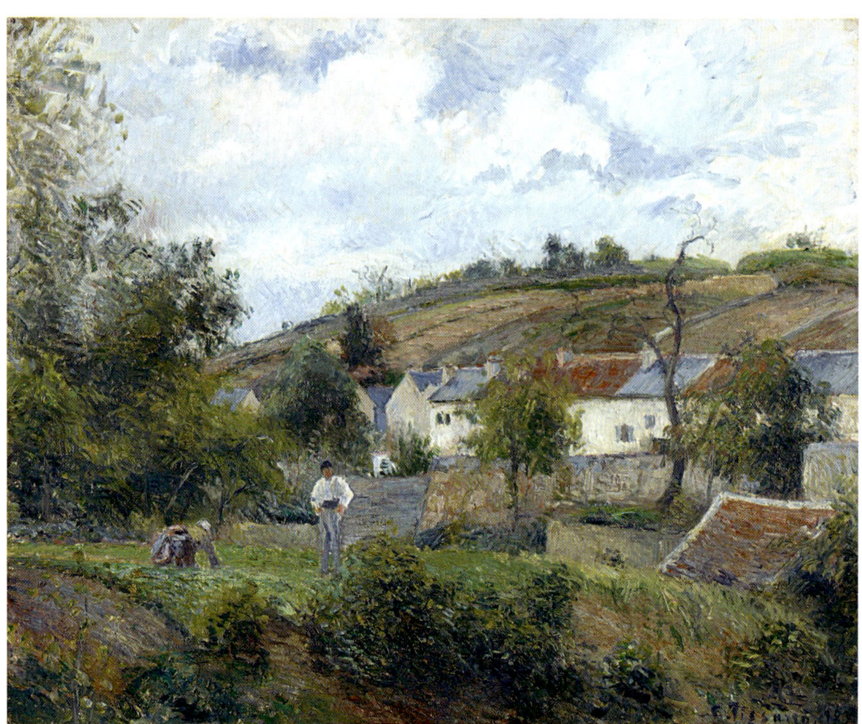

10. Camille Pissarro, *A Corner of the Hermitage, Pontoise* (*Un coin de l'Hermitage, Pontoise*), 1878, Kunstmuseum Basel, gift of a few amateurs acquired with the contribution of the Basel government, 1912

at the Kunsthalle für die Öffentliche Kunstsammlung Basel, became a small monument to remind us how the reception of Impressionism in Switzerland began. In a country whose museums did not systematically open up to recent art from abroad until forty years later, this early purchase was an act of huge symbolic significance – the start of an intensive and uninterrupted engagement with French Impressionism which has become part of Switzerland's own cultural identity.

1 Lukas Gloor, "A Historical Take on Modern Art Collections", in *The Emil Bührle Collection: History, Full Catalogue and 70 Masterpieces* (Munich–Zurich: Hirmer Verlag and Swiss Institute for Art Research, 2021), pp. 42–49.
2 For a complete list of exhibitions, see the websites of the three institutions, www.fondation-hermitage.ch, www.gianadda.ch and www.fondation.beyeler.ch
3 Franz Meyer, "Das 'Monet revival' der fünfziger Jahre" (The Monet Revival of the 1950s), in *Claude Monet: Nymphéas, impression, vision*, exhibition catalogue, Kunstmuseum Basel, 20 July – 19 October 1986 (Zurich: Schweizer Verlagshaus, 1986), pp. 145–55.
4 Gaston Diehl, *L'Extraordinaire Aventure de l'aube du XXe siècle: De l'impressionnisme à l'École de Paris* (Geneva: Petit Palais – Musée d'art moderne, 1988).
5 *Chefs-d'oeuvre des collections suisses de Manet à Picasso*, exhibition catalogue, Palais de Beaulieu, Lausanne, 1964 (Lausanne: Skira, 1964); *Chefs-d'oeuvre des collections suisses de Manet à Picasso*, exhibition catalogue, Orangerie des Tuileries, Paris, 1967 (Lausanne: Skira, 1967).
6 Lukas Gloor, "Emil Bührle and the Kunsthaus Zürich", in *The Emil Bührle Collection* cit., pp. 189–204.
7 *Carl Montag, Maler und Kunstvermittler (1880-1956)*, exhibition catalogue, Stiftung Langmatt Sidney et Jenny Brown, 17 June – 31 October 1992 (Baden: Buchdruckerei AG, 1992).
8 *La Peinture française du XIXe siècle en Suisse*, exhibition catalogue, Galerie Wildenstein, Paris–Zurich, May–July 1938 (Paris: La Gazette des beaux-arts, 1938).
9 Hans-Joachim Müller, *Nafea, Die Sammlung / La Collection Rudolf Staechelin, Basel / Bâle* (Basel: Wiese, 1990); *Von Rodin bis Tàpies: Werke der Sammlung Im Obersteg*, exhibition catalogue, Bündner Kunstmuseum Chur, 24 June – 17 September 2006 (Zurich: Scheidegger & Spiess, 2006).
10 Mariantonia Reinhard-Felice (ed.), *Sammlung Oskar Reinhart "Am Römerholz", Winterthur, Gesamtkatalog* (Basel: Schwabe, 2003).
11 Blanchet was supported by Oskar Reinhart, but also had international success. See Judith Zilczer, *"The Noble Buyer": John Quinn. Patron of the Avant-Garde* (Washington, D.C.: Smithsonian Inst. Press, 1978), p. 150.
12 *Sammlung Arthur Stoll, Skulpturen und Gemälde des 19. und 20. Jahrhunderts* (Zurich-Stuttgart: Swiss Institute for Art Research and Fretz & Wasmuth, 1961).
13 Lukas Gloor and Peter Wegmann (eds.), *Im Licht der Romandie: Oskar Reinhart als Sammler von Westschweizer Kunst*, exhibition catalogue, Museum Oskar Reinhart am Stadtgarten, Winterthur, 10 June – 28 October 2001 (Zurich–Ostfildern-Ruit: Swiss Institute for Art Research and Hatje Cantz, 2001). Oskar Reinhart later supplemented his collection with Swiss artists from the twentieth century.
14 Lukas Gloor, *Von Böcklin zu Cézanne: Die Rezeption des französischen Impressionismus in der deutschen Schweiz* (Bern: Peter Lang, 1986), pp. 217–25.
15 Paul-André Jaccard, "Le take-off du marché de l'art en Suisse romande durant la Première Guerre mondiale", *Traverse, Zeitschrift für Geschichte* 9, no. 1, 2002, pp. 81–104.
16 Friendly note from Alfred R. Sulzer, Hans Sulzer's grandson, who was able to determine the exact composition of the loan thanks to a request made to the Galerie Durand-Ruel. The author will publish the details in a forthcoming book on Hans and Lili Sulzer.
17 *Das gloriose Jahrzehnt: Französische Kunst 1910-1920 aus Winterthurer Besitz*, exhibition catalogue, Kunstmuseum Winterthur, 22 January – 1 April (Winterthur: Kunstmuseum Winterthur, 1991).
18 *Modernité – Renoir, Bonnard, Vallotton: Der Sammler Richard Bühler*, exhibition catalogue, Kunstmuseum Winterthur, 3 October 2020 – 21 February 2021 (Winterthur–Munich: Kunstmuseum Winterthur and Hirmer Verlag, 2020).
19 Margrit Hahnloser-Ingold, *La Collection Arthur et Hedy Hahnloser: Un regard partagé avec les artistes* (Lausanne: Bibliothèque des Arts, 2011).
20 Dieter Schwarz (ed.), *Die Sammlung Georg Reinhart*, exhibition catalogue, Kunstmuseum Winterthur, 24 May – 23 August 1998 (Winterthur: Kunstmuseum Winterthur, 1998), p. 5.
21 Gloor, *Von Böcklin zu Cézanne* cit., p. 148; Lukas Gloor, "Oskar Reinhart: Ein Sammler, zwei Museen", in *Im Licht der Romandie* cit., p. 38, fig. 1.
22 Eva-Maria Preiswerk (ed.), *Ein Haus fu□r die Impressionisten: Das Museum Langmatt, Stiftung Sidney und Jenny Brown, Baden, Gesamtkatalog* (Ostfildern-Ruit: Hatje Cantz, 2001); *Von München nach Paris: Die Sammlung Brown zwischen Sezession und Impressionismus*, exhibition catalogue, Stiftung Langmatt Sidney und Jenny Brown, Baden, 1998.
23 Gloor, *Von Böcklin zu Cézanne* cit., pp. 109–18.

CHAMPIONING IMPRESSIONISM IN THE AMERICAN MIDWEST: SARA TYSON HALLOWELL AND THE FORMATION OF THE BERTHA AND POTTER PALMER COLLECTION

CAROLYN KINDER CARR

Impressionism came to the East Coast of America in the early 1880s, nearly a decade after the first group exhibition in Paris of artists affiliated with this style. By then a few adventurous collectors, notably New Yorkers Erwin Davis, Henry O. and Louisine E. Havemeyer and Philadelphian Alexander Cassatt (the latter two advised by American expatriate artist Mary Cassatt) had purchased from French sources paintings by Édouard Manet, Edgar Degas, Claude Monet and Camille Pissarro. It made its first timid public appearance in Boston, Massachusetts in 1883, when the Durand-Ruel gallery included works by the Impressionists in a collection of French paintings sent to the American Exhibition of the Products, Arts and Manufactures of Foreign Nationals. No works were sold from that exhibition, and greater acceptance of Impressionism by an art-conscious audience living along the Atlantic seaboard had to wait until 1886. On 30 April of that year, the Durand-Ruel gallery, undaunted by its initial American venture, opened an exhibition of 289 paintings, pastels and watercolours in New York at the American Art Association. This exhibition, a version of which moved two weeks later to the National Academy of Design, featured more than 200 paintings by leading and lesser-known Impressionists. The relative commercial and critical success of this showing led Durand-Ruel to open a gallery in New York in 1887.[1]

Substantial physical distance and strong regional identities characterised America in the late nineteenth century, and Impressionism did not find a public audience in the Midwest until 1890, despite the efforts of the Durand-Ruel gallery in 1888 to expand its client base with a small exhibition of Barbizon and Impressionists paintings at the Thurber gallery in Chicago.[2] That year – 1890 – Sara Tyson Hallowell (1846–1924), who had gained a national reputation as curator of the art exhibitions at the Inter-State Industrial Expositions in Chicago during the 1880s, borrowed from the New York outpost of Durand-Ruel a collection of paintings that included six works by Claude Monet, four each by Camille Pissarro and Alfred Sisley, and three by Auguste Renoir.[3] Critical response, while not all favourable, was extensive, and Impressionism became part of the discourse in the Midwestern art world.[4]

A year before Hallowell became the first curator to publicly promote Impressionism in Midwest, her enthusiasm led her to encouraged Potter Palmer (1826–1902), a man who had made his fortune in Chicago as a merchant and real estate developer, and his wife, Bertha Honoré (1849–1918), to acquire works by the Impressionists for their personal collection.[5] In 1889, Hallowell was in Paris to select work for her forthcoming Inter-State Industrial Exposition and the Palmers, like most foreigners, were there to see the great Universal Exposition and to shop. After viewing the mammoth fair, the Palmers, with Hallowell as their cicerone, visited the studios of numerous artists and inspected the wares of various dealers. They came home with at least ten paintings and a selection of prints.[6] In this highly heterogeneous collection of art, which included paintings by several American expatriate artists, was a pastel by Edgar Degas, *Ballet Girls (On the Stage)* (*Danseuses en scène*) (1876–77), which they had acquired from the Durand-Ruel gallery.[7] Auguste Renoir also captured their fancy and shipped to them from abroad was *Madame Renoir in the Garden (Aline at the Gate)* (*Femme dans un jardin [Aline à la barrière]*) (1884, private collection).[8] With these two purchases, the Palmers became among the earliest American collectors of French Impressionism and the first in the Midwest to add this style of art to their collection.[9] With Hallowell's guidance during the following decade, the Palmers would build one of the great collection of Impressionism in America.

This fruitful collaboration had its roots in the decision by the Palmers in about 1886 to build a ninety-foot addition to their recently completed forty-two-room mansion at 1350 North Lake Shore Drive. This elegant addition to what was then the largest house in Chicago was to serve as both a ball room and an art gallery.[10] The unspoken but apparent goal of the Palmers was to assemble an art collection that would equal or surpass those being formed by their social peers.

The Palmers were not new to collecting art. On their six-month European honeymoon begun in August of 1870, they commissioned busts of themselves from the noted American sculptor Hiram Powers (1871). A large marble by Harriet Hosmer of *Zenobia in Chains* (*Zénobie enchaîné*) (1862, location unknown) dominated the main hall of their crenelated

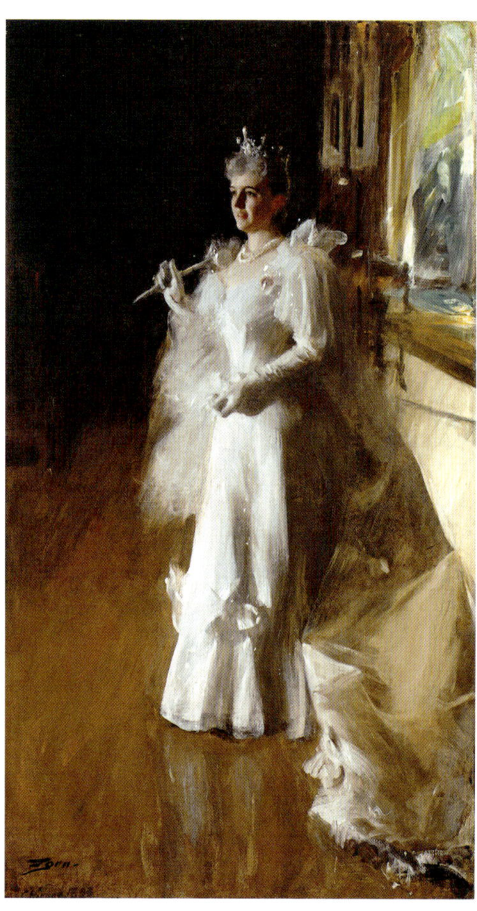

1. Anders Zorn, *Mrs Potter Palmer*, 1893, oil on canvas, 258 × 141.2 cm, Potter Palmer Collection, Art Institute of Chicago, 1922.450

2. Mary Fairchild, *Portrait of Mlle S. H. (Sara Tyson Hallowell)*, 1886, oil on canvas, 97.2 × 111.8 cm, Collection of Robinson College, Cambridge University, gift of Marion Hardy
Courtesy of ArtUK. Reproduced by kind permission of the Warden and Fellows of Robinson College

mansion.[11] In 1878 they loaned to the elite Calumet Club Thomas Buchanan Read's, *Sheridan's Ride* (1871, National Portrait Gallery, Washington, D.C.), a painting which reflected their political sympathies.[12]
In her day, Bertha Palmer was known as the "Queen of Chicago", a characterisation convincingly captured in her portrait by Anders Zorn, commissioned to celebrate her amazing administrative talent as President of the Board of Lady Managers at the 1893 World's Columbian Exhibition (fig. 1).[13] She was a woman with an acute sense of style and a perfectionist. As she contemplated the new addition to her home, she must have acknowledged that the art works that she and her husband possessed were inadequate for the space soon to be available to them. She may have suspected, too, that many of the paintings they owned were not up to the standards of those being collected by other wealthy Americans.[14]
Accustomed to having only the best, whether it be furniture from Herter Brothers in New York or dresses from Worth's in Paris, Bertha Palmer quickly realised that to create an important collection, she needed the advice of an

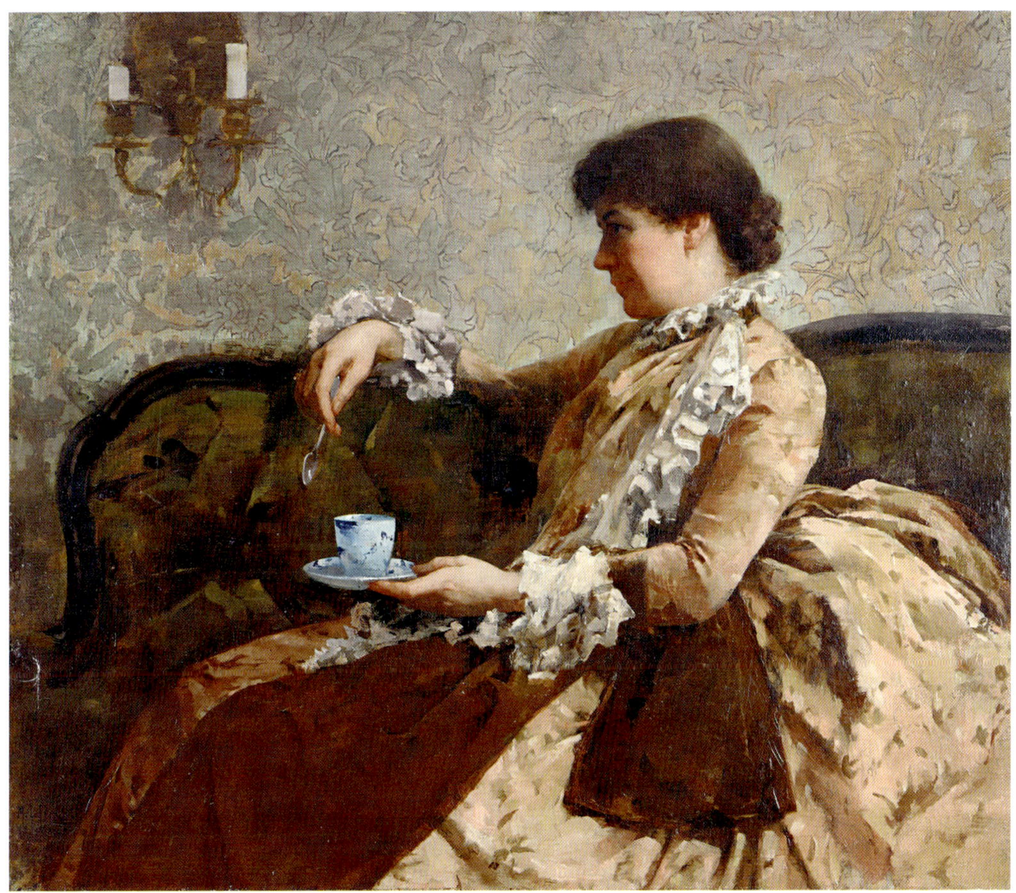

expert. Instinctively, she sought out Philadelphia-born Sara Tyson Hallowell, the curator of the critically acclaimed art exhibitions at the Inter-State Industrial Expositions. Not only had the Inter-State art exhibitions put Hallowell in touch with America's leading painters and its prominent collectors, but in the spring of 1887, the forty-year-old curator had just returned from a yearlong stay in Paris, a sabbatical that had given her recent contact with artists and dealers in this city, then the capital of the art world.

Why, one might ask, did Bertha Palmer turn to Hallowell? Why did she not choose a male advisor, as for instance, William T. and Henry Walters of Baltimore did, when they were forming their extensive collection?[15] Palmer not only admired Hallowell's eye for art, she also trusted her. Palmer and Hallowell were like two sides of the same coin, separated only by access to wealth. They were women of the same class. Although family circumstances led Hallowell to seek paid employment, she came from a distinguished Quaker family, whose ancestors traced their presence in America to the time of William Penn.[16] Both women were intelligent, organised and capable of managing large projects. Palmer would later describe Hallowell as "a woman of high birth and breeding", which is the image that Mary Fairchild (later MacMonnies) captured in her 1886 portrait of the popular curator (fig. 2).[17] Palmer also understood that Hallowell was a skilled professional. She knew that she was "a pioneer in a new field of work for a woman" and that "there was no man in America that has her experience in securing exhibitions and returning pictures from all parts of this country and Europe".[18] Hallowell would later tell sculptor Auguste Rodin that Bertha Palmer was "the Isabelle d'Este of my country. A woman with intelligence, taste, and fortune".[19] Beginning in 1887, the two soon formed a mutual admiration society, as well as a lifelong friendship.

Sara had a vision for the Palmer collection, which they embraced. She suggested that they create a collection of modern European and American art from 1860 to the present. Initially, she peppered their collections with paintings by Barbizon artists, such as Camille Corot, Narcisse Virgilio Díaz de la Peña and Charles-François Daubigny, and the Naturalists, among them Jules Bastien-Lepage, Pasqual-Adolphe-Jean Dagnan-Bouveret, and Jean-Francois Raffaëlli.[20] She also encouraged the Palmers to buy *The Sacred Grove, Beloved of the Arts and the Muses* (*Bois sacré, cher aux arts et aux muses*) (1884–89) by the great muralist Pierre Cécile Puvis de Chavannes. Only one artist led the Palmers to stray from this concept. From time to time, neither they nor Sara could pass up the opportunity to add a work by Eugène Delacroix, and paintings such as *The Combat of the Giaour and Hassan* (*Combat du Giaour et du Pacha*) (1826) became part of their growing assemblage of modern art. It was as if today an advisor told his client to collect nothing before the year 2000, unless, of course, a great Jackson Pollock came on the market.

The Palmers' American acquisitions would include equally great names. Among their American selections were at least six paintings by George Inness, five works by William Merritt Chase, and two paintings and a drawing by James McNeill Whistler. Representations of Dutch peasant life by American expatriates Gari Melchers, George Hitchcock and Walter MacEwen graced their walls as well.

Neither Hallowell nor the Palmer had considered adding Impressionism to their growing collection of modern art until 1889. Surprisingly, after their initial burst of interest, evidenced by their purchase of *Ballet Girls* (*Danseuses [Sur la scène]*) by Degas and Renoir's *Madame Renoir in the Garden* (*Femme dans un jardin*), the Palmers acquired no additional paintings by the French Impressionists until late spring of 1891 when they and Hallowell were together again in Paris. If their earlier commitment to this style of art had been tentative, work by the Impressionists now recaptured their imagination and made a substantial dent in their pocket book.

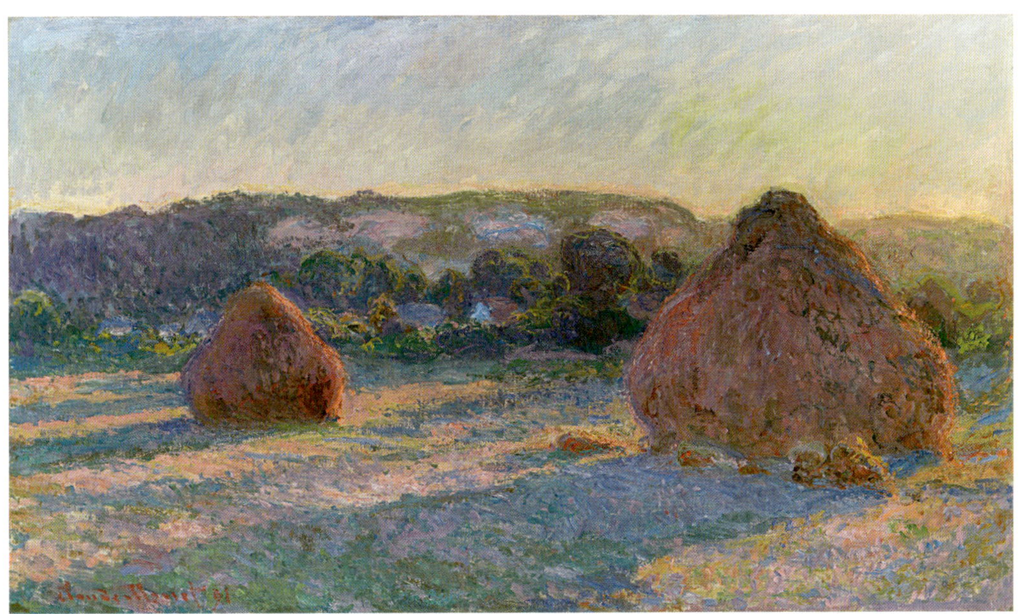

3. Claude Monet, *Stacks of Wheat (Sunset, Snow Effect)* (*Meules, effet de neige, soleil couchant*), 1891, oil on canvas, 60 × 100.5 cm, gift of Arthur M. Wood, Sr., in memory of Pauline Palmer Wood, Art Institute of Chicago

In May of 1891 Bertha Palmer, now President of the Board of Lady Managers, was in Europe seeking international support for women's activities at the forthcoming World's Columbian Exposition. Hallowell had returned to Paris the previous month to seek solace among her numerous friends in this European art capital, when it became apparent that she would be denied the prestigious position of chief of the Department of Fine Arts at the 1893 Chicago fair, despite her experience and wide-spread support, simply because she was a female. Being a woman was, as one newspaper reported "an insuperable objection".[21] When not in an official meeting, Bertha turned her attention to augmenting her picture gallery in time for the opening of the 1893 fair. She was well aware that this international exposition would bring a substantial number of important visitors to Chicago and to their home.

At the Durand-Ruel gallery the Palmers and Hallowell greatly admired the Claude Monet show, which opened on 4 May 1891. Their enthusiasm led the Chicago couple to purchase at least seven paintings by Monet from

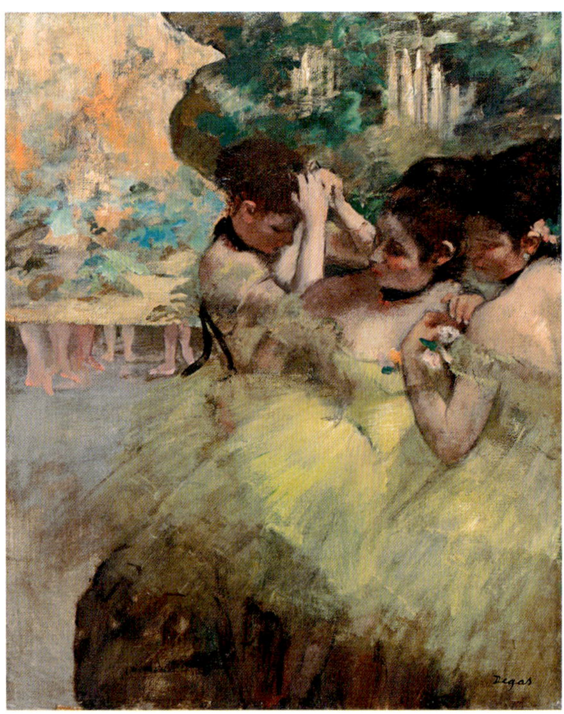

4. Edgar Degas, *Yellow Dancers (In the Wings)* (*Danseuses jaunes [dans les coulisses]*), 1874–76, oil on canvas, 73.5 × 59.5 cm, Art Institute of Chicago, gift of Mr and Mrs Gordon Palmer, Mrs Bertha P. Thorne, Mr and Mrs Arthur M. Wood, and Mrs Rose M. Palmer

the gallery before they left France in mid-June of 1891. Their choices ranged from the charm-filled *Artist's House at Argenteuil* (*Maison de l'artiste à Argenteuil*) (1873) to the sun-infused landscape, *The Willows* (*Les Saules*) (1880, National Gallery of Art), to the more emotionally turbulent *Petite Creuse River* (*La Petite Creuse*) (1889). *Stacks of Wheat, End of Day, Autumn* (*Deux meules, déclin du jour, automne*) (1890–91) was one of two grainstack, haystack or stacks of wheat paintings – the terms are used interchangeably – they acquired from Monet's most recent series. They had seen *Stacks of Wheat, End of Summer* (*Meules de foin, fin d'été*) (1890) in his Paris show, but it had been initially purchased by Charles Fairchild of Boston (fig. 3). When he returned it to Durand-Ruel's satellite gallery in New York in August of 1891, they became its proud owner.[22] Durand-Ruel was not the only dealer to benefit from the Palmers revitalised pleasure in art by the Impressionists. The Knoedler gallery sold the Palmers Monet's great Mediterranean landscape *Bordighera* (1884), which they saw in Paris but did not pay for until it arrived at their New York gallery in September.[23] Similarly, they saw Edgar Degas's *Yellow Dancers (In the Wings)* (*Danseuses jaunes [dans les coulisses]*) (1874–76) (fig. 4) in Paris at Goupil & Cie, but only finalised the purchase in September with the gallery's New York affiliate, the Boussod, Valadon & Cie.[24]

The acquisitions of paintings by the Impressionists that the Palmers made in the spring and summer of 1891 were merely a warm up for 1892. In the first three months of the year, the Durand-Ruel and the Knoedler galleries did a brisk business with this Chicago couple. In February and March, the Durand-Ruel gallery sent from France directly to the Palmers, three recent paintings of poplars by Claude Monet, of which *Row of Poplars on the Banks of the Epte, Cloudy Day* (*Peupliers au bord de l'Epte, temps couvert*) (1891, Ise Cultural Foundation, Tokyo) was one of the two they kept. The New York branch of Durand-Ruel then added six paintings by Monet to their collection, among them *Stacks of Wheat (Sunset, Snow Effect)* (*Meules, effet de neige, soleil couchant*) (1890–91) (fig. 3) and *Path on the Island Saint Martin, Vétheuil* (*Sentier sur l'île Saint-Martin, Vétheuil*) (1881, Philadelphia Museum of Art) (fig. 5). This buying spree from Durand-Ruel saw their first acquisition of a painting by Camille Pissarro, when they paid 750 dollars for his *Woman and Child at the Well* (*Femme et enfant au puits*) (1882). Just before they left for Europe on April 8, the Palmers acquired two additional paintings by Auguste Renoir, *Boatman's Luncheon* (*Le Déjeuner des rameurs*) (1875), for which they paid 1,100 dollars, and *Near the Lake* (*Près du lac*) (1879–80) for 900 dollars. New also to their collection were two paintings by Alfred Sisley, one of which was *View of Marly-le-Roi from Coeur-Volant* (*Vue de Marly-le-Roi depuis Coeur-Volant*) (1876, The Metropolitan Museum of Art).

The Knoedler gallery in New York did an equally robust business with the Palmers. In their shipment to Chicago, in the winter months of 1892, were four more grainstack paintings by Claude Monet. It included *Grainstacks in the Sunlight, Midday* (*Meules au soleil, milieu du jour*) (1890, National Gallery of Australia), as well as *Haystack, Last Ray of the Sun* (*Meules, derniers rayons de soleil*) (1891, private collection). The latter, purchased on 7 March, was like a coda to *Haystacks* (*Meules*) (1891, private collection), a painting with a receding line of stacks of wheat, acquired on the same day from Durand-Ruel.[25] Thus in two years, the Palmers had purchased nine paintings from this important series, of which they would keep six. As Richard Brettell has pointed out, they (a pronoun which also must include Hallowell) were the first Americans to realise the importance of Monet's serial imagery.[26] Adding to this cache of paintings by Monet were three more sun-filled landscapes, including *Monte Carlo, View of Roquebrune* (*Monte-Carlo vu de Roquebrune*) (c. 1884, private collection), as well as Alfred Sisley's *Canal du Loing* (1885, private collection).[27]

What, one can ask, was Sara's role in these acquisitions, given that she was not physically present? Was Bertha the ideal pupil? Had she learned her lessons well and gained the confidence to make decisions on her own? A reading of the situation, based on the Durand-Ruel check list of sales to the Palmers and the digitation of the Knoedler and Goupil stock books by the Getty Research Institute, suggests that the collaboration continued, and that the spring 1892 purchases were either works Hallowell and the Palmers had seen previously in Europe, or works that Hallowell selected for the Palmers' approval, which the galleries then shipped to America.

On 9 April 1892, the Palmers set sail for Europe. Shortly after they arrived in Paris, their buying spree continued. This year Mrs Palmer's primary task on behalf of the Board of Lady Managers was to select the two artists for the major murals in the Women's Building. Hallowell recommended Mary Fairchild MacMonnies, the artist who painted her portrait in 1886, and Mary Cassatt. Mrs Palmer was happy to accept her advice.[28] With this decision behind them, the two women, with Mr Palmer in tow, turned their attention to completing the Palmers' picture gallery.

At Durand-Ruel, the trio was warmly welcomed, deservedly so. Beginning around 28 April and over the next several weeks, their enthusiasm for Claude Monet remained unabated. They acquired an additional five paintings by him, ranging in date from 1868 to the late 1880s. *The Manneporte near Étretat* (*La Manneporte près d'Étretat*) (1886, The Metropolitan Museum of Art), *On the Banks of the Seine, Bennecourt* (*Sur les bords de Seine, Bennecourt*) (1868) and *Still Life with Pheasants and Plovers* (*Faisans et pluviers, nature morte*) (1879, Minneapolis Museum of Art) were among their new possessions. The latter painting, like so many other works in the Palmer collection, had a distinguished history, for it was shown in the seventh Impressionist exhibition in 1882.[29] Striking here, and evident earlier as well, is the breadth of the Palmers' interest in a wide variety of subject matter and in paintings covering nearly a twenty-year period in the artist's career. In time, this noted French painter would become the artist most fully represented in their collection of nearly 300 works of art.

Among the works in the packing case from Durand-Ruel in the summer of 1892 were five paintings by Pissarro, ranging from the landscape *View of the Village of Osny* (*Vue sur le village d'Osny*) (1883, private collection) to the figurative composition *Young Peasant Woman having her Café au Lait* (*Jeune paysanne prenant son café*) (1881), as well as two paintings by Sisley, both of which were made in Moret, the historic town where he lived at the end of his life.[30] To this bounty they added a suite of colour etchings and a pastel, *Young Mother* (*Jeune mère*) (1888) by Mary Cassatt. The latter selections were undoubtedly abetted by Sara and Bertha's pleasure in their recent decision to select Cassatt as a muralist for the Woman's Building at the great fair. Renoir, too, captured the fancy of this three-some and seven paintings by this artist were shipped from Paris to Chicago, among them *Acrobats at the Cirque Fernando (Francis-*

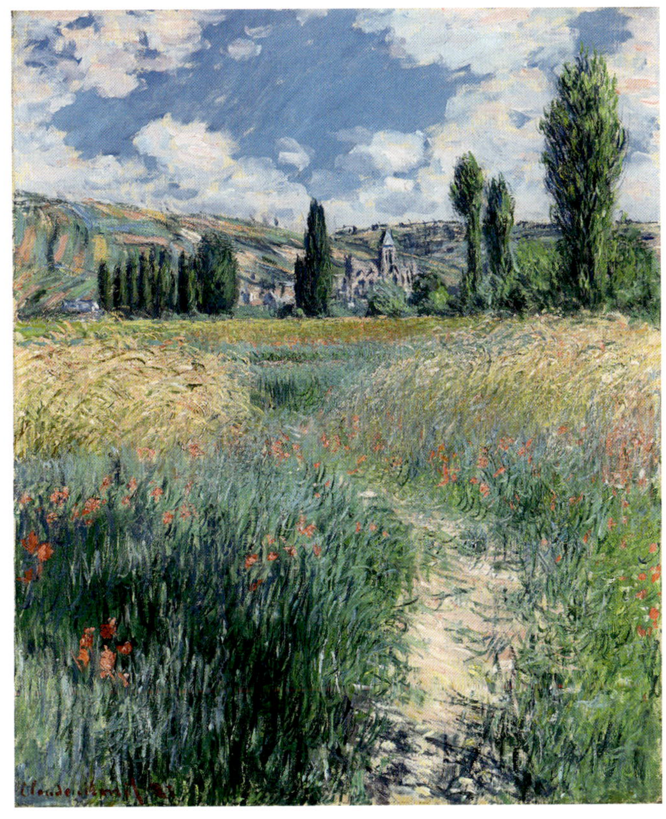

5. Claude Monet, *Path on the Island of Saint Martin, Vétheuil* (*Sentier sur l'île de Saint-Martin, Vétheuil*), 1881, oil on canvas, 73.7 × 59.7 cm, Philadelphia Museum of Art, gift of John C. Haas and Chara C. Haas, 2011

ca and Angelina Wartenberg) (*Acrobates au cirque Fernando [Francisca et Angelina Wartenberg]*) (1879), *Promenade* (1875–76, Frick Collection, New York), *Seated Bather* (*Baigneuse assise*) (1883–84; Fogg Museum, Cambridge, Massachusetts) and *Peonies* (*Pivoines*) (1880, Francine and Sterling Clark Art Institute, Williamstown, Massachusetts, fig. 6).

In early September of 1892 Sara Hallowell left France, after living there for nearly eighteen months. She had been invited back as an Assistant Chief in the Department of Fine Arts at the Columbian Exposition. Her job at the Chicago fair was to organise a loan collection of foreign masterpieces owned in the United States.[31] Sara sailed from Liverpool on 3 September aboard the *Aurania* and arrived in New York on 10 September 1892.[32] In her luggage were Mary MacMonnies's sketches for her Woman's Building mural, which Mrs Palmer had been eager to see; two still-life paintings by Paul Cézanne, *Milk Can and Apples* (*Pot de lait et pommes*) (1879–80, Museum of Modern Art, New York) and *Still Life with Milk Can, Carafe and Coffee Bowl* (*Les Fruits*) (1879, Hermitage Museum, St Petersburg) – the first paintings by this artist to grace the shores of America; and Alfred Sisley's *Street in Moret* (*Rue à Moret*) (1885–90).[33] Upon arrival Hallowell wrote the Palmers to say these works had escaped fumigation.[34] In 2020, nations were trying to stop the coronavirus; in 1892, the world sought to halt the cholera epidemic, then plaguing Europe.

The history of *Street in Moret* reinforces the notion that Hallowell, while abroad, was intimately involved in selecting pieces both seen and unseen for the Palmers' approval. Even in America she continued to be participate in this painting's ultimate acquisition; it was not until 16 November 1892, by which time Hallowell had returned to New York from Chicago to solicit loans for her forthcoming exhibition, that the Palmers finalised payment with the New York branch of Durand-Ruel.

Hallowell's role as a catalyst for the augmentation and refinement of the Palmer collection is underscored when one looks at the list of paintings returned and new works purchased by the Palmers in the last two months of 1892 and the early months of 1893. All these transactions occurred when it can be shown that Hallowell was on the East Coast and working in New York on behalf of her exhibition for the Chicago fair. On 16 and 22 November, Durand-Ruel booked four paintings by Claude Monet to the Palmers, among which was *Trees by the Sea at Antibes* (*Arbres au bord de la mer, Antibes*) (1888, private collection).[35] In December, at the request of Monet and presumably at the instigation of Sara prior to her departure from France, Durand-Ruel Paris sent four paintings by the artist to New York, which arrived on 21 December. This shipment included *Departure of the Boats, Étretat* (*Le Départ des bateaux, Étretat*) (1885), as well as *Church at Belle-Coeur* (*L'Église à Belle-Coeur*) (1881, private collection).[36] As part of this frantic push to complete their gallery, the Palmers also purchased two additional landscapes by Monet from Boussod, Valadon & Cie.

After the great fair ended the Palmers' purchases slowed considerably. It may be that they had a full house. Moreover, the need to entertain and impress visitors had diminished considerably. In March of 1894, after returning the art in her loan show, reinstalling the Palmer collection, visiting Philadelphia and selling her small art collection, including the two Cézanne's for which she had found no buyer, Hallowell returned to France, where she would live for the rest of her life. Upon her arrival, she must have seen the paintings by Pissarro that were in his March 1894 exhibition at Durand-Ruel and encouraged the Palmers to purchase additional works by him. In June, the New York branch sold them two works from this show, one of which was *Place du Havre* (1893). While abroad, the Palmers asked Hallowell to purchase a Manet from critic Théodore Duret and something by Bertha Morisot and the late Marie Batkirtcheff, but she had no luck with any of these acquisitions.[37] In 1896, the Palmers added to their collection Manet's *Races at Longchamp* (*Courses à Longchamp*) (1866), which they purchased from Durand-Ruel in New York. In

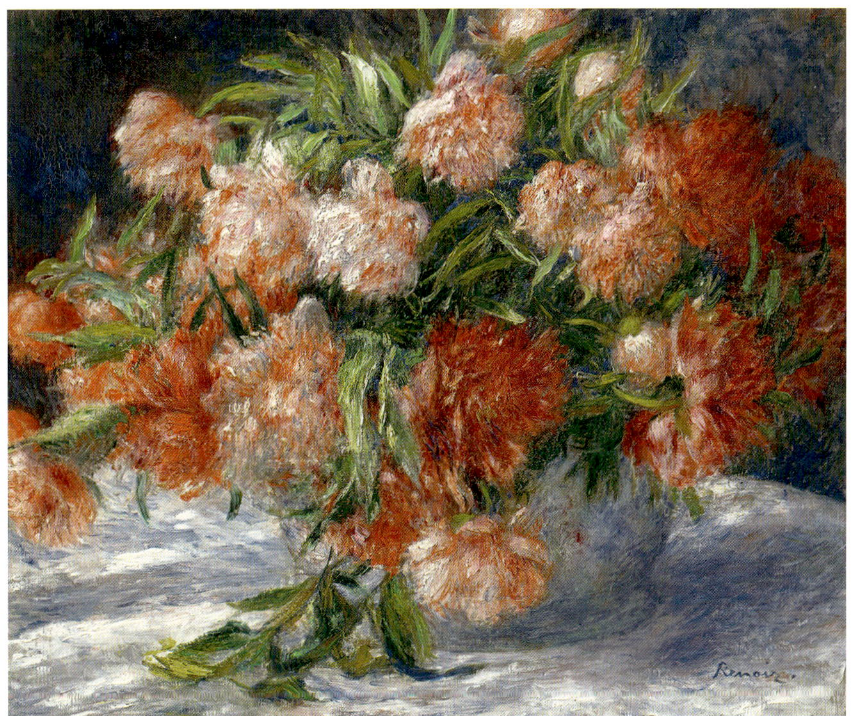

6. Pierre-Auguste Renoir, *Peonies* (*Pivoines*), c. 1880, oil on canvas, 55.3 × 65.7 cm, Sterling and Francine Clark Art Institute, Williamstown, Massachusetts, 1955.585

France in 1896, on their way to the coronation of Nicholas II as Czar, the Palmers acquired three pastels from Durand-Ruel, one of which was Degas's wonderful *The Morning Bath* (*Bain du matin*) (1887–90).

After what appears to be hiatus of several years, in 1901 and early 1902, the Palmers purchased several works by Claude Monet, perhaps impelled by a desire to replicate the psychological pleasure they had initially as they built their collection, or possibly to cash out the credit they had received from returning paintings. In 1901, they added Monet's *Rouen Cathedral, Morning Fog* (*La Cathédrale de Rouen, brouillard matinal*) (1894, Folkwang Museum, Essen), which Knoedler purchased at auction on their behalf. It may well have been one that Sara had seen in 1894, just as Monet was beginning the series.[38] In 1902, they added the second Rouen cathedral, *Rouen Cathedral Façade and Tour d'Albane (Morning Effect)* (*Cathédrale de Rouen, façade et tour d'Albane [effet du matin]*) (1894, Museum of Fine Arts, Boston), as well as Monet's *Morning on the*

Seine at Giverny (*Matin sur la Seine près de Giverny*) (1896, Museum of Fine Arts, Boston), paintings which demonstrate their appreciation for Monet's increasingly abstract style. In 1902, a second Manet, *Steamboat Leaving Boulogne* (*Bateau à vapeur quittant Boulogne*) (1887–1890), likewise became part of their collection.

Potter Palmer, twenty-three years older than his wife, died on 4 May 1902. Monet's *The Guibel Rock, Port-Domois* (*La Roche Guibel, Port-Domois*) (1886, private collection) appears to be the only Impressionist painting Mrs Palmer purchased after his death. She acquired it in March of 1903 from the sale of the collection of William Fuller, another American who was an early enthusiast of French Impressionism.[39] It clearly wasn't for lack of money that Mrs Palmer retreated from the art market. Moreover, in the late fall of 1902, she acquired a house in Paris. This could easily have sent her on a buying spree, but she appears to have furnished this home mainly with paintings sent from Chicago.[40]

I think this speaks to the role played by Potter Palmer. He was more than the legal buyer of record, the man who paid the bills; more than a man pleased that Hallowell's recommendations turned out to be good financial investments, he was their cheer leader. His enthusiasm and encouragement added to their pleasure when making acquisitions. With his death, an important psychological component of the process was missing.[41]

Hallowell and Bertha Palmer saw each other whenever Mrs Palmer was in France. Shortly after Palmer's death on 5 May 1918, sixteen years almost to the day after her husband's death, Hallowell wrote her cousin in Philadelphia, reminiscing about their friendship and noting that Bertha had thanked her for "turning her and Mr Palmer in the right direction in Art Matters".[42]

Bertha Palmer left a major portion of her collection to the Art Institute of Chicago and her heirs have added to her initial bequest. Her gift set the stage for the museum to become one of the great repositories of Impressionist painting in America. Vestiges of Hallowell's eye for art and the Palmers willingness to be turned in the right direction in terms of Art Matters can also be seen in other museum throughout America, as these institutions came to possess works that had belonged at one time to the Palmers and were returned to the marketplace, either by them, their heirs, or the Art Institute of Chicago.

1 Jennifer A. Thompson, "Durand-Ruel and America", in *Inventing Impressionism: Paul Durand-Ruel and the Modern Art Market*, edited by Sylvie Patry (London: National Gallery Company, 2015), 139–48.

2 "Art and Artists", *Daily Inter Ocean*, 20 May 1888: 14. The exhibition seemingly passed unnoticed, as neither the *Chicago Tribune* nor the *Daily Inter-Ocean*, the city's leading newspapers, provided an informative a discussion of the works on view.

3 Carolyn Kinder Carr, *Sara Tyson Hallowell: Pioneer Curator and Art Advisor in the Gilded Age* (Washington, D.C.: Smithsonian Institution Scholarly Press, 2019), 19–45, 53–67. *Catalogue of the Paintings Exhibited by the Inter-State Industrial Exposition of Chicago: Eighteenth Annual Exposition, Open from September 3d until October 18th, 1890* (Chicago: Rand McNally, 1890). 1890 was the last Inter-State Industrial art exhibition, as the glass-enclosed pavilion was torn down to make way for a building that would be ultimately become the home of the Art Institute of Chicago.

4 "Opening of the Exhibition", *Daily Inter Ocean*, 2 September 1890: 6; "The Fine Arts", *Chicago Tribune*, 12 September 1890: 38; "Pictures at the Exhibition", *Chicago Daily News*, 4 October 1890: 2; "Comments Upon Art", *Chicago Herald*, 26 October 1890: 27; "The Fine Arts", *Chicago Tribune*, 28 December 1890: 7; Harriet Monroe, "The Chicago Art Exhibition", *Art Amateur*, 23, no. 5 (October 1890): 84.

5 Biographical information on the Palmers is extensive. For Potter Palmer, see Donald L. Miller, *City of the Century: The Epic of Chicago and the Making of America* (New York: Simon and Schuster, 1996), 137–41 ff.; "Death of Potter Palmer", *New York Times*, 5 May 1902: 9; for Bertha Palmer, see Ishbel Ross, *Silhouette in Diamonds, The Life of Mrs. Potter Palmer* (New York: Harper, 1960).

6 Carr, *op. cit.*, 77–80.

7 Unless a location is designated, works of art mentioned in this essay are in the collection of the Art Institute of Chicago. The museum's website provides extensive documentation on these works.

8 François Daulte, *Auguste Renoir: Catalogue raisonné de l'œuvre peint* (Lausanne: Durand-Ruel, 1971), no. 464. Daulte provides a purchase date, but no source for the acquisition of this work.

9 Anne Distel, *Impressionism: The First Collectors* (New York: Abrams, 1990), 240–43.

10 The Palmer residence was designed by Cobb and Frost, architects. Photograph of the exterior and interior can be found in the Historic Architecture and Landscape Image Collection, Ryerson and Burnham Archives, The Art Institute of Chicago, digital files nos. 60409, 60400 and 60415.

11 Historic Architecture and Landscape Image Collection, *op. cit.*, digital files nos. 60384 and 60389. Hosmer's *Zenobia in Chains* was sold in 1942 (*Important Art Property, Notably Tapestries and Paintings, Bronzes, Marbles and Furniture, Formerly of the Bendix Foundation, Chicago*, 3 June 1942 (Chicago: Grant's Art Galleries, 1942), no. 14. The size listed, 66 inches, may include the base. Variants of this sculpture can be found at the Saint Louis Art Museum and at The Huntington. San Marino, California.

12 "The Calumet Club", *Daily Inter Ocean*, 19 October 1878: 8. In all likelihood, *Sheridan's Ride*, now in the National Portrait Gallery, Washington, D.C., belonged to the Palmers. It was given to the Smithsonian Institution by their nephew Ulysses S. Grant III (1881–1968).

13 "Queen of Chicago", *Daily Inter Ocean*, 19 May 1895: 14, is merely one example of the use of this term.

14 Edward Strahan [Earl Shinn], *Art Treasures of America: Being the Choicest Works of Art in Public and Private Collections of North America*, 3 vols. (Philadelphia: George Barrie, 1879).

15 William R. Johnston, *William and Henry Walters: The Reticent Collectors* (Baltimore: Johns Hopkins University Press, 1999).

16 Carr, *op. cit.*, 1–8.

17 Bertha H. Palmer to Chauncey Depew, January 1891, quoted in Jeanne Madeline Weimann, *The Fair Women* (Chicago: Academy, 1991), 184–85. Hallowell met Mary Fairchild, a young painter from St. Louis, Missouri, shortly after she arrived in Paris. The Fairchild's portrait of Hallowell was admitted to the 1886 Salon, much to the pleasure of both artist and sitter (Carr, *op. cit.*, 48–49).

18 Bertha H. Palmer to Chauncey Depew, Weimann, *op. cit.*, 184–85.

19 Sara T. Hallowell to Auguste Rodin, 26 December [1903], Musée Rodin, Paris.

20 Carr, *op. cit.*, 69–86. I have identified nearly 300 works in the Palmer collection from various sources. To develop this data base, I have relied on the archives and curatorial files of the Art Institute of Chicago, on Potter Palmer's account books in the Chicago History Museum, on newspaper and magazine reports, auction catalogues, exhibition catalogues, and catalogue raisonnés devoted to American and European painters, as well as provenance research conducted by museums that became the recipient of paintings acquired by the Palmer. Most recently the online publication by the Getty Research Institute of the stock books of the Knoedler and Goupil galleries has immeasurably expanded knowledge of the Palmer collecting history.

21 "World's Fair Anomalies", *New York Times*, 24 October 1890: 8. Carr, *op. cit.*, 87–100, provides an overview of Hallowell's failed campaign to become director of art at the 1893 World's Columbian Exposition.

22 This essay suggests the pace of the Palmers purchases of paintings, drawings, and prints by the Impressionists in the early 1890s and later, but it by no means enumerates all the works of art by the Impressionists which the Palmers acquired. The dates of the Palmers' purchases at the Durand-Ruel galleries in Paris and New York are listed in "Palmer Account, Durand-Ruel Gallery", Curatorial Archive, Art Institute of Chicago.

23 Getty Research Institute, Provenance Index, Dealer Stock Books, Knoedler Gallery Archive, Stock book 4, no. 6897. The information regarding Palmer purchases from the Knoedler Gallery, unless otherwise noted, is based on the data found in this online resource.

24 Getty Research Institute, Provenance Index, Dealer Stock Books, Goupil & Cie/Boussod, Valadon & Cie, Stock book 12, no. 21586. This is the source of information on Palmer purchases from these collaborating galleries, unless otherwise noted.

25 The "Palmer Account" does not record the initial sale of *Haystacks* on 7 March 1892 to the Palmers. Sotheby's (New York), *Impressionist & Modern Art Evening Sale*, no. 10067, 14 May 2019, lot 8 provides an updated provenance. *Haystacks, Last Ray of the Sun* most recently sold at Christie's (New York), *Impressionist & Modern Art Evening Sale*, no. 12145, 16 November 2016, lot 9B.

26 Richard R. Brettell, "Monet's Haystacks Reconsidered", *Art Institute of Chicago Museum Studies* 11, no. 1 (Autumn 1984): 4–21.

27 Daniel Wildenstein, *Monet*, 4 vols. (Köln: Taschen, Wildenstein Institute, 1996), 2, no. 892. Christie's (New York) *Impressionist and Modern Evening Sale Including Property from the John C. Whitehead Collection*, no. 3737, 14 May 2015, lot 18C provides a provenance for Sisley's *Canal du Loing*, but fails to note that the painting was owned by the Palmers before it was sold to Vincent H. Bendix (Grant's Art Galleries, *op. cit.*, no. 10).

28 Carr, *op. cit.*, 116–17; 171–75. The bibliography on these murals is extensive. For a recent analysis of their significance see, Wanda M. Corn, Charlene G. Garfinkle, and Annelise K. Madsen, *Women Building History: Public Art at the 1893 Columbian Exposition* (Berkeley: University of California Press, 2011), 113–14, 33–49, 167–78.

29 Charles S. Moffett (ed.), *The New Painting: Impressionism 1874-1886*, exhibition catalogue, National Gallery of Art, Washington, D.C.; The Fine Arts Museums of San Francisco (San Francisco: The Fine Arts Museums of San Francisco, 1986), p. 381. Wildenstein, *Monet* cit., vol. 2, no. 550.

30 Joachim Pissarro, Claire Durand-Ruel Snollaerts, Alexia de Buffévent, *Pissarro: Critical Catalogue of Paintings*, 3 vols. (Paris: Wildenstein Institute Publications, 2005), 2, no. 703. *View of the Village of Osny* most recently sold at Christie's (Paris), *Art Impressionniste et Moderne*, no. 5517, 21 May 2008, lot 50.

31 World's Columbian Exposition, *Official Catalogue. Part X. Department K. Fine Arts*. Edited by the Department of Publicity and Promotion. Chicago: W.B. Conkey, 1893.

32 S. T. Hallowell, *UK and Ireland Outward Passenger Lists, 1890–1960*, Ancestry. Com.

33 Carr, *op. cit.*, 128; John Rewald and Frances Weitzenhoffer, *Cézanne and America: Dealers, Collectors, Artists and Critics*

1891–1921 (Princeton, N.J.: Princeton University Press, 1989), pp. 11–13, 28; John Rewald, *The Paintings of Paul Cezanne: A Catalogue Raisonné*, 2 vols. (New York: Abrams, 1996), 1, nos. 426, 427.

34 Sara T. Hallowell to Bertha H. Palmer, 12 September 1892, Bertha H. Palmer Correspondence, Burnham Library, Art Institute of Chicago; Bertha H. Palmer to Sara T. Hallowell, 20 and 27 September, Board of Lady Manager Papers, Chicago History Museum.

35 Wildenstein, *op. cit.*, 3, no. 1188.

36 Wildenstein, *op. cit.*, 3, no. 989.

37 Sara T. Hallowell to Bertha H. Palmer, 9 August 1895; Theodore Duret to Sara T. Hallowell, 25 October 1895, Palmer Correspondence, *op. cit.*, Art Institute of Chicago.

38 Potter Palmer to Durand-Ruel, 21 January 1894, Archives Durand-Ruel © Durand-Ruel & Cie; Wildenstein, 3, no. 1352.

39 Wildenstein, *op. cit.*, 3, no. 1106.

40 Sara T. Hallowell to Thomas Morris Perot, Jr., 7 March 1919, Perot Family Papers, Historical Society of Pennsylvania.

41 As Anne Higonnet noted in the discussion of papers presented at the symposium, *Collecting Impressionism*, 10–13 November 2020: "The history of collecting reveals that only women who have a legal right to money can officially collect". As in the Palmer family, a married women may have instigated collecting activity, but she was legally not allowed to be the buyers of record. In the Durand-Ruel, Knoedler and Goupil/Boussod, Valadon & Cie records only Potter Palmer's name appears as a purchaser. This quaint tradition of ascribing a collection solely to a man when his wife may have been the driving force behind their acquisitions is often perpetuated in museum records.

42 Sara T. Hallowell to Thomas Morris Perot, Jr., 22 November 1921, Perot Family Papers, *op. cit.*

HOW DID HOLLYWOOD VIEW IMPRESSIONISM?

THÉO ESPARON

From the late nineteenth century on, New York and Chicago became the main centres of Impressionism in the United States thanks mainly to the work of Durand-Ruel. Art flooded into these two cities via the collections of personalities such as the Havemeyers in New York and the Potter Palmers in Chicago, followed by Adolph Lewisohn (New York), Chester Dale (New York) and Albert C. Barnes (Philadelphia). Their collections were eclectic and were not exclusively made up of Impressionist works: they perceived the movement as the awakening of modernism and juxtaposed Impressionist artists with others in order to trace their origins (Delacroix, Corot, Courbet) and track their descendants (Cézanne, Gauguin, Van Gogh). In the 1920s, collections like Adolphe Lewisohn's, for example, also boasted artists from the contemporary French schools such as Picasso, Modigliani, Derain, Rouault and Matisse. In 1922, the Potter Palmers donated part of their collection to the Art Institute of Chicago and in 1929, the Havemeyers followed suit by donating theirs to the Metropolitan Museum in New York. As René Brimo has pointed out, from this moment on "Impressionism, which was mocked in its early days, suddenly became 'museum art'".[1] This wave of "collectionism" did not hit the West Coast with the same force as in the East. In the 1930s, Los Angeles was no longer just a drop in the ocean and had already attracted an impressive community of rich film stars, but art collectors were rare. And so, throughout the 1940s, it was still often described as a cultural desert compared to San Francisco, where museums and galleries had begun showing modern French works as early as the late 1910s. Los Angeles and Hollywood seemed a world away from the source of French art whose strong artistic movements were already greatly appreciated by the Americans. This delay and distancing was partly linked to the history and even the geography of the city, but there were some celebrities keen to create large collections of works. The volume and quality of the works in their collections was no match however for the Havemeyers or the Lewisohns. Initially, the main barrier towards French Impressionism was partly due to the Californian "Impressionist" movement led by Guy Rose (1867–1925) who had visited Giverny, along with William Wendt (1865–1946), Edgar A. Payne (1883–1948) and Joseph Kleitsch (1882–1931). These "second lineage" painters broadly borrowed open-air methods, style, palette and brushwork from Monet or Renoir, and in the 1940s they all belonged to the "Society of Sanity in Art" which fought against modern and foreign art. In the 1920s and 1930s, the Los Angeles Museum, part of the Science Museum in Exhibition Park, still mainly exhibited local painters.

In 1923, an exhibition at the museum presented contemporary French art for the first time. Impressionism was included in the historical layout of the exhibition as a means of explaining French modernity which, according to the catalogue, was led by "Matisse, Picasso, Derain, Lhote, Laprade, Chabaud, Maillol". There were some Impressionist oils on show at the *Contemporary French Art* exhibition:[2] a Cézanne, Degas's dancers, a seascape by Monet, a study by Morisot, two works by Pissarro and two by Sisley. The best-represented artist was Renoir with seven works on show.

In 1926, William Preston Harrison travelled to France and stayed with André Lhote. He started an art collection which he then donated to the Los Angeles Museum in 1929, the same year that the Museum of Modern Art was inaugurated in New York and the Havemeyer collection was exhibited at the Metropolitan Museum. This major ensemble of modern works became a reference in Los Angeles and the central core of the museum's collection. Once again, Impressionism figured essentially as the starting point for more contemporary French painting, from Pointillism to Cubism, which was the real focus of the collection. Only two works on paper can be qualified as "Impressionist": *Woman in Blue* (*Une femme en bleu*) by Degas (1886, private collection) and a *Peasant Girl* (*Paysanne*) by Pissarro (LACMA, similar to the 1882 *Peasant Girls Seated on the Ground* [*Jeunes Paysannes assise sur le sol*] housed at the National Gallery of Art in New York [fig. 1]).

Like Hesperides, these two women in blue echo each other, one standing and the other sitting, one facing us and the other seen from behind. In the introduction to the beautiful catalogue published by the collector, André Lhote wrote that for William Preston Harrison the works on paper were the ones that truly revealed "the liveliest expression of this current effort to reject out-dated formulas".[3] Impressionism was the second group out of eleven in the exhibition which brought together "Pissarro, Guillaumin,

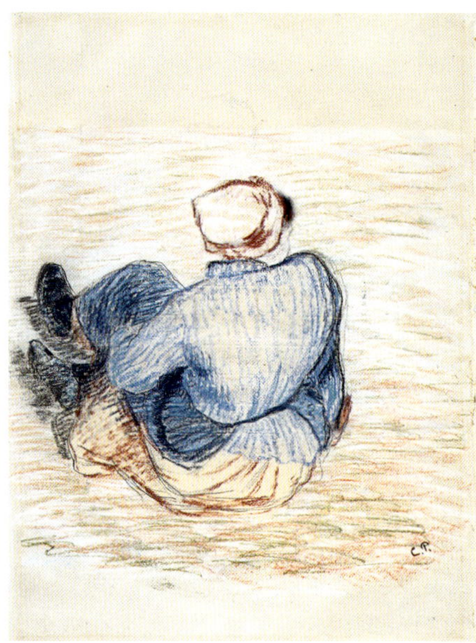

1. Camille Pissarro, *Peasant Girl Seated on the Ground* (*Paysanne assise*), c. 1882, drawing, pastel, 60 × 44.45 cm, LACMA, Los Angeles, Mr and Mrs William Preston Harrison Collection

2. Anonymous, *Edward G. Robinson with his collection*, promotional photograph for the film *Illegal*, c. 1955, The Kobal Collection: Dolfy/ Aurimages

Le Sidanier and Signac". This first permanent loan to the Los Angeles Museum was enriched with the addition of Aline Barnsdall's collection in 1937. Barnsdall was a wealthy heiress from Chicago and one of the founders of the bohemian art scene in Los Angeles. Her home, the Hollyhock House, was designed by Frank Lloyd Wright and served as a gallery for the California Art Club. Although she had an eclectic taste, Impressionism played a central role. Her collection boasted around a dozen paintings by Monet: according to the catalogue raisonné of the artist by Wildenstein,[4] she had acquired these works in the 1930s from Durand-Ruel, the long-standing art dealer of the Impressionists. Renoir was the other best-represented Impressionist artist in her collection. The group of five works came mostly from the sale of the artist's estate in the 1920s. They were late works such as the exceptionally luminous *Gabrielle in the Garden* (*Gabrielle au jardin*) from 1910 (private collection) and sketches like *Haystack* (*Les Meules*) from 1883 (location unknown) or *Sketch of Five Figures in a Landscape* (*Esquisse de cinq personnages dans un paysage*) dated 1893 (location unknown).[5]
At the same time Aline Barnsdall loaned her collection to the Los Angeles Museum, Edward G. Robinson had just returned from Europe with a very fine group of works. The famous actor from Mervyn LeRoy's *Little Cesar* (1931) was to become the most fervent and well-known art collector in Hollywood. Impressionism remained central to his collection[6] (fig. 2) which also included "Pre-Impressionist" works (Corot or Delacroix) and modern figurative painters: those who followed on from Impressionism (like Gauguin or Van Gogh), or who were contemporary with the actor himself

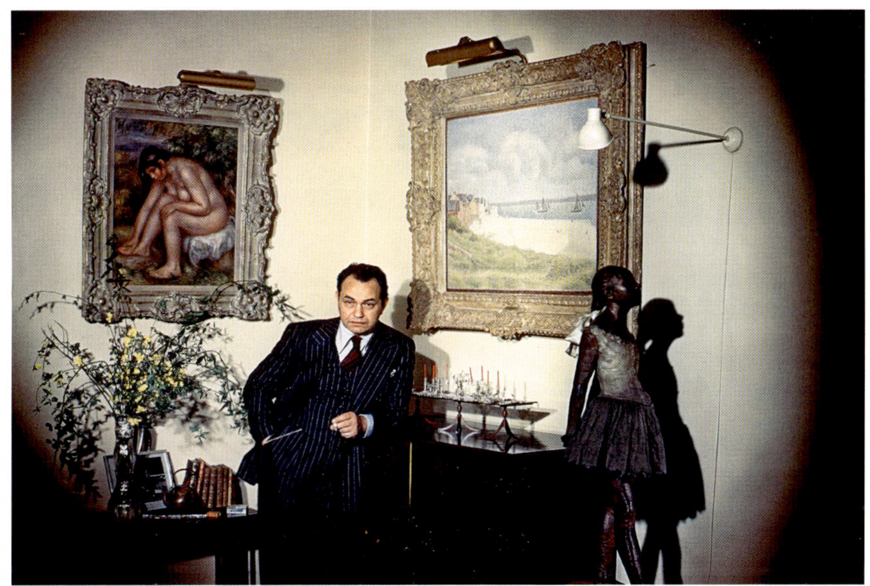

(like Grant Wood or Diego Rivera). And so, Impressionism was both central and a starting point. He began collecting in 1933, frequenting the New York galleries where he bought works by Renoir and Pissarro, two Impressionist artists who, along with Bonnard, remained the key artists in his collection. Robinson had seen Pissarro's *Boulevard des Italiens, Afternoon* (*Boulevard des Italiens, l'après-midi*) (1897, private collection) when he visited the Lewisohn collection and a certain number of works, like this one, had prestigious origins. In 1936, the star visited the Wildenstein Gallery in London and Paris and acquired a large part of what became his collection, including *Before the Theatre* (*Avant le théâtre*) by Berthe Morisot (1875, private collection) and *Italian Woman* (*L'Italienne*) by Jean-Baptiste Corot (around 1870, National Gallery, London). The works shown at Wildenstein's came from the Oscar Schmitz collection. The actor recalled:

> In its muted, severe, yet utterly sumptuous gallery the pictures of Oscar Schmitz shimmered and glowed in the light of the afternoon. Schmitz? Who was he and how did he come to these treasures? The catalogue says: ... a man who "can influence the artistic climate of a milieu, of a city, of a country". Was it possible with movies? No. Was this goal I had been seeking for despite autograph hunters and Warner Brothers? I still do not propose to answer the question because I have no answer. Schmitz had one. Not one. Sixty-two. Sixty-two Boudins, Daumier, Géricaults, Monets, Lautrecs, and Van Goghs – and every other now famous name.[7]

In 1933, the Wildenstein Gallery organised an exhibition at the Los Angeles Museum entitled *Five Centuries of European Painting*.[8] The nineteenth-century section comprised works by Corot, Manet, Monet, Renoir, Degas, Gauguin, Cézanne and Van Gogh and only the last two artists were illustrated in the catalogue with *The Black Marble Clock* (*La Pendule noire*) by Cézanne (1869–70, private collection) and *Portrait of Père Tanguy* (*Le Père Tanguy*) by Van Gogh (1887, private collection). Robinson, who had visited the exhibition at the time with Georges Gershwin, remembered it and in the late 1930s acquired these two paintings which were the pride of his collection. The actor was later known as something of a connoisseur in Hollywood and his Impressionist collection was frequently exhibited. In 1956 and 1957, it was shown across America for the last time, before the collection was split up following the actor's divorce. It was sold at Knoedler's and the best part bought by the billionaire Stavros Niárchos.
And so, it was not until the late 1930s and early 1940s that a real enthusiasm for French Impressionism manifested itself in Los Angeles. The new director of the Los Angeles Museum, Roland McKinney, enforced new policies based on the various local collections to present major exhibitions. In 1940, one of them retraced *The Development of Impressionism*[9] and was the prelude to an exhibition held the following year, *From Cezanne to Picasso*.[10] In 1941, Robinson's collection was part of the *Paintings of France since the French Revolution* travelling exhibition, with works on loan from museums but above all from a number of Parisian private collections. Finally, in 1943, thinking of settling in Hollywood, Erich Maria Remarque, author of *All Quiet on the Western Front*, lent his collection to the museum: it included a number of Cézannes as well as some beautiful paintings by Renoir and Degas. Personalities immigrating or travelling to America fuelled a taste for Impressionist art. Collectors wanted to create a community of art enthusiasts and, via the Los Angeles Museum, build an art centre for the promotion of modern art. This core grouped around a shared penchant for French painting and a fundamental taste, in the founding sense of the term, for Impressionism.
Works from Edward G. Robinson's collection (with its Pissarros), Willliam Preston Harrison's (for its works on paper) and Aline Barnsdall's (in particular *Gabrielle in the Garden*) were shown at *The Development of Impressionism* exhibition. But there were also works from other collectors. The Arensbergs, a famous couple of amateur modern art enthusiasts who had lived in Hollywood since 1921, lent a nude by Renoir (1817–18, Philadelphia Museum of Art). Stanley N. Barbee, the Coca-Cola mogul, lent a drawing by Manet and a work by Renoir (he sold a large part of his collection in 1944). Finally, George Gard De Sylva (known as Buddy De Sylva), the songwriter and Paramount director who worked in music-hall, lent works from

3. Claude Monet, *In the Woods at Giverny; Blanche Hoschedé at her Easel with Suzanne Reading* (*Dans le Marais de Giverny, Suzanne lisant et Blanche Hoschedé peignant*), 1887, oil on canvas, 91.44 × 97.79 cm, LACMA, Los Angeles, Mr. and Mrs. George Gard De Sylva Collection

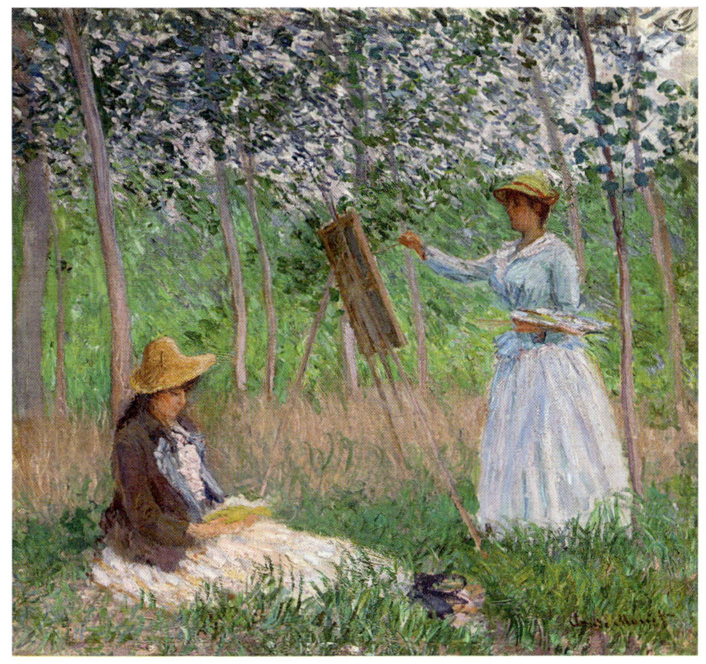

his small but dazzling collection of Impressionist painters. As *Life* magazine commented,[11] he started collecting in 1938 "using the same principles he employed in publishing and song writing" and his collection read like a gallery of number one hits. In 1946, the complete collection was put on show at the Los Angeles Museum[12] and William R. Valentiner, the museum's new director, negotiated a donation from De Sylva which included Degas's portrait of the Bellelli Sisters (1865–66, LACMA), *In the Woods at Giverny, Blanche Hoschedé at Her Easel with Suzanne Reading* (*Dans le Marais de Giverny, Suzanne lisant et Blanche Hoschedé peignant*) by Monet (1887, LACMA) (fig. 3) and *Place du Théâtre Français* by Pissarro (1898, LACMA). De Sylva had acquired two works from the Monet collection: *Woman in a Fur Coat* (*Femme à la fourrure*) by Manet (1879, today lost) and a bather by Renoir (1892, The Metropolitan Museum of Art, New York). The 1946 exhibition also included his own portrait, painted by Paul Clemens (1911–1992), a fashionable artist in Los Angeles who imitated Renoir's style.

After seeking exile in the United States in 1939, Erich Maria Remarquhe met a dealer named Sam Salz, who helped him with his future acquisitions.[13] Salz had remained in Los Angeles to find a new clientele and escape the New York scene, already occupied by Paul Rosenberg, Germain Seligman or Wildenstein. The galleries in Los Angeles invested in organising bigger exhibitions that reflected the taste for Impressionist works. It was not so much the historical movement itself that interested buyers but

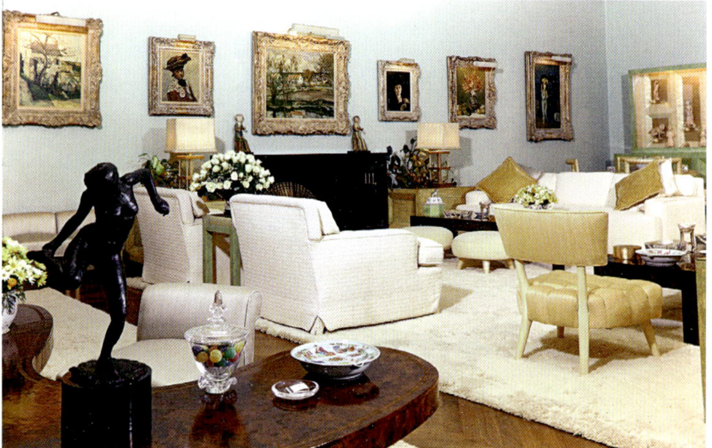

4. Interior of the Goetz house photographed by Eliot Elisofon, 1969

the prestigious names of the artists themselves. Earl Stendahl, the owner of one of the oldest galleries in Los Angeles, developed from showing works by local Impressionist painters to international, more modern even contemporary artists and sometimes acted as the distributor for some of the better-known art dealers such as Wildenstein. Dalzell-Hatfield moved back to Los Angeles in 1939 and specialised in "nineteenth-century French masters".[14] The gallery organised the first exhibition of Renoir's works in 1940 and a second one in 1943: Gabrielle, the painter's model who became Mrs. Conrad Slade, presented the collection of paintings and drawings that Renoir gave her. *Art Digest* reports: "As usual with Hatfield shows, the opening was attended by a large and brilliant group from Los Angeles' film and social circles. Among the guests were M. Jean Renoir, son of the artist and Hollywood motion picture director (who lent a painting of the Renoir Garden at Cagnes)".[15] The latter signs a moving foreword about his father in the exhibition catalog.[16] However, the presence of Jean Renoir in Hollywood from 1941 onwards does not seem to have been effective in spreading the recognition of his father and the growth of collections of his works.

In the middle of the 1940s, Edith Goetz, Samuel Goldwyn Mayer's daughter, and her film producer husband, William Goetz, established a large collection over a period of just four years.[17] They began by buying a Renoir in the early 1940s from Dalzell-Hatfield and it rapidly grew from 1946 on, mainly through the intermediary of Sam Salz, with works by Degas, Cézanne, Manet and Sisley. Impressionism was now a sound investment, more academic than modern. Collectors in the late 1940s preferred French modernism to the Impressionists (Braque, Rouault, Modigliani for example).[18] Around the time Robinson had commissioned Sam Marx to design his private art gallery, the Goetz were exhibiting their works on the colourful walls of their private home (fig. 4). The projection screen itself was located underneath the paintings. Whilst Robinson was looking to "influence the artistic climate of a milieu, of a city, of a country" and his Impressionist collection served a historical conception of art when it was shown, for the couple, collecting these works simply enabled them to luxuriously decorate their home and promote a form of social distinction. Edith Goetz was the sister of Irene Selznick, who was married to film producer David O. Selznick. Irene was supposedly more cultivated than Edith and the rivalry between the two sisters seems to have equally had an influence on their collections: they both bought similar bouquets painted by Renoir in 1889, one from Durand-Ruel, the other from Sam Salz. In 1956, Joshua Logan made a series of photographs of Marilyn Monroe against a backdrop of the works in the Goetz collection, hoping to find a resonance between the actress's face and poses and the works on show. So, is there a relationship, a parallel, between the works shown and motion pictures?

Edward G. Robinson was mainly known for his gangster roles but he also played a surprising number of art collectors in the movies. In fact, he embodied an art enthusiast in *The Woman in the Window* (1944), directed by Fritz Lang, and in *The Stranger* (1946) by Orson Welles. Although the artworks collected by the characters he played were different to those Robinson owned in reality, we can nevertheless see the collector's interest in his works. In both *The Woman in the Window* and *Laura* (1944) by Otto Preminger, figurative painting is used as a way of embodying the painted character through a form of diegesis: Joan Bennett's reflection in the window of an art gallery is cast onto a painting, the double and the embodiment. The painting highlighted refers more to the narrative it evokes than the painting itself, its materiality or style: there is just one step, one shot between the painted character and her extraordinary apparition. The works in the decor seem to mirror and reflect the narrative created by the film. *Scarlet Street* (1945), directed by the same Fritz Lang and starring once again Joan Bennett and Edward G. Robinson, is like the other side of the same coin: the main character in *The Woman in the Window* is an amateur, while *Scarlett Street* is the portrait of an artist who, on his own admission, loves Cézanne. In this adaptation of the novel *La Chienne* by Georges de La Fouchardière, already brought to the silver screen by Jean Renoir in 1931, Cross, an amateur painter and meek town cashier, falls in love with a woman who tricks him, signing his paintings, usurping both his identity and success, and forcing him to steal to provide for her. And so, the signature and the life of the painter are faked, distorted and romanticised. The focus of the story is nothing more than a lie, an object of fiction. Cross's works enabled a different narrative to

be told about the paintings and the painters. A few years before Robinson's collection was split up, part of it was used in Lewis Allen's film *Illegal* (1955), in which he plays a crooked lawyer. For the promotion of the film, the actor was photographed with his own paintings (fig. 2). There are very few actors who have played such similar roles between their persona and real life, taking on their real personality as a collector in their role as performers. *Laura*, *The Woman in the Window*, *Scarlett Street* and even *The Stranger*: all of these films "noirs" were produced by William Goetz presumably before he began collecting, at a key moment when he had left 20th Century Fox and created International Pictures, shortly before becoming president of Universal.
Another more formal parallel might be made between cinema and the phenomenon of collecting Impressionist works (in a broader sense, at least in terms of Van Gogh and Gauguin): the arrival of colour on our screens and the popularisation of Technicolor. The two moments were perfectly synchronous. Is this more than just a mere coincidence? Beyond the reconstructions of the Belle Époque and other later uses of a "multi-coloured" Technicolor, could this technology, its invention and diffusion, be linked to Impressionism? Not exactly, if we believe Nathalie Kalmus, Technicolor advisor on most of the films, who wrote in her 1935 manifesto "Color Consciousness":

> The principles of colour, tone, and composition make painting a fine art. The same principles will make a coloured motion picture a work of art. The precision and detail of Holbein and Bougereau [*sic*], the light effects of Rembrandt, the atmosphere and arrangements of Goya, the colour of Velasquez [*sic*], the brilliant sunlight of Sorolla, the mysterious shadows of Innes – all these artistic qualities can eventually be incorporated into motion pictures through the medium of colour. The design and colours of sets, costumes, drapes, and furnishings must be planned and selected just as an artist would choose the colours from his palette and apply them to the proper portions of his painting.[19]

The painters cited as the sources of inspiration in the article are rather traditional, even academic. According to Kalmus, Technicolor initially contented itself with "loud" or "clashing" colours. And so, in *The Trail of the Lonesome Pine* (1936), directed by Henry Hathaway, the first Technicolor film shot outdoors in the San Bernardino National Forest, is bursting with shades of greens, greys and browns. We could compare the autumnal hues of the Kentucky forests in the film to Pissarro's colour palette. And perhaps we can find the same dense greens used by Monet in, for instance, *Blanche and Suzanne*[20] (*Hoschedé Blanche et Suzanne Hoschedé*), a work

5. Vivien Leigh in *Gone with the Wind*, promotional photograph, 1939

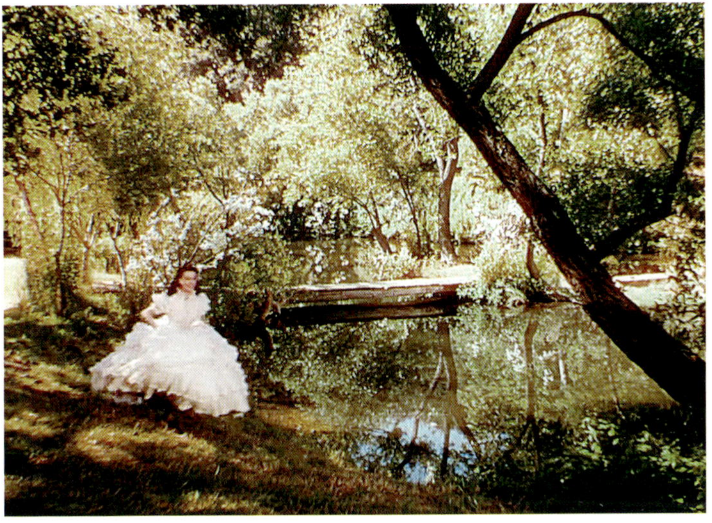

from the Georges Gard De Sylva collection (fig. 3), in the first scenes of Victor Fleming's *Gone with the Wind* (1939), produced by David O. Selznick, and in particular in the famous bucolic barbecue scene with the white gowns splayed out on the lawn (fig. 5). The more flamboyant reds and blacks throughout the rest of the film appear more Fauve than Impressionist. For his first colour film, *Meet Me in St. Louis* (1944), Vincente Minnelli progressively and surely moved closer to Renoir. The film is cut into seasonal chapters and, just like flicking through an album, each season begins with a photo that bursts into colour and literally comes to life. The film carefully echoes the changing tonalities of the seasons and, similarly to Impressionism, creates colourful atmospheres. In the indoor scenes, a deep reddish glow echoes the powdery pinks of the women's flesh, and the scene where the two sisters are playing the piano resonates with the *The Piano Lesson* (*Leçon de Piano*) (1892). One version of this famous painting was shown at *The Development of Impressionism* exhibition: the composition and the use of the colours seem to mirror the painter's style. Likewise, the film is reflected through Renoir's painting; a sculpture above the piano echoes the two sisters playing the piano. Minnelli was not a collector but a painter, boldly citing artworks throughout his films, seeking a certain picturality in the honest colour palette of French painting. Later films in the 1940s and 1950s, and notably musicals, continued referring to Impressionism, for example Degas in *A Star Is Born* by George Cukor in 1954. There were also other more general pictorial references to French art, for example Raoul Dufy in *An American in Paris*, directed by Minnelli in 1951.

In Minelli's 1953 film *The Band Wagon*, Fred Astaire plays a declining film star and art collector. In his hotel room, a Degas is placed next to a painting of

a bouquet of flowers by Odilon Redon, a Modigliani and a Miro. Just as Edward G. Robinson is filmed in a scene from *Illegal* a few years later, in front of a pastel from his collection by Degas, Tony Hunter's dance partner (Cyd Charisse) resonates with the *Dancers Practicing at the Barre* (*Danseuses à la barre*) by Degas, a well-known masterpiece from the Phillips collection (Washington, D.C.) acquired in 1944. Used in the musical, the painting takes on both a fictional and paradoxical authenticity: the work is clearly designated as the original even though it is obviously a copy, reproduced by the film. Although the actress reads the date of 1877 and deduces it to be "an early Degas" it is clearly one of the artist's later works. The painting in the decor has its own polluted story which marries with and echoes the real narrative. In *The Band Wagon*, it resonates with the differences between the dancers: she is a ballerina whilst he is a simple music hall dancer. Hollywood tastes, not unlike the colourful, popularist tastes, can be seen as the antithesis of the ballet and Broadway avant-garde with its romantic and symbolic style. However, these styles of shows and dance find themselves tied together in the work of Degas just as they are bound together in the musical itself. When talking about himself, Tony Hunter ironically said: "Don't be fooled. I don't know anything more about art than I do dance. I am just one of those Hollywood actors". Staging collections did not just allow characters to be categorised: the sets, the paintings, resonate directly with the films, the bodies of the characters and their stories.
Impressionism and Technicolor are outmoded tastes. They describe an out-dated, passé and fantasised story in colour. In contrast to film "noir" and black and white photographs in newspapers, the colours are not "realistic", in touch with the present. Technicolor films often make us think of postcards and other chromolithographs rather than Impressionist painting.[21] But to fully comprehend the Hollywood vision, it seems nevertheless essential to understand the history of the art collections, the tastes of the film directors, producers, scenarists and actors and look in parallel at how the films were produced, their techniques and forms. From the 1940s on, the number of collectors increased in Hollywood: Vincent Price, Charles Laughton, Greta Garbo or even George Cukor were just some of those who established small collections. Hollywood celebrities were definitively and more directly interested in painting than we may initially have thought and studio filmmakers saw and collected more works than might have been apparent. These recent comparisons between paintings and photograms allow us to imagine the unknown impact of Impressionism on motion pictures and more broadly the relationships created between painting and cinema.

1 R. Brimo, *L'Évolution du goût aux États-Unis* (Paris: James Fortune, 1938), p. 159.
2 *Catalogue of an exhibition of Contemporary French Art*, Los Angeles Museum of History, Science and Art, Exhibition Park, Los Angeles, 1923. This exhibition was organised thanks to the support of Mr H. Oelsnitz and Mr L. Hermanos.
3 A. Lhote, Introduction to *A Catalogue of the Mr. And Mrs. William Preston Harrison Gallery of Modern French Art*, private edition, 1929.
4 D. Wildenstein, *Monet: Catalogue raisonné*, 4 vols. (Cologne: Taschen and Wildenstein Institute, 1996).
5 G-P. and M. Dauberville, *Renoir: Catalogue raisonné des tableaux, pastels, dessins et aquarelles* (Paris: éd. Bernheim-Jeune, 2007–14): *Haystack* (Les Meules) (1883, no. 889), *Sketch of Five Figures in a Landscape* (Esquisse de cinq personnages dans un paysage) (1893, no. 963a). See also "Barnsdall Estate, 1952-1953", Frank Perls papers and Frank Perls Gallery records, Box 7, Folder 22, Archives of American Art.
6 *The Gladys Lloyd Robinson and Edward G. Robinson Collection*, Los Angeles County Museum, 11 September – 11 November 1956; California Palace of The Legion of Honor, San Francisco, 30 November – 13 January 1957.
7 E. G. Robinson, *All my yesterdays* (London-New York: W. H. Allen, 1973), pp. 173–75.
8 *Five Centuries of European Painting: A Collection of European Paintings from Early Renaissance to the Modernists Loaned by Wildenstein & Company*, Los Angeles Museum, 25 November – 31 December 1933.
9 *The Development of Impressionism*, Los Angeles Museum, 12 January – 28 February 1940. The exhibition catalogue is kept at the LACMA.
10 *Aspects of French Painting from Cezanne to Picasso*, Los Angeles Museum, 15 January – 2 March 1941. The exhibition catalogue is kept at the LACMA.
11 Noel F. Bush, "Close-up: Buddy De Sylva", *Life*, 30 December 1940, p. 55.
12 *Collection Mr. And Mrs. George Gard De Sylva*, Los Angeles County Museum, October 1946.
13 Inge Jaehner, Thomas F. Schneider, *Remarque's Impressionists: Art Collecting and Art Dealing in Exile* (Göttingen: Vandenhoeck & Ruprecht, 2013).
14 "Among Other Things", *California Arts and Architecture*, November 1940, p. 12.
15 "Notable Renoir Exhibition in Los Angeles", *Art Digest* 18, no. 1, 1 October 1943, p. 14.
16 Renoir, Dalzell Hatfield Galleries, 15 September – 15 October 1943, Los Angeles.
17 *The Collection of Mr. & Mrs. William Goetz*, California Palace of the Legion of Honor, Lincoln Park, San Francisco, 18 April – 31 May 1959; *Important Impressionist and Modern Paintings and Sculpture, Proprety from the Collection of William & Edith Goetz*, 14 November 1988, Christie's New York.
18 "Great Art... in Four Californian Houses", *Vogue*, 1 February 1945, pp. 128–37; "Art in Hollywood", *Life*, 1 March 1948, pp. 64–68.
19 Nathalie M. Kalmus, "Colour Consciousness", *Journal of the Society of Motion Picture Engineers*, August 1935, p. 140.
20 Formerly entitled *In the Woods at Giverny, Blanche Hoschedé at Her Easel with Suzanne Reading*.
21 Laurent Le Forestier, "La couleur, naturellement ? Débats sur la couleur en France au sortir de la Seconde Guerre mondiale", *1895. Mille huit cent quatre-vingt-quinze* 71, 2013.

THE SPREAD OF IMPRESSIONISM AND COLLECTORS IN CHINA FROM SUN PEICANG TO MODERN DAY

MARIE LAUREILLARD

Today considered as the first Chinese collector of modern Western art, Sun Peicang 孫佩蒼 (1890–1942) was recently brought into the spotlight thanks to the hard work of his grandson Sun Yuan 孫元, who has written two books about him, published in 2014 and 2018. Sun Peicang made two trips to France and his eclectic tastes attracted him to artists such as the Orientalist Henri-Émilien Rousseau and the Symbolist Eugène Carrière, as well as Poussin, Delacroix, and Repin. But what about Impressionism? The "School of Impression" (印象派 *yinxiang pai*) became known in China from the 1920s and Sun Peicang's collection only includes works from a precursor of Impressionism, Díaz de la Peña (1807–1876), and a follower, Louis-Édouard Garrido (1893–1982). Was this due to a lack of finances or opportunities?

Although the Japanese became fond of this artistic movement very early on, we have failed to find evidence of a similar passion in twentieth-century China. However, the Chinese people did welcome Impressionism with a kind of curiosity, undoubtedly encouraged by the movement's success in Japan, at this time at the forefront of avant-gardism in Asia. Its subjectivity was even compared to traditional Chinese painting[1] and it inspired several artists like Liu Haisu 劉海粟 (1896–1994), before fading into oblivion. After a long gap, today, Impressionism is once again attracting new collectors who acquire Monet's and Van Gogh's without even batting an eyelid.

The Story of a Chinese Collector in the First Half of the Twentieth Century

Over a period of almost twelve years, Sun Yuan carried out in-depth research into his grandfather, a man who has been overlooked by history and who died in mysterious circumstances in 1942. He recounts his meticulous investigation in two books, *Xunzhao Sun Peicang* 尋找孫佩蒼 (*Looking for Sun Peicang*, 2014) and *Zoujin Sun Peicang* 走进孙佩苍 (*Sun Peicang's Approach*, 2018). The painter and writer Chen Danqing 陳丹青, who in 1978 managed to discover some thirty Western works then on loan to the Central Academy of Fine Arts in Peking where he was studying, paid tribute to the collector in the preface of the first book.[2] He tells how original European paintings (absolutely exceptional in China at the time) were presented to the students not as having been brought together "by the former director, Xu Beihong, during his stay in France, but by a civil servant on a mission to France during the Warlord Era ... Given that they dated from the Warlord Era and according to current political policies, they belonged to the State and so it was quite natural for them to be housed at the Central Academy of Fine Arts. I remember that nobody questioned the origins of the paintings, and even less the name of the collector".[3]

Sun Peicang was a true pioneer in the world of collecting. He travelled to France on two occasions, firstly when he was studying at the École des Beaux-Arts in Paris between 1920 and 1926, then from 1930 to 1934, when he was working as a diplomat and director of the Franco-Chinese Institute in Lyon. He was passionate about Western art history, assiduously visiting museums and churches and, despite his modest finances, he threw himself into collecting European painting dating from the seventeenth century to 1920. He continued his mission during his second stay.

Originally from Shenyang (Liaoning), in Manchuria, a region under Japanese control from 1932, Sun Peicang headed off for France in October 1920 on board the Porthos, a maritime communications ship, with 179 other Chinese students, including Zhou Enlai. They all belonged to the Association d'éducation sino-française and they were going to take part in the Diligent Work-Frugal Study Movement. Sun was quickly accepted into the École nationale supérieure des beaux-arts in Paris under Lucien Simon (1861–1945), a member of the group nicknamed "La Bande noire" who opposed the light filled tonalities of the Impressionists and who were more concerned with composition than the effects of light. Lucien Simon appreciated Manet as much as Velasquez or Frans Hals, and adopted a naturalist and intimist style of painting similar to the Impressionists with its use of colour and lively brushwork, as can be seen in his *Evening Conversation* (*Causerie du soir*) (1902) in the Nationalmuseum Stockholm.

Having himself painted some realist paintings inspired by photographs, Sun Peicang quickly abandoned artistic practice for a more theoretical approach due to his age and his former academic training. During his first trip, in his free-time he began his collection by frequenting the book stalls along the banks of the Seine and visited around a hundred churches and European museums. He travelled to ten countries including Italy, England, Germany, the Soviet Union, the Netherlands and Spain. "Sun Peicang couldn't afford to buy books at auction even if the prices were nowhere near as high as today. Thanks to the knowledge and perspicacity in terms of the works and artists he had acquired during his travels across Europe, he had the time, space and capacity to glean some rare gems in the markets, galleries and art stalls."[4] Employed to carry out an enquiry into European artistic education, the money he earned from this job undoubtedly helped towards his acquisitions. Sun Peicang was looking to promote culture and spirituality and improve the level of artistic teaching in China: at this key period, reviving art seemed a priority in order to adapt to the new society. In an essay he wrote several years later, *The Relationship Between Art and Life* (*Meishu yu rensheng de guanxi* 美術與人生的關係, 1928), Sun explained the essential role of art, closely tied to the project for national modernisation.[5]

In her memoirs, Jiang Biwei 蔣碧薇 (1899–1978), wife of the painter Xu Beihong 徐悲鴻 (1895–1953), told how Sun Peicang became friends with her husband and took advantage of the devaluation of German currency to acquire works relatively cheaply in Berlin. Xu Beihong, who travelled with him, was impressed by his perseverance and discernment.[6] In France, Sun also knew the painter Sanyu 常玉 (1901–1966), the poet Shao Xunmei 邵洵美 (1906–1968), the writer Zhang Daofan 張道藩 (1897–1968) – a future eminent member of Chiang Kaï-shek's government, whom he followed in his fall to Taiwan in 1949 – or furthermore Guo Youshou 郭有守 (1901–1978), who become a diplomat and collector of Chinese modern art.[7] All of these students belonged to an association known as "Chiens célestes", founded in Paris in 1921, which united their intellectual affinities in an attempt to reflect upon the future of art in China (天狗會 *tiangou hui*).

In January 1927, Sun Peicang returned to China where he taught in the arts and literature department at the North-East University and at the Department of Law and Engineering. In October 1927, he was involved in the creation of the influential Art Research Society at Mukden Palace in Shenyang. At the end of 1930, he was nominated director of the Franco-Chinese Institute in Lyon (founded in 1921) by the Nankin nationalist government's minister of education and as the Republic of China's representative for education on the youth committee at the League of Nations. During this period, Sun continued studying and collecting European paint-

ing, bringing together originals and reproductions, encouraged all the while by the National Research Institute in Peking.
On his return to China, he was named director at the offices of the North-East's Kuomintang party, then senator of the first and second National Council from 1938. From 1 to 7 January 1942, an art exhibition was organised by the Sichuan Fine Arts Association at the Sichuan province library in Chengdu. It was divided into two sections: "Oil paintings. Eight modern Chinese painters" and "Western art and reproductions: Mr Sun Peicang's collection". The then president of the association, Guo Youshou, director of the department of culture in Sichuan and friend of Sun Peicang since his trip to France, wrote an article on the exhibition published on 2 January 1942 in the *Central Daily News* (中央日報) of Chengdu, which specified the origins of Sun Peicang's collection and his desire to open a museum in Sichuan.
Against all expectations, Sun Peicang died suddenly at the age of fifty-two on 3 January 1942 in a public hospital in Chengdu, supposedly from health reasons. According to a newspaper of the time, he had been the victim of an aggression following a disagreement among members of the Kuomintang party, which had led to a fatal haemorrhage. Some of the works, his notebooks and a history of world art he had written disappeared.
In 1969, in the midst of the Cultural Revolution, Sun's family, who had retrieved part of the collection, were forced to hand it over to the Central Academy of Fine Arts, where it was placed under lock and key for nine years. It was there that it was rediscovered in the late 1970s. It was returned to his descendants in 1986 and they still own the collection today. A rapid examination reveals its diversity and eclecticism. It includes traditional works along with others on the boundaries of Impressionism: limited finances probably stopped Sun Peicang from being able to buy works from the great masters of the movement such as Monet or Renoir.

A Look at Sun Peicang's Collection

At first glance, you might think you recognise two works by Rembrandt but in reality, they are copies commissioned, and brilliantly executed by Xu Beihong from two paintings by the Dutch master, *Young Woman Leaning Against a Door* (*Jeune femme à la porte ouverte*) (c. 1656, Gemäldegalerie, Berlin) and *The Blinding of Samson* (*L'Aveuglement de Samson*) (1636, Städel Museum, Frankfort).
You can also admire the realist style of a lost work by the Russian painter Ilya Repin (1844–1930), as well as a pencil drawing by one of the key

figures of Romanticism, Alexandre-Gabriel Decamps (1803–1860), entitled *The Cart* (*Le Chariot*) (15 × 25 cm).
There are equally some works by a well-loved teacher at the École des Beaux-Arts, Jean-Paul Laurens (1838–1921), a master of history painting with an irreproachable technique that could be classed as academic, entitled *Roman Soldier* (*Soldat romain*) (oil on canvas, 57 × 43 cm) and *Woman* (*Femme*) (1898, 49 × 30 cm). The dramatic staging and clever use of empty space gives these paintings a powerful and evocative force which makes the characters look like they are performing on a stage.
You will also find an early work by Gustave Courbet (1819–1877) and a watercolour by Henri-Émilien Rousseau (1875–1933), an Orientalist who was passionate about horses and devoted himself to North African subjects such as *Arabs on Horseback* (*Arabe à cheval*, 48 × 64 cm). Other paintings, such as those by Vassili Sourikov (1848–1916), undoubtedly acquired during Sun Peicang's trip to the Soviet Union, belong to the *pleinairism* movement which, whilst having the same ambitions as Impressionism, remained faithful to smooth brushwork and dark, broken colours.
Several works in the collection are in a similar vein to Impressionism. Eugène Delacroix for example, who opened the way for this movement by influencing Degas, Signac or Van Gogh. Sun Peicang only managed to acquire one watercolour on paper by Delacroix, less expensive than an oil on canvas – *Othello and Desdemona* (*Othello et Desdémone*) (c. 1847–49, 38 × 46 cm), which catches the light and creates an illusion of depth in a palette of brownish, virtually monochrome hues. A landscape artist from the École de Barbizon, whom Sun Peicang was particularly fond of, Narcisse Díaz de la Peña (1807–1876) also produced aesthetic effects which heralded the luminosity and instantaneity of Impressionism. Although he was friends with many of the artists from this movement, he was unable to participate in their first exhibition in 1874 due to ill health, and died two years later.
A Mother and Child (*Mère et enfant*) (oil on canvas, 52.5 × 56.5 cm) by Eugène Carrière (1849–1906) also caught the collector's eye (fig. 1). Although the characteristic monochrome palette of this work was probably no surprise to someone accustomed to the use of ink in Chinese painting, he was undoubtedly struck by the subtle effects of light which gave the figures a mysterious feel. Amidst the predominant shades of grey and browns, the blurred outlines of the mother and child and in particular their faces and hands, create a homogeneous group appearing to emerge from the darkness, ghostlike, as if the light emanates from inside them. This style expressed "a new beauty, nothing like the one Impressionism tries to achieve in expressing the luminous moment, fleeting aspects ... The appearance of forms that are signs with a higher meaning; discovering

1. Eugène Carrière, *A Mother and Child* (*Mère et enfant*), n.d., oil on canvas, 52.5 × 56.5 cm, Sun Peicang Collection (now the Sun Family Collection)

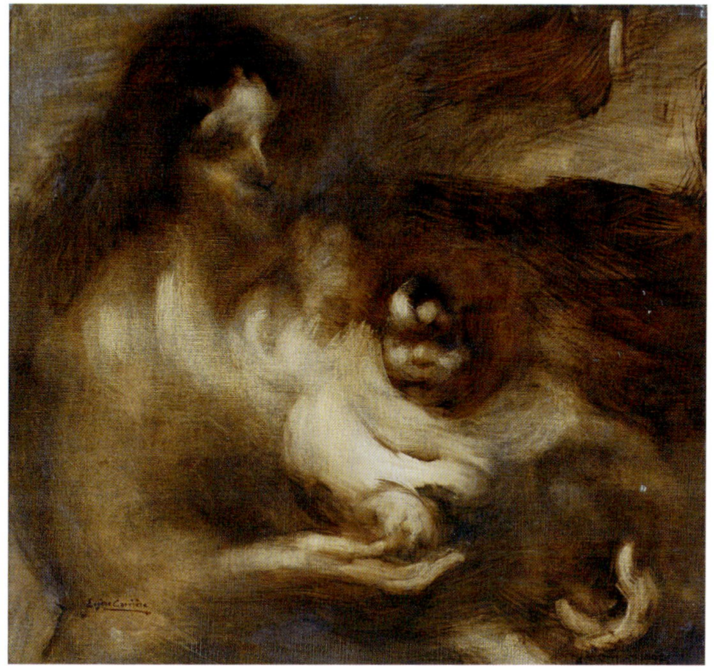

this hidden meaning is the artist's triumph".[8] Indeed, unlike Impressionist paintings dominated by colour and a taste for outdoor scenes bathed in sunlight, from 1876–1880, Eugène Carrière progressively eliminated colour from his palette.[9] However, the aesthetics of this admirer of Monet are closer to the Impressionists than they might appear, because "Carrière knew about his contemporary's preoccupation with colour: like them he was looking to render the sensation of light, not through the radiance of colour but by opposing light and dark which made his characters emerge and created a more palpable atmosphere ... Like them, Carrière drew directly with his brush and adopted spontaneous, vibrant brushstrokes and autonomous colours ... he paints infinite shades of light using an *atmospheric technique* comparable to works by Monet, Renoir, Degas".[10]

As for Louis-Édouard Garrido (1893–1982), he was clearly closer to the Post-Impressionists in style. A painter of countryside scenes, seascapes or figures, he might even have been labelled an Impressionist if he had been of the same generation as his grand elders Monet, Pissarro or Sisley, who had a huge impact on his work. His *Half-length Portrait of a Woman* (*Femme en buste*) (oil on canvas, undated, 46 × 38 cm) figures a dashing young woman elegantly dressed in a shimmering blouse and feather hat. Painted with lively and rapid brushstrokes, Garrido skilfully translates the young woman's vivacity and rebellious temperament (fig. 2).

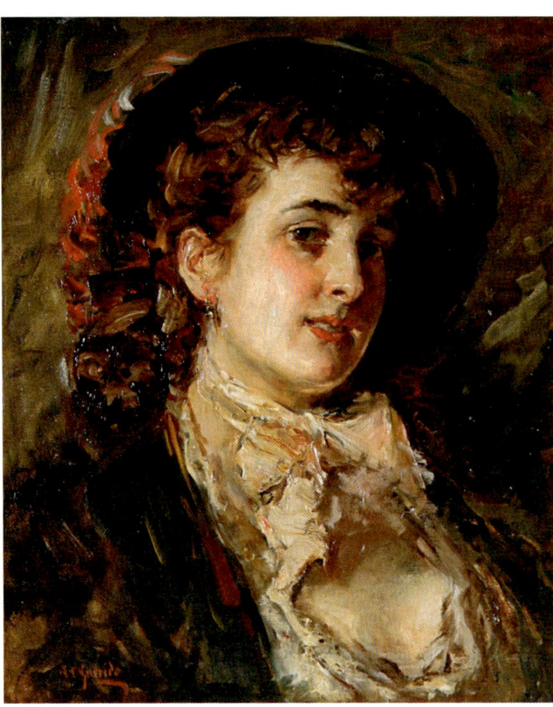

2. Louis-Édouard Garrido, *Half-length Portrait of a Woman* (*Femme en buste*), n.d., oil on canvas, 46 × 38 cm, Sun Peicang Collection (now the Sun Family Collection)

And so, unlike Xu Beihong who was exclusively attached to classical European painting, Sun Peicang showed his taste not just for a smooth, detailed, realistic facture, but also for other aesthetic trends that were progressively freeing themselves from the concept of *mimesis*. He enjoyed landscapes and figurative works – less perhaps still life – and played a major role in the history of Chinese collectionism thanks to his enthusiasm and foresight, even if his lost notebooks mean that today we are lacking precious information on the origins and prices of his acquisitions. He appears to be one of the rare collectors of Western art during the Republican era, along with the writer Lu Xun 魯迅 (1881–1936), fervent supporter of European engraving in his time, and the teacher Cai Yuanpei 蔡元培 (1868–1940), who in the 1910s, bought around fifteen Cubist engravings which were later lost during the Sino-Japanese War.[11] The latter, who studied philosophy in Leipzig from 1908 to 1911, was convinced that an aesthetic education would "replace Confucianism" (*yu meiyu dai zongjiao* 與美育代宗教) and that traditional Chinese art could no longer satisfy the demands of a modern society.[12] Chen Danqing rightly highlighted the exceptional nature of Sun Peicang's contribution: "In terms of riches and power, spending across the world and experience in politics and business, Mr Sun couldn't compare with his modern-day homologues, but who amongst them has managed to achieve as much as he did? Who could boast such a collection? ... Sun Peicang was not wrong about his study trip to Europe in the 1930s and he made the decision to start collecting completely independently".[13]

A Chinese Vision of Impressionism

But apart from this specific collection, how was Impressionism viewed in China? In the art world of the time, there were two distinct camps: the Western camp and those who were adepts of *guohua* 國畫 or national painting – a neologism that appeared at the end of the Qing dynasty to distinguish traditional Chinese painting from an art characterised by Western techniques and style. Within this context, well-informed Chinese people were aware of the artistic movements that had emerged in Europe such as Impressionism, Post-Impressionism, Fauvism, Expressionism, Cubism, Dadaism or Surrealism. Many artists and intellectuals discovered them though the Japanese prism: since the reforms of the first Meiji era (1869–1912), Japan had had a head start in learning about Western culture, from both a geographical and linguistic point of view Japan was much more accessible for the Chinese than Europe, which some like Sun Peicang were nevertheless lucky enough to visit. For those who stayed behind, their vision of all of these movements and in particular the "School of Impression" 印象派 *yinxiang pai* (a term taken from Japanese) or "Inner School of Impression"内印主义 *neiyin zhuyi* was reliant on poor quality reproductions, often in black and white, seen in the publications of the time. An article in *Arts and Life* (*Meishu shenghuo* 美術生活 (no. 5, August 1934), one of the main art magazines during the 1930s, rightly described Monet as a "colourist" (彩色家 *caisejia*) and a "landscape artist of light" (一片光芒的风景画家 *yi pian guangmang de fengjing huajia*), whilst in the photograph accompanying the text, the bright colours were transformed into a simple gradation of greys offering nothing more than a vague idea of the original painting. The subject was also discussed in books such as *Claude Monet* by the painter Liu Haisu 劉海粟 (1896–1994), published by Zhonghua Shuju in 1936. Liu Haisu, who had also studied in France, drew inspiration in terms of subjects and techniques from Claude Monet, as we can see in his works *Notre-Dame de Paris* (1930) and *Sunset at Westminster* (*Coucher de soleil à Westminster*) (1935). Books and magazines of the time show then that this pictorial trend was not unknown to the urban cultivated Chinese public. However, the influence of Impressionism would soon be reduced to zero by the Sino-Japanese War and a new preference for realism, following the ideas of the artist Xu Beihong. Founded on a direct observation of the subject, academic realism appeared to the Chinese to be a manifestation of science, considered as the force behind the development of a new society. This aesthetic direction soon triumphed with the rise to power of the communists, who rapidly associated it with the Soviet inspired "socialist realism". On the other hand, in Taiwan, Impressionist-style painting continued to be appreciated and practised by talented artists like Yang San-lang 楊三郎 (1907–1995) or Liao Chi-chun 廖繼春 (1902–1976), who had both sojourned in France. Introduced by the Japanese at the time of the colonisation (1895–1945), it reflected a pro-western and anti-communist stance.[14]

Taiwan's Pioneering Role

A few decades later, thanks to the economic rise of Hong Kong and Taiwan in the 1980s, some collectors began episodically buying French Impressionist works. Born in 1928, Kho Bun-liong 許文龍 was a rich industrialist and director of Chimei Electronics in 1998 who then went into the food industry in 2010. In 2011, Kho Bun-liong fulfilled his lifetime dream of founding the Chimei Museum in Taiwan, near Tainan, to show his private collection of Western art which covered the period from the Renaissance to the nineteenth century. Among the Impressionists, Kho had a preference for Gustave Caillebotte, more affordable on the art market than a Monet or a Cézanne, and you can see for example *Woman with a Rose* (*Femme aux roses*) at the Chimei Museum.[15] "Taking into account recent scientific research into various artists and their works, the Chimei collection could help to highlight the diversity of Impressionist painting. The strange characteristics of *Woman with a Rose* (1884, oil on canvas, 72.7 × 60.3 cm) is highly enlightening for studying the urban themes of Impressionism."[16]

Born in 1949, Frank Huang 黃崇仁, a mogul of the IT industry in Taiwan and head of Powerchip Technology Corporation, is passionate about Ming-Qing porcelain and modern and Impressionist painting. *Woman Playing a Guitar* (*Femme à la guitar*) (fig. 3) by Auguste Renoir (1896-1897) is a fine example of one of his costly acquisitions: a woman is shown sitting in an armchair, a sign of bourgeois comfort, playing the guitar with a concentrated air in an intimist atmosphere. Next to her on a table, is a Chinese or Japanese vase that can be seen in another work from the same series, housed at the National Gallery of Victoria in Melbourne and which reminds us just how fascinated the Impressionists were with Japanese culture. Carefully divided into areas of warm pinks, brownish oranges and cold blues and greens, the composition is dominated by the undulating lines of the woman's dress, the guitar, the armchair and the vase, con-

3. Auguste Renoir, *Woman Playing a Guitar* (*Femme à la guitare*), 1896–97, oil on canvas, 65.8 × 54.6 cm, Frank Huang Collection, date of acquisition unknown

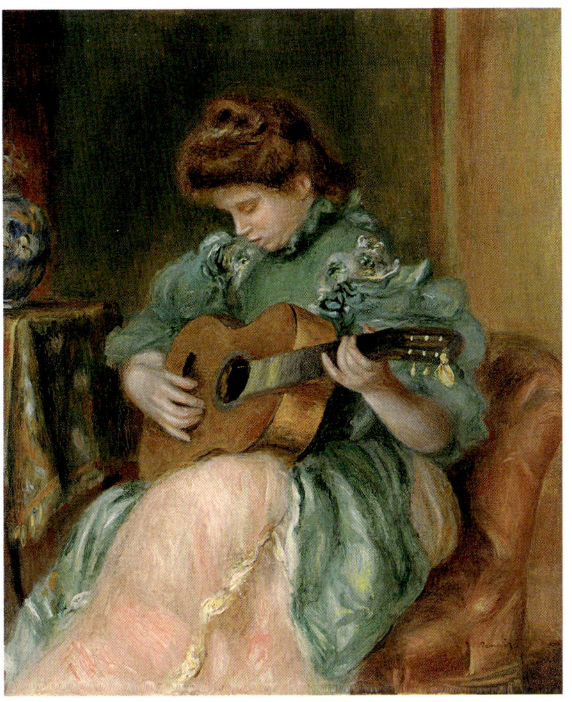

trasting with the vertical lines of the background and the table. The dress is modelled with gradations of white and green. Shades of pink and grey suggest the light shimmering across the fabric, echoing the pearly complexion of her face, hands and arms. Renoir admired the figures of Camille Corot, who also painted women playing musical instruments set in timeless atmospheres.

Born into an educated Taiwanese family versed in the arts, Frank Huang has claimed he doesn't collect artworks to make money, but because of his taste for art. He learnt to paint at the age of ten, enthralled by local artists Liao Chi-chun 廖繼春 (1902–1976), a talented colourist known for his landscapes and still lifes, and Guo Xuehu 郭雪湖(1908–2012), author of what are known in Taiwan as "national treasures". Despite being attracted to painting, Frank Huang studied medicine in New York, the American capital of art and music. "My brother and I studied painting and my two sisters music, but I never had the chance to pick up my brush again after obtaining my diploma at university in New York. Later, when I had earned money in business, I started buying artworks."[17] After obtaining his PhD in medicine in New York, Huang taught at the Taipei Medical College for ten years. Purely by chance, at the age of thirty-eight, he went into the very lucrative IT industry. "I have done everything in my life, I was a doctor, teacher, high-tech entrepreneur and art collector, I really can't complain, he declared. Perhaps one day I will give my collection to a museum, or I will create my own. I don't think I will ever sell my artworks, I will undoubtedly leave them to Taiwan so that everyone can enjoy them."[18] Perhaps he will follow in the fosters of Mr Kho and the Chimei Museum.

Van Gogh's Success

Individuals have only been allowed to acquire artworks in the People's Republic of China since 2002 – a luxury which had been reserved up until then for museums. And so, encouraged by the auction houses and galleries, mainland collectors began turning their sights towards the Impressionists. In September 2006, for the first time, Christie's started offering masterpieces from the movement on the Beijing Peninsula. In 2010, the French art dealer Édouard Malingue opened a gallery of the same name in Hong Kong in an attempt to promote Impressionism and more widely, modern art, amongst East Asian clients. For the first time, Sotheby's Hong Kong also organised shows and auctions of Impressionist works in Peking and Hong Kong aimed at Asian collectors and to test out the market. In 2007, the Beijing Huachen Auction House organised a major auction of oil paintings and Western sculpture on the continent.
This resulted in a purchase that caused a sensation at Sotheby's New York in 2007 by the promoter and real estate investor from Hong Kong Joseph Lau 劉鑾雄 (b. 1951), of *Morning* (*Te Poipoi*) by Gauguin (1892) for a price of 39,241 million dollars.
Even more spectacular was the acquisition of a Van Gogh by Wang Zhongjun 王中军 (b. 1960), seven years later at the same auction house for nearly 62 million dollars. In November 2014, the president of the giant Huayi Brothers Media Group, bought the famous *Still Life, Vase with Daisies, Cornflowers and Poppies* (*Nature morte, vase aux marguerites, bleuets et coquelicots*) (1890) by the Dutch painter, with its beautifully-balanced composition and lively lines, which, in an explosion of colours, perfectly conveys the freshness of the wild flowers bundled together in a dense harmonious bouquet (fig. 4). The complementary colours of the poppies and cornflowers are magnified through their opposition. The work is dated June 1890, when Van Gogh had returned to Auvers-sur-Oise to stay under the watchful eye of doctor Gachet, shortly before his tragic death.
Wang Zhongjun was highly criticised by some internet users: "It's a painting by a madman bought by another madman", wrote a Sina Weibo user. Someone else posted the following comment: "Here's another way of spending investors' money, what a waste!"[19]

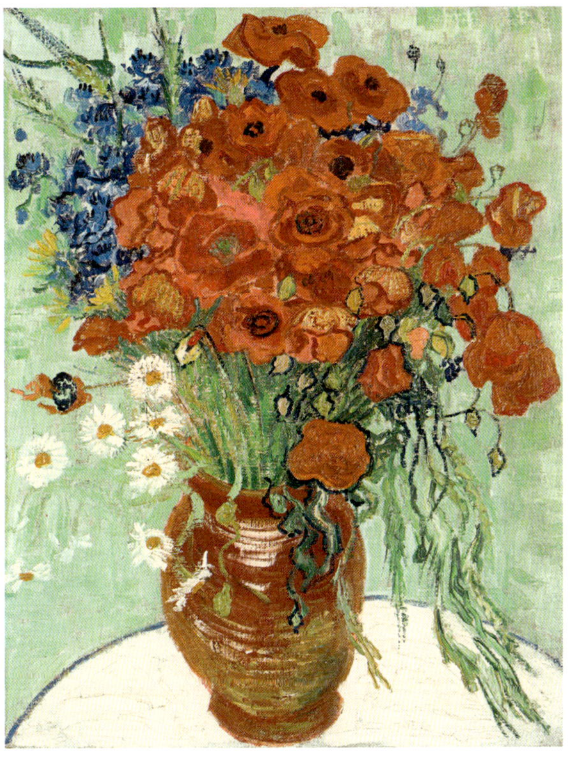

4. Vincent Van Gogh, *Vase with Daisies and Poppies (Vase avec marguerites, bleuets et coquelicots)*, 1890, oil on canvas, 66 × 51 cm, Wang Zhongjun Collection, bought for 61.765 million dollars at Sotheby's New York, November 2014

The acquisition of the Van Gogh brought the businessman into the spotlight, himself a painter and long-time collector of modern and contemporary Chinese art. His collection is spread throughout his numerous homes in Hong Kong, Los Angeles and Péking. Wang Zhongjun, who has always described himself as being passionate about painting, made his fortune in 1998 which has enabled him to buy works from artists like Wu Guanzhong 吳冠中 (1919–2010), Luo Zhongli 羅中立 (b. 1948) or Ai Xuan 艾軒 (b. 1947). His tastes have gradually evolved. It was only around 2011-2012 that he moved towards Impressionist art, securing artworks by Monet, Renoir, Pissarro and Cézanne: "I buy works of art in a really casual way, including the Van Gogh, he said. It was at the preliminary exhibition at Sotheby's that I felt I wanted to own it. I followed my instinct. The name of Van Gogh, associated with the fact that no work of this kind had been on the market for years, made me realise I had to seize the opportunity. But it wasn't essential and if the price had been even higher, I probably would have given up the idea. I was deeply satisfied with this purchase. Acquiring such an object in your life is really meaningful."[20] Although today the work hangs in his home in Hong Kong, reserved for his own appreciation and his circle friends, Wang Zhongjun

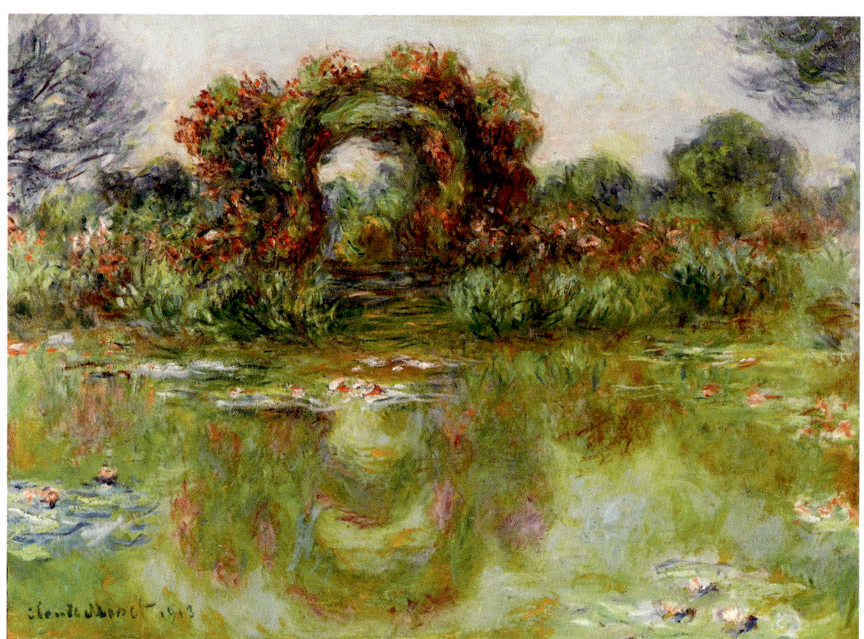

5. Claude Monet, *Lily Pond with Roses* (*Étang aux nymphéas et roses*), 1913, oil on canvas, 73 × 100 cm, Wang Jianlin Collection (Wanda Group), bought for 20.41 million dollars at Sotheby's New York, May 2015

hasn't given up the idea of one day presenting it to the public through the bias of a museum.

The following year, in May 2015, another Van Gogh, *L'Allée des alyscamps*,[21] made in Arles in November 1888, came into the possession of the Taiwanese gallery owner Robert Wu 吳青峰 for 66.33 million dollars at Sotheby's New York. In November 2017, an anonymous Chinese collector outdid this by buying *Labourer in a Field* (*Laboureur dans un champ*), painted in Saint-Rémy in September 1889, for the sum of 72 million dollars, one of the highest prices ever paid at auction for a Van Gogh. This success might be explained by the fascination for the painter's personality in China: his madness, perceived in a positive way, appears to be considered as a sign of this famous creator's sheer genius.[22]

Monet or Communion with Nature

Impressionism appears to be provoking increased enthusiasm in twenty-first-century China, if we consider the recent success of the One Art Museum exhibition in Shanghai of around fifty works on loan from the Musée Marmottan Monet, including the famous *Impression, Sunrise* (*Impression, soleil levant*) (1872–73) by Claude Monet. Although today, only moguls and magnates are able to acquire the masterpieces from this movement still circulating on the art market, the Chinese public, with a sensibility for this art that attempted to capture the light and transcribe fleeting sensations with fragmented brushstrokes, are impatient to see the originals close up. Crowds flock to admire *Water Lilies* (*Nymphéas*), a series by Monet that reflected the rhythm of the changing seasons in his garden at Giverny, moved by the genius of this artist for whom nature was, just like in China, a place for contemplation.

In May 2015, an Asian millionaire, Wang Jianlin 王健林 (b. 1954), at the head of the Wanda Group – a conglomerate involved in tourism activities, hospitality and cinema – reflected this interest by buying a painting by Claude Monet for 20.4 million dollars at Sotheby's New York: *Water Lily Pond with Rose Bushes* (*Bassin aux nymphéas, les rosiers*) (1913), which, created out of "the enchantment of Giverny",[23] depicts a rose arbour on the edge of a pond scattered with water lilies and bathed in sunlight (fig. 5). Mirroring the sky and flora, the pond was created by deviating an arm of the Epte River and fascinated the artist to such an extent that it absorbed him for the last thirty years of his life. The exuberance of the soft green vegetation, infinitely multiplied by its reflection in the water, is beautifully rendered by light vibrant touches blurring the forms. This idyllic scene for contemplation, exalts the "water garden" by transporting us into an aquatic and organic universe bathed in calm and serenity. This acquisition by the Wanda group followed the earlier purchase of *Claude and Paloma* (*Claude et Paloma*) by Pablo Picasso for 28.2 million dollars in 2013. This action was highly criticised at that time by some Chinese people who questioned Wang's patriotism and the true value of the work.

Haunted by the urgency of modernising China, Sun Peicang's pedagogical or patriotic motives have today been replaced by the pride of imposing oneself on the international art market and a desire for personal pleasure, which can also sometimes lead to a desire to share this pleasure. Looking at his collection today, if Sun Peicang had been lucky enough to dispose of greater financial means in his day, he would have undoubtedly bought works by the masters of Impressionism, already singled out by his discerning eye. Today, only a few billionaires in China have the luxury of being able to obtain these kinds of works, making up to some extent for the lack in the past. Because, as Chen Danqing points out, "although today in China, there are art schools, teaching and research institutions focusing on oil painting, associations and an amazing industry of auction houses, over the last hundred years not a single museum has brought together original Western paintings".[24] Perhaps every now and then, Wang Jianlin, takes time to enjoy his prestigious acquisition, just like the ancient Chinese scholars who marvelled before the spectacle of nature, to peacefully contemplate his work, far from the hustle and bustle of crowds and the world of business, captivated by the glimmering water and the shimmering light.

1 See Marie Laureillard, "La perception sensible du peintre et théoricien chinois Feng Zikai à l'époque républicaine", in Véronique Alexandre Journeau et Christine Vial Kayser (eds.), *Notions esthétiques (II): la perception sensible organisée*, L'Univers esthétique (Paris: L'Harmattan, 2015), pp. 399–415.

2 For more on Chen Danqing (b. 1953), a realist-style painter and key media figure in the art world in China, see Xu Zhiyuan, *Étranger dans mon pays* (Arles: Picquier, 2019), pp. 249–72, as well as Mei Mercier, "De la peinture à l'écriture le 'phénomène Chen Danqing'", *Art Asie Sorbonne*, 2022.

3 Sun Yuan, *Xunzhao Sun Peicang* 尋找孫佩蒼 (*Looking for Sun Peicang*) (Guilin: Guangxi shifan daxue chubanshe, 2014), pp. 1, 2.

4 Sun Yuan, *Zoujin Sun Peicang* 走进孙佩苍 (*Sun Peicang's Approach*) (Shenyang: Shenyang chubanshe, 2018), p. 173.

5 Ibid., pp. 382–88. Text published in the *Shengjing shibao* 盛京時報, 1 October and 8 October 1928.

6 Jiang Biwei, *Jiang Biwei huiyilu*, 蒋碧微回忆录 (*Memoirs of Jiang Biwei*) (Shanghai: Huadong shifan daxue chubanshe, 2014), p. 59.

7 On collecting activities and Guo Youshou's role with the Musée Cernuchi, see Éric Lefebvre, "Collecting as an Ambassade: Guo Youshou and the Introduction of Modern Chinese Painting in Post-War France", in Michaela Pejcochova and Clarissa von Spee (eds.), *Modern Chinese Painting & Europe: New Perceptions, Artists Encounters, and the Formation of Collections* (Berlin: Reimer, 2017), pp. 81–94.

8 Charles Morice, *Eugène Carrière: l'homme et sa pensée, l'artiste et son œuvre* (Paris: Mercure de France, 1906), p. 213.

9 Valérie Bajou, *Eugène Carrière, 1849-1906: portrait intimiste* (Lausanne: S. Acatos, 1998), p. 83.

10 Ibid., pp. 83, 88, 93.

11 Sun Yuan, *Xunzhao Sun Peicang* cit., p. 3.

12 *Nouvelle jeunesse* (*Xin qingnian* 新青年), 3/6, 1 August 1917, Shanghai.

13 Sun Yuan, *Xunzhao Sun Peicang* cit., p. 11.

14 On this subject see Marie Laureillard, "La peinture à Taiwan des années 1930 aux années 1950: échos artistiques du contexte socio-politique", *Monde Chinois Nouvelle Asie*, no. 58, 2019, pp. 70–82.

15 Liu Chiao-mei, "Les œuvres d'art occidental du musée Chimei à Taiwan", in Marie Laureillard and Cléa Patin (ed.), *À la croisée de collections d'art entre Asie et Occident (du XIXe siècle à nos jours)* (Paris: Maisonneuve Hémisphères, 2019), pp. 351–60.

16 Ibid., p. 353.

17 https://tw.news.yahoo.com (accessed 21 July 2021).

18 Ibid.

19 http://french.peopledaily.com.cn/Culture/n/2014/1106/c31358-8805539.html (accessed 21 July 2021).

20 https://www.carriegoodmansf.com/the-man-who-brought-van-gogh-to-china/ (accessed 21 July 2021).

21 92 × 73.5 cm

22 During the Republican period (1912–1949), Feng Zikai already presented Van Gogh's madness in a positive light in his biography dedicated to the artist in 1929, by implicitly comparing him to other eccentric painters from Chinese history, whose anti-conformism readily made people think they were mad. We should emphasize the fact that classical Chinese aesthetics closely links the value of a work to the temperament of the artist. See Marie Laureillard, "La perception sensible du peintre" cit., p. 407.

23 Ségolène Le Men, *Monet* (Paris: Citadelles & Mazenod, 2010), p. 366. The Chinese translation of the book was published in 2020 in Peking by Beijing meishu sheying chubanshe.

24 Sun Yuan, *Xunzhao Sun Peicang* cit., p. 8.

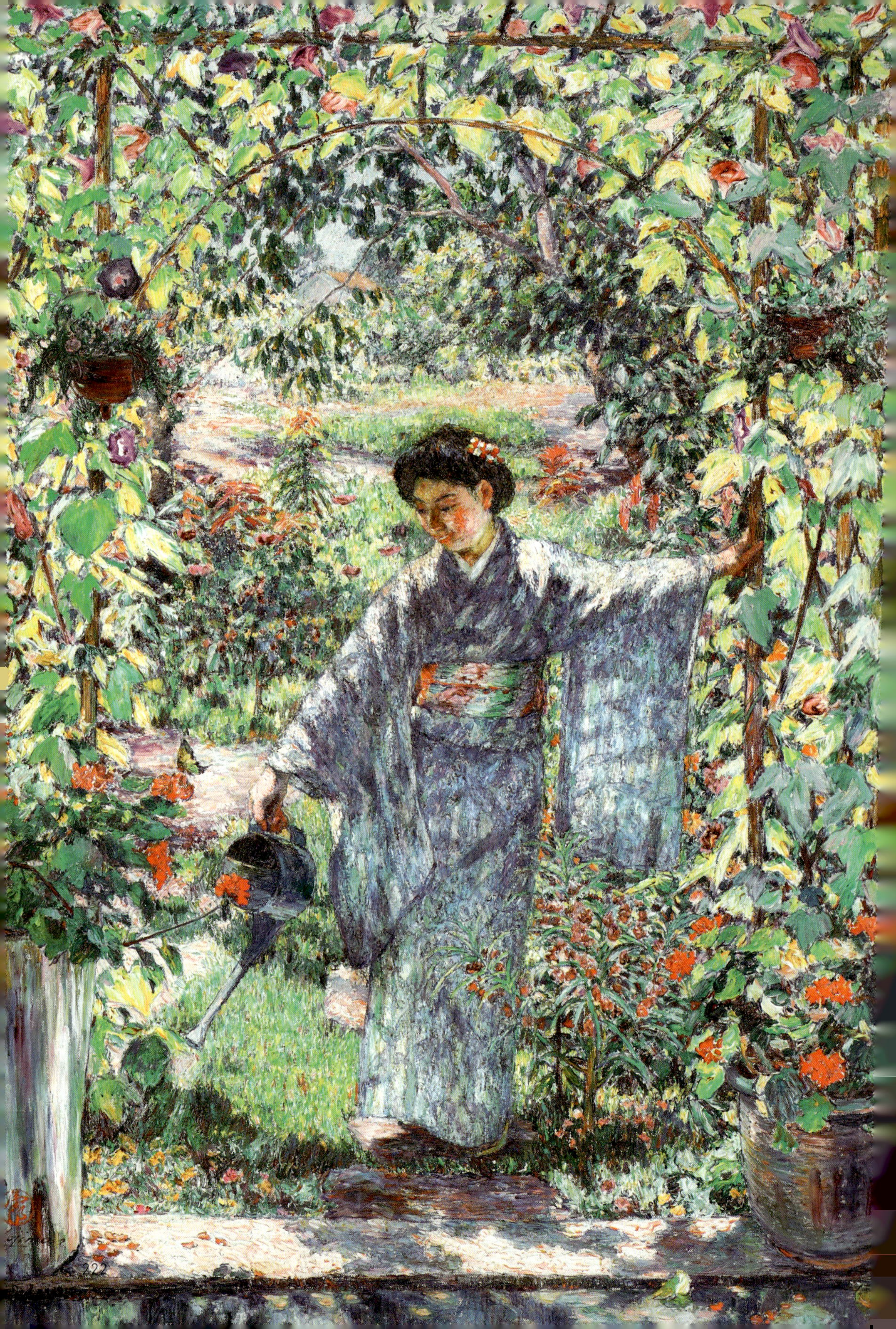

Impressionism and the Construction of Identities: From Collections to Museums

Studying a collection involves transcribing the encounter between an individual and a work, a style or a movement. Although the spread often originated in a collection, making works lose their belonging to a group to become simple units again, many collections went beyond the individual scale and encountered a collective fate. The concern for leaving a legacy for the majority, a desire to perpetuate their heritage or to make Impressionism known for others... there were multiple motivations behind collectors who donated their collections to a museum or who created one for their works. In all of these cases, the shift from private to public was not insignificant. It had an impact not just on the history of the movement but also on the society that welcomed it.

In twentieth-century Europe, where national identities were constructed and sometimes crystallised, the opening of an Impressionist collection to the public questioned local identity, whether it was on a regional or national level, and provoked artistic, economic and social reactions. Today, whilst Impressionism might appear like a movement from the past whose reception has been acquired and digested, a renewed historiography of the movement has revealed its modern-day relevance and its ability to still provoke a reaction.

Torajirō Kojima,
Morning Glory (diptych)
(*Belle de matin [diptyque]*),
1920, detail, Ohara Museum
of Art, Kurashiki

THE ÉCOLE DE ROUEN CREATED BY ITS COLLECTORS

NOÉMIE PICARD

The first occurrence of the name "École de Rouen" dates back to 1889. In his article "Les impressionnistes à Rouen", Eugène Brieux, a journalist at the *Nouvelliste de Rouen*, wrote about this first generation of painters: "These are the four representatives of the École de Rouen".[1] Later, the term was used again by the art critic Arsène Alexandre "to designate the Rouen Impressionist sensibility"[2] at the Paris exhibition of one of the artists in 1902. It was their benefactor and collector, François Depeaux, who validated the name we know today by organising an exhibition in their honour in Swansea, Wales, entitled *The École de Rouen, Its Painters and Wrought-Iron Craftsmen*.[3] The first denomination "the Rouen Impressionists" – which was more a reference to the local disciples of the movement – made way for a term that gave the group a real identity. The term "school", which indeed suggested a "shared apprenticeship, common exhibition habits, coherent iconography, transmission and legacy",[4] suited our artists from Rouen perfectly. This concept existed long before the period considered here as it was developed during the nineteenth century within the context of "peripheral-centres" to distinguish between local and national art production. It was concerned with classifying, studying and highlighting art by fitting it into an overall hierarchy, as Vojtech Jirat-Wasiutynski reminds us about the Marseille school: "At that time, the system was dominated by national schools ... and the regional schools were subordinate to them".[5] This artistic regrouping was based on a stylistic unity which was inseparable from a regional attachment.[6] These groups developed around the site of their shared apprenticeship. In the case of these regional groups, the "recognition of a school outside of Paris was determined by the same criteria, by re-establishing the higher teachings

of the Beaux-Arts, and often, a provincial academy".[7] Up until the late nineteenth century, this is where the name "École de Rouen" came from because it designated students of the town's École des Beaux-Arts. The shift towards its current definition came later.
How and why did this denomination contribute to forging an identity that ensured these artists were recognised? And to what extent does the way these artists were collected reflect this identity? The study of François Depeaux's collection seems central in answering these questions as it was a determining factor in the construction of the École de Rouen's identity. As for this regional attachment, it was either rejected to make a career outside of the provinces and in the Parisian collections, or it was fully embraced in order to continue working in Normandy.

The École de Rouen Seen through François Depeaux's Collection

The École de Rouen was made up of two generations of painters: the first – which included Charles Angrand (1854–1926), Charles Fréchon (1856–1929), Joseph Delattre (1858–1912) and Léon Jules Lemaitre (1850–1905) – represented the local Impressionist movement; the second, which gravitated around Robert Antoine Pinchon (1886–1943) and Pierre Dumont (1884-1936), inherited the legacy of the local masters and moved towards Post-Impressionism. They immersed themselves in Impressionist techniques in a bid to free themselves from artistic teaching, still strongly influenced by academism. In fact, similarly to the town's École des Beaux-Arts, the artistic milieu in Rouen was still firmly attached to its tradition and was wary about painters from the École de Rouen. Nevertheless, a small group of important town folk (journalists, gallery owners and collectors) came together and supported them. The key figure was François Depeaux (1853–1920) who set to work shaping the artistic group.
Félix-Célestin Depeaux's son, François Depeaux, came from a prosperous industrialist background and in 1840, founded Maison Depeaux Frères along with his brothers. In addition, he took over the running of the family coal business at the age of just twenty-seven. In his bibliographic work on the businessman, Marc-Henri Tellier explains that a study of his marriage contract to Eugènie Décap, dated 23 September 1880, reveals his early interest in art, but that "his taste had not yet led him towards the pictorial avant-garde".[8] Some of the works mentioned in this contract – Paul Coquand, *The Plains at Belle-Croix, Fontainebleau Forest* (*Plateau de la Belle-Croix, forêt de Fontainebleau*); Louis Le Poittevin, *Wild Flowers* (*Fleurs des champs*) and *Lilies* (*Lilas*); Paul Vallois, *Cliffs at Etretat* (*Falaises d'Etretat*) – were moreover identified in the catalogue for the town exhibi-

tion at the École des Beaux-Arts in Rouen in 1878 by François Lespinasse.[9] This information offers a glimpse of the future collector's love of the artistic and cultural life of his hometown.

During the 1880s, François Depeaux became interested in the first Impressionist paintings, and also got to know the young Rouen painters of the future "École de Rouen". He began promoting, supporting and diffusing the work of these artists. Good friends with Joseph Delattre and Albert Lebourg (1849–1928), in the early days of his collection, he also bought works by Charles Fréchon. The desire of these artists to teach – mainly Joseph Delattre and Charles Fréchon, who by the end of the century were giving classes in the open-air – enabled a second generation to emerge who were in turn supported by the collector.

Depeaux had a strong interest in both the Impressionist masters and local painters and this is clearly reflected in the various sales catalogues of his collection. We will analyse some of them here.

On 25 April 1901, François Depeaux organised an auction of part of his collection at the Hôtel Drouot for reasons which are difficult to pinpoint. Perhaps he had cash flow problems? In fact, the collector had bought works at many other sales the same year.[10] At the sale in April 1901, paintings by Charles Fréchon and Joseph Delattre (three and nine works respectively) were juxtaposed with paintings by Guillaumin, Claude Monet, Auguste Renoir, Camille Pissarro and Alfred Sisley. Although works by two Rouen artists were presented, this auction mainly focused on works by Impressionist masters. On the other hand, in 1903, when the divorce between the collector and Eugénie Décap was settled, a large number of works from the École de Rouen were listed.[11]

In 1906, a separate two-day sale within the context of their divorce was held at the Georges Petit Gallery for the partnership of aquests Depeaux-Décap.[12] The Rouen artists were underrepresented: on the first day, there were only works by Albert Lebourg next to those by Armand Guillaumin, Berthe Morisot and Monet, for example. On the second day there were fifty-three paintings by Joseph Delattre, two by Charles Fréchon and nine by Albert Lebourg. Once again, they were shown alongside a large number of works by Impressionist masters, including ten by Alfred Sisley, one of Depeaux's favourite artists.[13] We know that François Depeaux bought fifty-five paintings in total at this auction. After this, he continued to acquire works, reconstituting his collection and buying paintings from new local artists.

Following the death of the Rouen collector, several auctions were held in 1921. The last three, which took place in Paris,[14] Le Havre and Rouen, reveal, on the one hand, the perfect quantitative balance between works by Rouen painters and those of the Impressionists and, on the other hand, the collector's desire to have local, second-generation artists in his collection. Hence, we find works by Armand Guillaumin, Claude Monet, Camille Pissarro or Alfred Sisley. Also on sale were sixteen paintings by Albert Lebourg, forty by Robert Antoine Pinchon, as well as several by Marcel Couchaux (1877–1939), Narcisse Guilbert (1878–1942) and Narcisse Hénocque (1879–1952).

Throughout his life, François Depeaux collected a large number of Impressionist works as well as of Rouen artists, disciples of the movement, whom he particularly loved. The increasingly strong presence of local artists in the auction catalogues of his collection and the way the lots were organised – Impressionist masters on the first day and their followers on the second – contributed to constructing the identity of the École de Rouen as a regional variant of Impressionism.

For François Depeaux, just collecting works by Rouen artists was not enough. He also became their benefactor and used his network to create exhibition opportunities outside of Rouen. In the early 1900s, the businessman made it his job to promote the painters in the capital. Thanks to his connections with the Parisian art dealer Paul Durand-Ruel, who was also a collector, he organised solo exhibitions for some of his Rouen protégées.

And so, Joseph Delattre's first solo exhibition was held at the Durand-Ruel Gallery from 23 April to 5 May 1900. The event was not a huge success; frequentation was very low and no works were actually sold. François Depeaux repeated the experience with Charles Fréchon the following year but the result was much the same.[15] From 18 to 31 December 1902, he organised a second solo exhibition for Joseph Delattre, also at the Durand-Ruel Gallery.[16] Despite a positive review written by Arsène Alexandre in *Le Figaro*,[17] the work of the Rouen painter was not a hit in the capital. The collector did not organise another event in Paris until 1909, when he promoted the work of a young promising artist from Rouen by the name of Robert Antoine Pinchon. The artist's first solo exhibition was held from 15 to 25 March 1909 at the Galerie des Artistes Modernes, run by the experts Chaine and Simonson.[18] Although there is little information about its eventual success, François Depeaux speaks about it very positively in a letter to his protégé's father dated 17 March 1909, two days after the show opened.[19]

A passionate collector and devoted patron, François Depeaux never stopped supporting the painters from the École de Rouen. He collected, exhibited and promoted their work. Desirous to durably anchor the painters' identity in a Normandy school of Impressionism, he put their work in the museum alongside the masters of the movement.[20] This donation was evoked as early as 1903 but had not been carried out due to

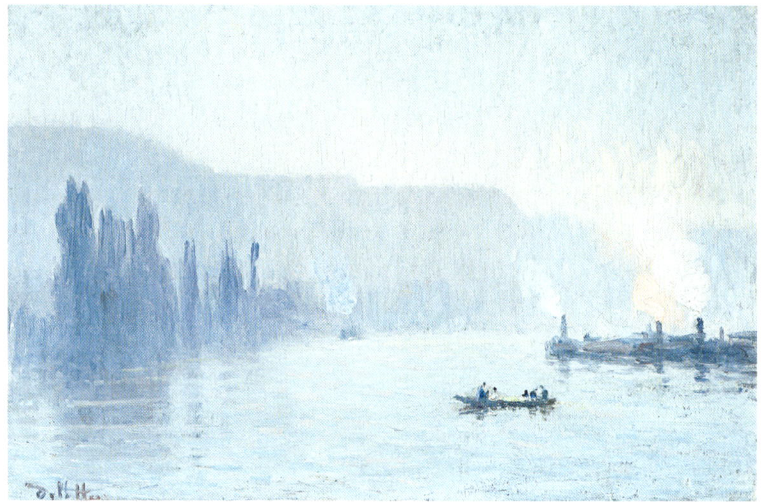

1. Joseph Delattre, *Tugboats, Mist on the Seine* (*Les Toueurs, brume sur la Seine*), 1909, oil on canvas, Musée des Beaux-Arts in Rouen, François Depeaux Donation

his divorce.[21] It was only after having reconstituted part of his collection that the businessman finally decided to make his donation.[22] The description he gave of his collection and Impressionism left little room for doubt in terms of the filiation he wanted to highlight between the masters and the Rouen painters:
"... this collection still appears to me to give a fair idea of what was called Impressionism, but which would be more appropriately called the open-air school ... I am happy to think that my hometown will be one of the first, if not *the* first, provincial town ... to open wide the doors of its museum to this art which, although criticised at its debuts ... thanks to its authentic techniques and the ardent convictions of its followers, Claude Monet, Sisley, Renoir, Degas, Cézanne, Pissarro, Guillaumin, Lebourg and all the younger ones who have followed, found its place among the most beautiful works of human genius."[23]
The three Depeaux exhibition rooms were inaugurated on 13 November 1909. Among the fifty-three works in the donation, half were paintings by artists from the École de Rouen: Marcel Couchaux, Joseph Delattre (fig. 1), Charles Frechon (fig. 2) or furthermore Albert Lebourg and Robert Antoine Pinchon.[24]

The Breakthrough of Certain Artists in Parisian Collections

Albert Lebourg (1849–1928), a Normandy painter born in the Eure, has frequently been associated with the first generation of the École de Rouen. His studies at the École des Beaux-Arts in Rouen, his attachment to the

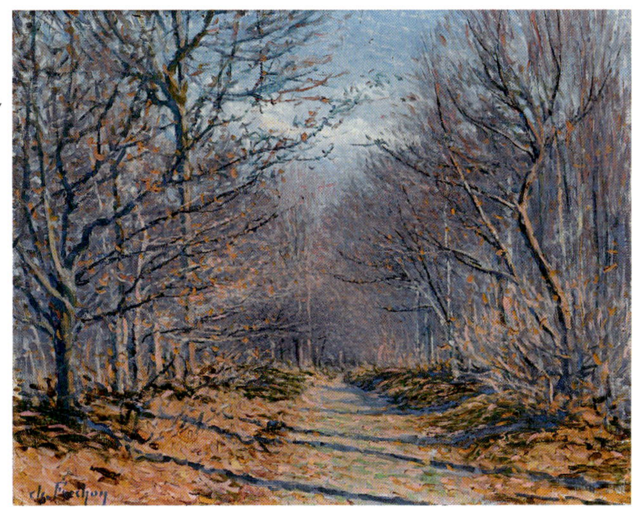

2. Charles Fréchon, *Woodland Scene in Winter* (*Sous-bois en automne*), oil on canvas, Musée des Beaux-Arts in Rouen, François Depeaux Donation

landscapes of Normandy and his Impressionist brushwork made him the perfect candidate. His career path differs somewhat however from his colleagues from Rouen. In the early 1870s, an amateur called Mr Laperlier spotted one of his paintings in the window of the Legrip Gallery.[25] The latter offered him a job teaching in Algeria where he worked between 1872 and 1876.[26] When he returned to France, after a difficult start, he was noticed by Alphonse Portier, an art dealer also known by the name of "Père Portier",[27] who introduced him into the Parisian Impressionist circles. Lebourg took part in the 1879 and 1880 exhibitions. In 1887, he was invited to participate in the Groupe des XX exhibition in Brussels and then later at the Salon National des Beaux-Arts from 1890 to 1893. We should also mention his participation in the Libre Esthétique exhibition in Brussels in 1901.

It was undoubtedly thanks to this series of exhibitions outside of Normandy that enabled Albert Lebourg to become associated with the Parisian Impressionist movement rather than the Normandy artists. And so, it is not surprising to find traces of his work in some major private collections and in particular those belonging to Antonin Personnaz and Étienne Moreau-Nélaton.

Antonin Personnaz (1854–1936)[28] collected Impressionist works from 1870 and up until the end of the First World War. He created a large collection of paintings which he bequeathed on his death, to state museums. Three works by Albert Lebourg were part of this bequest: *The Port of Algiers* (*Le port d'Alger*) (1876) (fig. 3), today at the Musée d'Orsay, and the two others, *View of Rouen* (*Vue de Rouen*) and *The Seine at Rouen* (*La Seine à Rouen*), housed at the Musée Bonnat-Helleu in Bayonne where Antonin Personnaz was the curator.

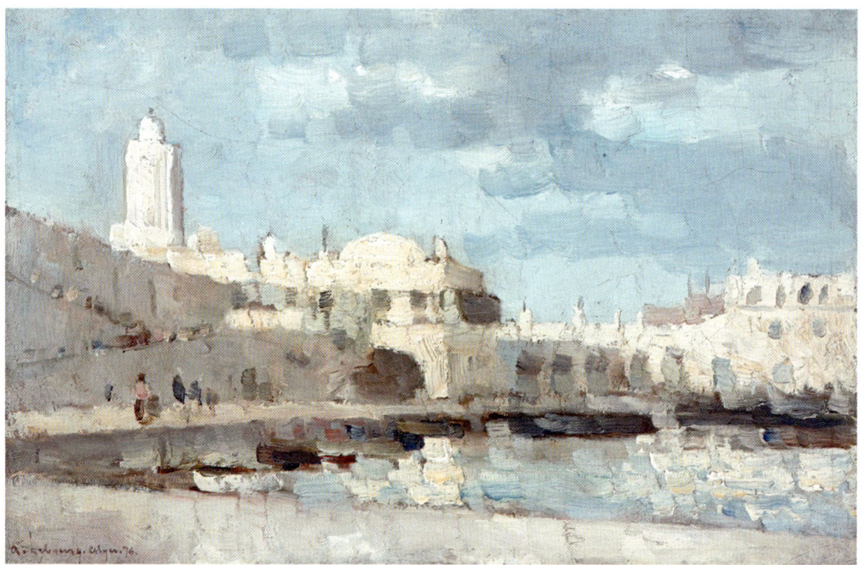

During his lifetime, the artist and art historian Étienne Moreau-Nélaton (1859–1927) gathered together a very large collection of Romantic paintings, works from the École de Barbizon as well as some very large Impressionist works. When he bequeathed his collection to the State, alongside Édouard Manet's *Déjeuner sur l'herbe* or Claude Monet's *Poppies* (*Coquelicots*), there came to be two works by Albert Lebourg: *Edge of the Ain River* (*Bords de l'Ain*), painted in 1897 (fig. 4), and *Road on the banks of the Seine at Neuilly in Winter* (*Route au bord de la Seine, à Neuilly en Hiver*), housed at the Musée d'Orsay.

Albert Lebourg's evolution among the Parisian Impressionist artists, along with the diversity of his painted subjects, enabled him to figure in some of the greatest art collections of his day and to free himself of his regional identity. It would appear therefore that Parisian collectors only bought Lebourg's work because he was identified as an Impressionist and not as part of the École de Rouen.

Charles Angrand (1854–1926) arrived in Rouen in 1873 where he studied under Philippe Zacharie (1849–1915)[29] at the municipal drawing school. Angrand rapidly developed a sensibility for the Impressionist movement. Although Zacharie was not completely against it, he remained convinced that it was not the best path for an artist. He expressed this opinion in a letter he wrote to Charles Angrand in 1882: "I hope that without becoming a true academic painter, which I would deplore, the countryside will have a positive influence on you nevertheless and that you will see painting somewhat less like a telegraph operator... Impressionism is the height of impotency".[30]

3. Albert Lebourg, *The Port of Algiers* (*Le Port d'Alger*), 1876, oil on canvas, Paris, Musée d'Orsay, Antonin Personnaz Collection

4. Albert Lebourg, *Edge of the Ain River* (*Bords de l'Ain*), 1897, oil on canvas, Paris, Musée d'Orsay, Etienne Moreau-Nélaton Collection

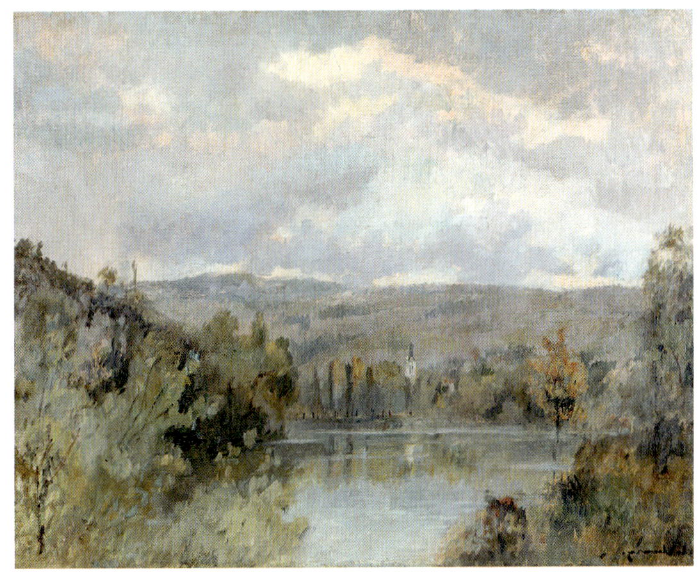

The painter became definitively part of the Impressionist movement in 1880 at the Salon in Rouen, where he exhibited *View of Gramont Bridge from Saint Sever Station* (*Gare Saint-Sever vue du Pont Grammont*) (today lost). The critic from the *Journal de Rouen*, Alfred Darcel, wrote: "But the real, pure [Impressionist], the one who sees blue harmonies, is Mr Angrand. Look at *Saint-Sever Station*, the trains are blue. It is true that there are scholars who insist that black is just an intense blue, a false black. He associated this blue with the purple of the sky, purple being a blue modified by red, the yellows of the ballast harmonising perfectly in contrast with this purple. All of this is intentional but is not factual, and it is in this sense that this landscape – and what a landscape! – belongs to the Impressionist school".[31] After meeting Georges Seurat (1859–1891), he moved towards Neo-Impressionist techniques whilst continuing to paint his Normandy landscapes.[32] Along with Seurat, he was involved in founding the Société des Artistes Indépendants in 1884 and exhibited at the Salons des Indépendants organised later by the Société. Not unlike Albert Lebourg, it was by ridding himself of his regional label that Charles Angrand became part of Oscar Ghez's collection a few decades later, shown at the Musée du Petit-Palais in Geneva.

Oscar Ghez (1905–1998) was a French entrepreneur who began buying works of art in the 1950s. Although he purchased nineteenth-century art, he mainly acquired works by artists from the early twentieth century. Among others, he was interested in the Fauves, the École de Paris, but also the Post-Impressionists. This was how he acquired seven drawings

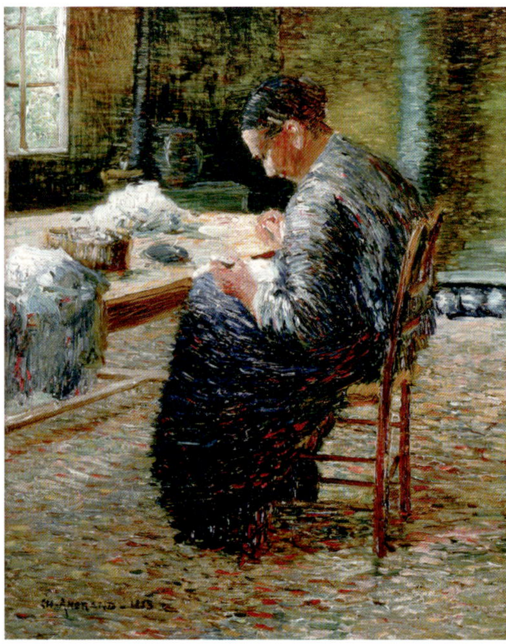

5. Charles Angrand, *The Artist's Mother Sewing* (*La Mère de l'artiste cousant*), 1885, oil on canvas, Geneva, Musée du Petit Palais – Modern Art Foundation, Oscar Ghez Collection

6. Léon-Jules Lemaitre, *Law Courts Courtyard* (*La Cour du Palais de Justice*), c. 1890, oil on canvas, Musée de Louviers, Constant Roussel Donation

in Comté crayon, five pastels as well as four oil paintings by Charles Angrand (fig. 5).

Similarly to Albert Lebourg, it was once again his association with the Parisian artistic circles, due to his Pointillist works and his participation in various group exhibitions that enabled him to enter some major private collections and obtain recognition outside Normandy.

Despite François Depeaux's attempts at promoting Normandy Impressionism outside of the region, it appears that in the end, it was more of a disadvantage for these artists. These two examples show the fragility of the Normandy identity and being identified with the École de Rouen for artists who wanted to have a career outside of their region.

The École de Rouen in Normandy Collections

Normandy landscapes, previously painted by the masters, were the main source of inspiration for the first- and second-generation artists of the École de Rouen. But how did representing this region affect the desire to collect works from the École de Rouen?

Let us take for example Constant Roussel, the main benefactor of the Musée de Louviers. In 1904, he bequeathed his collection which was made up mainly of academic landscapes but also several works from the

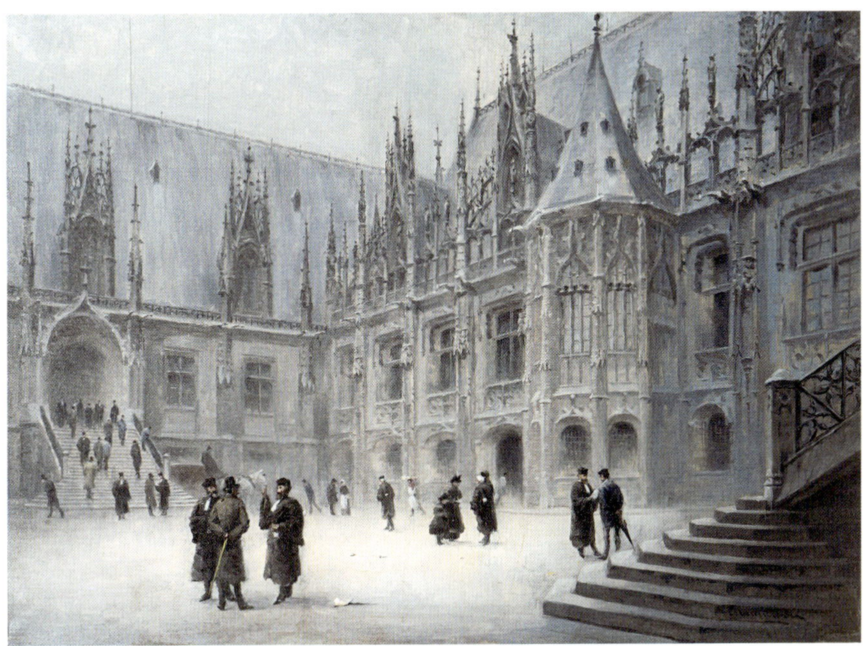

École de Rouen. Son of a dyer from La-Ferrière-sur-Risle, Constant Roussel (1814–1904) came from an ordinary background and although he was destined to take over his father's business, an event made him change his mind.[33] His uncle, Prosper Roussel, initially a travelling salesman for Jean-Baptiste Labelle, a haberdashery merchant from Rouen, became Labelle's associate and son-in-law. He asked his nephew to join him in Rouen. When his uncle died, Constant Roussel became very close to the Labelle family and remained so throughout his life. Passionate about art, over time he brought together a large collection of works (paintings, sculptures, drawings, furniture). Painting seems to have been the keystone of his collection with 200 or so works, mainly by contemporary artists. Despite this high number, there were no Impressionists in his collection. It would in fact appear that the collector did not really appreciate their style of painting and that his tastes were more traditional. He particularly liked "landscapes of a classical facture and especially views of familiar places".[34] Moreover, he regularly visited local exhibitions in Rouen, where the moderns were little represented and it seems that this was where most of his collection was compiled.
Despite all of this, the inventory of his bequest lists five paintings by Léon-Jules Lemaître (fig. 6), four by Charles Fréchon (fig. 7) and two by Joseph Delattre. Constant Roussel's taste for works with a strong regional bias by painters from the École de Rouen led him to include them in his collection and donate them to the Musée de Louviers when he died. The

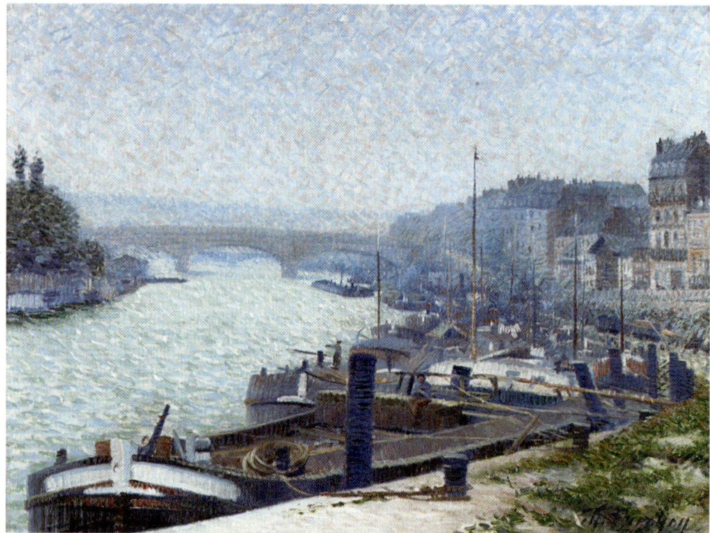

7. Charles Fréchon, *Le Pré-aux-Loups (Rouen)*, c. 1893–1894, oil on canvas, Musée de Louviers, Constant Roussel Donation

painters' taste for their region and their manner of representing it appears to have got the better of the few Impressionist works in the collection.

During our research on collectors of the École de Rouen, we found two sales catalogue for collections of artists which included a large number of works by the group. Commenting on these collections, Olivier Bonfait wrote: "A collection, a stock of models, can be a symbolic or economic investment".[35] Keeping these words in mind, we are going to try and understand the motivations of Magdeleine Hue (1882–1944) and Pol Pitt (1885–1921) for creating their collections. To what extent can these collections be explained through the group's regional ties and the relationship between the artists in the group?

Magdeleine Hue, originally from Bernay (in the Eure), began her studies at the École des Beaux-Arts in Rouen in the 1910s and exhibited for the first time in 1915 at the show *Pour nos soldats, pour nos artistes*, organised by Pierre Dumont, a second-generation artist from the École de Rouen. The sale of her studio collection took place on 30 September 1974 at the auction rooms in Rouen. Studying the catalogue reveals that Joseph Delattre was the only first-generation artist present, with three paintings. On the other hand, there were a lot of second-generation painters: Pierre Dumont and Robert Antoine Pinchon but also Léonard Bordes (1898–1969), Marcel Couchaux (1877–1939), Narcisse Guilbert (1878–1942), or furthermore Maurice Louvrier (1878–1954). Insofar as she herself was a member of this second generation and friends with one of its leading figures: Robert Antoine Pinchon, this studio collection might also reflect the link and strong solidarity between members of the École de Rouen.

The second catalogue studied is the sale of Pol Pitt's collection (1885–1921). Paul Pitrais, also known as Pol Pitt, was an artist-caricaturist from Rouen. In 1906, he joined the 39th Infantry Regiment in Rouen along with Robert Antoine Pinchon, and it is highly likely that the caricaturist frequented artists from the second generation of the École de Rouen. On 18 November 1924, a sale of the artist's collection was held at the auction rooms in Rouen. In total, the catalogue contained forty works up for auction of which the majority were works by artists from the École de Rouen. It should be noted that Joseph Delattre, Narcisse Guilbert, as well as Robert Antoine Pinchon, were the best represented with ten works each for sale. It would appear that similarly to Magdeleine Hue's studio collection, Pol Pitt wanted to support the artists of the town by buying and collecting their works. These two collections seem to have been constituted on the basis of local proximity or even friendship between the Rouen artists. Or perhaps it was a symbolic investment for these two artists who wanted to support their entourage?

In this inventory[36] we have sought to understand the relationships between members of this regional artistic school and their collectors, as well as the way in which the latter could have influenced their group identity. We have been able to see how François Depeaux, a central figure in the development of the École de Rouen, enabled painters to enter local collections and develop their reputation in Normandy by assigning them a group identity, firmly anchored in the region. It would nevertheless appear that the patron's desire to extend this action to Paris was not enough to allow them to cross the provincial boundaries. Studying the collections on a national level has allowed us to see the price to be paid for erasing artists' regional identity. Indeed, it seems that this was one of the conditions of them entering Parisian collections but above all for becoming more famous. In contrast, whilst this regional identity seems to have been a disadvantage on the national art scene, in the provinces, it opened the door to local collections and offered painters a solid artistic network.

1 Eugène Brieux, "Les impressionnistes à Rouen", *Nouvelliste de Rouen*, April 1889, Archives départementales de Seine-Maritime, JPL 18.

2 Arsène Alexandre, "Exposition Delattre", *Le Figaro*, 22 December 1902

3 François Depeaux, "Dossier de personnalité 92N", Bibliothèque patrimoniale Jacques Villon.

4 Claire Maingon, "De l'école de Rouen à la Société des artistes rouennais : affirmation et reconnaissance d'un (im)possible impressionnisme normand", in Frédéric Cousinié (ed.), *L'impressionnisme, du plein air au territoire* (Mont-Saint-Aignan: PURH, 2013), p. 83, available online, https://books.openedition.org/purh/4988?lang=fr

5 Vojtech Jirat-Wasiutynski, "École de Marseille: région et histoire de l'art en France au XIXe siècle", in Christine Peltre and Philippe Lorentz (eds.), *La Notion d'école* (Strasbourg: Presses Universitaires de Strasbourg, 2007), p. 219, available online, http://books.openedition.org/pus/13030

6 Christine Peltre, "Des usages d'un outil", in Christine Peltre and Philippe Lorentz, *op. cit.*, p. 10.

7 Vojtech Jirat-Wasiutynski, *op. cit.*, p. 221.

8 Marc-Henri Tellier, *François Depeaux, le charbonnier et les impressionnistes*, edited by the author, Rouen, 2010, p. 27.

9 François Lespinasse, "Depeaux et l'école de Rouen", in Sylvain Amic and Joanne Snrech (eds.), *François Depeaux, collectionneur des impressionnistes* (Paris–Rouen: Musée des Beaux-Arts de Rouen and In Fine éditions d'art, 2020), p. 140.

10 Caroline Durand-Ruel Godfroy, "François Depeaux et Paul Durand-Ruel", in Sylvain Amic and Joanne Snrech, *op. cit.*, p. 196.

11 François Lespinasse, *op. cit.*, p. 146.

12 Catalogue of modern paintings – watercolours, pastels, drawings by Besnard, Courbet, Fantin-Latour, Guillaumin, Lebourg, Lépine, Monet, Pissarro, Rafaelli, Renoir, Sisley, Toulouse-Lautrec, etc. – *The Ball* (Le Bal) by Renoir, 46 works by Sisley, major paintings by Claude Monet: making up the Depeaux partnership of aquests DEPEAUX-DECAP collection which was liquidated by decree from the Court of Appeal in Rouen on 7 February 1906. Auction, Paris, Galerie Georges Petit, 31 May and 1 June 1906, Nmm 79 Depeaux, Bibliothèques patrimoniales Jacques Villon, Rouen.

13 Joanne Snrech, "François Depeaux et Alfred Sisley: une relation particulière", in Sylvain Amic and Joanne Snrech, *op. cit.*, pp. 76–84.

14 Catalogue of modern paintings – watercolours, pastels, drawings by Allongé, Bracquaval, Dauchez, Doré G., D'Espagnat, Forain, Guillaumin, Lebourg, Martin L., Monet Claude, Montenard, Morerod, Moret Henri, Ottman, Pinchon Robert, Pissarro, Sisley, Stettlet, Vauthier – ancient paintings by Hendriks, Van Huysem: making up Mr Depeaux's collection on his death. Auction, Paris, Hôtel Drouot, 30 June 1921, Nmm 79 Depeaux, Bibliothèque patrimoniale Jacques Villon, Rouen.

15 François Lespinasse, *op. cit.*, p. 147.

16 Ibid., p. 146.

17 Arsène Alexandre, "Exposition Delattre", Le Figaro, 22 December 1902, available online, https://gallica.bnf.fr/ark:/12148/bpt6k286094k (accessed 6 July 2021).

18 Laurent Salomé (ed.), *Une ville pour l'impressionnisme. Monet, Pissarro et Gauguin à Rouen* (Paris: Skira Flammarion, 2010), p. 356.

19 François Lespinasse, "François Depeaux, un collectionneur", in Frédéric Cousinié, *op. cit.*, pp.107–35.

20 Letter from François Depeaux cited by the mayor of Rouen, Auguste Leblond, in his report from 28 May 1909, published on 29 May 1909 in the *Journal de Rouen*, Archives départementales de Seine-Maritime, available online: http://www.archivesdepartementales76.net/rechercher/archives-en-ligne/journal-de-rouen/

21 Laurent Salomé, "Une ville pour ou contre l'impressionnisme", in Laurent Salomé, *op. cit.*, p. 19.

22 Letter from François Depeaux cited by the mayor of Rouen, Auguste Leblond, in his report from 28 May 1909, cit.

23 Ibid.

24 François Lespinasse, *op. cit.*, p. 148.

25 Obituary of Albert Lebourg, 7 January 1928, name of the review unknown, "Dossier de personnalité 92N", Bibliothèque patrimoniale Jacques Villon.

26 François Lespinasse, *Journal de l'école de Rouen*, edited by the author, Rouen, 2006, p. 32.

27 Gustave Coquiot, *Vincent van Gogh* (Paris: Ollendorf, 1923), p. 136, available online, https://gallica.bnf.fr/ark:/12148/bpt6k-9736304w (accessed 7 July 2021).
28 An exhibition focused on the work of the photographer at the Festival Normandie Impressionnisme 2020 at the Musée des Beaux-Arts in Rouen: Virginie Chardin and Sylvain Amic (eds.), *La Vie en couleurs : Antonin Personnaz, photographie impressionniste* (Cinisello Balsamo: Silvana Editoriale, 2020).
29 Philippe Zacharie was a Normandy painter who led his whole career in Rouen. A prolific academic artist, he was awarded third prize at the Salon des Artistes Français in Paris in 1883. His local fame led him to become a drawing teacher at the Ecole Régionale des Beaux-Arts in Rouen from 1882.
30 Letter from Philippe Zacharie to Charles Angrand, 7 February 1882, cited by François Lespinasse, *Journal de l'école de Rouen*, edited by the author, Rouen, 2006, p. 42.
31 Alfred Darcel, "Exposition municipale de Rouen", *Journal de Rouen*, 14 October 1880, p. 3, available online at the Archives départementales de Seine-Maritime website, http://recherche.archivesdepartementales76.net/?id=recherche_guidee_journal
32 Russell T. Clement and Annick Houzé, *Neo-Impressionist Painters: A Sourcebook on Georges Seurat, Camille Pissarro, Paul Signac, Théo Van Rysselberghe, Henri Edmond Cross, Charles Angrand, Maximilien Luce, and Albert Dubois-Pillet* (Westport, CT: Greenwood Press, 1999), p. 309.
33 The biographical elements are mainly taken from Claude Cornu's text written for the documentation of the Musée de Louviers.
34 Claude Cornu, "Constant Roussel (1814-1904), un mécène pour Louviers", documentation of the Musée de Louviers.
35 Olivier Bonfait, "Collectionnisme", Encyclopediae Universalis, online, http://www.universalis-edu.com.ezproxy.normandie-univ.fr/encyclopedie/collectionnisme/ (accessed 6 April 2021).
36 This inventory is taken from our current PhD research: *L'École de Rouen : la normandité de l'avant-garde ? Marchands, réseaux, diffusion*, supervised by Frédéric Cousinié at the Université de Rouen-Normandie.

PROVINCIALISING IMPRESSIONISM: THE DAVIES SISTERS, FRENCH IMPRESSIONISM AND WELSH IDENTITY IN 1913

SAMUEL RAYBONE

In February 1913, the National Museum of Wales staged "the greatest artistic event in the history of Wales", its first ever exhibition of paintings that "should be a milestone in Welsh artistic development", a truly "national affair" (fig. 1).[1] Over 26,000 visitors encountered fifty-nine works "which typify", its organisers explained, "what is greatest in the art of the last century".[2] They included Édouard Manet's plein air sketch of the *Church of Petit-Montrouge* (*Église du Petit-Montrouge*),[3] which exemplified his "personal observation of nature" and "spontaneity of effect", and justified his status as a "genius" "... who has created a great school... Impressionism".[4] Claude Monet's "analysis of light... atmospheric effects... [and] the colours of the spectrum" was demonstrated by three late Venetian scenes ("a misty morning", "a twilight scene" and an "opalescent effect") and a *Westminster Bridge* [*sic*] bathed in "the quiver of light..., the whirl of smoke, and the glitter of the water".[5] James Abbott McNeill Whistler's "melting [of form] into a liquid sky" was shown alongside the "mists of the valleys" captured by Jean-Baptiste-Camille Corot, "the bath of air and light" depicted by J. M. W. Turner and the "extreme simplicity" of Charles-François Daubigny.[6] Other *pleinairistes* in the exhibition included Eugène Boudin, Narcisse Virgilio Diaz, Jules Dupré and Anton Mauve.[7] Ostensibly adding to the exhibition's range, figure studies and groups by Honoré Daumier, Jean-François Millet and Adolphe Monticelli were also included, as was Auguste Rodin's bronze *The Kiss* (*Le Baiser*) and Ernest Meissonier's highly finished historical genre scene of a *A Main at Piquet*.[8] Sometimes interpreted as "a mixed spectacle" in which impressionism (defined narrowly as Manet and Monet) played a relatively minor role, the unassumingly titled *Loan Exhibition of Paintings* was in fact a coherent and ambitious argument in favour of "Impressionist Painting", "The Great French Modern Art".[9] Specifically, it proposed impressionism as the salve for particularly Welsh deficiencies, and catalyst for the revival of a distinctively Welsh art. In this way, "French" impressionism became intertwined with the politics of Welsh nationalism and became a reference point in debates about Welshness, the "place of art in [Welsh] life" and how that life might itself be visualised in the early twentieth century.[10] In the *Loan Exhibition*'s ambitions to "direct" the Welsh public in a more "noble standard of taste" and "give stimulus to the long-delayed revival in Welsh art", we can discern, I suggest, the evidence of a distinctly Welsh engagement with the polyvalent and global phenomenon that was impressionism in the early twentieth century.[11] Yet, while speaking to *national* desires and anxieties, the exhibition, its organisers and its patrons were participants in various forms of *transnational* exchange and mobility. These transnational lineaments were vital in shaping the vision of impressionism that was presented to the Welsh people and posited as a vehicle of their "enlightenment".[12]

The *Loan Exhibition* in Cardiff offers a case study of the promiscuity and lability of impressionism, which, as contemporary scholarship is showing, was decidedly a global and transnational phenomenon. The complex and creative rearticulation of impressionism that the exhibition effected – its appropriation and adaptation of global impressionism to speak to local identities and experiences of modernity – demonstrates the inadequacy of the dominant ways of thinking impressionism to date, which have insufficiently equipped art historians to understand the multiform engagement with impressionism in places beyond France on their own terms. New scholarship, informed by decolonial and transnational approaches, is dismantling centre-periphery models and challenging teleological and developmental narratives whereby discourses and practices of impressionism outside France (whether as painting, collecting, exhibiting, dealing, criticising or historicising) have been trapped in a "perpetual state of comparison" in relation to the supposed French original, articulated in terms of derivation, imitation and influence, or else ignorance, incomprehension and failure.[13] By relocating the focus of inquiry to new sites (supposed-peripheries) and new scales (networks rather than nations), we can provincialise supposed centres and pluralise standardised canons, allowing us to practice "an inclusion of equal pluralities" which attends to the "particularities and specificities" of global impressionisms in their "own historical contexts".[14]

"Impressionism" was a "polysemous term and dynamic concept without always clearly codified stylistic criteria", neither "associated solely with

France" nor with the Société anonyme.[15] impressionism was "a globalised aesthetic" and a "flexible cultural language" whose meanings "shifted from place to place".[16] While French impressionists were understood to be "importing and synthesising different national schools of painting", "artists and authors around the world" claimed "impressionism as part of their national, and so local, painterly traditions".[17] "As a global but concomitantly national and local artistic language, impressionism" "... acted as an indexical sign of modernity" that "dialogued with the formation of modern national and cultural identities" and allowed for "local assertions of global concerns".[18] Impressionism flowed around the "capitalist-colonial" circuits that constituted and globalised modernity, whereupon it was often (but not always) "translated" and "adapted" to speak to "contentious debates around modernism, cosmopolitanism and nationalism" and "reverberated with questions about how to be or become part of the modern... world".[19]

Contributing to these cutting-edge developments in the field, in this chapter I analyse the complex entanglements of the national and transnational, the local and the global, that came together when French impressionism was collected and exhibited for the first time in Wales. On the premise that impressionism was a flexible cultural language rather than a fixed style or circumscribed group, I undertake a close reading of the exhibition catalogue to recover the polyvalent and pluralistic standard of impressionism it presented to the Welsh public. Next, I follow the exhibition's organisers and patrons in and out of Wales to uncover the roots of the impressionism they constructed for Cardiff in the much-more-studied London marketplace of pictures and ideas. Yet, I refuse to interpret the *Loan Exhibition* as a straightforward imitation of more famous exhibitions, such as those staged by Paul Durand-Ruel in 1883 and 1905, or Roger Fry in 1910 and 1912. Instead, I articulate how it leveraged the malleability of impressionism and adapted it to respond to distinctively Welsh anxieties and ambitions. In the final section, I set the exhibition in a wider context and examine how its presentation of impressionism resonated with the ambivalent and conflicted identity of a stateless nation in the grips of rapid modernisation and national reawakening.

Impressionism in Cardiff

The *Loan Exhibition* was conceived and organised by Hugh Blaker and Murray Urquhart under the patronage of Gwendoline and Margaret Davies of Llandinam.[20] The Davies sisters were the first major collec-

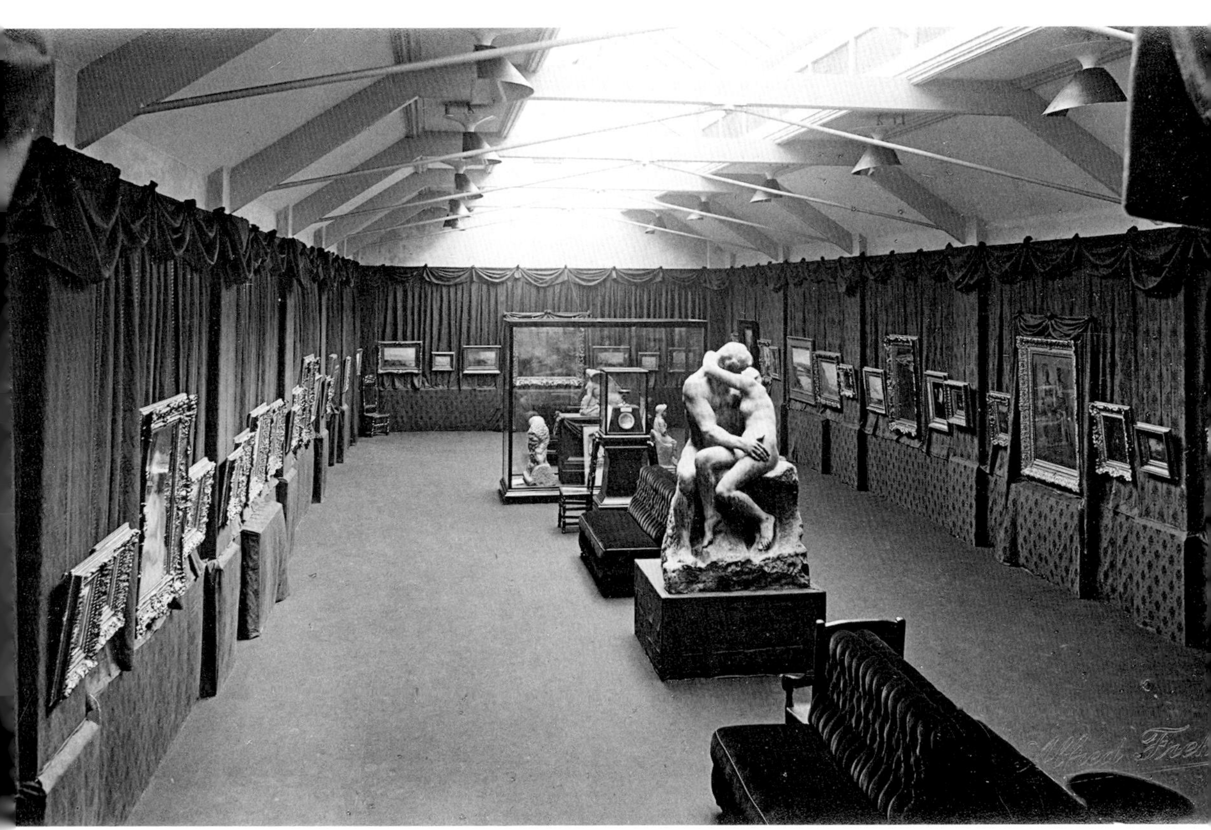

1. View of the *Loan Exhibition of Paintings*, Cardiff City Hall, 4 February – 28 March 1913, photograph, Amgueddfa Cymru – National Museum Wales

tors of impressionism in Britain after the Irish art dealer Hugh Lane; they lent thirty-eight of the fifty-nine works exhibited and defrayed the costs of its staging and educational activities, which included a series of gallery talks and a syllabus of lectures. Granddaughters of "self-made industrialist" David Davies of Llandinam, Gwendoline and Margaret were socialised into the Liberal and Nonconformist elite of turn-of-the-century Wales, a moment of "cultural reawakening", "buoyant national confidence", and a "tidal wave of economic expansion" that amounted to a "national renaissance".[21] Margaret was educated in art and art history, and both undertook studious tours of Italy and France.[22] They "began to collect in earnest" in 1912, purchasing works by Whistler, Monet, Manet, Boudin, Daumier, Millet and Rodin to complement those by Turner, Corot and David Cox they had acquired since 1906.[23] "By the eve of the First World War Gwendoline and Margaret had amassed a superb collection" that was "outstanding in Great Britain... [for the quantity of] French late nineteenth-century works".[24] After the war, they expanded their collection with progressive acquisitions of works by Vincent van Gogh and Paul Cézanne. During the war, the sisters served on the front running a Red Cross canteen for French troops; experiencing their suffering and returning to Wales to find "appalling need everywhere", they came to find art collecting a morally unsustainable "indulgence".[25] In the 1920s, they focused their resources on making their country home of Gregynog (near Newtown, then in Montgomeryshire) into "a centre for the arts and for discussion of social problems" that would "go some way to build a new Wales".[26] Upon her death in 1951, Gwendoline bequeathed her part of their joint collection to the National Museum of Wales; with the same intention, Margaret then resumed collecting, "working closely with staff at the National Museum" to put "the finishing touches" to her eventual bequest, which came in 1963.[27] The Davies sisters' collection "transformed completely the range, scale and quality of the [Welsh national] art collection".[28]

Blaker, the brother of the Davies sisters' governess and companion Jane, was a "painter, writer, art critic, museum curator, collector, dealer in Old Masters and... indefatigable advocate of avant-garde tendencies in art", especially championing Cézanne and the impressionists.[29] Urquhart, a childhood friend of the sisters' brother David, was a Scottish painter who trained in Paris and "loved the French Impressionists".[30] Frederick Wedmore and David Croal Thomson contributed to the catalogue. Wedmore, art critic for the *London Evening Standard*, had written the first significant English-language essay devoted to the impressionists in 1883.[31] Thomson was editor of the *Art Journal* from 1892 to 1902, manager of the Goupil Gallery between 1885 and 1897 and, from 1898 to 1908, a partner in Agnew's, where, through exhibitions and articles, he advocated Whistler and the Barbizon School.[32]

Since at least the 1880s, the Welsh public had been reading about impressionism thanks to the London correspondents of papers like the *Western Mail* and the *South Wales Daily News*, as well as reprints and clippings of articles and exhibition reviews originally published in London. The 1913 *Loan Exhibition* represented the first opportunity to actually see French impressionism in Wales, and the impressionism that visitors encountered was multifaceted and transnational. Centred on a *plein air* naturalism of loosely painted atmospheric effects, the capture of changing light, the suppression of pictorial detail and adherence to a subjective experience of nature, it also encompassed and interposed landscapes of a more narrowly scientific truth (based on the rigorous analysis of light) and paintings which transcended the optical to articulate the poetic resonance of high-key colouration and the purity of abstract form. More importantly, it combined these seemingly contradictory aesthetics in its articulation of individual artists and artworks. Not limited to a single aesthetic, neither was impressionism the exclusive property of France or the Société anonyme: the exhibition stressed the continuities and overlaps between artists of different generations and nations.

The longest entry in the exhibition catalogue was devoted to Monet and written by Wedmore; it offered a detailed explanation of impressionist theory and practice for the Welsh public unfamiliar with his pictures.[33] On the one hand, it presents impressionism as an art of "scientifically correct", natural vision founded on the rigorous "analysis of light... [which is] the chief motive of all his pictures": "The aim is to summarise the impressions of an effect" so as to replicate the way the eye sees, rather than falling into the trap of "individualis[ing] every detail in the picture" in the manner of a "photographic lens".[34] Such a definition fit best Monet's modern landscapes of the 1870s, but less the canvases exhibited in Cardiff, which all dated from the twentieth century. Thus, Wedmore also explained that "the emotion produced by colour is the artist's principal aim, in preference to the easier and more prosaic effects produced by scientific drawing".[35] He then enumerated a parallel "summary of the aims of impressionism" that focused less on natural vision and more on Monet's formal approach to colour.[36] By smoothing over the transformation that had occurred in Monet's art during the 1880s, Wedmore synthesised Monet's artistic development, opting to pluralise impressionism rather than historicise it, in order to mediate between what the Welsh public already knew of impressionism via the newspapers, and the physical examples he had available to show them (which were much less better known in Britain).

As the homology between Wedmore's emphasis on "the emotion produced by colour" and Roger Fry's influential emphasis on "the emotional elements of design" would suggest, the exhibition's plural impressionism manifest, too, in a formalist language which permeated the catalogue.[37] Thus, Honoré Daumier's *Coming out of School* (*La Sortie de l'École*) was described as "an unusually strong piece of colour... The simplicity of the forms should be noted, giving a breadth of effect which would probably have been lost had the artist painted direct from models".[38] Likewise, Jean-François Millet was praised for having "generalised the figure and landscape".[39] In *The Peasant Family* (*Une famille de paysans*), Millet "leaves us with the great outlines, the broad underlying facts" of the subject; in *Faggot-carriers* (*Bûcheronnes*) he presents a "splendid generalisation".[40] The presence of these Realist painters is sometimes understood as having diluted the impressionism of the exhibition, but viewed in the context of the formalist adoption of Daumier especially (Clive Bell would soon identify Daumier alongside Corot as a precursor to impressionism) and the critical cross-pollination between impressionism and Post-impressionism occurring in London, their prominence can instead be seen as lending weight to the exhibition's argument in favour of an impressionist tendency, broadly understood.[41] Indeed, the undecidability of Wedmore's Monet as a painter of scientific naturalism *and* expressive forms echoes in the description of Millet's formal generalisation as resulting in a "truer impression".[42]

In the same vein, Manet's biography in the catalogue presented him as "the senior member of the French impressionist group... [whose art was] based on a personal observation of nature", while notes about the *Church of Petit-Montrouge* (*Église du Petit-Montrouge*), described as a "quick sketch", stressed as well Manet's ability to boil his observations down to the "essentials of the subject', thus condensing the haste of execution associated with impressionism and the essentialism associated with Post-Impressionism.[43] Monet's "unerring power of selection", abstracting a scene to its bare "essentials", manifest in more than formal purity: "With the magic of a seer, Monet transmuted the Bridge of London almost into a fairy scene, so beautiful are the terms in which he has expressed it".[44] Similarly, Corot's value oscillated between his capture of "nature's varying effects", expression of "poetic beauty", and construction of "the perfect balance of the whole" composition seen in the abstract.[45]

The exhibition advocated impressionist approaches negatively as well as positively. The inclusion of Meissonier has sometimes puzzled, appearing as it does to cut against the main thrust of the exhibition. However, interpreted in light of the exhibition's argumentative remit, perhaps this stark contrast was exactly the point; perhaps it was included not on its own merits but as a teaching aid, to allow visitors to more clearly discern, by way of the contrast, the characteristics of impressionism that everywhere surrounded it. At least one attendee, artist John Witcombe, got the message. He wrote in the *Western Mail* that: "It is fortunate that the Meissonier... should be exhibited with the other pictures. It serves to show how much it loses by its unscientific camera vision, and how much the other works gain by the natural vision and record of one impression".[46]

In this plural and permeable frame, the exhibition's organisers did nevertheless acknowledge that the "school of impressionism" was "largely instituted by Monet and his followers, Renoir, Pissarro and Sisley", and that their "modern landscape[s]" constituted "one of the most revolutionary changes of modern times".[47] Yet, nuancing this picture, they also emphasised the evolutionary nature of this school and the timelessness of impressionism as an artistic principle with equal strength. As we have seen, "the senior member of the French impressionist group", Manet, and its most characteristic exemplar, Monet, were joined by French precursors in the form of Boudin, Monticelli, Corot, Daubigny, Díaz and Dupré, as well as painters from the Hague School, Mauve and Neuhuys, all of whom were framed by the language of impressionism.[48] Corot was a painter of "nature's varying effects", *Fête Champêtre* by Díaz offered "a little poem in colour" and Daubigny recorded "nature [at its]... simplest... [with an] extreme simplicity... of colour and form".[49] Monticelli was included for "the harmonious blending of his colour", which also expressed "surging emotions", and Boudin was the "stepping-stone between the impressionists and the French painters who preceded them".[50] Although beyond the scope of the exhibition, in the catalogue the exhibition's organisers took the opportunity to include the Old Masters, describing Manet as a "a modern Hals, painting with swiftness and certainty, and, like Hals, almost disregarding chiaroscuro".[51] At the evening lecture on the topic of "Impressionist painting", Hugh Blaker – taking the place of the advertised speaker George Moore – explained that "the impressionist movement is modern only in name, and dates back almost as far as the beginnings of art".[52]

The dependence of impressionism and its precursors on the British tradition was especially emphasised through the juxtaposition of Constable and Turner ("the greatest landscape artist the English school has seen") with the Barbizon painters and Monet.[53] The inclusion of Richard Wilson and Edward Burne-Jones (neither of whom were represented in the Davies sisters' collection at this time) was unjustifiable on aesthetic grounds, but introduced a specifically Welsh point of reference, and their work was attached, albeit tentatively, to the wider argument for impressionism.[54] The short entry on Wilson began with a quotation from John Ruskin: "With the name of Richard Wilson the history of sincere landscape art, founded as a meditative love of nature, begins for England", says Ruskin, and we may add "for Wales"; his (untraced) landscape was described as a "late afternoon effect".[55] Burne-Jones "takes us to a dreamland, a quiet world of beautiful unreality", echoing the description of Monet as a "seer... [who] transmutes the Bridge of London almost into a fairy scene, so beautiful are the terms in which he has expressed it".[56] The inclusion of Venetian scenes by Monet, Boudin and Whistler (the cosmopolitan American associated with the London impressionists and himself frequently called an impressionist), explicitly cross-referenced in the catalogue, encouraged viewers to identify a continuity and continuum of impressionism that spanned nationality and style.[57]

This pluralistic and polyvalent configuration of impressionism – a landscape art of personal observation *en plein air* that is delicate enough to capture atmospheric effects, scientific enough to conform to natural vision and poetic enough to stir the emotions; that is revolutionary for its modernity while not disconnected from tradition – drew from the complex and contradictory discourses generated by the regular exhibitions of impressionism in London.

Impressionism in London

First appearing in 1870, by 1913 impressionist paintings were a mainstay of the exhibition calendars and art markets of London and Glasgow.[58] Paul Durand-Ruel's 1883 exhibition at Dowdeswell & Dowdeswell's "was the first exhibition in Britain to devote itself explicitly to the Impressionists", marking "a turning point... in the reception of the Impressionists in England".[59] About fifty other exhibitions followed during the next decade – most importantly the monographic Monet exhibition by Goupil under the management of David Croal Thomson in 1889.[60] Even by 1887, London was so familiar with impressionism that the *Artist* reported: "Impressionism in some form or another is becoming the central idea in a very large proportion of modern picture production. The desire to paint effects rather than subjects is rapidly spreading".[61] Thus, even before Durand-Ruel's much larger and more famous 1905 exhibition at the Grafton Galleries, impressionism "no longer scandalised".[62]

The reference to "Impressionism in some form or another" is particularly revealing because the broad acceptance of impressionism in England at the turn of the century coincided with a precipitous pluralisation of its meanings. According to Kate Flint, "Impressionism was taken to mean a variety of things by a variety of people", and the boundaries of what counted as impressionism were permeable and shifting.[63] Whistler, for example, was readily annexed to impressionism, despite his protestations to the contrary; as Frank Rutter put it: "In England... Impressionism meant Whistler... The more we liked Whistler, the more we were tempted to dub 'Impressionist' all the paintings we liked".[64] Meanwhile, British artists like Turner and Constable, and even Old Masters like Velázquez and Hals were labelled impressionist. While some attributed this polyvalence to "the utter confusion of the English writers in the very use of the word [impressionism]", in France too "the term Impressionism itself had no clear unitary meaning at the time".[65] Thus, per John House, "the term Impressionist, loosely used, remained the most widely used broad category for modern French painting into the early years of the twentieth century".[66] As Wynford Dewhurst proclaimed in 1911: "We are all impressionists now".[67]

However, multiplicity does not mean meaninglessness: beyond the specificities of style, subject or technique, what united the diverse definitions of impressionism circulating around London was a general sense of impressionism as *modern*, that is, of impressionism as constituting a *break with tradition*. Indeed, the modernity of impressionism had been the focus of Wedmore's seminal article: "The adaptability of modern life to the purposes of Art has been tried... in France... [and] it has been tried best by the Impressionists"; whereas Degas's modernity lay in his choice of subjects ("the world of 1882", of "the jockey and the ballet girl"), "the modernité of Monet... is his method of actual painting... he, too, is unfettered. He sees with fresh eyes his autumn foliage, his shadows of the clouds and cliffs on brilliant summer waters. His impression is his own, and it is recorded while it is still vivid, and recorded fearlessly".[68] Alas, in England, arrayed against the painting of modern life "has been the force of traditions, in a country of tradition".[69]

English critics were still grappling with the modernity of impressionism when, at exhibitions staged in 1910 and 1912, Roger Fry introduced the complication of post-impressionism. Advocating the work of Gauguin, Van Gogh and Cézanne, Fry articulated a new paradigm of artistic modernity founded, as John House puts it, on "the Post-Impressionists' concern with expressive form, rather than with mere appearances".[70] Along with his "henchman" Clive Bell, Fry posited a new value system for assessing recent developments in art, not on the basis of conformity to natural vision (modernity as the repudiation of Academic formulae), but on the basis of their capacity to articulate "the emotional elements of design" (modernity as modernism).[71] Fry's influential formalist paradigm introduced yet another vector of polyvalence into English conceptions of impressionism, and, while the hostile critical reception to Fry's exhibitions contrasted sharply with the newly-established positive consensus on impressionism, the lines between impressionism and Post-Impressionism were not as clear-cut as Fry, or his critics, claimed: indeed, Fry himself would come to include Degas and late Renoir within his modernist territory.[72] Thus, the emergence of formalism after 1910 meant that critics had at their disposal multiple and hybrid ways of triangulating their varied interpretations of the stylistic and technical characteristics of impressionism between the poles of modernity and tradition.

Recent French painting thus "constituted a radical break with the past".[73] Just as it had in France in the 1870s, impressionism's modernist threat to artistic tradition merged with the spectre of political revolution.[74] Some Englishmen, as Walter Sickert reported, "use the word 'Impressionism'... with a sneer... much as a lady might use the word 'Socialist' in a drawing room".[75] The *foreignness* of impressionist modernity heightened the alarm: Ebenezer Wake Cook for example castigated an interest in impressionism as "anti-patriotism".[76] Since "modern art seemed... a threat to British values", traditions and the National School, efforts to secure the representation of impressionism in national museums sparked enormous controversy.[77]

In response to these xenophobic reactions – which conflated the modernity of impressionism with its foreignness – impressionism's supporters strategically stressed its emergence from (and thus conformity with) the very national traditions seemingly under attack. Thus, in his 1904 book *Impressionist Painting* Wynford Dewhurst effectively defined impressionism as a transnational "cult of sun-worship" – characterised by painting "in the open" to achieve "a closer verisimilitude to the varying moods of nature... [and] the problems of light" – that had originated in Britain.[78] The "Modern Impressionists" are simply the "French followers" of Turner, just as the Barbizon School had been "the direct result of Constable's power" in search of "sincerity and truth" a generation before.[79] Impressionism, broadly defined, was thus "British in its conception".[80] Other writers cast the net even wider: R. A. M. Stevenson characterised Velázquez as "the great Spanish Impressionist"; Wedmore concurred, adding Hals and Cox to the list.[81]

Thus, for England impressionism did not map straightforwardly to a coherent style or technique, but rather connoted a broad array of family resemblances which centred on a modernising attitude. After 1910, the array of overlapping characteristics (and thus the borders of impressionism) widened further to include (for some, if not Fry himself) the modernist priority for abstract and expressive form. The reception of impressionism was thus animated by the profound tension between its modernity and existing traditions. Yet, while celebrated or denigrated as a break with the past, impressionism was also understood as a timeless artistic principle, describing Velázquez and Hals as effectively as Monet and Degas. This tension between past and present was also influenced by a perceived antagonism between (modern) foreign art and the (traditions of the) National School. Thus, Constable, Turner and Whistler were cast as impressionists to reassure the "aggressively xenophobic [English] public" that impressionism had native roots and local practitioners.[82]

"The greatest artistic event in the history of Wales" thus presented French art to the Welsh people in a conceptual framework indebted to English aesthetic and institutional debates.[83] As we have seen, the exhibition's organisers and authors of its catalogue – Blaker, Urquhart, Thomson and Wedmore – were all active participants in the London art market and belligerents in the critical war for the acceptance of modern foreign art in England. Through their participation in the exhibition, they transported these debates to Wales.[84]

Wedmore was already part of the nascent Welsh art world. In 1883, at the invitation of T. H. Thomas (an artist at the centre of turn-of-the-century Welsh cultural nationalism), he adjudicated the art competitions at the 1883 Eisteddfod in Cardiff.[85] The following year, he was involved in the exhibition Thomas organised in support of the Royal Cambrian Academy.[86] Via Thomas, Wedmore became friendly with art collector and philanthropist James Pyke Thompson: in 1888, Thompson opened a gallery called Turner House on the grounds of his estate in Penarth, centred on his collection of Turner watercolours. In 1897, Wedmore executed Thompson's will, which provisioned for the donation of the Turner House collection to the Cardiff Museum and Art Gallery, whom, starting in 1905, Wedmore advised on acquisitions. When, in 1912, the Cardiff Museum and Art Gallery was absorbed into the new National Museum of Wales, Wedmore continued to advise the Museum, and in this role ensured the purchase of modern British and French works, including Gustave Courbet and multiple Boudins.[87]

As Wedmore travelled into Wales, the Davies sisters would look beyond it, to engage in the transnational networks that globalised impressionism. They were educated at a private residential school in England, where they were inculcated in the Francophile values of the British elite. After 1903 Margaret took art classes at the Slade, and in 1907–8 attended art history lectures in Germany, which acquainted her with the European canon from the Renaissance to Turner and Whistler. They each spoke French and travelled extensively in Europe, including to Italy in 1902, 1908 and 1909. On their return from this latter trip, they stopped in Paris to visit the Louvre, the Salon and the spring exhibition at the Grand Palais. They would return to France in 1911 and 1912, once again visiting Paris, where they encountered Monet's Venetian scenes at Bernheim-Jeune in May and June 1912. They owned a copy of Théodore Duret's *Les Peintres impressionnistes*, and in January 1918 Margaret translated Ambroise Vollard's 1914 biography of *Cézanne* from the French.[88]

These transnational experiences directly informed their collecting practice: they began collecting Turner immediately after Margaret completed her lecture course (and Whistler not long after); after visiting Bernheim-Jeune they bought three works from Monet's Venetian series; and in February 1918 Gwendoline purchased the sisters' first two Cézannes. More generally, the sisters purchased from major London- and Paris-based dealers via agents and advisors, but would receive sales catalogues and artworks for their consideration at home in Llandinam.[89] The Davies sisters thus engaged with impressionism through multiple modalities of transnational exchange: education, travel, exhibitions (both museum and commercial), criticism, art history and the art market. These concrete transnational mobilities help situate the Cardiff exhibition in a wider context and go some way to explain its framing of impressionism.

Impressionism for Wales

The 1913 exhibition of the Davies sisters' collection was one node in a manifold transnational network connecting Cardiff to London, Paris and beyond, around which discourses about impressionism circulated across national borders; it provided an important locus for these heterogeneous discourses to coalesce and take a concrete, public-facing form for the first time in Wales. Thus far, I have emphasised points of continuity between the polyvalent, ambivalently modern impressionisms presented to Wales and England. As we have seen, for the English, the promise (and threat) of impressionism consisted in its capacity to enhance (or destroy) the native art traditions and the National School. It is here that the significance of impressionism in the Welsh national context begins to diverge from the English, because, as it was understood at the time, there was no substantial native art tradition, and certainly no National School, to be imperilled. Indeed, the very purpose of the exhibition, stated explicitly by its organisers and widely recognised by both Welsh and English commentators, was "fostering national taste in art".[90]

Speaking at the opening, Urquhart expressed his wish that "the exhibition would direct a noble standard of taste" among the Welsh people, thereby spanning the "great gulf fixed" "... between the supreme art of the ages and the art of the popular imagination".[91] Ordinary visitors were effectively asked to suspend their ignorant prejudice for historical and religious art and catch up (with "the connoisseurs of Europe") to the fact that "Art must be pure in its aesthetic sense".[92] Lord Mostyn, president of the National Museum and patron of the Royal Cambrian Academy, preceding Urquhart on the bill, reiterated that "*Those best able to judge* are of the unanimous opinion that the present exhibition is the most important ever organised within the Principality".[93] When the *Western Mail's* art critic J. M. Staniforth expressed his unease with the "'Impressionist' school of painting", he was quickly criticised for his "parochial" attitude.[94] Nevertheless, while they disagreed about what constituted "the best in art" (Staniforth preferred Meissonier to the impressionists), everybody with an interest in the exhibition agreed that "wise guidance in [art] appreciation" was desperately needed to "enable Wales to shake off the trammels of artistic philistinism"; "[w]hen the... Welsh appreciation of the fine arts considered with that of her Scottish sister, it can only be lamented that a nation so rich and so eager for education generally is yet so lagging in the culture of the fine arts".[95] Cardiff, as the rest of Wales, was understood to offer such "uncongenial soil... [for] the cultivation of art" due to the poor state of art education, the City Council's "porcine indifference to art" and the "apathy" of its citizens, starved of "opportunity of seeing the best in art".[96] Thus, "an exhibition of that sort" – showcasing the progress made beyond Wales's border, staged in Cardiff Town Hall under the auspices of the National Museum and accompanied by an educational programme – "was one of the finest things on earth to stimulate and encourage true art in Wales".[97] "Certainly nowhere in England can such a group of modern masterpieces be seen. This, then, is the chance of young Cardiff".[98]

To ensure the exhibition was "as educational as possible", the Davies sisters agreed to defray the cost of offering free admission.[99] As we have seen, a catalogue was produced, providing biographies of each artist (explaining their art historical significance) and interpretative précis of each artwork (directing readers evidently imagined to lack expertise to notice the marks of technique and instructing them to draw apposite comparisons). This paratext was embodied – three times a week – by the exhibition's curators, who gave "informal talks about the paintings" in the gallery.[100] The most prominent and staunch advocates of impressionism in Britain were invited to give a series of formal evening lectures: Wedmore; the Irish critic and writer George Moore, author of *Modern Painting* (1893); and the Scottish critic and painter D. S. MacColl, member of the New English Art Club and author of *Nineteenth Century Art* (1902).[101] The first lecture set this artistic education in a civic framework: Laurence Housman spoke about "Art Training in Relation to Citizenship".[102]

This concrete and discursive framing of the Welsh public's first encounter with impressionism as the starting point for a national revival underscores the complexities and ambivalences that inhered to impressionism as it crossed national borders and assumed specific local meanings in global peripheries. On the one hand, those high-handed and elitist assumptions about popular Welsh ignorance were repetitions of a well-worn cliché about the congenitally "unvisual" Welsh that, as Peter Lord has long since argued, contributed to a wider colonial discourse about Welsh backwardness with respect to England that justified political inequalities between the two nations.[103] By mobilising French art seen, at least in part, through English eyes, the exhibition could be seen to participate in a colonial cultural politics, imposing the standards of the centre on the periphery and supressing indigenous culture.

Yet, on the other hand, since the very desire to articulate a positive vision of the Welsh nation had been catalysed by the infamous accusations of the *Blue Books* commissioners in 1847 (who characterised the Welsh as a primitive people being held back by their stubborn clinging to the Welsh language and led into moral turpitude by their religious Nonconformity), "Welsh backwardness" became a shibboleth of Welsh nationalism. Partisans of the vibrant and energised turn-of-the-century Welsh nationalist movement accepted that Wales was behind England (and even more worryingly, Ireland, Scotland and other small and stateless nations) in matters artistic, and acknowledged that "the widespread perception of the deficiency of the indigenous culture in visual art weakened the national argument".[104] Iona Williams, for example, saw a National School as necessary but as-yet-absent proof of the self-evident fact that "the Welsh are a living nation with a definite distinctive character... A people that is a nation should have an Art... [which] utters its vision to the world".[105] Tom Ellis – a Romantic and Hegelian nationalist who articulated an organicist vision of Wales as a unity of social values, popular traditions, history, literature, art and political institutions – admitted with "sorrow as well as with frankness – that not the most patriotic of us can claim for Wales the possession of a native school of art".[106] A National School needed an enlightened common people to support it, wealthy patrons to fund it, a national Museum to display it and progressive art schools to perpetuate it.[107] Thus, when Urquhart and Blaker spoke of "plac[ing] a true ideal before the Welsh people" to "give stimulus to the long-delayed revival in Welsh art", they were participating in this nationalist discourse and thus positioning impressionism as the most viable vehicle of nationalist cultural politics.[108]

The Davies sisters certainly supported this ambition. While they began collecting art in pursuit of pleasure, spurred by nostalgia for their travels in Europe (especially Venice), their first purchases of French impressionist canvases in 1912 (the three Venetian Monet's and Manet's church) nevertheless coincided with a shift in motivation away from "pleasure [... towards] buying with the view to the formulation of a collection which might benefit a greater number of people".[109] The Davies sisters were linked "by family ties and friendship" to the "leading lights of Welsh patriotism", and their collection and display of art, most significantly impressionist art, was just one aspect of a lifelong project centred on the cultural enlightenment and material amelioration of the Welsh people, ultimately culminating in their bequest of their collection to the National Museum of Wales in 1951 (Gwendoline) and 1963 (Margaret).[110]

The potential national significance of loan exhibitions of private collections in Wales had been proposed by William Cornwallis West of Ruthin Castle who, in 1868, organised "the first major historical art exhibition in Wales" on the model of the *Art Treasures of Great Britain* exhibition staged in Manchester in 1857 and in parallel with the Ruthin Eisteddfod, repeating the feat in Wrexham in 1876.[111] Borrowing works from Welsh gentry collections (which reflected their conservative, anglicised taste) and the studios of contemporary artists respected in England (including, for the Wrexham exhibition, George Frederic Watts and Frederick Leighton), Cornwallis West stressed "the beneficent effect of... works of art upon the population of a country. Their contemplation elevates the taste, they refine the mind, and lead the human soul to all that is pure, great and good. We trust... that the people of Wales, the intelligent and ingenious artisans, the... colliers, miners and slate quarrymen... will be enabled to visit this exhibition".[112] Yet, despite pleasing Welsh critics, Cornwallis West failed to attract the crowds and the 1876 show especially was a "financial disaster".[113] In 1881, Welsh artists T. H. Thomas, B. S. Marks and Edwin Seward organised a loan exhibition in Cardiff to raise funds for the Free Library, and again in 1884 in support of the Royal Cambrian Academy (founded in 1881 to advance Welsh art by a group of English-born painters active in North Wales). At the opening of the 1884 exhibition, Cardiff's mayor lauded the opportunity that the exhibition provided "to give the toiling thousands of our race the opportunities of coming in contact with the productions of the best painters and artists – a privilege now enjoyed by the few who can afford to travel long distances in order to gratify their taste and fancy... I believe in the elevating power of true art".[114] Yet, as in 1876, the toiling thousands failed to materialise and the exhibition was another "financial disaster".[115]

Exhibitions of contemporary Welsh art fared no better. Since 1862, artists working in Wales had exhibited competitively at the National Eisteddfod, but, despite the involvement and support of such prominent figures as Hubert Herkomer, Lawrence Alma-Tadema and Wedmore, the patchy quality of entrants and the absence of a wider institutional framework that might support prize-winning artists in forming a National School meant that the Eisteddfod "continued to disappoint patriotic intellectuals".[116] Similarly, the exhibition of works by artists of the Royal Cambrian Academy at South Wales University College in Cardiff in 1885 was another "fiasco"; those in the press who recognised that "a continuous flow of visitors, and not a few buyers", as would be guaranteed in "any of the English large towns", was needed to make the Academicians "the centre of a new Welsh School of Painters" were destined for disappointment.[117]

In terms of attendance, impressionism succeeded in 1913 where earlier attempts had failed. Understandably then, the Davies sisters continued to exhibit their collection, including at the Glynn Vivian in Swansea in 1914 and the Royal National Eisteddfod in Barry in 1920.[118] At this latter exhibition, Gwendoline (joined at the event by Blaker) spoke "on [the] place of art in life" and expressed her pleasure that "the public were now realising the importance of art": what Blaker called her "public spirit shown in the expression of taste and judgement" was rewarded by a large attendance and organised visits by local schools.[119] As with the 1913 exhibition, the content was impressionist, the framing was didactic and the context national (eisteddfodau being the primary vehicle of Welsh cultural nationalism): "Educational value attaches to the selections from the Llandinam collection of modern art. The works ... illustrate different tendencies in modern French art".[120]

Despite Blaker's praise, the popularity of the Davies sisters' collection cannot be attributed solely, or even mainly, to their taste and judgement. As Mark Evans has argued, "local opinion at the two principal art collections in Wales was already well disposed towards modern French painting immediately before the Davies sisters showed a similar inclination".[121] I have already discussed Wedmore's key role in shaping the National Museum's collecting policy in a broadly impressionist direction. In Swansea, this was achieved under the impetus of Rouennais industrialist, collector and patron, François Depeaux who, in 1911, donated six works by Rouen impressionists to the newly-opened Glynn Vivian Art Gallery (near to which Depeaux owned a coal mine), with the intention to "make known in [Wales]... the impressionist art... which... originated in France".[122] In 1914, forty-three École de Rouen paintings from Depeaux's collection were exhibited in parallel with the loan exhibition to which the Davies sisters contributed.[123] Looking beyond individual collectors to the context in which they collected, the question then is: why had modern French art, and impressionism specifically, seemingly proven itself more amenable to nationalist ambitions in Wales than works by either English or Welsh artists?

At the 1913 exhibition, reviewers perceived a uniformity that art historians have subsequently missed: "The promoters have confined themselves almost entirely to purely emotional art. There are practically no examples of literary or historical interest, the aesthetic and highest form of art alone being exhibited... [Monet's] splendid realisation of light and air in prismatic colours... will be generally admired".[124] For Edgar Jones, "[t]he choice of the selectors" to focus exclusively on "the poetry of colour" of Monet, Turner, Corot; the "musical rhythm" of Díaz and Monticelli, and the "spiritual insight" of Millet "testifies to their keen insight into the Welsh temperament... They all stimulate a certain emotion, and they may, therefore, be expected to appeal in a high degree to Welshmen".[125] Here, Jones was mobilising the racial standard of nationality and an antiquarian vision of Welshness, "shrouded in the swirling mountain mists of that Celtic twilight" "invented" by literary historian Matthew Arnold.[126] In his 1876 Oxford University lectures on Celtic literature, Arnold evoked "Wales, where the past still lives", inhabited by a Celtic race governed by "emotion" and "sentiment", and possessed of a "genius for poetry" ("where emotion counts for so much") with corresponding "difficulties [with] painting and sculpture" (where emotion must be tempered by a "sense of measure").[127] The "lyrical appeal" of impressionism wooed "[t]he Celt's love of poetry, of music, of mysticism, of spiritual ideas".[128] In this frame, the particular significance of impressionism for Wales lay in the emotional elements of design and the emotion produced by colour which, in so closely resonating with one aspect of (this racial configuration of) Welshness (the love of poetry), might provide stimulus for overcoming another (difficulties with painting) and so, by kindling an aesthetic sense among the toiling thousands, would cultivate more congenial soil for the flowering of a National School, which would finally attest to the world that the Welsh are a people that is a nation with an Art.[129]

Yet, this timeless, antiquarian Wales bore little resemblance to the concrete experiences of those toiling thousands, who had been "sucked into the pattern of life... pioneered" in Merthyr Tydfil and the South Wales coalfield: modernity.[130] The long nineteenth century was an era of rapid and intense modernisation for Wales, driven by industrialisation centred on the extraction of natural resources for export: the Davies sisters inherited fortune had been made in the South Wales coal industry, which was at its very zenith in 1913.[131] The claim of Cardiff to be the nation's capital, and thus rightful home to the National Museum, was predicated on its docks being "the most important coal port in the world".[132] A modern, class-based "industrial society" emerged that was difficult to reconcile with inherited ideas of Wales as an unspoiled and ahistorical natural Arcadia, where simple, Welsh-speaking and Liberal-voting folk lead simple, God-fearing lives, in touch with ancient traditions, governed by Nonconformist ethics and practices, animated by a passionate Celtic spirit, and predisposed to a love of song and poetry.[133] The shared language and religion which had (conceptually) bound the Welsh into an organic whole, were seemingly imperilled by the rapid, immigration-fuelled growth of multicultural and polyglot communities governed by values ostensibly inimical to Welsh national sentiment: socialism in the "working-class metropolis of Merthyr Tydfil", mercantilism in the "new middle-class world of Cardiff".[134] Thus, although by 1895 modernity "embodied reality for the majority of the inhabitants of Wales... this situation had come into being so rapidly that the image of Wales did not correspond with the substance of Wales".[135]

As we have seen, modernity was the overriding characteristic ascribed to impressionism by the London discourse imported and adapted by the organisers of the 1913 exhibition. With the impressionist artworks exhibited in Cardiff, they did not offer an image of modern Wales, but instead a modern aesthetic through which the Welsh might create one for themselves. The labile and plural impressionism it advocated had a foot on both sides of the fissure separating experiences of modernisation from imagined national identities. Thus, impressionism as "one of the most revolutionary changes of modern times", which abandoned "sham classicism and academic absurdities" in favour of the "personal observation of nature" and "scientifically correct" natural vision, connected with the desires of a booming nation to be "unfettered" by the baggage of the past and to see a changed world with "fresh eyes".[136] At the same time, the "magic" and "poetic beauty" of impressionism's "high key... tone and colour", the "rhythmic grace" of its abstracted forms, were meaningful for those who conceptualised their Welshness in terms of inherited Celtic traditions.[137] Similarly, while the Frenchness of impressionism was essential to its value as an outside agent capable of reactivating a moribund Welsh School, the desires and anxieties to which it spoke reflected the particularities and complexities of Welsh history and identity; thus, the exhibition's celebration of impressionism's novelty was tempered by the connections it drew between French, English and Welsh artists united (more or less tentatively) under the label of impressionism. This hybrid impressionism, which held the traditional and the modern, the local and the global, the national and the transnational in unresolved tension, was neither an imitation nor a misconception, but an authentically Welsh creation.

1 First and third quotations from Hugh Blaker, "The Loan Exhibition at the Welsh National Museum", *Western Mail*, 12 February 1913, p. 7. Cf Lord Mostyn, president of the National Museum: "The beautiful gallery of pictures he had just opened was the finest and most important exhibition ever held at Cardiff: perhaps it was the most important ever held in Wales." "Masterpieces of Art. First Work of National Museum. Exhibition in Cardiff. Gallery Opened by Lord Mostyn", *Western Mail*, 5 February 1913, p. 6. Second quotation from Hugh Blaker's diary (4 February 1913), reprinted in Murray Urquhart, "The Blaker Diary: Some Extracts with a memoir by Murray Urquhart", *Apollo*, vol. 78, no. 20, 1963, p. 294.

2 Visitor numbers given by John Ingamells, *The Davies Collection of French Art* (Cardiff: National Museum of Wales, 1967), p. 25; Mark Evans, "The Davies sisters of Llandinam and Impressionism for Wales, 1908–1923", *Journal of the History of Collections*, vol. 16, no. 2, 2004, p. 225. Quotation from *Catalogue of Loan Exhibition of Paintings (With Illustrations) February & March 1913* (Cardiff: Amgueddfa Genedlaethol Cymru – National Museum of Wales, 1913), p. 31.

3 The painting was presented under this title at the 1913 exhibition, but today it is known as *Effect of Snow on Petit-Montrouge* (*Effet de neige à Petit-Montrouge*).

4 Édouard Manet, *Effect of Snow on Petit-Montrouge* (*Effet de neige à Petit-Montrouge*), 1870–71, oil on canvas, 61.6 × 50.4 cm, Cardiff, Amgueddfa Cymru – National Museum of Wales, Gwendoline Davies Bequest. Quotations from *Loan Exhibition of Paintings*, pp. 22–23.

5 Claude Monet, *Charing Cross Bridge*, 1902, oil on canvas, 65.4 × 81.3 cm, Cardiff, AC – NMW, Margaret Davies Bequest; Claude Monet, *San Giorgio Maggiore by Twilight* (*San Giorgio Maggiore au crépuscule*), 1908, oil on canvas, 65.2 × 92.4 cm, Cardiff, AC – NMW, GD Bequest; Claude Monet, *The Grand Canal, Venice* (*Le Grand Canal*), 1908, oil on canvas, 73.2 × 89.7 cm, San Francisco, Legion of Honor, Fine Arts Museums of San Francisco; Claude Monet, *San Giorgio Maggiore*, 1908, oil on canvas, 59.2 × 81.2 cm, Cardiff, AC – NMW, GD Bequest. Quotations from ibid., pp. 33–35.

6 James Abbott McNeill Whistler, *Nocturne: Blue and Gold, St Mark's, Venice*, 1880, oil on canvas, 75.4 × 90.5 cm, Cardiff, AC – NMW, GD Bequest; Jean-Baptiste-Camille Corot, *Distant View of Corbeil, Morning* (*Corbeil vu de loin, le matin*), c. 1870, oil on canvas, 25.1 × 33.9 cm, Cardiff, AC – NMW, MD Bequest; Jean-Baptiste Camille Corot, *Castel Gandolfo, Dancing Tyrolean Shepherds by Lake Albano* (*Danse tyrolienne près du lac Albano*), date unknown, oil on canvas, 49.2 × 65.5 cm, Cardiff, AC – NMW, GD Bequest; including Joseph Mallord William Turner, *Margate Jetty*, c. 1840, oil on canvas, 47 × 37 cm, Cardiff, AC – NMW, GD Bequest; Joseph Mallord William Turner, *A Sailing Boat off Deal*, c. 1835, oil on millboard, 22.6 × 30.3 cm, Cardiff, AC – NMW, GD Bequest. Quotations from ibid., pp. 31, 9, 19, 25.

7 Eugène Louis Boudin, *Venice, the Molo* (*Venise, le Molo*), 1895, oil on canvas, 33.5 × 57 cm, Cardiff, AC – NMW, GD Bequest; Narcisse Virgilio Diaz, *Fête Champêtre*, 1844, oil on canvas, 24 × 32,4 cm, Cardiff, AC – NMW, MD Bequest; Jules Dupré, *Landscape* (*Paysage*), untraced; Anton Mauve, *Shepherdess* (*Bergère*), late nineteenth century, oil on canvas, 30.3 × 50.6 cm, Cardiff, AC – NMW, MD Bequest.

8 Including, for example, Jean-François Millet, *Winter, The Faggot Gatherers* (*Hiver : les Fagoteuses*), 1868–75, oil on canvas, 82 × 100 cm, Cardiff, AC – NMW, GD Bequest; Jean-François Millet, *The Peasant Family* (*La Famille du paysan*), 1871–72, oil on canvas, 110.4 × 81 cm, Cardiff, AC – NMW, MD Bequest; Honoré Daumier, *The Night Walkers* (*Promeneurs de la nuit*), 1842–47, oil on board, 28.9 × 18.7 cm, Cardiff, AC – NMW, GD Bequest; Jean Louis Ernest Meissonier, *Innocents and Card Sharpers* (*Un jeu de piquet*), 1861, oil on board, 24.2 × 32.2 cm, Cardiff, AC – NMW, MD Bequest; Adolphe Monticelli, *Group of Figures* (*Groupe de personnages*), untraced, from the collection of J. J. Cowan. In September 1913, Gwendoline Davies purchased a different Monticelli: *Summer Court*, date unknown, oil on board, 39.3 × 59.7cm, Cardiff, AC – NMW, GD Bequest. Auguste Rodin, *The Kiss* (*Le Baiser*), cast 1902, bronze, 182.9 cm, Cardiff, AC – NMW, gift of GD.

9 First quotation from J. Ingamells, *Davies Collection*, p. 24.Ingamells, *Davies Collection* cit., p. 24. Cf Madeleine Korn, "Exhibitions of modern French art and their influence on collectors in Britain 1870–1918: the Davies sisters in context", *Journal of the History of Collections*, vol. 16, no. 2, 2004, p. 191. Later quotations are titles of lectures related to the exhibition given by Hugh Blaker (taking the place of the advertised George Moore) and Frederick Wedmore on

26 and 19 February 1913, respectively. For the full syllabus see *Loan Exhibition of Paintings*, p. 41.

10 Gwendoline Davies spoke on this subject at the opening of the *Arts & Crafts* exhibition at the Eisteddfod in Barry in 1920. "Welsh Arts and Craft", *Western Mail*, 26 July 1920, p. 5. See also *Eisteddfod Genedlaethol Frenhinol Cymru, Barri, 1920, Awst 2, 3, 4, 5, 6, 7: y rhaglen swyddogol = The Royal National Eisteddfod of Wales, Barry, 1920, August 2, 3, 4, 5, 6, 7: the official programme* (Barry: Eisteddfod Genedlaethol Cymru, 1920), pp. 9, 189.

11 First quotation Murray Urquhart, speaking at the opening of the exhibition, quoted in "Masterpieces of Art", *op. cit.*, p. 6. Second quotation Hugh Blaker, "Loan Exhibition", p. 7.

12 "Masterpieces of Art", *op. cit.*, p. 6.

13 This phrase belongs to Nada Shabout, which she uses to discuss Eurocentric histories of modernism more generally, but which amply applies to histories of impressionism specifically. Catherine Grant and Dorothy Price, "Decolonizing Art History", *Art History*, vol. 43, no. 1, 2020, p. 52. Two recent edited volumes are at the forefront of these new developments: Emily C. Burns and Alice M. Rudy Price (eds.), *Mapping Impressionist Painting in Transnational Contexts* (Abingdon: Routledge, 2021); Alexis Clark and Frances Fowle (ed.), *Globalizing Impressionism: Reception, Translation, and Transnationalism* New Haven and London, Yale University Press, 2020. See Samuel Raybone's book reviews of *Globalizing Impressionism: Reception, Translation, and Transnationalism*, edited by Alexis Clark and Frances Fowle, and *Mapping Impressionist Painting in Transnational Contexts*, edited by Emily C. Burns and Alice M. Rudy Price, in *Nineteenth-Century Art Worldwide* 20, no. 3, 2021.

14 Nada Shabout in Catherine Grant and Dorothy Price, "Decolonizing Art History", pp. 52–53. A recent locus for these discussions was the session I convened at the Association for Art History's 2021 Annual Conference on "Provincializing Impressionism", https://eu-admin.eventscloud.com/website/2065/provincializing-impressionism/.

15 Alexis Clark and Frances Fowle, "Introduction: "What Is Impressionism?", in Clark and Fowle, *Globalizing Impressionism: Reception, Translation, and Transnationalism* (New Haven–London: Yale University Press, 2020).

16 First and third quotations ibid. Second quotation Emily C. Burns and Alice M. Rudy Price, "Mapping Impressionist Constellations", in Burns and Price (eds.), *Mapping Impressionist Painting in Transnational Contexts* (Abingdon: Routledge, 2021), p. 5.

17 Clark and Fowle, "What Is Impressionism?", *op. cit.*

18 Final quotation from Partha Mitter, "Decentering Modernism: Art History and Avant-Garde Art from the Periphery", *Art Bulletin*, vol. 90, no. 4, 2008, p. 540, quoted in Burns and Price, *Mapping Impressionist Constellations* cit., p. 4. Earlier quotations from Clark and Fowle, "What Is Impressionism?" cit.

19 First and third quotations Burns and Price, *Mapping Impressionist Constellations* cit., pp. 6, 5. Other quotations Clark and Fowle, "What Is Impressionism?" cit. "[I]mpressionist aesthetics connected with imperialist circuits... In its application to landscapes... the stylistic attributes of Impressionism enact a possession of colonised and Indigenous landscapes through representation... Artists in colonised territories infrequently embraced Impressionist aesthetics and did so in uneasy contexts." "Many, if not most, nineteenth-century cultures did not value the type or tradition of artmaking that includes impressionism." Burns and Price, *Mapping Impressionist Constellations* cit., pp. 6–10.

20 The Davies sisters are well known and much studied in Wales. After they bequeathed their collection to the National Museum of Wales in 1951 and 1963, that institution became a locus for scholarship on the sisters and their collection, especially via catalogues, collection guides, exhibitions and publications by its keepers of art and curators: Ingamells, *Davies Collection*; Peter Cannon-Brookes, "The Davies Sisters of Gregynog", *Apollo* vol. 109, no. 205, 1979; Peter Hughes, *French Art from the Davies Bequest* (Cardiff: National Museum of Wales, 1982); Mark Evans and Oliver Fairclough (eds.), *The National Museum of Wales: A Companion Guide to the National Art Gallery* (Cardiff: National Museum of Wales in association with Lund Humphries, 1993); Bethany McIntyre, *Sisters Select: Works on Paper from the Davies Collection* (Cardiff: National Museums & Galleries of Wales, 2000); Ann Sumner, *Colour and Light: Fifty Impressionist and Post-Impressionist Works at the National Museum of Wales* (Cardiff: National Museum of Wales, 2005); Oliver

Fairclough (ed.), *'Things of Beauty' What Two Sisters Did for Wales* (Cardiff: National Museum Wales Books, 2007); Bryony Dawkes, Ann Sumner and Oliver Fairclough, *Turner to Cézanne: Masterpieces from the Davies Collection* (Cardiff: National Museum Wales, 2009); Oliver Fairclough (ed.), *A Companion Guide to the Welsh National Museum of Art* (Cardiff: Amgueddfa Cymru – National Museum of Wales, 2011). A special issue of the *Journal of the History of Collections* collected scholarship on the sisters in a wider context: Mark Evans, "Impressionism for Wales", pp. 219–253; Madeleine Korn, "Exhibitions of modern French art", pp. 198–218; Robert Meyrick, "Hugh Blaker: doing his bit for the moderns", *Journal of the History of Collections*, vol. 16, no. 2, 2004, pp. 173–89. The best biography of the Davies sisters remains Eirene White, *The Ladies of Gregynog* (Cardiff: University of Wales Press, 1985).

21 First quotation Ann Sumner, *Colour and Light*, p. 21. Later quotations Kenneth O. Morgan, *Rebirth of a Nation: Wales 1880-1980* (Oxford: Oxford University Press, 1981), pp. 121, 123, 124, 94.

22 Ann Sumner, "'Much that is beautiful': art, travel and learning", in Oliver Fairclough, *Things of Beauty*, pp. 41–56.

23 Sumner, "Much that is beautiful", *op. cit.*, p. 57. Their very first recorded purchase was a watercolour by Hercules Brabazon Brabazon of *An Algerian*, which Margaret acquired from the Goupil Gallery, London in December 1906. See Mark Evans, "Impressionism for Wales", p. 240; Bethany McIntyre, "Gwendoline and Margaret Davies – Collectors of Works on Paper", in McIntyre, *Sisters Select: Works on Paper from the Davies Collection* (Cardiff: National Museums & Galleries of Wales, 2000), p. 9.

24 Sumner, "Much that is beautiful", *op. cit.*, p. 58; Ingamells, *Davies Collection*, p. 5.

25 First quotation Gwendoline Davies letter to Thomas Jones, November 1921, quoted in Oliver Fairclough, "'Knocked to Pieces': The Impact of the Great War", in Oliver Fairclough, *Things of Beauty*, pp. 79. Second quotation Fairclough, "Knocked to Pieces" cit., p. 76.

26 Fairclough, "Knocked to Pieces" cit., p. 79; Robert Meyrick, "'Wealth Wise and Culture Kind': Gregynog in the 1920s and 1930s", in Fairclough, *Things of Beauty* cit., p. 98.

27 Sumner, *Colour and Light* cit., p. 28. "Although the sisters bought individually, they saw the collection as one." Louisa Briggs, "'An All Consuming Drive': Margaret's Later Collecting", in Fairclough, *Things of Beauty* cit., p. 150.

28 Oliver Fairclough, "Building a national art collection", in Fairclough, *A Companion Guide to the Welsh National Museum of Art* (Cardiff: Amgueddfa Cymru – National Museum of Wales, 2011), p. 8. This brief précis of the Davies sisters" cultural and philanthropic activities is by no means comprehensive; in the interests of concision, it focuses on their collecting practice in order to help elucidate upon the individuals behind the collective endeavour of the 1913 exhibition. In reality, and as noted below, their art collecting was just one element (and arguably far from the most important one) of a much broader project of contribution to Welsh culture fuelled by a sense of philanthropic duty borne of religious faith and textured by Ruskinian ideas (fashionable among the turn-of-the-century nationalist intelligentsia) about the inherently improving nature of beauty on ordinary people and the national condition.

29 Robert Meyrick, "Hugh Blaker" cit., p. 173.

30 "With two or three brushstrokes, he could summon and retain a sunny seaside or an overcast winter day in the Scottish highlands." Brian Urquhart, "My Father Murray Urquhart", *The New York Review*, 21 February 2013.

31 Frederick Wedmore, "'The Impressionists', *Fortnightly Review*, January 1883, pp. 75–82", in Kate Flint, *Impressionists in England: The Critical Reception* (London, Boston, Melbourne and Henley: Routledge and Kegan Paul, 1984), pp. 46–55.

32 On Thomson's practice as a dealer at the forefront of the "professionalization of art dealing', alongside Durand-Ruel, Georges Petit, Alexander Reid, Theo van Gogh and others, and in context in which "art history, art criticism, and art dealing were nebulous and overlapping fields of knowledge", see Anne Helmreich, "David Croal Thomson: The Professionalization of Art Dealing in an Expanding Field", *Getty Research Journal*, no. 5, 2013, pp. 89–100, 90.

33 On Wedmore's authorship see Korn, "Exhibitions of modern French art" cit., p. 192.

34 *Loan Exhibition of Paintings*, pp. 32–35.

35 Ibid., p. 34.

36 Ibid.

37 Roger Fry, "An Essay in Aesthetics", in Fry, *Vision and Design* (London: Chatto & Windus, 1920), p. 22.

38 *Loan Exhibition of Paintings*, p. 9.
39 Ibid., p. 27.
40 Ibid., pp. 28, 30.
41 "Fry's Grafton Galleries exhibition had enabled some to see in Daumier's oils a precedent for 'the rigid simplification' of the Post-Impressionists." Ingamells, *Davies Collection*, p. 12. Clive Bell, *Art* (New York: Frederick A. Stokes, 1914), p. 178.
42 *Loan Exhibition of Paintings*, p. 27.
43 Ibid., pp. 22–23. In his 1910 exhibition Fry had of course privileged Manet's early work as a pre-cursor to Post-Impressionism while, in subsequent essays, side-lining his more Impressionist later work. Robert Fry, "The French Exhibition – III", *New Statesman and Nation*, 23 January 1932, p. 93 cited in John House, "Modern French Art for the Nation: Samuel Courtauld's Collection and Patronage in Context", in House, *Impressionism for England: Samuel Courtauld as Patron and Collector* (London: Courtauld Institute Galleries, 1994), p. 33, note 91.
44 *Loan Exhibition of Paintings*, p. 34.
45 Ibid., pp. 9–10.
46 John Witcombe [R.B.A.], "Letters from Readers. The Paintings at the Cardiff Museum", *Western Mail*, 4 March 1913, p. 6.
47 *Loan Exhibition of Paintings*, pp. 136–137.
48 Ibid., p. 22. In the Netherlands, the Hague School was understood to be impressionism. Joost van der Hoeven, "'Impressionism' as a Contested Term in Dutch Art Criticism, 1870–1900", in Clark and Fowle, *Globalizing Impressionism* cit.
49 *Loan Exhibition of Paintings*, pp. 9, 13–14, 11, 25.
50 Ibid., pp. 18, 15.
51 Ibid., p. 22.
52 Although his remarks were not recorded, I have been able to discover Blaker's angle thanks to an oblique press reference that, to my knowledge, has not been noticed before: during this period the *Liverpool Echo* ran a regular column entitled "Wisps of Wisdom", a compendium of pithily paraphrased remarks on matters of topical interest. We read the above quoted comments from "Hugh Blaker at Cardiff" on 27 February 1913, the day after Blaker's lecture. "Wisps of Wisdom", *The Liverpool Echo*, 27 February 1913, p. 4. In the very same column, Roger Fry offered the insight that "poetry need not have sense to be thoroughly enjoyed, and pictures need not convey facts to give pleasure to the emotions".
53 *Loan Exhibition of Paintings*, p. 19.
54 To early twentieth-century historians and curators in Wales, "the art history of Wales began with Richard Wilson". Oliver Fairclough, "Building a national art collection" cit., pp. 7–8. Although his connection to Wales was tenuous, Burne-Jones was considered a Welsh artist at this moment, thanks to his Welsh ancestry (which the exhibition catalogue made a point of noting). *Loan Exhibition of Paintings*, p. 32.
55 *Loan Exhibition of Paintings*, p. 29.
56 Ibid., pp. 31, 34.
57 On Whistler in London see Anna G. Robins, *A Fragile Modernism: Whistler and His Impressionist Followers* (New Haven–London: Yale University Press, 2008).
58 Korn, "Exhibitions of modern French art" cit., pp. 191–218; Frances Fowle, *Van Gogh's Twin: The Glasgow Art Dealer Alexander Reid* (Edinburgh: National Galleries of Scotland, 2010).
59 Quotations in order Korn, "Exhibitions of modern French art", cit. p. 199; Kate Flint, "Introduction", in Flint, *Impressionists in England* cit., p. 6.
60 Korn, "Exhibitions of modern French art" cit., p. 200.
61 *Artist*, August 1887, vol. 8, p. 258 quoted in Flint, "Introduction" cit., p. 8.
62 Ibid., p. 20. On the 1905 Durand-Ruel exhibition, see John Rewald, "Jours sombres de l'impressionnisme: Paul Durand-Ruel et l'exposition des impressionnistes, a Londres, en 1905", *L'Oeil*, vol. 223, 1974, pp. 14–19.
63 Flint, "Introduction" cit., p. 12.
64 Frank Rutter, "Impressionism as a Word in the Vocabulary of Art Criticism", in *Art in My Time* (London: Rich and Cowan, 1933), pp. 57–58, quoted in Frances Fowle, "British Impressionism and the Glasgow Boys", in Clark and Fowle, *Globalizing Impressionism* cit. See also Flint, "Introduction" cit., p. 12.
65 *Saturday Review*, quoted in Flint, "Introduction" cit., p. 12; John House, "Impressionism and its Contexts", in House, *Impressionism for England: Samuel Courtauld as Patron and Collector* (London: Courtauld Institute Galleries, 1994), p. 5.
66 House, "Impressionism and its Contexts" cit., p. 5.
67 Wynford Dewhurst in *Contemporary Review*, March 1911 quoted in Flint, "Introduction" cit., p. 8.
68 Wedmore, "The Impressionists" cit., pp. 49–50.
69 Ibid., pp. 49.
70 House, "Modern French Art for the Nation" cit., p. 25.
71 Ingamells, *Davies Collection* cit., p. 10; Fry,

72 "Studying the reception of Impressionist painting in England means examining the growth of formalist art criticism." Flint, "Introduction" cit., p. 1. See Robert Fry, "The Post-Impressionists", in Fry, *Manet and the Post-Impressionists* (London: Ballantyne & Company, 1910), reprinted in J. B. Bullen (ed.), *Post-Impressionists in England: The Critical Reception* (London: Routledge, 1988), pp. 94–99; Robert Fry, "Renoir", in Fry, *Vision and Design* cit., pp. 175–178; R. Fry, "Retrospect", in Fry, *Vision and Design* cit., pp. 188–199. Despite reservations about Fry's skill as a painter, Hugh Blaker wholeheartedly endorsed his formalist aesthetics and his advocacy for "the moderns – the Post Impressionists", especially Cézanne. Murray Urquhart, "The Blaker Diary", pp. 296–97.

73 House, "Modern French Art for the Nation" cit., p. 26.

74 Stephen F. Eisenman, "The Intransigent Artist *or* How the Impressionists Got Their Name", in Charles S. Moffett, *The New Painting. Impressionism 1874-1886* (Oxford: Phaidon, 1986), pp. 51–91.

75 Walter Sickert, "The Language of Art", in *A Free House!*, 1947, pp. 92–93, quoted in Flint, "Introduction" cit., p. 14.

76 Quoted in Flint, "Introduction" cit., p. 14. As early as 1870 *The Art Journal* worried that a surfeit of dealer exhibitions means "we may be going too far with our patronage of Continental Art". Quoted in ibid.

77 Ingamells, *Davies Collection* cit., p. 9. On the solidification of "the nationalistic meaning of 'school' in response to the Frenchification of British art, at a time when Impressionism was capturing the world market", see Julie Codell, "From English School to British School: Modernism, Revisionism, and National Culture in the Writings of M. H. Spielmann", *Nineteenth-Century Art Worldwide*, vol. 14, no. 2, 2015. The acrimony that met Hugh Lane's offer to loan his collection of modern European paintings is well known, as is the diatribe it met in response from National Gallery Trustee Lord Redesdale: "The National Gallery is – and should remain – a great Temple of Art. It should open its doors to what is highest and best: never to the productions of a degraded craze ... I should as soon expect to hear of a Mormon service being conducted in St. Paul's Cathedral as to see an exhibition of the works of the modern French Art-rebels in the sacred precincts of Trafalgar Square". Quoted in House, "Modern French Art for the Nation" cit., pp. 10–11.

78 Wynford Dewhurst, "*Impressionist Painting*, 1904, pp. 3–6", in Flint, *Impressionists in England* cit., p. 191.

79 Ibid., p. 190.

80 Dewhurst did acknowledge that in their compositional references to Japanese art and their use of modern pigments to achieve a "purified... palette... [of] new and brilliant combinations" were genuine innovations of the modern French Impressionists. Ibid., p. 192.

81 R. A. M. Stevenson, *The Art of Velasquez* (London: G. Bell, 1895), p. 29 Quoted in Flint, "Introduction" cit., p. 16. Wedmore, "The Impressionists" cit., p. 51. These strategies mirrored those being used by French writers (accessible in English via translation): Théodore Duret acknowledged the influence of Constable and Camille Mauclair that of Turner, stressing that impressionism was "neither an isolated manifestation, nor a violent denial of the French traditions, but nothing more or less than a logical return to the very spirit of these traditions". Camille Mauclair, "*The French Impressionists 1860-1900*, 1903, trans. P. G. Konody, pp. 4–9; 16–21; 22–33; 203–11", in Flint, *Impressionists in England* cit., p. 179. As Alexis Clark notes, "French art writers readily appreciated that influence ebbed and flowed across the Channel... For French writers, English precedent did not negate the Frenchness of impressionism. To them, impressionism as a synthesis of different national traditions spoke to the supposed universalism of the French tradition". Alexis Clark, "Making an Art-Historical Empire: French Histories of Impressionism in Translation", in Clark and Fowle, *Globalizing Impressionism* cit. The Davies sisters owned a copy of Duret's *Les Peintres impressionnistes*, which remains at Gregynog.

82 Flint, "Introduction" cit., p. 1.

83 Blaker, "Loan Exhibition" cit., p. 7.

84 Blaker, Urquhart and Thomson maintained an ongoing relationship with the Davies sisters: they, alongside Émile Bernheim of Bernheim-Jeune, acted as the Davies sisters' advisors and agents in acquisitions. Evans, "Impressionism for Wales" cit., p. 230.

85 Christabel Hutchings, "T. H. Thomas (1839–1915): A Founding Father of the National Museum of Wales", *Friends of the National Museum of Wales Newsletter and Magazine*, March 2014, pp. 9–12; Peter Lord, *The Visual Culture of Wales: Imaging the Nation* (Cardiff: University of Wales Press, 2000), p. 302.

86 *A Catalogue of the Fine Art Loan Exhibition, at the Cardiff Public Hall, in aid of the*

fund for establishing the Royal Cambrian Academy of Arts at Cardiff (Cardiff: South Wales Printing Works, 1884).

87 Evans, "Impressionism for Wales" cit., pp. 222–23.

88 On the sisters' formation, see Sumner, "Much that is beautiful" cit., pp. 41–59.

89 Including *inter alia* Colnaghi, Grosvenor Gallery, Leicester Galleries; and Bernheim-Jeune, Durand-Ruel, Georges Petit, Wildenstein's. As Gwendoline wrote to Thomas Jones: "The great joy of collecting anything is to do it yourself, with expert opinion granted, but one does like to choose for oneself. All the time we have been collecting our pictures we have never bought one without having seen it or at least a photograph before purchase". Gwendoline Davies letter to Thomas Jones, 29 January 1925, quoted in White, *Ladies of Gregynog* cit., p. 36. For a complete inventory of the Davies Sisters' purchases, see Evans, "Impressionism for Wales" cit., pp. 240–51. The sisters' most important advisor was Hugh Blaker, to whom – we can infer from his reply – they wrote in or shortly before August 1912 asking him to source "some examples of the Impressionists of 1870". As Blaker replied: "Very few English collectors, except Hugh Lane have bought them at all, although much of their best work is an America already. I expect you also know the work of Sisley, Pissarro and Renoir. These can still be got quite cheaply". Quoted widely and in Sumner, "Much that is beautiful" cit., p. 57. On Blaker, see Meyrick, "Hugh Blaker" cit., pp. 173–89; Robert Meyrick, *Hugh Blaker* (Aberystwyth: The University College of Wales, 1991); Ingamells, *Davies Collection* cit., pp. 19–22. Bernheim-Jeune sent a *Vétheuil* landscape to Llandinam, but the sisters preferred instead to buy *St Georges Majeur*. Ibid., p. 10.

90 "Welsh Picture Exhibition. Fostering National Taste in Art", *The Liverpool Echo*, 17 February 1913.

91 "Masterpieces of Art" cit., p. 6.

92 Blaker, "Loan Exhibition" cit., p. 7; "Masterpieces of Art" cit., p. 6.

93 "Masterpieces of Art" cit., p. 6. Emphasis mine.

94 For Staniforth an Impressionist painter was one who "endeavours to hide, by a plenitude of gaudy colours, his ignorance of some of the other branches of knowledge which go to the making of a work of art". Joseph Morewood Staniforth, "Art Culture in Wales. Some Masterpieces at Cardiff. Loan Exhibition of Pictures", *Western Mail*, 6 Febraury 1913, p. 8. Second quotation Edgar Jones, "Art Apathy in Wales. Masterpieces at City-Hall. Lyrical Appeal. A Critic's Opinions Assailed", *Western Mail*, 10 February 1913, p. 4.

95 Final quotation Staniforth, "Art Culture in Wales" cit., p. 8. Earlier quotations Jones, "Art Apathy in Wales" cit., p. 4.

96 First two quotations Staniforth, "Art Culture in Wales" cit., p. 8. Last two quotations Jones, "Art Apathy in Wales" cit., p. 4.

97 "Masterpieces of Art"cit., p. 6.

98 J. Witcombe (R.B.A.), "Letters from Readers" cit., p. 6.

99 Murray Urquhart, speaking at the opening of the exhibition, quoted in "Masterpieces of Art" cit., p. 6.

100 *Loan Exhibition of Paintings*, p. 4.

101 On the importance of whose criticism for winning support for impressionism in England, see Flint, "Introduction" cit., pp. 1–30. The lectures series was clearly integral to the exhibition for its organisers: "It is hoped', they explained in the catalogue, "that as many as can will attend this course of lectures and thereby obtain the greatest amount of benefit from the Exhibition of Paintings". *Loan Exhibition of Paintings*, p. 41.

102 *Loan Exhibition of Paintings*, p. 41.

103 Peter Lord, *The Aesthetics of Relevance* (Llandysul: Gomer, 1993), p. 7, passim.

104 Peter Lord, *Clarence Whaite and the Welsh Art World: The Betws-y-coed Artists" Colony 1844-1914* (Aberystwyth: National Library of Wales, 1998), p. 170.

105 Iona Williams, "Welsh Art", *The Welsh Review*, vol. 1, 1906, p. 97.

106 T. E. Ellis [Thomas Edward Ellis], "Domestic and Decorative Arts in Wales", *Young Wales*, vol. 55, no. July, 1899, p. 145. John Davies, *A History of Wales* (London: Penguin, 2007), p. 435; Morgan, *Rebirth of a Nation* cit., pp. 113–114.

107 On the national importance of the Welsh people's artistic taste see, for example, T. E. Ellis, "Domestic and Decorative Arts in Wales" cit., pp. 145–52. On the want of private patronage see, for example, James Milo ap Griffith, "The Eisteddfod and its relation to Art, paper presented to meeting of the Cymmrodorion Society", *Western Mail*, 9 August 1883, p. 6. On calls for a national museum see, for example, Arlunydd Penygarn [pseud. Thomas Henry Thomas], "A National Museum for Wales", *Young Wales*, vol. 91, no. July, 1902, pp. 145–47. On the importance of remedying the poor state of art education in Wales see, for example, C. Williams, "Wales and Art", *Cardiff Times and South Wales Weekly News*, 28 September 1907, p. 4.

108 Murray Urquhart, speaking at the opening of the exhibition, quoted in "Masterpieces of Art" cit., p. 6; Blaker, "Loan Exhibition" cit., p. 7.

109 Bryony Dawkes, "A taste for modernity: the Davies Sisters as art collectors", in Simon Grennan, *Becoming Modern* (Newtown: Oriel Davies, 2008), n.p.

110 Prys Morgan, "Introduction: The World of the Davies Family", in Oliver Fairclough, *Things of Beauty* cit., p. 16. Other aspects of their activity included resettling Belgian refugee artists (including George Minne, Valerius de Saedeleer and Gustave van de Woestyne) in Wales during the First World War to help them "continue their work... [and] bring a specific talent to the Welsh people". Daughter of George Minne quoted in Oliver Fairclough, "Knocked to Pieces" cit., p. 65. In line with the Ruskinian and Arts and Crafts principles that informed the cultural politics of Welsh nationalism at this moment, the sisters were also committed to supporting the learning, appreciation, and practice of craft as well as fine art. They patronised the Brynmawr Experiment, including furnishing Gregynog with Brynmawr pieces; in 1923 they founded the Gregynog Press, which united craftsmen and artists in the production of limited-edition volumes in Welsh and English, illustrated by wood engravings, and intended to "help cultivate a love of beautiful things in the people of Wales". John R. Kenyon, "'The Gaiety of these Books': The Gregynog Press", in Oliver Fairclough, *Things of Beauty* cit., p. 134. In August 1923 they hosted a Summer School of Arts and Crafts at Gregynog, run by Blaker and Urquhart and making use of the sisters' art collection. Meyrick, "Wealth Wise and Culture Kind" cit., p. 106. They also funded the establishment and teaching collection of a Department of Arts and Crafts at the University of Wales, Aberystwyth to "instruct and inspire for the welfare of the coming generations". Dan Jones, drawing master and later Head of Department of Arts and Crafts, quoted in Eveline Holsappel, "'The Beauty of Simplicity': Arts and Crafts Ideals for Wales", in Oliver Fairclough, *Things of Beauty* cit., p. 86. The sisters shared the same ambition for music as they did the visual and decorative arts: stimulating a Welsh cultural reanissaince by cultivating a love of beauty among the Welsh people and improving the quality of art in Wales, guiding ordinary taste and artistic practice by exposing the public and artists to the latest European developments. On their musical activities see Bryony Dawkes, "'Flinging Songs Across the Ether': The Sisters, Gregynog and Music for Wales", in Oliver Fairclough, *Things of Beauty* cit., pp. 113–31.

111 Peter Lord, *Betws-y-coed* cit., p. 109.

112 *Carnarvon and Denbigh Herald*, 8 August 1868, quoted in Lord, *Imaging the Nation* cit., p. 273. Mobilising the colonial discourse of Welsh backwardness and stereotypes of Welsh aesthetic insensitivity, the *Spectator*'s review of the 1876 exhibition instead found it "strange" that "Art should *se nicher* in a region which we associated chiefly with coal and slate", which is "ugly and uninteresting... crowded with people who are unbeautiful exceedingly, and whose talk is so unpleasant to hear... The visitor will probably be attacked by a profound melancholy, as the result of his first few minutes' observation, especially as the other visitors, and most noticeably the excursionists, are of the limpest order of sight-seers, wearing an air of being there only as the result of a painful effort which, on the whole, they now wish they hadn't made. People have different ways of enjoying themselves, however, and this may be the Welsh way... one would be inclined to pronounce the aesthetic fare offered to the people at Wrexham much too fine and delicately flavoured for their taste or comprehension... they seemed dull and unimpressed, and made one think that a philanthropist who knew something, and would just "go round" with them... would be a vast addition to their pleasure. [Yet, if the English visitor can overcome his revulsion at the ignorant Welsh], he will find there... a very rich feast spread for him... in the rare and beautiful Art Collection". "The Art-Exhibition at Wrexham", *The Spectator*, 28 October 1876, pp. 1339–41.

113 Lord, *Imaging the Nation* cit., p. 275.

114 *Western Mail*, 15 February 1884, p. 3, quoted in Lord, *Betws-y-coed* cit., p. 126.

115 Lord, *Betws-y-coed* cit., p. 126.

116 Lord, *Imaging the Nation* cit., p. 275.

117 Lord, *Betws-y-coed* cit., p. 129; Hypolite [pseud.], *Red Dragon*, vol. 8, 1885, p. 252, quoted in ibid., p. 130.

118 *Catalogue of the special loan exhibitions* (Swansea: Glynn Vivian Art Gallery, 1914); *Eisteddfod, Barry, 1920: official programme*. Such exhibitions were not limited to Wales: the 1913 exhibition travelled to the Holburne of Menstrie Museum in Bath, of which Blaker had been the curator since 1905.

119 Gwendoline Davies and Hugh Blaker paraphrased in "Welsh Arts and Crafts", *Western Mail*, 26 July 1920, p. 5.

120 Ibid.
121 Evans, "Impressionism for Wales" cit., p. 224.
122 Mr Jacqueline, Depeaux's representative, speaking at the inaugural ceremony, quoted in Evans, "Impressionism for Wales" cit., p. 224.
123 For more on Depeaux, see Sylvain Amic and Joanne Snrech, *François Depeaux: collectionneur des impressionnistes* (Paris-Rouen: In Fine and Réunion des musées métropolitains Rouen Normandie, 2020).
124 "Welsh Picture Exhibition. Fostering National Taste in Art."
125 The sole exception to this uniformity of focus noted by Jones was Meissonier. Jones, "Art Apathy in Wales" cit., p. 4.
126 Morgan, *Rebirth of a Nation* cit., p. 3.
127 Matthew Arnold, *On the Study of Celtic Literature* (London: Smith, Elder and Co., 1867), pp. 2, 100–4.
128 Jones, "Art Apathy in Wales" cit., p. 4.
129 This racial standard of Welshness dominated the interpretation and delimitation of Welsh art and its history in the early twentieth century. Indeed, it was the organising principle behind the very next exhibition staged by the National Museum, *Exhibition of Works by Certain Modern Artists of Welsh Birth or Extraction*, which ran from December 1913 to February 1914 and was organised by the Museum's Keeper of Art Isaac Williams, as well as the first book of Welsh art history, T. Mardy Rees, *Welsh Painters, Engravers and Sculptors, 1527–1911* (Carnarvon-Newport: Welsh Pub. Co. and J.E. Southall, 1912). In those works, unity was provided by shared Welsh ancestry rather than a shared aesthetic as with the 1913 *Loan Exhibition*.
130 Davies, *A History of Wales* cit., p. 317.
131 David Jenkins, "'Whatsoever thy hand findeth to do': the 'Top Sawyer's' legacy", in Fairclough, *Things of Beauty* cit., p. 125.
132 Davies, *A History of Wales* cit., p. 420.
133 Peter Lord, *The Visual Culture of Wales: Industrial Society* (Cardiff: University of Wales Press, 1998); Lord, *Imaging the Nation*, cit.
134 Morgan, *Rebirth of a Nation* cit., pp. 9, 127. On the intertwining of Welshness, Cymraeg, and Nonconformity in the nineteenth-century and its enduring impact in ideas of Wales, see Matthew Cragoe, "Wales", in Chris Williams, *A companion to nineteenth-century Britain* (Oxford: Wiley-Blackwell, 2008), pp. 521–33.
135 Davies, *A History of Wales* cit., p. 448.
136 First and fourth quotations *Loan Exhibition of Paintings*, pp. 32–33; second, third and fifth quotations ibid., p. 22; final quotation Wedmore, "The Impressionists" cit., pp. 49–50.
137 First and third quotations *Loan Exhibition of Paintings*, p. 34; second and fourth quotations ibid., p. 10.

THE ŌHARA-KOJIMA COLLECTION: WESTERN ART FOR EARLY-TWENTIETH-CENTURY JAPAN

CHIKAKO TAKAOKA

The Ohara Museum of Art is a window to the world and a place where art is spotlighted ahead of its time. Two people were involved in the creation of the museum: Magosaburō Ōhara (1880–1943) and Torajirō Kojima (1881–1929). The first was a talented businessman at the head of some spinning mills in the town of Kurashiki (Okayama Prefecture) who also made his name as a social entrepreneur, inspiring and promoting a large number of projects of public interest. As for Kojima, he was a Western-style painter who made an impact on the art of his time.

The Ohara Museum of Art collection was created from works Ōhara and Kojima collected in Europe around 100 years ago, in order to realise Kojima's dream of bringing authentic European masterpieces into the Japanese art world. Indeed, at that time, although many Japanese people were very curious about European art, there were still no specific museums for this art in Japan. It was Ōhara himself who financed this initiative. The two men began collecting works for the Japanese public after the First World War. With Ōhara's financial support and the cooperation of several French artists, Kojima moved to Paris and purchased artworks to send back to Japan. The initial group of works collected was made up of around 150 paintings and other types of objects.

A lot of research has been carried out on the collecting activities of Ōhara and Kojima.[1] However, there still remains unpublished material and there is a lot left to do in order to examine the importance of their activities in terms of how Western art was perceived in Japan. As we will see, this study is based on documents such as Kojima's diary, letters, photos and other archives to analyse just how Impressionist works

were collected and shown by a businessman and a painter and to understand the meaning of such a collection in Japan.
Kojima considered it was not enough to just temporarily show the Impressionist paintings in Japan and that a permanent collection was essential for the transmission of modern European art.[2] With this objective in mind, he attempted to visit Claude Monet (1840–1926) and buy one of his paintings directly from him.[3] In addition, in 1914, Ōhara had personally acquired *Woman at the Spring* (*Femme à la fontaine*) (1914, Ohara Museum of Art) by Pierre-Auguste Renoir (1841–1919).[4] The majority of works the two men brought together, including the Impressionist paintings, represented "contemporary European art" in their eyes and the collection they created in the early 1920s had a major impact in Japan because they did not just keep the collection for themselves and immediately showed it to the Japanese public. Finally in 1930, the one year after Kojima's death, the Ohara Museum of Art, the first museum of Western art in Japan, was inaugurated with artworks Kojima had brought together on the international stage, at last fulfilling his dream. However, the Ōhara and Kojima collection was only partly representative of European art of the time but it was, in some ways, a mirror of social conditions in Japan and the Japanese vision of European art in the early twentieth century. Unlike a traditional private collection, it was not established with personal tastes in mind but exclusively in the interests of the Japanese public and in this sense, its contents partly represent Japanese attitudes toward European art of the time.

The Origins of the Ōhara-Kojima Collection

Magosaburō Ōhara was born in 1880 and he was involved in promoting many large-scale social projects such as the creation of hospitals and research institutes. He supported the oldest orphanage in Japan whilst at the same time managing his business. Born in 1881, Torajirō Kojima was also from the Okayama Prefecture. He studied at the Tokyo School of Fine Arts (today the Tokyo University of the Arts) from 1902 onwards. That same year, during a visit to the Ōhara family to obtain a scholarship, he met Magosaburō. Kojima studied under Seiki Kuroda (1866–1924), the first painter to have introduced the French Impressionist style into Japan, and Takeji Fujishima (1867–1943). On Kuroda's advice, Kojima exhibited two paintings at the *Tokyo Industrial Exhibition* in March 1907: *The Garden of Charity* (*Le Jardin de la charité*) (1907, Sannomaru Shōzōkan/Museum of the Imperial Collections) and *Watermill in the Village* (*Le Moulin à eau du village*) (1906, Ohara Museum of Art). Realist in style, *The*

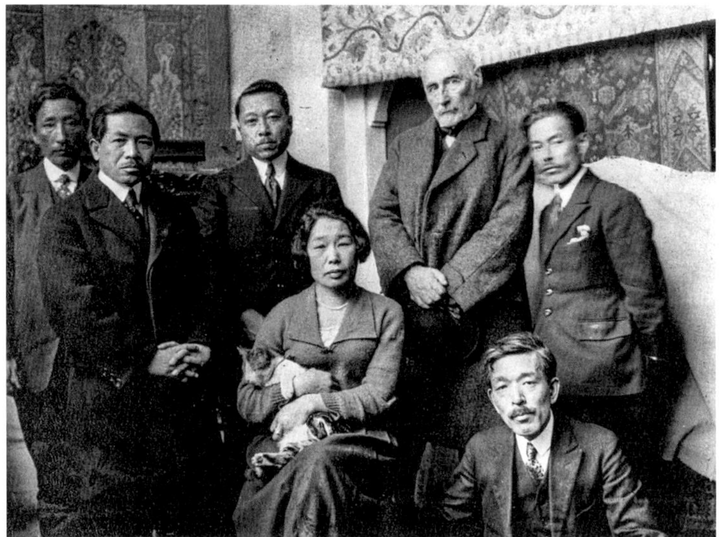

1. Aman-Jean, Kojima and the Japanese painters in Aman-Jean's studio, Paris, March 1923 (Kojima, second on the left), private collection

Garden of Charity skilfully used contrasts between light and shade to illustrate daily life at the Okayama orphanage. It was awarded first prize in the Western-style painting category. Ōhara was impressed by this excellent result and suggested the painter go to study in Europe.

Ultimately, Ōhara sent Kojima to Europe three times during the first half of the twentieth century. Kojima embarked on his first trip in January 1908, leaving from the port of Kobe and arriving at Marseille around two months later. While in Europe, Kojima stayed in Paris, then sojourned in Grez-sur-Loing for a year from June 1908 before moving to Ghent, Belgium. In October 1909, he began studying at the Royal Academy of Fine Arts in Ghent, immersing himself in Belgian Impressionist style.[5] In this way, Kojima could directly appreciate Western art and take lessons from the European masters. He submitted his *Belgian Girl in Kimono* (*Fillette belge en costume japonais*) (1911, Ohara Museum of Art) to the Salon de la Société Nationale des Beaux-Arts (SNBA) in Paris and it was accepted in March 1911.[6] In February of the following year, wanting to show his paintings at the SNBA Salon again, he returned to Paris with several of his paintings and visited the French painter Edmond-François Aman-Jean (1858–1936). He had been introduced to Aman-Jean by Jean Delvin (1853–1922), director of the Royal Academy of Fine Arts in Ghent and a painter himself. On this occasion, Aman-Jean advised him on his work and Kojima was able to rely on the help of this French painter throughout the rest of his life[7] (fig. 1).

His experience and direct contact with artists in Europe convinced Kojima of the importance of learning about real European painting with-

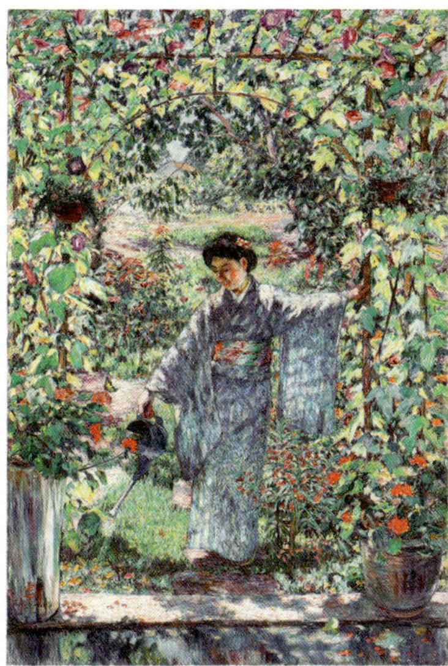
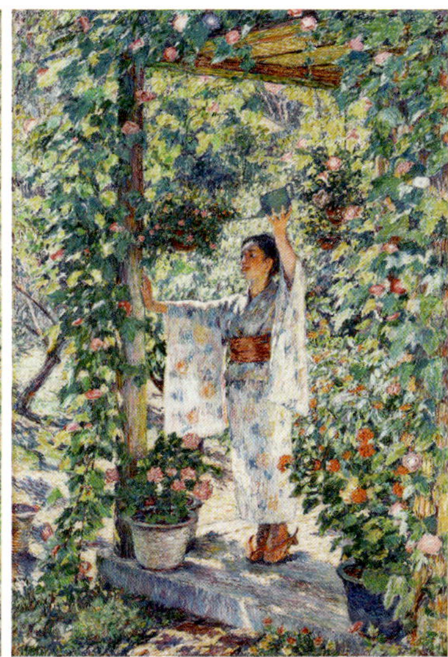

2. Torajirō Kojima, *Morning Glory (diptych)* (*Belle de matin [diptyque]*), 1920, oil on canvas, 197.2 × 131.5 cm (on the left), 1916/1920, oil on canvas, 197.4 × 135.5 cm (on the right), Ohara Museum of Art, Kurashiki

out any intermediary. He suggested Ōhara buy some works of European art in order to inspire Japanese artists. Along with Kunishirō Mitsutani (1874–1936), another painter who had obtained a scholarship from the Ōhara family, Kojima sent a letter to Ōhara asking him to consider buying a painting by Aman-Jean, *Hair* (*La Chevelure*) and transport it back to Japan. "It is not only a desire on our part. It is a desire expressed after considering that it would be beneficial for the world of art in Japan".[8] As his comments show, his aim was to share European art not just with the artistic milieu but also with the ordinary Japanese people. He was motivated by the public good.

With Ōhara's financial support, Kojima bought *Hair* (c. 1912, Ohara Museum of Art) by Aman-Jean in July 1912 and the painter returned to Japan with the work in November of the same year. It became the first painting in the Ōhara-Kojima collection.[9]

The Development of the Ōhara-Kojima Collection

In May 1919, a year after the First World War had ended, with the help of Ōhara, Kojima set off again from the port of Kobe for Europe. Although Ōhara had sent him to Europe to learn more about European art, the necessity of bringing back works for the Japanese art world became clearly obvious to Kojima during this second trip.

He arrived in Paris in July 1919. In the March of the following year, he exhibited three works brought from Japan at the SNBA Salon: *Morning*

Glory (diptych) (*Belle de matin [diptyque]*) (fig. 2), depicting a Japanese lady posing in a *yukata* (summer kimono) in Impressionist style, *Autumn* (*Automne*) (1920, Centre Pompidou – Musée national d'Art Moderne) and *Little Cowherd* (*Opéra dynastie Ming, Chohannue*) (1920, Ohara Museum of Art), which represented a scene from Chinese theatre.[10] Among these paintings, *Autumn*, which depicted a Korean woman, was bought by the French government.[11] Following this, Kojima was elected member of the SNBA.

Kojima's different experiences at this time, notably the presentation of his oriental subjects at the Salon and the recognition he gained among the French art world, confirmed his firm belief of the need to acquire European artworks and exhibit them in Japan. Once again, he managed to persuade Ōhara to collect more artworks.

Around August 1920, he began collecting works seriously. While continuing to paint, he actively visited art galleries, dealers, and exhibitions to buy works, then left Europe, heading back to Japan from Marseille in January 1921. Immediately after Kojima's return, he and Ōhara presented their collection at an exhibition entitled *French Art Exhibition: Twentieth Century Painting*, which was held in March at a primary school in Kurashiki. The exhibition featured twenty-seven paintings newly arrived from Europe and was a huge success.

Moreover, when he returned to Japan, Kojima continued to buy works with the help of Aman-Jean. The Ohara Museum of Art has several purchase receipts indicating the French painter as the buyer.[12] There are also thirteen letters from Aman-Jean and his wife Thadée to Kojima, dated from 1919 to 1923, one which mentions that the French painter Lucien Simon (1861–1945) and Thadée equally took part in collecting the paintings instead of Aman-Jean, who had fallen ill, at the end of 1921.[13]

In January 1922, Ōhara and Kojima organised the *Second French Art Exhibition: Twentieth Century Painting* in Kurashiki. With thirty-four paintings, it included the new collection acquired by Aman-Jean and the works presented at the first exhibition.[14]

The event was once again a huge success and even had repercussions on a social level. Ōhara, undoubtedly convinced of the social impact of presenting European art to the Japanese public, sent Kojima to Europe once again in the hope of enriching the collection further. Kojima left in May 1922 for his third trip to Europe. He not only stopped off in Belgium and France, but also Germany, Switzerland and Sweden. He returned to Japan in May 1923. In August, the *Third Exhibition of Famous European Painters* was held, again in Kurashiki, with fifty-six paintings.[15]

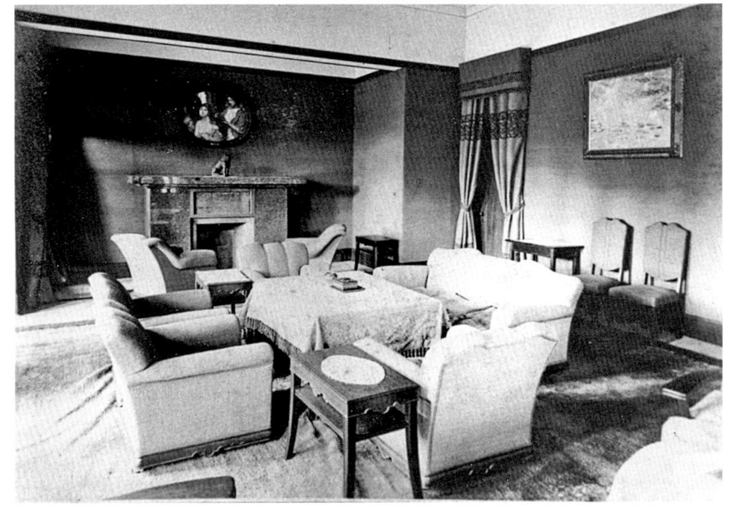

3. Western-style room at Yūrinsō villa, Kurashiki, c. 1928 (we can see *Hair* [*La Chevelure*] on the left and *Water Lilies* [*Les Nymphéas*] on the right), Ohara Museum of Art, Kurashiki

The Collection Between Private and Public Motives

Hair by Aman-Jean, the first work in the Ōhara-Kojima collection, was exhibited to the public on several occasions within the framework of various exhibitions, notably in Kurashiki in the early 1920s. It was also hung in the Western-style salon at Villa Yūrinsō, which belonged to the Ōhara family, a half-Japanese, half-Western-style house completed in April 1928. Monet's *Water Lilies* (*Les Nymphéas*) (c. 1906, Ohara Museum of Art) and *Courtyard at the "Rondest House", Pontoise* (*Une cour à Eragny, maison Rondest*) (1880, Ohara Museum of Art) by Camille Pissarro (1830–1903) were also hung in this same room[16] (fig. 3). In other words, these paintings, initially bought to be shown to the Japanese public, were also kept and appreciated in a private context. During the late nineteenth century and early twentieth century, the demand for European works of art to decorate interiors rapidly grew. This paralleled the arrival of Western-style architecture in Japan.

Ōhara himself never went to Europe. However, he actively sent young promising Japanese men there in the 1920s. Among them there were researchers, scientists, musicians, architects, as well as two painters, Mitsutani and of course Kojima. On 11 November 1913,[17] mandated by Ōhara, Mitsutani went to visit Renoir in Cagnes to commission a painting from him and this is how Ōhara acquired *Woman at the Spring* the following year.[18] This painting is one of the rare European works Ōhara bought on his own initiative, as he essentially collected traditional Japanese paintings and objects related to the tea ceremonial. The original

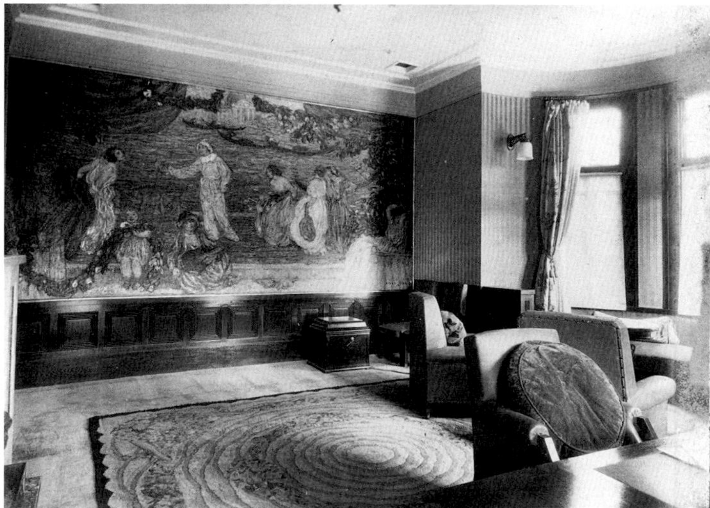

4. *Carnival of Venice* (*Fête de Venise*) hanging inside the Ōhara's home in Osaka, Yurinkai Ohara Memorial Foundation, Kurashiki

vocation of the Renoir painting is unclear but it may have been intended to decorate the interior of one of his Western-style homes.

On the other hand, we know for certain that for the décor of his new house in Osaka, Ōhara asked Aman-Jean, through the intermediary of Kojima, to create some paintings. Photographs of the house, completed in late 1922, show the works by Aman-Jean – *Swallows Farewell* (*L'Adieu aux hirondelles*) (1923, on loan to the Mitsubishi Museum Ichigokan) and *Festival of Venice* (*Fête de Venise*) (1923, Ohara Museum of Art) – installed in the Western-style salon (fig. 4). These two paintings, along with *Spring* (*Printemps*) (current location unknown) were commissioned by Ōhara from Aman-Jean with the unique objective of decorating his house and not for being exhibited to the public. Some letters from Kojima to Ōhara specify the conditions of how these paintings were commissioned. In a letter from 22 June 1922, Kojima reported to Ōhara that he had asked Aman-Jean to make some wall paintings and that the latter had agreed.[19] The letter dated 9 July 1922 indicates the sum for the three works by Aman-Jean and specifies that the French painter wanted to exhibit one of these masterpieces in France before sending them to Japan and he hoped Ōhara would also allow them to be shown at the Salon the following year.[20] Ōhara seems to have accepted this request, because Aman-Jean presented *Festival of Venice* at the first exhibition at the Salon des Tuileries.[21] Lastly, a receipt dated 27 February 1923 stipulated that Ōhara had bought "three decorative panels" by Aman-Jean for 60,000 francs.[22] Other photographs reveal that Ōhara's house in Osaka was also decorated with other European paintings – e.g., two paintings by Paul

Sérusier (1864–1927) and a Henri Matisse (1869–1954). They were all paintings Kojima had bought in France.[23]

As we have just seen, Ōhara decorated his homes in a Western style with some paintings directly bought in Europe by Kojima for the Japanese public. The paintings commissioned from artists were, on the contrary, works acquired for purely personal ends. Moreover, in April 1928, when Osaka's land and house were sold in order to make up his companies' losses, these works remained in his possession, including *Festival of Venice*. They only became part of the Ohara Museum of Art collection in 1930. Renoir's painting and the other paintings from Villa Yūrinsō followed. It is therefore possible to say that, before 1930, the Ōhara-Kojima collection was formed on the basis of both public and private motives. Although collected for different purposes, these works were finally brought together for the Japanese public when the museum of Western art was completed.

Visiting Monet for the *Water Lilies*

The letter from Aman-Jean to Kojima dated 30 June 1921 testifies to discussions with three Japanese men: Kōjirō Matsukata (1866–1950), Sanji Kuroki (1884–1944) and a certain Higashi.[24] They were some of the few people in direct contact not just with Aman-Jean but also with Monet,[25] not including Kojima, of course. From 1919 to 1922, Kuroki carried out some research on the international monetary situation in Paris for the Japanese Ministry of Finance. During his stay in Paris, he visited Monet several times and bought four works from him, opening the way for other Japanese collectors. It was Kuroki who introduced Matsukata to Monet. At this time, in the 1920s, Matsukata was collecting works in Europe to establish the main collection for the National Museum of Western Art in Tokyo which would open in 1959. It was also through Kuroki that Kojima was able to visit Monet, obtaining a painting he wanted to show the Japanese public in 1920 (fig. 5). Kojima wrote about this first visit in his diary:

> With Saitō, I went to Monet's home in Giverny by the one o'clock train in the afternoon. We arrived at the station in Vernon at half past two. We travelled five kilometres by car before arriving at Monet's house. After having toured the three studios and the garden, he offered us tea. Monet had just built the big new studio and was working on his large-scale works. There were between twenty and thirty panels measuring two metres high and four metres wide; all representing parts of his garden. I took some photos. We took the train back at half past six in the evening and we arrived back in Paris at half past eight.[26]

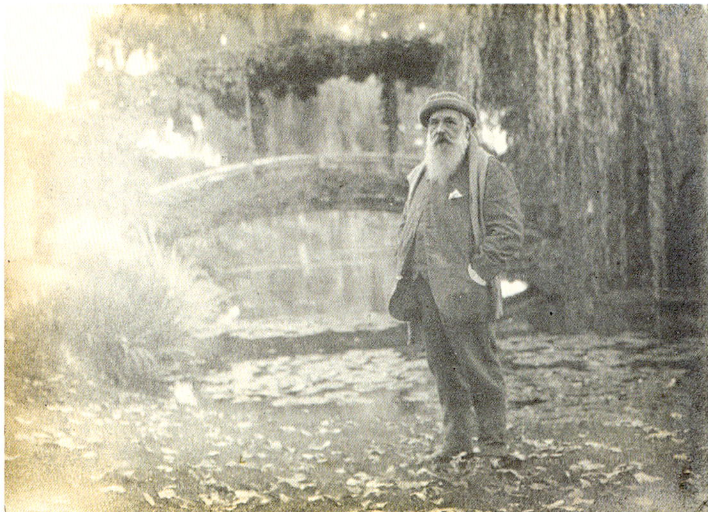

5. Monet at Giverny, October 1920 (photographed by Kojima), private collection

As his diary recounts, Kojima visited Monet's studio on 21 October 1920 with Toyosaku Saitō (1880–1951). This Japanese painter was one of the people who supported Kojima's collection. The description made in the diary emphasises that Monet was working on what would appear to be the *Water Lilies* series, but it does not mention the choice of paintings to be made in the studio. Also, about a month later, on 23 November, Kojima visited Monet again accompanied by Saitō and Kuroki. Kojima noted in his diary:

> I left the Saint-Lazare station at one in the afternoon to visit Monet in Giverny with Saitō and Kuroki. The budget fixed was 10,000 francs, but I could only have bought a small painting for that sum, so I bought *Water Lilies*, canvas size no. 30, for 20,000 francs. We went back to the station in the evening and we waited for the half past six train. We arrived in Paris at half past eight in the evening. Since our last visit, Monet has painted several large works.[27]

Water Lilies, which Kojima acquired on this occasion, was shown at the *French Art Exhibition: Twentieth Century Painting*, held in March 1921 in Kurashiki. It was the first time that a painting by Monet was shown publicly in Japan. At the time, there were only two people who owned paintings by Monet in Japan: Tadamasa Hayashi (1853–1906),[28] an art dealer who had opened a boutique in Paris around 1883, and Kichizaemon Sumitomo (1864–1926, pseudonym: Shunsui), the fifteenth generation head of the Sumitomo family, the founding family of the Sumitomo Zaibatsu.. But the four paintings they owned were never presented to the public.[29]

Monet's name appeared in some artistic reviews in Japan in the late nineteenth century. At the start of the following century, Monet's art was still only known indirectly and in a general way,[30] but it was almost impossible to see it directly. The Japanese people had no other choice than to learn about Monet through the Impressionist style works by Japanese artists who had returned from France, or imported books and reproductions. Monet's example perfectly illustrates the relationship between Japanese and European art in the early twentieth century. Being one of the rare Japanese painters to have assimilated Impressionism into his art practice by staying in Europe, Kojima collected European art in order to offer this experience to a wider audience. That is why he wanted to share Monet's work with the public immediately after acquiring it.

Aman-Jean and Renoir in Japan Before the First World War

As we have seen, Ōhara and Kojima started buying and showing European works to the public before the First World War. Later, in the 1920s, they organised a series of exhibitions. On analysing the list of works acquired by Kojima, we notice a high number of artists linked to the SNBA. For example, there are Aman-Jean, Charles Cottet (1863–1925), Simon, Henri Le Sidaner (1862–1939), Paul Albert Besnard (1849–1934), Maurice Denis (1870–1943) and George Desvallières (1861–1950). As Kojima was the first Japanese artist to have been elected a member of the SNBA in 1920, it must have been relatively easy for him to collect works by artists connected to this society.[31] Because he did not only want to take into account his personal taste and had set himself the task of introducing contemporary European art into Japan, he used the SNBA to develop his selection criteria. In addition, painters from the SNBA had actively been introduced to Japan by painters and critics who had studied in Europe, mostly before the First World War. This might also explain why Kojima collected so many works by painters from the SNBA.
Why, for example, did Kojima buy a painting by Aman-Jean in the first place? It is true that this artist was introduced to him by Delvin during his first trip to Europe, but it might also be linked to the views of his former teacher at the Fine Arts School in Tokyo, Fujishima, who highly esteemed the talent of Aman-Jean and had actively presented his art in Japan. After studying in Europe, Fujishima had returned to Japan in 1910. He presented the contemporary French paintings in the art review *Bijutsu Shinpō* [Art News] in March of the same year. In an article, he placed Aman-Jean at the top of a list of modern masters and sang the praises of the SNBA as being the most promising salon.[32] In April 1912, he

published a review of the painter in the same magazine, praising his rich expressive colours and poetic style.[33] Kojima translated this article into French and showed it to Aman-Jean,[34] proving that Kojima, who was in Europe at that time, was familiar with Fujishima's point of view. Kojima acquired *Hair* by Aman-Jean in July 1912 and went back to Japan at the end of the same year. The painting was immediately shown at the *Second Exhibition of Kōfūkai* in Tokyo from February to March 1913. It was the first presentation of Aman-Jean's original work to the public, which up until then had only been seen through reproductions. This presentation had an impact on the Japanese art world and *Hair* was praised by critics, one of whom affirmed that this work was truly stimulating for Japanese painters.[35]

As for the works by Renoir owned by Japanese collectors before the First World War, it is well known that Hayashi was the first to have bought one and he actually owned three.[36] However, these were sold again at auction in the United States in 1913, without having been shown in Japan. The painter Shintarō Yamashita (1881–1966) visited Renoir in Paris in July 1909 and bought *Bather* (*Baigneuse*) (1907, Artizon Museum) directly from him for 500 francs.[37] This painting was presented at the *Fourth Exhibition of Shirakaba* in Tokyo in February 1912. It was the first time an original painting by Renoir was shown to the Japanese public. But the public's attention was mainly drawn to the work of Auguste Rodin (1840–1917) shown at the same exhibition, and the first reactions of the Japanese public to Renoir's painting was rather timid. Similarly, in 1914, when the painter Ryūzaburō Umehara (1888–1986) presented the small painting *Rose* (before 1913, private collection) by Renoir, with whom he had studied before returning to Japan in 1913,[38] at the *Art Exhibition for Soldiers*, organised to help sick and wounded soldiers, it went relatively unnoticed.[39]

Woman at the Spring, bought by Ōhara in 1914, was the biggest and most recent painting by Renoir exhibited in Japan before the First World War. This canvas was shown during the *Twelfth Exhibition of Taiheiyōgakai* in Tokyo in March 1915 (fig. 6). However, as some artists lamented,[40] this event did not receive the attention hoped for, because Renoir was not yet well-known enough to the public. Despite this poor reception, nevertheless, some Japanese painters, who had direct access to the art of the master Impressionists on these occasions, were already adopting characteristics of Renoir's style in their paintings.[41]

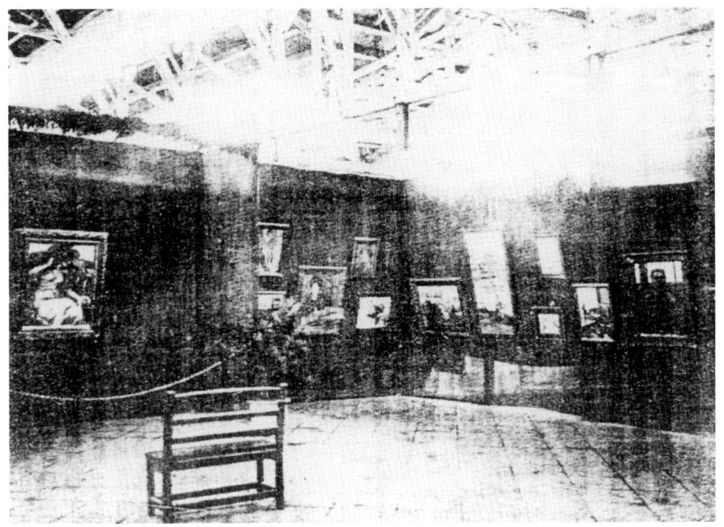

6.Room at the *Twelth Taiheiyōgakai exhibition* (we can see *Woman at the Fountain* [*Femme à la fontaine*] on the left), reproduced by *Bijutsu shūhō* [Weekly art review], vol. 2, no. 25, March 1915, p. 3

Conclusion

We have explored the specificities of Impressionist painting and other works that constituted the Ōhara-Kojima collection, as well as the history of the Ohara Museum of Art, the first museum of Western art in Japan created in 1930. Whilst the aim of the two men's collecting activities was initially to enrich the Japanese art world, until the "Western art museum" had actually become a reality, it can be considered that their collection had both private and public motives. This might also be explained by the situation in Japan at the time, where it was difficult to grasp the social impact of collecting European artworks and sharing them with the public. The early twentieth century was also a period of transition towards the Japanese public really gaining an understanding of the social importance of European art. It is then possible to say that, at least before the First Word War, Japanese painters living in Japan were very rarely confronted with the direct influence of Impressionist painting because the number of works of European art visible in Japan was minimal and original Impressionist paintings were virtually nonexistent. There was only an indirect contact with these works through publications and reproductions.
Within this context, Ōhara and Kojima's desire not just to collect but also to immediately show their Western artworks is even more remarkable and clearly stands out from the activities of other Japanese collectors at the same period. Through his experience of Impressionist style, acquired in Paris and Belgium, Kojima rapidly realised this shortfall and it pushed

him, along with Ōhara, to introduce Impressionist paintings into the latter's collection and show them to the public. Conversely, the modest number of true Impressionist paintings out of the total works collected by Ōhara and Kojima would seem to reflect, on the one hand, the high prices of these works and, on the other, the weakness of understanding of the necessity of Impressionists art in Japan at this time. Showing original artworks truly participated in the evolution of this conception of Western art and today it is impossible to retrace the history of Western art in Japan without evoking Impressionism. Ōhara and Kojima's collecting activities, as well as their consistent practice of sharing the fruit of their discoveries with the public in the 1910s and up until the early 1920s, shows that this period marked the dawning of a veritable exchange between European painters – notably the Impressionists – and Japanese society.

* I would like to thank Mrs Ségolène Le Men, Mrs Félicie Faizand from Maupeou, Mr Kaitarō Kojima, Mrs Lucile Audouy, Mr Yann Farinaux-Le Sidaner, Mr Pierre Vaisse and the researchers at the Yurinkai Ohara Memorial Foundation for their precious advice. I would also like to thank my colleagues at the Ohara Museum of Art.

1 Aomi Okabe, *Origine de la collection du Musée Ohara, archetype de musée d'art contemporain au Japon*, research diploma at the École du Louvre supervised by Michel Hoog, 1987, pp. 11–19; Shūji Takashina, "Impact-ten no Imi suru Mono" ["Signifiers of the Impact Exhibition"], in *Impact: Higashi to Nishi no Kingendai, Mōhitotsu no Ohara Bijutsukan* [*Impact: Modern and Contemporary, Eastern and Western, Another Aspect of the Ohara Museum*], exh. cat., Kurashiki, Ohara Museum of Art, 2006, pp. 5–7; Hideyuki Yanagisawa, "The Ohara Museum of Art—85 Years of History", in *The Best Selection of the Ohara Museum of Art*, exh. cat., Tokyo, The National Art Center, 2016, pp. 26–38.

2 The following references provide more information on the relationship between the painters and collectors in Japan and the French Impressionists. Shūji Takashina, "Eastern and Western Dynamics in the Development of Western-Style Oil Painting During the Meiji Era", in Shuji Takashina and J. Thomas Rimer, with Gerald D. Bolas (eds.), *Paris in Japan: The Japanese Encounter with European Painting*, exh. cat., St. Louis, Washington University, 1987, pp. 21–31; Atsushi Miura, "Japan and the Impressionists: The Collection of French Painting and the Interrelation between French and Japanese Art", in Beat Marks-Hanssen (ed.), *Japan's Love for Impressionism: From Monet to Renoir*, exh. cat., Bonn, Kunst- und Ausstellungshalle der Bundesrepublik Deutschland, 2016, pp. 12–27; Atsushi Miura, "Japon et impressionnisme: peinture japonaise moderne et collections de tableaux impressionnistes au Japon", *Japon pluriel 12, autour de l'image: arts graphiques et culture visuelle au Japon* (Arles: Éditions Philippe Picquier, 2018), pp. 21–45.

3 Ōhara bought a painting from Monet through the intermediary of Kojima on 23 November 1920 for 20,000 francs. The Ohara Museum of Art owns a note written in French about this purchase. It says: "Giverny the 23 November 1920/a painting by Claude Monet present 'Nymphœa' price of twenty thousand francs (20,000)".

4 There is no confirmation of this purchase receipt, but there are articles relating to this sale. Kunishirō Mitsutani, "Gaiyū Issekiwa" ["A Brief Story of my Trip Abroad"], *Bijutsu Shinpō* [*Art News*], vol. 13, no. 5, March 1914, pp. 7–8; Anonymous, "Yosekizaiku" ["Marquetry"], *Bijutsu Shinpō* [*Art News*], vol. 14, no. 7, May 1916, p. 32. In the last one, there is a large illustration of *Woman at the Spring*, a special painting from the *Taiheiyōgakai Exhibition*. According to these articles, Ōhara asked Renoir to make a painting for 5,000 yens.

5 To find out more about Kojima's activities in Belgium, see Tomoko Matsuoka, "Torajiro KOJIMA et la Belgique", *Bulletin de la Société franco-japonaise d'art et d'archéologie*, no. 18, 1998, pp. 19–34.

6 This painting figured in the catalogue for the Salon as "no. 758, Fillette au costume japonais".

7 Patrick-Gilles Persin, *Aman-Jean: peintre de la femme* (Paris: La Bibliothèque des arts, 1993), pp. 172–95; Tomoko Matsuoka, "Kojima Torajirō to Edmond-François Aman-Jean Bijutsu-hin Shūshū Katsudō wo Chūshin ni" ["Torajirō Kojima and Edmond-François Aman-Jean: their activities as art collectors"], *Kindai Gasetsu*, no. 6, 1997, pp. 40–52; Yann Farinaux-Le Sidaner, "Les Derniers impressionnistes - les temps de l'intimité, in *The Last Impressionists: Time of Intimacy*, exh. cat., Tokyo, Seiji Togo Memorial Sompo Japan Nipponkoa Museum of Art et al., 2015–16, pp. 130–45. When Kojima contacted Léonce Bénédite, almost certainly to commission some sculptures by Rodin, he introduced himself as a student of Aman-Jean. Musée Rodin historical archives, KOJ-3486.

8 "Ce n'est pas seulement un souhait de notre part. C'est un souhait formulé après avoir pensé que ce serait le plus bénéfique pour le monde de l'art au Japon." Ohara Museum of Art Archives, letter from Kojima and Mitsutani to Ōhara, 30 May 1912. Author's translation.

9 There is no confirmation of this purchase receipt, but the letter from Kojima and Mitsutani indicates that the price was 4,000 francs. Ibid. According to Kojima's diary, 12 July 1912, he visited Aman-Jean, who was staying at Château-Thierry, in order to buy *Hair* (La Chevelure). Private collection, Kojima's diary, 12 July 1912.

10 The numbers of these paintings in the Salon catalogue are 630, 631 and 632. It should be noted that Kojima painted three paintings *Morning Glory* of almost the same size, and it is now difficult to specify which of these paintings was exhibited at the Salon as *Morning Glory (diptych)*. However, it is assumed here that *Morning Glory (diptych)* consists of two paintings with signatures (fig. 2).

11 *Autumn* became part of the collection at the Musée du Luxembourg and was included in its catalogue. Léonce Bénédite, *Le Musée du Luxembourg : peintures, pastels, aquarelles et dessins des écoles étrangères* (Paris: H. Laurens, 1924), p. 104.

12 For example, *Man in Rose-Colored Robe* by Paul Albert Besnard (1911, Ohara Museum of Art) and *Good Thief* by George Desvallières (1913, Ohara Museum of Art).
13 Letter from Thadée Aman-Jean to Kojima, 6 December 1921, Tomoko Matsuoka, *Kojima Torajirō Kenkyū* [*Study of Kojima Torajirō*], Tokyo, Chuo Koron Bijutsu Shuppan, 2004, pp. 478–80. There is also a letter from Simon to Ōhara showing that Ōhara gave Simon a gift. Yurinkai Archives Ohara Memorial Foundation, letter from Simon to Ōhara, 29 June 1922.
14 The exhibition also included a painting by Henri Le Sidaner, *Fishing Boats* (Barques de pêche) (c. 1921, location unknown), that Kojima had not been able to send before he left for Japan in January 1921.
15 Following this, and before the opening of the Ohara Museum of Art in 1930, the Ōhara-Kojima collection was presented at the *Exhibition of Western Masterpieces* held in 1927 at what is today the National Museum of Kyoto and, in 1928, at the current Museum of Metropolitan Art in Tokyo.
16 The Western-style room, where Western artworks were hung, functioned as a kind of salon, a specific "place", as if the tea room had been westernised. It is interesting to note that Yūrinsō's western-style room was also equipped with an oven for the tea ceremony.
17 Senyō Ogawa (1882–1971), a Japanese painter who accompanied Mitsutani, specified in his diary that they had visited Renoir on 11 November. Sayoko Ueda, Masubuchi Kyōko, "Honkoku Ogawa Senyō "Taiō Nikki" (Ge) (2)" ["Reprint Ogawa Senyo "Diary in Europe" Part 2 (2)"], *SUZAKU: Bulletin of the Museum of Kyoto*, no. 31, 2019, pp. 84–85.
18 Kunishirō Mitsutani, *op. cit.*, March 1914, pp. 7–8. In this issue, a letter was published from Renoir to Mitsutani, 8 November 1919. It read: "I would be delighted to make your acquaintance before we leave for Japan", and it appears that it was sent before Mitsutani's visit.
19 Yurinkai Archives Ohara Memorial Foundation, letter from Kojima to Ōhara, 22 June 1922.
20 Yurinkai Archives Ohara Memorial Foundation, letter from Kojima to Ōhara, 9 July 1922.
21 The work figures in the catalogue for the Salon as "no. 14, *L'Offrande, panneau décoratif pour un palais, au Japon*".
22 Ohara Museum of Art Archives, receipt of sale from Aman-Jean to Ōhara, 27 February 1923.
23 On the other hand, the *Exhibition of Contemporary French Art*, organised by the art dealer Herman d'Oelsnitz almost every year from 1922 to 1931, in Tokyo and Osaka, was undoubtedly the first occasion to acquire works of European art in Japan. It seems that Ōhara or Kojima had visited these exhibitions, which is suggested for example, by the painting *Woman in a Straw Hat* supposedly by Jules Flandrin, visible in a photograph of the house in Osaka, which was considered to have been acquired at one of these exhibitions.
24 Tomoko Matsuoka, *op. cit.*, pp. 485–87. "Higashi" was undoubtedly the future Japanese prime minister, Naruhiko Higashikuni (1887–1990).
25 Yui Hayashi, "Monet wo Giverny ni Tazuneta Nihonjin" ["The Japanese Man who Visited Monet in Giverny"], in *Monet: Inshōha no Kyoshō, Sono Isan* [*The Art of Monet and it's Posterity*], exh. cat., Tokyo, The National Art Center, 2007, pp. 209–16.
26 "Avec Saitō, je suis allé chez Monet à Giverny par le train d'une heure de l'après-midi. Nous sommes arrivés à la gare de Vernon à deux heures et demie. Nous avons suivi cinq kilomètres de route en voiture avant d'arriver à la maison de Monet. Après avoir fait le tour des trois ateliers et du jardin, il nous a servi du thé. Monet venait de construire un nouveau grand atelier et travaillait sur des œuvres d'envergure. Il y avait de vingt à trente panneaux de deux mètres de haut et quatre mètres de large ; tous représentaient des coins de son jardin. J'ai pris plusieurs photos. Nous avons repris le train de six heures et demie le soir et nous sommes arrivés à Paris à huit heures et demie." Private collection, Kojima's diary, 21 October 1920. Author's translation. Kojima's diary has never been published.
27 "Je suis parti de la gare Saint-Lazare à une heure de l'après-midi pour rendre visite à Monet à Giverny avec Saitō et Kuroki. Le budget d'achat prévu était de 10,000 francs, mais je n'aurais pu acheter qu'un petit tableau pour cette somme, alors j'ai acheté *Les Nymphéas*, format de la toile no. 30, pour 20,000 francs. Nous nous sommes rendus à la gare dans la soirée et avons attendu le train de six heures et demie. Nous sommes arrivés à Paris à huit heures et demie du soir. Depuis notre précédente visite, Monet avait peint plusieurs grandes œuvres." Private collection, Kojima's diary, 23 November 1920. Author's translation.
28 On Tadamasa Hayashi and his collection, see Brigitte Koyama-Richard, "Hayashi Tadamasa III. Retour au Japon (1901-1906)", *Cahiers Edmond et Jules de Goncourt*, no.

7, 2000, pp. 165–75; Akiko Mabuchi, "Hayashi Tadamasa's Western Art Collection and Berthe Morisot", in The Committee of Hayashi Tadamasa Symposium (ed.), *Hayashi Tadamasa: Japonism and Cultural Exchanges* (Tokyo: Brücke, 2007), pp. 339–49; Marianne Mathieu, "Tadamasa Hayashi, Kōjirō Matsukata and the Western Collectors and Collections", *op. cit.*, pp. 120–23; Atsushi Miura, *op. cit.*, pp. 21–23.

29 Katsumi Miyazaki, *Seiyō Kaiga no Tōrai: Nihonjin wo Miryōshita Monet, Renoir, Cézanne nado* [*The Arrival of Western Painting: Monet, Renoir, Cézanne and Others Who Fascinated the Japanese*] (Tokyo: Nikkei Publishing, 2007), pp. 154–56.

30 Katsumi Miyazaki, *op. cit.*, pp. 164–173; Tomoko Matsuoka, "Mone to Nihon no Inshōha: Kojima Torajirō wo Chūshin ni" ["Monet and Japanese Impressionism: A Look at Torajirō Kojima"], *Bijutsu Forum 21*, vol. 23, 2011, pp. 61–64.

31 For example, *Fishing Boats* by Le Sidaner, which Kojima bought, was shown at the SNBA Salon in 1921.

32 Takeji Fujishima, "Taiō Kenbun Sūsoku" ["My Knowledge Acquired during my Stay in Europe"], *Bijutsu Shinpō* [*Art News*], vol. 9, no. 5, March 1910, p. 11.

33 Takeji Fujishima, "Aman-Jean no E ni tsuite" ["About Aman-Jean's Paintings"], *Bijutsu Shinpō* [*Art News*], vol. 11, no. 6, April 1912, p. 2.

34 Torajirō Kojima, "Taiō Gadan" ["Views on the Painting I Saw during my Stay in Europe"], *Bijutsu Shinpō* [*Art News*], vol. 12, no. 8, June 1913, pp. 13–14. In this article, Kojima talks about an article by Fujishima he translated and showed to Aman-Jean, an illustration of *Hair* and a message from Aman-Jean to Kojima were published.

35 Sōhachi Kimura, "Aman-Jean no E" ["The Paintings of Aman-Jean"], Takeji Fujishima, "Aman-Jean-shi no Sakuhin" ["The Works of Aman-Jean"], Tōkoku Kōno, "Kōfūkai Zatsu Inshō" ["The Various Impressions of Kōfūkai"], *Gendai no Yōga* [*The Yoga of Today*], vol. 2, no. 1, April 1913, pp. 8–10, 13. A large illustration of *Hair* was published in this issue. To find out more about how Aman-Jean's work was received in Japan, see Sara Durt, "Aman-Jean to Cottet: Nihon de no Juyō" ["Aman-Jean and Cottet: their Works in Japan"], in *op. cit.*, Kurashiki, 2006, pp. 194–201.

36 Katsumi Miyazaki, *op. cit.*, p. 201.

37 Shintarō Yamashita, "Ōshū Yūgaku Zatsuwa ["About my Stay in Europe"], *Bijutsu Shinpō* [*Art News*], vol. 9, no. 9, July 1910, pp. 9–10.

38 Ryūzaburō Umehara, "Renoir-okina no Tsuitō" ["In commemoration of Renoir"], *Bijutsu Shashin Gahō* [*Art and Photo Bulletin Bulletin d'art et de photo*], vol. 1, no. 2, February 1920, pp. 62–79.

39 Katsumi Miyazaki, *op. cit.*, pp. 202-7.

40 Hakutei Ishii, "Bijutsu Tenrankai no Kankyaku" ["Exhibition Visitors"], *Kaiga Sōshi* [*The Painting Collection*], no. 334, June 1915, p. 12.

41 For example, Tsune Nakamura (1887–1924). Masahiro Yasugi, "Renoir and Japanese Painters: A Master's Visage in Words", in *Renoir, Tradition and Innovation*, exh. cat., Tokyo, The National Art Center, 2010, pp. 288–93.

IMPRESSIONIST COLLECTION – WHERE NOW?

ANNE HIGONNET

Where in public do collections of Impressionist art now belong? Together, I believe, with other collections of nineteenth-century art. Paintings, prints and sculptures of this beloved artistic movement are now displayed by museums as if their collection were self-evident. And yet, if we exercised exactly the sort of critical scepticism at the heart of the greatest Impressionist art, we might think differently. We could imagine museums and galleries which heeded the global power dynamics that circulated art in the late nineteenth century, and started displaying their effects. What if we began to consider the collection of Impressionism as an integral part of a global collecting history?

To re-think the collection of Impressionism, let us begin by remembering the individual audacity of the first collectors of Impressionism. Many, if not most, collections of Impressionism originate in personal motives. As Baudrillard so memorably said: "One always collects oneself". Putting aside the biographical details of collectors' histories, consider their hopes for immortality through donation of Impressionist works to public institutions.

Gustave Caillebotte's great 1894 donation of sixty-eight of his colleagues' paintings to the French state, with Auguste Renoir as his executor, comes immediately to mind, along with Monet's 1891 subscription campaign to donate Manet's 1863 *Olympia* to the French state and, on the other side of the Atlantic, Louisine Havemeyer's great 1929 donation to the Metropolitan Museum of Art in New York. Scholars continue to discover new aspects of these early donations, notably Gloria Groom and Kathryn Krenmitzer about Bertha and Potter Palmer on the occasion of a recent exhibition at the Art Institute of Chicago, *Monet and Chicago*, or James McAuley about Isaac de Camondo's donations to the French state in his recent book, *House of Fragile Things*.

The hopes collectors of Impressionism have had for themselves and for the reputation of Impressionism have always been predicated on the civic functions of the museum. Jurgen Habermas, Michel Foucault and many others have pointed out that the public sphere requires institutions, of which the museum, Tony Bennet observed, is one of the most important. Each of the examples of collecting and donating Impressionism already mentioned demonstrates not only a personal motive, but also a desire to enlarge a public's critical capacity. Well aware of the stylistic and ideological challenges the finest Impressionist art presented, each of these donors hoped to push a public toward the acceptance of new ideas.

Monet, notably, hoped that the collective pressure of the many prominent French intellectuals who subscribed to the purchase of *Olympia* would accelerate the acceptance of a modern aesthetic. Perhaps Monet also hoped *Olympia* would foster the critical attitude towards modern society articulated by Baudelaire in his *Le Peintre de la vie moderne* and amplified so controversially by Manet in *Olympia*.

Such individual faith in the civic purpose of difficult art was entirely appropriate to the collection of Impressionism. The movement itself had struck a remarkable balance between individualism and collective aspiration. Each of the Impressionists had a distinct aesthetic personality. Yet, in shifting configurations, each of them participated in the Impressionist exhibitions as well as in the private sociability that consolidated their professional alliance. Respect for each other's unique style bound them together. The Impressionists cultivated a resistance to orthodox thought entirely in keeping with the generation that took France out of Napoleon III's autocracy and into the Third Republic. How else to come out from under an Imperial regime and into elected government? How else to challenge the tenets of the Académie des Beaux-Arts and inaugurate Modernism?

The hallmark of the greatest Impressionist works was a fundamentally political resistance to habit, which has prompted critical inquiry ever since. We have been reminded by *Olympia*, notably, at least three times over of Impressionism's ability to call anything and everything into question. Just recently, in 2018 and 2019, the painting yielded new productive race critique, through Denise Murrell's scholarship and an exhibition that travelled, in variant forms, from Columbia University's Wallach Gallery to the Musée d'Orsay as *Le Modèle noir*, to ActeMemorial in Guadeloupe. Before that, *Olympia* had instigated strong gender critique from feminist art historians, and before that, class critique from social art historians.

Olympia remains perhaps the single most disputed paintings of the Impressionist movement, but many less well-known works were socially difficult in ways which also required courageous collecting. To move again across the Atlantic from the Musée d'Orsay to the Met – between the collecting poles of Paris and New York – take the example of Mary Cassatt's 1883 *Lady at the Tea Table*, in the collection of the Met. In this painting, Cassatt expressed her scepticism about the femininity of tea rituals, tea sets and cosmetic beauty standards. She contradicted what was supposed to be pretty, dainty, neat and tight with a bold, gestural, painting technique. She flaunted her identification with the authorial individualism of Impressionist style. In so doing, she rebelled against the gendered social expectations of her extended family and suffered their insulting refusal of the painting. Mrs Riddle, the subject of the portrait, along with her daughter, flatly turned it down. They could have politely accepted it and then hidden it. Instead, they chose to insult Cassatt. Luckily, Cassatt's mother and Edgar Degas supported her and defended the portrait. Nonetheless, Cassatt consigned it to a closet, where it languished for almost thirty years before Havemeyer pulled it into the public domain for an exhibition in support of women's suffrage, and then urged Cassatt to donate the painting to the Met.

Cassatt's conventionally feminine family members refused the painting because it actually was troubling, which helps explain why Cassatt hid it for so long. An unflattering image of Mrs Riddle's face was the least of the painting's social offenses. Fundamentally, Cassatt was refusing her society's masculine gendering of professionalism, creativity, wit and scepticism itself. Cassatt and her colleague Berthe Morisot may well have been the most daring of all the Impressionists, because they called into question the most fundamental organising principle of European society: its gendered division into masculine versus feminine.

Donations of Impressionist art encountered resistance which can be explained by its critical attitude, though not excused. Caillebotte's bequest was only accepted after strenuous argument, and then only partially. McAuley's new account of reaction against Isaac de Camondo's donation makes us painfully aware of that the association of Jews with cosmopolitan modernity could be toxic. Nor, as McAuley reminds us, did generous donation to France of Impressionist art keep the families of Jewish donors from being murdered during the Holocaust, with the willing collaboration of the Vichy regime.

The Impressionists themselves sometimes internalised social conventions, to be sure. Degas became an anti-semite and crossed the street rather than greet Camille Pissarro. Cassatt was truly mortified by her family's refusal of *Lady at the Tea Table*. Morisot encouraged Monet to take the lead public role in the campaign to buy *Olympia* for the state, rather than conduct the campaign herself. We have evidence that she was a driving force behind the scenes, but she clearly deferred to him. Caillebotte had included work by neither woman in the collection he bequeathed to the

French state. Morisot's friends noticed, however, and in 1894 organised to have the state buy one of her paintings, her 1879 *Young Girl in a Ball Gown* (*Jeune femme en toilette au bal*).

Those who donated difficult or troubling Impressionist art did so because they believed in the future. They had the confidence to imagine that in the future ideas would be different. Better, they had the confidence to move works of art into the public domain in order to help that change happen. The very act of donation implies a vision for the future, a belief that in the public domain works of art will eventually change people's minds.

The movement of collections into the public sphere of museums allows public pressure to relay, supplement or redirect private pressures. The anthropologist Arjun Appadurai has memorably called the history of objects "The Social Life of Things". We have tended to think that the social life of art things ends when they enter museums. Museums promise to withdraw art from public markets, to keep them perpetually safe. From an anthropologist's point of view, museums do withdraw art from many forms of exchange. From an art historical point of view, however, the collection of art by museums accelerates the social life of art things. In museums, opportunities to alter the meanings of works of art expand. Qualitatively, the ways in which museums choose to publish, label, research and exhibit their collections can produce radically new meanings for existing objects. Quantitatively, those meanings reach ever-expanding audiences: in galleries, through programming and now online.

Museums continue to elicit new meanings from their collections which invite new audiences. Look at the Musée d'Orsay in one recent season, the summer of 2019. *Le Modèle noir* exhibition and the first truly national monographic exhibition of a woman Impressionist overlapped. (In 1941, a Morisot exhibition took place during the Nazi occupation.) Musée d'Orsay director Laurence des Cars and curators Geneviève Lacambre, Sylvie Patry and Isolde Pludermacher achieved heroic breakthroughs, luckily not long before Covid-19 closed down public access to museums all over the world.

Let the pause Covid-19 imposed on all of us become a historical swerve. In the United States, especially, where the unequal effects of Covid have been so pronounced, there have been dramatic calls for social justice and for deep change in all domains. Our moment is being called a plastic moment, one in which we can imagine greater change than in any normal time. A plastic moment could allow us to imagine a fundamental conceptual change in the history of collecting.

This collective book is supposed to be about the collection of Impressionism. But that subject itself acts as a boundary I want now to call into question. I have become sceptical of a subject called the collection of Impressionism. I no longer believe as I once did in the boundaries that protect

Impressionism within museum galleries of European paintings within the Musée d'Orsay, or within the galleries of major American museums like the Met. It seems to me now that those boundaries have been made all too real by the design of entire museum institutions and by the distribution of art works among them.

My purpose is not to lament the origins of those boundaries. Nor do I want to spend energy on critiques of a past which can never be undone. My questions are to some extent about the effects the boundaries around Impressionism have on our society in the present. Mostly, my questions are about what we can do now to change the future.

Because Impressionism was born in Paris, and because the Musée d'Orsay houses such a splendid collection of Impressionist art, I turn first to the issue of Paris museums. What is the effect of there being, in one city, along the same river, a Musée d'Orsay which houses one sort of collection of late nineteenth-century art, and then, in a completely different institution, the Musée du Quai Branly, which houses other sorts of collections of late nineteenth-century art? In one collection are works by white people. In the other, works by people of colour. In one collection, Europe, mostly France. In the other, non-Europe. Lines as thick as museum walls separate the two. In one collection are works of art made by people who were full citizens of European nations, mostly of France. In the other collection are works of art taken by French citizens, in the name of France, from people who were not French. The two museums separate art that was made in Europe from art that was taken for Europe.

But they are both French art collections. They are both effects of the French aesthetics of the late nineteenth century. The same French culture produced Impressionism, as well as the military, ethnographic and anthropological missions that took art from its places of creation and claimed them for France. If art objects were not directly channelled into national French collections by those missions, they were indirectly channelled there by the private collectors and dealers who were also parts of the same French art system. One and the same culture fostered the collection both of Impressionism and of African, Polynesian and Latin American art. If these arts from different continents are now all possessions of the French state, then they all belong within the same national history of collection.

Though the issue of Paris museums is perhaps the most important, I do not want to call only the French national museum system into question. In New York City, where I work, two separate museum collections also produce a remarkable difference. On one side of Central Park is the Met, which houses collections of art from the whole world, and on the other side of Central Park the Museum of Natural History, which houses no European art, but collections of some non-European art together with collections of natural objects. Moreover, following standard museum practice, houses its collections of European art in one set of galleries and its collections of other galleries.

The totality of this arrangement cannot be fairly treated in a single essay. Rather, I am just drawing attention to the separation of French Impressionism from the arts taken during the Impressionist decades from their places of origin by force, especially those now in the Musée du Quai Branly. I find it extremely thought-provoking that the arts of East Asia, whose history of collecting is more complicated, belong to yet another museum, the Musée Guimet. But that is also another subject, though related.

Art historians, both curators and academics, will quickly respond that the current distribution of art into different museums of galleries reflects their place of origin. Certainly, place of origin is a crucial part of an object's history. I would be the last person to suggest abolishing all public displays of art sorted according to a history of origins. And yet, as Appadurai said, the social life of things does not end when they are made. There are other histories of objects besides their place of origin, and I do want to suggest that some of those other histories need to be seen in public museums.

I will go so far as to say that in some cases, the carving of art history solely according to place of origin presents a view of history which we should change for the future. By separating art according to who made it, we are in fact denying the deep structures of collecting. To collect and exhibit Impressionism, going forward, must be to ask how museums will represent the era of Impressionism in the future. What responsibilities for a vision of our heritage will the state take in France, where the great museums are ultimately run by the state? What responsibilities will Trustees, directors and curators take in the Unites States, where museums are essentially privately run? Now is the moment to reckon with a late nineteenth-century European and North American culture whose aesthetic included both making and taking. They need to be seen as one, in one place, in the same museum, in the same galleries.

This question is all the more timely to ask of French museums because an important discussion about the Musée du Quai Branly has been recently been begun by the pioneering Sarr-Savoy report. The 2018 Sarr-Savoy report weighed the possible restitution of works of art to Africa, notably from the Musée du Quai Branly. The report did an extraordinary job of re-thinking the philosophical concepts underlying possession and restitution. It brilliantly questions the assumption that all works of art belong forever in museums. Perhaps some works of art, the report suggests, need to circulate in the geographic locations from which they were taken, and not to rest in museums (as Europeans define museums) but even to move through educational circuits. Perhaps some art objects belong in schools, rather than in museums.

The Sarr-Savoy report was charged with assessing the issues of restitution. I have no quarrel with that charge. Restitution is a crucial option to consider. It is not, however, the only option we could consider. Restitution leaves in place the assumption that the only history of an art object that matters is its place of origin. Restitution leaves two museums along the Seine, the Musée d'Orsay and the Musée du Quai Branly, which both house Impressionist-era collections. Alongside the possibility of restitution, I suggest a reorganisation of collections within French museums, beginning with Impressionist collections.

Whatever its good intentions, whatever its past meanings, the Musée du Quai Branly is indeed, for our moment and moving forward, a monument to colonialism. Its separation from the Musée d'Orsay is now, in and of itself, a monument to racial distinctions founded on inequality. So are the distinctions in a museum like the Met between galleries dedicated to the effects of one culture on the art of white people and the effects of that same culture on the art of people of colour. Any collection of art created by human hands in a museum called a Natural History Museum, is now, in our moment, a practice beyond redemption.

Somehow – not always, not everywhere, but somehow – we need to see the making and the taking of art together, in the same galleries, in the same museum. The great art made by the North-West Indian peoples now in the Museum of Natural History belongs alongside Impressionism. The great N'kisi sculptures of Central Africa belong alongside Impressionism.

Edward Said, the great theorist of Orientalism, called for a "contrapuntal history". In a contrapuntal collection of art, we should be able to see the causes and the effects of a culture's aesthetic values. We need to recognise that our aesthetic values govern what we make and what we take.

Moves have been made in this direction by some museums. Curiously, these have often been in the areas of seventeenth- and eighteenth-century art, rather than the nineteenth or the twentieth. Over the summer of 2020, the British Museum re-installed its bust of slave-owning founder Hans Sloane, and now the text of its website is far more historically inclusive than it was. Many galleries devoted to porcelain now exhibit Chinese, Japanese and European porcelains together in order to exhibit the relationships among them cause by global trade and style feedback loop; the Freer Gallery staged a "chinamania" exhibition in 2010 that addressed the craze for Chinese and Japanese blue and white porcelain during the Impressionist period.

Theorists of museums have long adopted Foucault's concept of the "heterotopia" to explain the distorted mirrors that museum exhibitions provide societies. In the heterotopia, we see our ourselves, but in a glass, darkly. For many who study art museums, that distortion has been for the worse. Museum heteropias, they say, concealed colonialism and the subordination of women, excuses the abuse of power, the inequalities of gender and race. Quite apart from the negative social effects of museum heterotopias, museum critics help us understand that we have constructed our collection and exhibition of Impressionism. Because we have always constructed a vision of Impressionism through collection and exhibition, I want to emphasise, we can alter that vision. We made it. We can re-make it.

The distortions of the heterotopia can be for the better as well as for the worse. If we want our society to change, then let us construct a heterotopia in the image of our hopes. Let us use the mirroring devices of the museum to create an interpretation of Impressionism that proclaims its place in a united world. We can re-commit to Impressionism's faith in the social good of individual scepticism and ceaseless, restless inquiry. Or, in the charming malapropism invented by Richard Brindsley Sheridan: let our retrospection be all to the future. May our collecting and our museum practice serve a very simple goal: a vision of one, equal human race.

This essay is dedicated to the 115 Columbia University art history graduate students who wrote a letter to the art history faculty during the summer of 2020 asking that the department advance the cause of social justice.

TIMELINE 1850–1960

	LIFE OF THE COLLECTIONS	HISTORY ECONOMY SCIENCE
1850		• 2 Dec. 1851: Coup d'Etat by Napoleon Bonaparte. • 1852: 2nd Republic is proclaimed the 2 December. • 1852: creation of Bon Marché, the first Parisian department store. • 1853: start of Haussmann's major construction work in Paris.
1860	• 1865: Mary Cassatt arrives in Paris.	• 1861: start of the American Civil War. • 1864: the Le Havre-New-York transatlantic line opens. • 1864: law allowing the right to strike. • 1868: start of the Meiji period, marking Japan opening up to the West. • 17 Nov. 1869: the Suez Canal is inaugurated.
1870	• 1876: Captain Henry Hill buys Whistler, *Nocturne in Blue and Gold: Valparaiso Bay* by Whistler, one of the major paintings in his collection which would become the core of the Brighton Art Museum. • 1875: Louisine Elder buys *Scène de ballet* by Degas (1875), undoubtedly the first Impressionist painting to cross the Atlantic. • 1878: Ernest Hoschedé is forced to sell his collection after his business goes into bankruptcy. • 1879: Charpentier exhibits Renoir at his magazine's gallery.	• 19 July 1870: France declares war on Prussia. • 4 Sept. 1870: the Republic is declared. • Nov. 1870: Frédéric Bazille is killed on the battlefield • 28 Jan. 1871: armistice signed with the Prussians. • March-May 1871: Paris Commune. • 1871: treaty of Frankfurt sanctioning the loss of Alsace and part of Lorraine. • 7 Jan. 1873: death of Napoleon III. • 1875: first steam-powered automobile. • 1876: invention of the telephone. • 1879: Edison invents the electric lightbulb.
1880	• In the 1880s Renoir stays at Wargemont with the Bérards, who commission some major works. • 1880: Carl Bernstein buys some Impressionist works through the intermediary of his cousin Charles Ephrussi. • 1884: Manet's studio is sold. • 1889: Erwin Davis donates *La Femme au perroquet* (*Woman with a Parrot*) by Manet (1866) to the Metropolitan Museum.	• 1881: the Jules Ferry law makes primary education free and accessible to all. • 1882: Union générale crash.
1890	• Death of Georges Bellio. • 19 March 1894: Duret auction. • 1994: Caillebotte bequest. • 1896: The Nationalgalerie in Berlin acquires, through the intermediary of its director, Hugo von Tschudi, *Le Moulin sur la Couleuvre à Pontoise* (*Mill on the Couleuvre at Pontoise*) by Cézanne (1881). • 26 March 1896: Emmanuel Chabrier auction. • July 1899: auction of Victor Chocquet's and Count Doria's collections.	• 1894: start of the Dreyfus Affair which destabilised France up until 1906. • 13 January 1898: within the context of the Dreyfus Affair, Zola publishes *J'accuse* in *L'Aurore* newspaper.

CULTURAL LIFE

• 1851: the first World fair opens in London.
• 1855: Paris World Fair.
• 1855: Courbet's Realism Pavilion.
• 1856: *Mme Bovary* by Gustave Flaubert is published.
• 1856: Turner bequest to the National Gallery.
• 1857: *Fleurs du mal* by Charles Baudelaire is published.
• 1858: Nadar, first aerial photograph.
• 1859: Millet paints *l'Angélus* (*The Angelus*).

• 1860: Louis Martinet gallery opens at Bd des Italiens.
• 1861: invention of colour photography.
• 1862: *Misérables* by Victor Hugo and *Salammbô* by Flaubert are published.
• 1863: Salon des Refusés.
• 1865: Richard Wagner.
creates *Tristan and Yseult*.
• 1865-1869: *War and Peace* saga by Leo Tolstoy is published.
• 1867: World Fair in Paris.
• 1867: solo exhibitions by Manet and Courbet.
• 1867: *Grammaire des arts et du dessin* by Charles Blanc is published.
• 1867: *Manette Salomon* by the Goncourt brothers is published.
• 1869: Charles Cros photographed in colour.

• 1871: World Fair in London.
• 1873: *A Season in Hell* by Arthur Rimbaud is published.
• 1874: first solo exhibition of Whistler's work at the Flemish gallery.
• 1874, 1876, 1877, 1879: 1st, 2nd, 3rd and 4th Impressionist exhibition.
• 1874: *Diabolics* by Barbey d'Aurevilly is published.
• 1875: the Opéra Garnier is inaugurated.
• 1875: Georges Bizet creates *Carmen*.
• 1877: World Fair in Paris. Tribute paid to Japan and ironwork architecture.
• 1879: Pasteur discovers the principle of vaccination.

• 1880: Rodin sculpts *Le Penseur* (The Thinker).
• 1880, 1881, 1882 and 1886: 5th, 6th, 7th and 8th Impressionist exhibition.
• 1881: the Société des artistes français is created and organises the Salon from then on.
• 1881: International Electricity Exhibition in Paris.
• 1881: *Bouvard and Pécuchet* by Flaubert is published posthumously.
• 1881: *La Maison d'un artiste* by Edmond de Goncourt is published.
• 1884: Manet retrospective at the Ecole des Beaux-arts.
• 1884: first salon de la Société des Indépendants.
• 1884: Salon des XX is founded in Brussels by Octave Maus.
• 1884: *A Rebours* by Huysmans is published.
• 1885: death of Victor Hugo.
• 1886: symbolist manifesto by Jean Moréas.
• 1886: *l'Œuvre* by Emile Zola is published.
• 1886: the term Neo-Impressionism is coined by Félix Fénéon.
• 1888: birth of synthetism.
• 1889: World Fair in Paris.
• 1889: Monet/Rodin at the Georges Petit gallery.
• 1889: first issue of *La Plume* newspaper.

• 1890: the Société nationale des Beaux-arts is founded.
• 1890: Manet's *Olympia* is donated to the nation.
• 1890: first issue of *Mercure de France*.
• 1891: Van Gogh retrospective at the Salon des Indépendants.
• 1891: *Revue Blanche* is founded by the Natanson brothers.
• 1892: first Salon de la Rose+Croix.
• 1982: Debussy writes *Prelude to the afternoon of a faun*.
• 1893: first exhibition of the Munich Secession.
• 1893: the Vollard gallery opens.
• 1895: publication in Berlin of *Pan* magazine.
• 1895: first film showing by the Lumière brothers in Paris.
• Late 1895: Bing opens the *L'art nouveau* gallery.
• 1896: in Brussels, 1st Salon of *la Libre Esthétique* which replaced the *Société des XX*.
• 1898: first Vienna Secession exhibition.
• 1899: *De Eugène Delacroix au Néo-impressionnisme* by Signac is published.
• 1899: Salon des Cent in Paris.
• 1899: first Berlin Secession exhibition.

LIFE OF THE COLLECTIONS

1900	• 1902: Hayashi and Faure auctions. • May 1905: auction of Paul Bérard's collection. • 1908: opening of the Dublin City Gallery The Hugh Lane. • 1908: in Moscow, Chtchoukine opens his collections to the public.	• 1909: François Depeaux donates his collection to the town of Rouen. • 1906, 1919 and 1927: Etienne Moreau-Nelaton makes several bequests to the nation.
1910	• 1910: the Johannesburg Art Gallery opens in South Africa showing works by French Impressionists. • On his death, Isaac de Camondo bequeaths his collection to the Louvre. • 1912: Henri Rouart's and Jean Dollfus' collection are sold at auction. • 1913: at the last Rouart auction, Durand-Ruel	buys Les *Danseuses à la barre* (*Dancers Practicing at the Barre*) by Degas for Louisine Havemeyer. • 1913: the Metropolitan Museum of Art buys a Cézanne *Vue du Domaine Saint-Joseph* (*View of the Domaine Saint-Joseph*), 1887. • Auction of Degas' collection. • 1918: nationalisation of the Morozov collection.
1920	• 1922: the Palmer collection is donated to the Chicago Art Institute. • 1925: inauguration of the Barnes Foundation in Philadelphia. • 1926–27: Matsukata Kojiro's 3rd and final trip to Europe during which he creates an immense collection of Western art which was later split up.	A part of it formed the core of the Tokyo National Museum of Western Art. • 1929: the Havemeyer collection enters the Metropolitan Museum of Art.
1930	• 1930: the Ohara Museum of Art opens. • 1930: Duncan Phillips moves, leaving the entire building devoted to his collection. • 1932: the Courtauld Institute is founded.	
1940	• From the 1940s and following in the footsteps of his father, who founded it, Paul Mellon makes numerous donations to the National Gallery of Art in Washington, D.C.	• A large number of private collections are dispersed during the Second World War and by Nazis exactions.
1950	• The Davies sisters make a donation to the National Museum Cardiff. • Georges de Bellio's descendants make an important bequest to the Musée Marmottan Monet.	• 1952: Bridgestone Museum of Art opens. • 1959: National Museum of Western opens based on Matsukata's collection which France gave back to Japan.
1960		

HISTORY ECONOMY SCIENCE	CULTURAL LIFE
• 1900: inauguration of the first Parisian metro line. • 1903: Pierre and Marie Curie are awarded the Nobel Prize for physics. • 9 December 1905: laws separating the Church and the State. • 1909: Louis Blériot flies across the Channel.	• 1900: World Fair in Paris including a section devoted to the impressionists. • 1903: the Salon d'automne in Paris is created. • 1904: Matisse paints *Luxe, calme et volupté.* • 1907: Picasso paints *Les Demoiselles d'Avignon.* • 1909: Diaghilev's *Les Ballets Russes* is performed at Châtelet.
• 3 August 1914: Germany declares war on France. • 1917: Clemenceau is appointed War Minister. • 1917: communist regime established in Russia. • 11 November 1818: first World War Armistice. • 1919: creation of the League of Nations.	• 1913: *Alcools* by Apollinaire. • 1913: *The Right of Spring* by Stravinski at the Théâtre des Champs-Elysées. • 1913: Marcel Proust, *Swann's Way.* • 1917: death of Rodin. • 1917: *Fontaine* by Marcel Duchamp is shown, first ready-made.
• 1928: penicillin is discovered. • 1929: stock market crash. .	• 7 February 1922: Durand-Ruel is buried. • 1924: publication of the Surrealist manifesto. • 1926: death of Monet. • 1927: the *Nymphéas* (*Water-Lily*) panels are installed at the Orangerie, officially opened the 17 May.
• 1933: proclamation of the III Reich in Germany. • 1936: in France the Front populaire are elected. • 1936: in Spain, Franco takes power. • 1939: start of the Second World War. • 8 May 1945: armistice of the Second World War. • August 1945: Japan drops two nuclear bombs on the United States.	• 1936: release of Charlie Chaplin film *Modern Times.* • 1937: *Correspondence of Cézanne* by John Rewald is published. .
• 1945: creation of the UN. • 1949: advent of communism in continental China. .	• 1942: *L'Etranger* by Albert Camus is published. • 1946: *Existentialism is a Humanism* by Jean-Paul Sartre is published. • 1949: Simone de Beauvoir writes *The Second Sex*.
• 1953: Elisabeth II takes the throne.	• 1951: *Memoirs of Hadrian* by Marguerite Yourcenar is published. • 1953: first Waiting for Godot by Samuel Beckett. • 1958: Jacques Tatie films *Mon Oncle*.
• 28 August 1863: Martin Luther King's speech. • May 1868: social and student movement. • 1969: first man on the moon.	

BIBLIOGRAPHY

This bibliography does not claim to be exhaustive nor to examine all aspects of the history of collecting, but it seeks to address the conjunction between Impressionist studies and collections. It also includes the main references given by the authors in the various contributions.

Aitken, Geneviève and Marianne Delafond, *La Collection d'estampes japonaises de Claude Monet à Giverny*, Paris, Bibliothèque des arts, 1983.

Alexandre, Arsène, *La Collection Henri Rouart*, Paris, Goupil, 1912.

Alexandre, Arsène, "La Collection de M. Jean Dollfus", *Les Arts*, 1904, January, no. 25, pp. 6–16 and February, no. 26, pp. 3–12.

Assante di Panzillo, Maryline, *Cézanne et l'argent : salons, marchands et collectionneurs*, Paris, RMN-Grand Palais, 2011.

Baetens, Jan Dirk and Dries, Lyna (eds.), *Art Crossing Borders: The Internationalisation of the Art Market in the Age of Nation States, 1750-1914*, Leiden, Brill, 2019.

Bailey, Colin B., "The Origins of the Barnes Collection, 1912–15", *The Burlington Magazine*, vol. 150, no. 1265, 2008, pp. 534-543.

Barilli, Renato, *Impressionismo italiano*, Milan, Mazzotta, 2002.

Baudrillard, Jean, *Le Système des objets*, Paris, Gallimard, 1968.

Berson, Ruth, *The New Painting, Impressionism 1874-1886*, 2 vols., San Francisco, Fine Arts Museums of San Francisco, 1996.

Biasi, Pierre-Marc de, "Système et déviances de la collection à l'époque romantique", *Romantisme*, dossier "Déviances" (ed. Marc Eigeldinger), no. 27, 980, pp. 77-93.

Blot, Eugène, *Histoire d'une collection de tableaux modernes : cinquante ans de peinture (de 1882 à 1932)*, Paris, Éditions d'art, 1934.

Bodelsen, Merete, "Early Impressionist Sales 1874–94 in the Light of Some Unpublished "Procès-Verbaux"", *The Burlington Magazine*, vol. 110, no. 783, 1968.

Bodelsen, Merete, "Gauguin, the Collector", *The Burlington Magazine*, vol. 112, no. 810, 1970, pp. 575-587, 589.

Boime, Albert, "Les hommes d'affaire et les arts en France au XIXe siècle", *Actes de la recherche en Sciences sociales*, no. 28, 1979, pp. 57-75.

Boulouch, Nathalie, "Antonin Personnaz ou l'aventure d'un autochromiste", *Histoire de l'art*, no. 13-14, 1991, pp. 67-76.

Bourdieu, Pierre, "Le marché des biens symboliques", *L'Année Sociologique*, vol. 3, no. 22, 1971, pp. 49-126.

Brettell, Richard R., Selz, Peter and J. Roberts, Norma, *Impressionism and European Modernism: The Sirak Collection*, Columbus, Ohio, Columbus Museum of Art, 1991.

Broude, Norma (dir.), *L'impressionnisme dans le monde : un mouvement international, 1860-1920*, Paris, Nathan, 1990.

Burns, Emily C. and Rudy Price, Alice M., *Mapping Impressionist Painting in Transnational Contexts*, Abingdon, Routledge, 2021.

Burty, Philippe, "Exposition de la Société anonyme des artistes", *La République française*, 25 April 1874.

Cabanne, Pierre, *Les grands collectionneurs, Tome I : Du Moyen Âge au XIX*e *siècle*, Paris, les Éd. de l'Amateur, 2003.

Catalogue de la collection Moreau (tableaux, dessins, aquarelles et pastels) offerte à l'État français et exposée au Musée des Arts Décoratifs, Paris, imprimerie Frazier-Soye, 1907.

Clark, Alexis and Fowle, Frances (dir.), *Globalizing Impressionism: Reception, Translation, and Transnationalism*, New Haven, Yale University Press, 2020.

Cooper, Douglas and Blunt, Anthony, *The Courtauld Collection: A Catalogue and Introduction, by Douglas Cooper, with a Memoir of Samuel Courtauld, by Anthony Blunt*, London, University of London, 1954.

Cousinié, Frédéric (ed.), *L'impressionnisme, du plein air au territoire*, actes de colloque, Mont-Saint-Aignan, PURH, 2013.

De Nittis, Giuseppe, *Notes et souvenirs du peintre Joseph De Nittis*, Paris, Librairies-Imprimeries Réunies, 1895.

Degas inédit, proceedings of the symposium *Degas*, Paris, musée d'Orsay, 18-21 April 1988, Paris, La Documentation française, 1989.

Dewhurst, Wynford, *Impressionist Painting, Its Genesis and Development*, London, G. Newnes, 1904.

Dilworth, Leah (dir.), *Acts of Possession: Collecting in America*, New Brunswick, NJ, Rutgers, 2003.

Distel, Anne, *Les Collectionneurs des impressionnistes : amateurs et marchands*, Paris, Bibliothèque des arts, 1989.

Duret, Théodore, *Critique d'avant-garde*, Paris, Charpentier, 1885.

Duverget, Chantal, *George Besson: critique d'art et collectionneur (1882-1971)*, Villeneuve-d'Ascq, Presses universitaires du Septentrion, 1999.

Evans, Mark, "The Davies Sisters of Llandinam and Impressionism for Wales, 1908–1923", *Journal of the History of Collections*, vol. 16, no. 2, 2004, pp. 219-253.

Faizand de Maupeou, Félicie, *Monet et l'exposition. Une stratégie de carrière à l'avènement du marché de l'art*, Rouen, PURH, 2018.

Fletcher, Pamela M. and Helmreich, Anne, *The Rise of the Modern Art Market in London, 1850-1939*, Manchester-New York, Manchester University Press, 2011.

Flint, Kate, *Impressionists in England: The Critical Reception*, London, Boston, Melbourne and Henley, Routledge & Kegan Paul, 1984, pp. 46-55.

Gaehtgens, Thomas W. and Marchesano, Louis, *Display & Art History. The Düsseldorf Gallery and Its Catalogue*, Los Angeles, The Getty Research Institute, 2011.

Gee, Malcolm, *Dealers, Critics, and Collectors of Modern Painting: Aspects of the Parisian Art Market Between 1910 and 1930*, New York, Garland, 1981.

Georgel, Chantal (ed.), *Jacques Doucet : collectionneur et mécène*, Paris, Les Arts décoratifs, 2016.

Gilson, Sophie, *La fin de siècle au musée d'Ixelles : collection Octave Maus*, Ixelles, musée d'Ixelles, 2008.

Gimpel, René, *Journal d'un collectionneur marchand de tableaux*, Paris, Calmann-Lévy, 1963.

Gloor, Lukas, *Von Böcklin zu Cézanne. Die Rezeption des französischen Impressionismus in der deutschen Schweiz*, Bern-New York, P. Lang 1986.

Goncourt, Edmond de, *La maison d'un artiste*, Paris, G. Charpentier, 1881.

Goncourt, Edmond and Jules de, *Journal des Goncourt*, Paris, G. Charpentier and E. Fasquelle, 1887-1896.

Guillerme, Jacques (ed.), *Les collections : fables et programmes*, Seyssel, Champ Vallon, 1993.

Haskell, Francis, *La norme et le caprice. Redécouvertes en art : aspects du goût, de la mode et de la collection en France et en Angleterre, 1789-1914*, Paris, Flammarion, 1993.

Hayashi, Yui, "Monet wo Giverny ni Tazuneta Nihonjin [The Japanese who visited Monet in Giverny]", in *Monet : Inshōha no Kyoshō, Sono Isan* [Monet's art and its posterity], cat. exp., Tokyo, The National Art Center, 2007, pp. 209-216.

Hauptman, William and Norgaard Larsen, Peter (eds.), *Impressions du Nord : la peinture scandinave, 1800-1915*, Lausanne-Milan, Fondation de l'Hermitage-5 Continents, 2008.

Henriet, Frédéric, "Étienne Moreau-Nélaton", *Annales de la Société historique et archéologique de Château-Thierry*, 1906.

Hook, Philip, *The Ultimate Trophy. How the Impressionist Painting Conquered the World*, London, Prestel, 2012.

House, John, *Impressionism for England: Samuel Courtauld as Patron and Collector* [exh. London, Courtauld

Institute Galleries, 1994], London, Courtauld Institute Galleries, 1994.

Joyeux-Prunel, Béatrice, *Nul n'est prophète en son pays ? L'internationalisation de la peinture des avant-gardes parisiennes, 1855-1914*, Paris, N. Chaudun, 2009.

Joyeux-Prunel, Béatrice, *Les avant-gardes artistiques, 1848-1918 : une histoire transnationale*, Paris, Gallimard, 2015.

Kosinski, Dorothy, Pissarro, Joachim and Stevens, Maryanne (dir.), *From Manet to Gauguin: Masterpieces from Swiss Private Collections*, London, Royal Academy of Arts, 1995.

Kuhrau, Sven and Wolff-Thomsen, Ulrike, *Öffentliches und privates Kunstsammeln in Deutschland 1871-1933*, Kiel, Ludwig, 2011.

Lecomte, Georges, *L'Art impressionniste, d'après la collection privée de M. Durand-Ruel, 36 eaux-fortes, pointes sèches et illustrations dans le texte, par A.-M. Lauzet*, Paris, impr. de Chamerot et Renouard, 1892.

Lefèvre, Géraldine (ed.), *Monet, les années décisives au Havre*, Paris, Hazan, 2016.

Lenman, Robin, "Painters, Patronage and the Art Market in Germany 1850-1914", *Past & Present*, vol. 123, 1989, pp. 109-140.

Lobstein, Dominique, *Défense et illustration de l'impressionnisme Ernest Hoschedé et son « Brelan de Salons » (1890)*, Dijon, l'Échelle de Jacob, 2008.

Long, Véronique, *Mécènes des deux mondes : les collectionneurs donateurs du Louvre et de l'Art Institute de Chicago, 1879-1940*, Rennes, Presses universitaires de Rennes, 2007.

Madeline, Laurence, *Musée de l'Orangerie : la collection Walter-Guillaume et les « Nymphéas » de Monet*, Paris, Nouvelles éditions Scala, 2017.

Maingon, Claire, "La collection Isaac de Camondo au Louvre (1914-1950) : le "musée" retrouvé", *La Revue du Louvre et des musées de France*, no. 4, 2015, pp. 91-101.

Malouvier, Emilie, "Les catalogues de la collection des ducs de Leuchtenberg : rédaction et diffusion de savoirs muséographiques européens", numéro spécial *Musée, Musées* de *Romantisme* (ed. Ségolène Le Men, avec Philippe Hamon and Paule Petitier), no. 173, 2016-3, pp. 88-97.

Michel, Patrick, *Peinture et plaisir. Les goûts picturaux des collectionneurs parisiens au XVIIIe siècle*, Rennes, Presses universitaires de Rennes, 2011.

Miura, Atsushi, "Japon et impressionnisme : peinture japonaise moderne et collections de tableaux impressionnistes au Japon", in Julien Bouvard and Cléa Patin (eds.), *Japon Pluriel 12, autour de l'image : arts graphiques et culture visuelle au Japon*, Arles, Éditions Philippe Picquier, 2018.

Miyazaki, Katsumi, *L'arrivée de la peinture occidentale : Monet, Renoir, Cézanne et autres qui ont fasciné les Japonais*, Tokyo, Nikkei Publishing, 2007.

Montout-Richard, Marie-Hélène (eds.), *L'œil d'un collectionneur : catalogue raisonné de la collection d'Henry Vasnier au musée des Beaux-Arts de Reims*, Paris, Somogy, 2003.

Monneret, Sophie, *L'impressionnisme et son époque*, Paris, Robert Laffont, [1978] 1987.

Moreau-Nélaton, Étienne, *Mémorial de famille*, Paris, published by the author, 1918.

Moscatiello, Manuela, *Le japonisme de Giuseppe De Nittis : un peintre italien en France à la fin du XIXe siècle*, Bern, Peter Lang, 2011.

Nerlich, France, *La peinture française en Allemagne 1815-1870*, Paris, Éd. de la Maison des sciences de l'homme, 2010.

Ott, John, "How New York Stole the Luxury Art Market: Blockbuster Auctions and Bourgeois Identity in Gilded Age America", *Winterthur Portfolio*, vol. 42, no. 2/3, 2008, pp. 133-158.

Paret, Peter, *German Encounters with Modernism, 1840-1945*, New York, Cambridge University Pres, 2000.

Perec, Georges, *Un cabinet d'amateur. Histoire d'un tableau*, Paris, Balland, 1979.

Pety, Dominique, *Les Goncourt et la collection : de l'objet d'art à l'art d'écrire*, Geneva, Droz, 2003.

Pety, Dominique, *Poétique de la collection au XIXe siècle : du document de l'historien au bibelot de l'esthète*, Nanterre, Presses universitaires de Paris Ouest, 2010.

Poe, Edgar, "La Philosophie de l'ameublement", *Histoires grotesques et sérieuses*, by Edgar Poe, translated by Charles Baudelaire, Paris, Michel Lévy frères, new edition, 1871.

Praz, Mario, *Histoire de la décoration d'intérieur. Philosophie de l'ameublement*, Paris, Thames & Hudson, 1994 (Italian ed., 1981).

Preti-Hamard, Sénéchal, Monica and Philippe (eds.), *Collections et marché de l'art en France, 1789-1848*, actes du colloque [Paris, INHA, 4-6 December 2003], Rennes-Paris, Presses universitaires de Rennes-INHA, 2005.

Raybone, Samuel, *Gustave Caillebotte as Worker, Collector, Painter*, New York, Bloomsbury Visual Arts, [2020].

Rewald, John, *Cézanne and America: Dealers, Collectors, Artists and Critics, 1891–1921*, London, Thames & Hudson, 1989.

Rewald, John, *Histoire de l'impressionnisme*, Paris, A. Michel, [New York, Museum of Modern Art, 1946], 1986.

Rheims, Maurice, *Les collectionneurs de la curiosité, de la beauté, du goût, de la mode et de la spéculation*, Paris, Ramsay, [1981], 2002.

Rizzo, Cettina, *Le collectionnisme au XIXe siècle : Théophile Gautier et les Préfaces aux catalogues des ventes aux enchères*, Paris, L'Harmattan, 2015.

Romantisme. Revue du XIXe siècle, no. 112, special issue on "La collection", ed. Dominique Pety, 2001.

Rougeot, Magali, *Gustave Fayet (1865-1925), itinéraire d'un artiste collectionneur*, thesis in art history [Université Paris Nanterre, ed. Ségolène Le Men – École du Louvre, ed. Rodolphe Rapetti], 2013.

Russian Impressionism: Paintings from the Collection of the Russian Museum : 1870s-1970s, New York, Palace Editions, 2000.

Saint-Raymond, Léa and Viraben, Hadrien, "The Virtual Collection of Alexandre Berthier, Prince of Wagram", *Nineteenth-Century Art Worldwide*, vol. 19, no. 2, 2020, https://doi.org/10.29411/ncaw.2020.19.2.4.

Saint-Raymond, Léa, "Vers une histoire élargie des collections ? Les annuaires artistiques des collectionneurs au prisme des humanités numériques", *Histoire de l'art*, no. 87, 2021, pp. 1-12.

Saint-Raymond, Léa, *À la conquête du marché de l'art. Le Pari(s) des enchères (1830-1939)*, Paris, Garnier, 2021.

Theuveny, Christian and Petit-Castelli, Claude, *George Viau, un amateur : 50 ans de collection d'un ami des impressionnistes*, Louviers, HB impressions, 2018.

Vaisse, Pierre, *Deux façons d'écrire l'histoire : le legs Caillebotte*, Paris, Inha – Éd. Ophrys, 2014.

Valéry, Paul, *Degas, Danse Dessin. Illustrations d'Edgar Degas*, Paris, Ambroise Vollard, 1936.

Venturi, Lionello, *Les Archives de l'impressionnisme. Lettres de Renoir, Monet, Pissarro, Sisley et autres. Mémoires de Paul Durand-Ruel. Documents*, 2 vols., Paris-New York, Durand-Ruel, 1939.

Viraben, Hadrien, *Le savant et le profane : Documents et monuments de l'impressionnisme, 1900-1939*, Dijon, Les Presses du réel, 2021.

Vollard, Ambroise, *Souvenirs d'un marchand de tableaux*, [1937], Paris, A. Michel, 2007.

Watson, Janell, *Literature and Material Culture from Balzac to Proust: The Collection and Consumption of Curiosities*, Cambridge, Cambridge University Press, 1999.

White, Harrison and Cynthia, *La Carrière des peintres au XIXe siècle. Du système académique au marché impressionniste*, Paris, Flammarion, 1991.

Wildenstein, Daniel, *Monet : Catalogue raisonné*, Paris-Lausanne, Wildenstein Institute, 1974-1991, 5 volumes.

Exhibition catalogues

Monet et ses amis : le legs Michel Monet, la donation Donop de Monchy (exh. Paris, musée Marmottan, 1971), Daulte Françoise and Richebé Claude(ed.), Paris, musée Marmottan-Bibliothèque des arts, 1971.

Les Impressionnistes de la collection Courtauld de Londres (exh. Paris, musée de l'Orangerie, October 1955 – January 1956), Anthony Blunt, Douglas Cooper and Charles Sterling (eds.), Paris, musée de l'Orangerie, 1955.

Deutsche Impressionisten: Liebermann, Corinth, Slevogt (exh. Schaffhausen, Museum zu Allerheiligen, 23 April – 24 July 1955), Schaffhausen, Buchdruckerei Meier & Cie, 1955.

Centenaire de l'impressionnisme (exh. Paris, Grand Palais, 21 September – 24 November 1974), Hélène Adhémar (ed.), Paris, Éd. des musées nationaux, 1974.

Degas (exh. Paris, Galeries nationales du Grand Palais, 9 February – 16 May 1988; Ottawa, musée des Beaux-Arts du Canada, 16 June – 28 August 1988; New York, The Metropolitan Museum of Art, 27 September 1988 – 8 January 1989), Henri Loyrette and Michael Pantazzi (eds.), Paris, Éd. de la Réunion des musées nationaux, 1988.

Landschaft im Licht. Impressionistische Malerei in Europa und Nordamerika 1860-1910 (exh. Cologne, Wallraf Richartz Museum, 6 April – 1 July 1990; Kunsthaus Zürich, 3 August – 21 October 1990), Götz Czymmek (ed.), Cologne-Zürich, Wallraf-Richartz-Museum-Kunsthaus, 1990.

Deutsche Impressionisten aus dem Niedersächsischen Landesmuseum Hannover (exh. Baden-Baden, Staatliche Kunsthalle, 15 June – 28 July 1985), Staatliche Kunsthalle, 1985.

The New Painting: Impressionism 1874–1886 (exh. Washington, National Gallery of Art, 19 January – 6 April 1986; The Fine Arts Museums of San Francisco, 19 April – 6 July, 1986), Charles S. Moffett (ed.), Seattle, University of Washington Press, 1986.

Masterpieces of Impressionism and Post-Impressionism: The Annenberg Collection (exh. Philadelphia, Philadelphia Museum of Art, 21 May – 17 September 1989), Philadelphia, Philadelphia Museum of Art, 1989.

De Corot aux impressionnistes, donations Moreau-Nélaton (exh. Paris, Grand Palais, 1991), Pierre Rosenberg and Françoise Cachin (eds.), Paris, Réunion des musées nationaux, Bibliothèque nationale, 1991.

Claude Monet et ses amis : œuvres choisies du Musée Marmottan et de collections privées (exh. Lausanne, Fondation de l'Hermitage, 28 May – 26 September 1993), Lausanne-Paris, Fondation de l'Hermitage and Bibliothèque des arts, 1993.

La collection Havemeyer : quand l'Amérique découvrait l'Impressionnisme (exh. Paris, musée d'Orsay, 20 October 1997 – 18 January 1998) Sylvie Patin (ed.), Paris, Réunion des musées nationaux, 1997.

The Private Collection of Edgar Degas. A Summary Catalogue (exh. New York, The Metropolitan Museum of Art, 1 October 1997 – 11 January 1998), Ann Dumas, Colta Ives, Susan Alyson Stein and Gary Tinterow (eds.), New York, The Metropolitan Museum of Art, 1997.

Un ami de Cézanne et Van Gogh : le docteur Gachet (exh. Paris, Galeries nationales du Grand Palais, 28 January – 26 April 1999; New York, The Metropolitan Museum of Art, 17 May – 15 August 1999; Amsterdam, Van Gogh Museum, 24 September – 5 December 1999), Anne Distel, Susan Alyson Stein and Andreas Blühm (eds.), Paris, Réunion des musées nationaux, 1999.

Impressions du Nord. La peinture scandinave 1800-1915 (exh. Lausanne, Fondation de l'Hermitage, 27 January – 22 May 2005), William Hauptman, Peter Larsen and Juliane Willi-Cosandier (eds.), Milan, 5 Continents, 2004.

Au cœur de l'impressionnisme : La famille Rouart (exh. Paris, musée de la Vie romantique, 2004), Solange Thierry (ed.), Paris, Paris musées, 2004.

De Courbet à Matisse. Donation Senn-Foulds (exh. Le Havre, musée Malraux, 13 March – 12 June 2005), Annette Haudiquet and Géraldine Lefebvre (eds.), Le Havre, musée Malraux and Somogy éditions d'art, 2005.

Cézanne to Picasso : Ambroise Vollard, Patron of the Avant-Garde (exh. New York, The Metropolitan Museum of Art, 13 September 2006 – 7 January 2007; Chicago, The Art Institute, 17 February – 13 May 2007; Paris, musée d'Orsay, 18 June – 16 September 2007), Maryline Assante di Panzillo, Douglas W. Druick and Rebecca A. Rabinow (eds.), New Haven, Yale University Press, 2006.

Masters of Light: Selections of American Impressionism from the Manoogian Collection (exh. Vero Beach Museum of Art, Florida, 30 January – 23 April 2006), Jennifer A. Bailey and Lucinda H. Gedeon (eds.), University of Washington Press, 2006.

Cézanne in Florence: Two Collectors and the 1910

Exhibition of Impressionism (exh. Florence, Palazzo Strozzi, 2 March – 29 July, 2007), Francesca Bardazzi (ed.), Milan, Electa, 2007.

Manet to Matisse: Impressionist Masters from the Marion and Henry Bloch Collection (exh. Kansas City, The Nelson-Atkins Museum of Art, 9 June – 9 September 2007), Richard R. Brettell and Joachim Pissarro (eds.), Kansas City, Nelson-Atkins Museum of Art, 2007.

À l'apogée de l'impressionnisme : La collection Georges de Bellio (exh. Paris, musée Marmottan Monet, 10 October 2007 – 3 February 2008), Marianne Delafond and Remus Niculescu (eds.), Lausanne, Bibliothèque des arts, 2007.

Impressionism and Scotland (exh. Edinburgh, National Gallery Complex, 19 July – 12 October 2008; Glasgow, Kelvingrove Art Gallery and Museum, 31 October 2008 – 1 February 2009), Frances Fowle and Vivien Hamilton (eds.), Edinburgh, National Galleries of Scotland, 2008.

La Splendeur des Camondo : de Constantinople à Paris 1806-1945 (exh. Paris, musée d'art et d'histoire du judaïsme, 2009-2010), Anne Hélène Hoog (ed.), Paris, musée d'art et d'histoire du judaïsme, Skira Flammarion, 2009.

De Renoir à Sam Szafran, parcours d'un collectionneur (exh. Martigny [Switzerland], Fondation Pierre Gianadda, 10 December 2010 – 13 June 2011), Marina Ferretti Bocquillon (ed.) Martigny, Fondation Pierre Gianadda, 2010.

Chefs-d'œuvre de la peinture française du Sterling and Francine Clark Art Institute : de l'école de Barbizon à l'impressionnisme (travelling exhibition, 2010–12), James A. Ganz and Richard Robson Brettell (eds.), Williamstown-Paris, Sterling & Francine Clark Art Institute, Skira Flammarion, 2011.

De Delacroix à Marquet. Donation Senn-Foulds. Dessins (exh. Le Havre, musée Malraux, 12 March – 22 May 2011), Annette Haudiquet and Géraldine Lefebvre (eds.), Le Havre-Paris, MuMa and Somogy, 2011.

Le Cercle de l'art moderne : collectionneurs d'avant-garde au Havre (exh. Paris, musée du Luxembourg, 19 September 2012 – 6 January 2013), Annette Haudiquet and Géraldine Lefebvre (eds.), Paris, musée du Luxembourg-Sénat and Réunion des musées nationaux-Grand Palais, 2012.

Collection David et Ezra Nahmad : impressionnisme et audaces du XIXe *siècle* (exh. Sète, musée Paul Valéry, 29 June – 27 October 2013), David Nahmad and Maïthé Vallès-Bled (eds.), Sète, Éd. Au fil du temps, 2013.

L'impressionnisme et les Américains (exh. Giverny, musée des impressionnismes, 28 March – 29 June 2014; Edinburgh, National Galleries of Scotland, 19 July – 19 October 2014; Madrid, Museo Thyssen-Bornemisza, 4 November 2014 – 1 February 2015), Richard Brettell and Frances Fowle (eds.), Giverny-Malakoff, musée des impressionnismes and Hazan, 2014.

Les impressionnistes en privé : cent chefs-d'œuvre de collections particulières (exh. Paris, musée Marmottan Monet, 13 February – 6 July 2014), Marianne Mathieu (ed.), Paris, Hazan, 2014.

Cézanne et la Modernité : Chefs-d'œuvre de l'art européen, la collection Pearlman (exh. Oxford, Ashmolean Museum of Art and Archaeology, 13 March – 22 June 2014; Aix-en-Provence, musée Granet, 12 July – 5 October 2014; Atlanta, High Museum of Art, 25 October 2014 – 11 January 2015), Paris, Aix-en-Provence, Artlys, musée Granet and Pays d'Aix, 2014.

Paul Durand-Ruel, le pari de l'impressionnisme (exh. Paris, musée du Luxembourg, 9 October 2014 – 8 February 2015; London, National Gallery, 4 March – 31 May 2015, Philadelphia, Philadelphia Museum of Art, 24 June – 13 September 2015), Sylvie Patry (ed.), Paris, Réunion des musées nationaux-Grand Palais and musée du Luxembourg-Sénat, 2014.

Victor Chocquet : ami et collectionneur des impressionnistes Renoir, Cézanne, Monet, Manet (exh. Winterthur, Sammlung Oskar Reinhart "Am Römerholz", 21 February – 7 June 2015), Mariantonia Reinhard Felice (ed.), Munich, Himmer Verlag, 2015.

Japan's Love for Impressionism: From Monet to Renoir (exh. Bonn, Bundeskunsthalle, 8 October 2015 – 21 February 2016), Atsushi Miura (ed.), Munich-London-New York-Bonn, Prestel and Bundeskunsthalle, 2015. In particular Marianne Mathieu, "Tadamasa Hayashi, Kōjirō Matsukata and the Western Collectors and Collections" and Atsushi Miura, "Japan and the Impressionists: The Collection of French Painting and the Interrelation between French and Japanese Art".

Icônes de l'art moderne : La collection Chtchoukine (exh. Paris, Fondation Louis Vuitton, 22 October 2016 – 20 February 2017), Anne Baldassari (ed.), Paris, Gallimard and Fondation Louis Vuitton, 2016.

Les impressionnistes à Londres : artistes français en exil (exh. London, Tate Britain, 2

November 2017 – 7 May 2018; Paris, Petit Palais-musée des Beaux-Arts de la Ville de Paris, 20 June – 14 October 2018), Caroline Corbeau-Parsons (ed.), Paris, Paris musées et Petit Palais-musée des Beaux-Arts de la Ville de Paris, 2017.

Collections privées : un voyage des impressionnistes aux fauves (exh. Paris, musée Marmottan Monet, 13 September 2018 – 10 February 2019), Marianne Mathieu and Claire Durand-Ruel Snollaerts (eds.), Paris, Hazan and musée Marmottan Monet, 2018.

Le jardin secret des Hansen. La collection Ordrupgaard : Degas, Cézanne, Monet, Renoir, Gauguin, Matisse (exh. Paris, musée Jacquemart-André, 15 September 2017 – 22 January 2018), Pierre Curie and Anne-Brigitte Fonsmark (eds.), Paris-Bruxelles, Culturespaces - Fonds Mercator, 2017.

Monet collectionneur (exh. Paris, musée Marmottan Monet, 14 September 2017 – 14 January 2018), Marianne Mathieu and Dominique Lobstein (eds.), Paris, Hazan and musée Marmottan Monet, 2017.

Collection Burrell : chefs-d'œuvre réalistes et impressionnistes (exh. Marseille, musée Cantini, 18 May – 23 September 2018), Paris, Lienart, 2018.

Mary Cassatt : une impressionniste américaine à Paris (exh. Paris, musée Jacquemart-André, 9 March – 23 July 2018), Nancy Mowll Mathews, Pierre Curie and Flavie Durand-Ruel Mouraux (eds.), Brussels, Fonds Mercator, 2018.

Trésors impressionnistes. La Collection Ordrupgaard : Degas, Cézanne, Monet, Renoir, Gauguin, Matisse (exh. Martigny, Fondation Pierre Gianadda, 8 February – 16 June 2019), Anne-Birgitte Fonsmark (ed.), Martigny, Fondation Pierre Gianadda, 2019.

La collection Courtauld : le parti de l'impressionnisme (exh. Paris, Fondation Louis Vuitton, 20 February – 17 June 2019), London-Paris, The Courtauld Gallery - Fondation Louis Vuitton, 2019.

La collection Emil Bührle (exh. Paris, musée Maillol, 20 March – 21 July 2019), Lukas Gloor (ed.), Paris, Gallimard, 2019.

De l'impressionnisme à Bonnard et Picasso : collection Nahmad (exh. Le Cannet, musée Bonnard, 6 July – 3 November 2019), Véronique Serrano (ed.), Cinisello Balsamo-Le Cannet, Silvana Editoriale and musée Bonnard, 2019.

François Depeaux : collectionneur des impressionnistes (exh. Rouen, musée des Beaux-Arts, 3 April – 7 September 2020), Sylvain Amic (ed.), Paris, In Fine-Réunion des musées métropolitains Rouen Normandie, 2020.

La vie en couleur : Antonin Personnaz, photographe impressionniste (exh. Rouen, musée des Beaux-Arts, 3 April – 7 September 2020), Virginie Chardin, Sophie Harent and Sylvie Patry (eds.), Cinisello Balsamo, Silvana Editoriale, 2020.

Camille Moreau-Nélaton, une femme céramiste au temps des impressionnistes (exh. Rouen, musée de la Céramique, 3 April – 15 November 2020), Alexandra Bosc and Xavier de Massary (eds.), Cinisello Balsamo-Rouen, Silvana Editoriale and Réunion des musées métropolitains, 2020.

Icônes de l'art moderne : la collection Morozov (exh. Paris, Fondation Louis Vuitton, 22 September 2021 – 22 February 2022), Anne Baldassari (ed.), Paris, Gallimard and Fondation Louis Vuitton, 2021.

Signac collectionneur (exh. Paris, musée d'Orsay, 12 October 2021 – 13 February 2022), Marina Ferretti-Bocquillon and Charlotte Hellman (eds.), Paris, Gallimard, 2021.

Julie Manet : la mémoire impressionniste (exh. Paris, musée Marmottan Monet, 19 October 2021 – 20 March 2022), Marianne Mathieu (ed.), Vanves-Paris, Hazan and musée Marmottan Monet, 2021.

PHOTO CREDITS

Cover
The Barnes Foundation

Félicie Faizand de Maupeou, Ségolène Le Men
Fig. 1: Museum of Fine Arts, Boston
Fig. 2: Bibliothèque nationale de France

Ségolène Le Men
Fig. 1: Museo Nacional del Prado
Fig. 2: The Metropolitan Museum of Art
Fig. 3: Hervé Lewandowski © 2022. RMN-Grand Palais / Dist. Foto Scala, Firenze
Fig. 4: Musée de l'ancien Évêché - Évreux (France)
Fig. 5: Photo Archives Durand-Ruel © Durand-Ruel & Cie.
Fig. 6: Photo Archives Durand-Ruel © Durand-Ruel & Cie.
Fig. 7: The Barnes Foundation
Fig. 8: The Metropolitan Museum of Art / Art Resource / Scala, Firenze
Fig. 9: Bibliothèque nationale de France
Fig. 10: Musée Nissim de Camondo, Paris
Fig. 11: Yohann Deslandes / Réunion des Musées Métropolitains Rouen Normandie
Figs. 12-15: Private collection, all rights reserved
Fig. 16: 2022. RMN-Grand Palais / Dist. Foto Scala, Firenze
Fig. 17: 2022. RMN-Grand Palais / Dist. Foto Scala, Firenze
Fig. 18: Private collection, all rights reserved
Fig. 19: 2022. RMN-Grand Palais / Dist. Foto Scala, Firenze
Fig. 20: Bibliothèque nationale de France
Fig. 21: The Barnes Foundation
Fig. 22: The Barnes Foundation

Gwendoline Corthier-Hardouin
Fig. 1: Courtier-Hardouin
Fig. 2: The Metropolitan Museum of Art / Art Resource / Scala, Firenze

Fausto Minervini
Fig. 1: Collection of Shelburne Museum, gift of Dunbar W. and Electra Webb Bostwick. 1981-82.
Fig. 2: Stéphane Maréchalle © 2022 RMN-Grand Palais / Dist. Foto Scala, Firenze
Figs. 3-4: Getty Research Institute, Special Collections
Fig. 5: The Philadelphia Museum of Art / Art Resource / Scala, Firenze
Fig. 6: © 2022 The National Gallery, London / Scala, Firenze
Fig. 7: © 2022 Scala, Firenze
Fig. 8: Petit Palais, musée des Beaux-Arts de la Ville de Paris

Alexandre D'Andoque
Fig. 1: Private archives
Fig. 2: Henri Gaud © MAGFF
Fig. 3: © 2022. RMN-Grand Palais / Dist. Foto Scala, Firenze
Fig. 4: Musée de Beaux-Arts de Rennes
Fig. 5: Archives Fayet
Fig. 6: Private collection
Fig. 7: Collection Senn-Foulds
Fig. 8: Dominic Büttner

Anne Distel
INHA

Catherine Méneux
Fig. 1: Tony Querrec © 2022 RMN-Grand Palais / Dist. Foto Scala, Firenze
Fig. 2: Carnegie Museum of Art, Pittsburgh, acquired through the generosity of the Sarah Mellon Scaife Foundation
Fig. 3: Patrice Schmidt © 2022 RMN-Grand Palais / Dist. Foto Scala, Firenze
Fig. 4: Artefact / Alamy Stock Photo
Fig. 5: © 2022 The Metropolitan Museum of Art / Art Resource / Scala, Firenze
Fig. 6: The Metropolitan Museum of Art / Art Resource / Scala, Firenze

Léa Saint-Raymond
Figs. 1-4: Léa Saint-Raymond
Fig. 5: Jean-Gilles Berizzi, Paris, musée d'Orsay © 2022. RMN-Grand Palais / Dist. Foto Scala, Firenze

Lukas Gloor
Fig. 1: Fondation Beyeler, Riehen / Basel
Figs. 2-3: Private collection
Fig. 4: © Oskar Reinhart Collection "Am Römerholz", Winterthur
Fig. 5: Kunstmuseum Solothurn
Fig. 6: SIK-ISEA, Zürich (Philipp Hitz)
Fig. 7: Kunstmuseum Winterthur, Ankauf, 1916 © Hermann Linck
Fig. 8: SIK-ISEA, Zürich (Jean-Pierre Kuhn)
Fig. 9: Museum Langmatt
Fig. 10: Kunstmuseum Basel, Martin P. Bühler

Carolyn Kinder Carr
Fig. 1: 2022 The Art Institute of Chicago / Art Resource, NY / Scala, Firenze
Fig. 2: With kind permission of the Warden and Fellows of Robinson College
Fig. 3: 2022 The Art Institute of Chicago / Art Resource, NY / Scala, Firenze
Fig. 4: 2022. The Art Institute of Chicago / Art Resource, NY / Scala, Firenze
Fig. 5: 2022 The Philadelphia Museum of Art / Art Resource / Scala, Firenze
Fig. 6: Massachusetts, Sterling and Francine Clark Art Institute

Théo Esparon
Fig. 1: Los Angeles County Museum of Art
Fig. 2: The Kobal Collection / Aurimages
Fig. 3: Los Angeles County Museum of Art
Fig. 4: Harry Ransom Center – The University of Texas at Austin
Fig. 5: All rights reserved

Marie Laureillard
Fig. 1: Collection Sun Peicang
Fig. 2: Collection Sun Peicang
Fig. 3: 2022 Album / Scala, Firenze
Fig. 4: Christie's Images - Bridgeman Images
Fig. 5: 2022 Album / Scala, Firenze

Noémie Picard
Fig. 1: Agence Albatros / Réunion des Musées Métropolitains Rouen Normandie
Fig. 2: C. Lancien, C. Loisel / Réunion des Musées Métropolitains Rouen Normandie
Fig. 3: Hervé Lewandowski © 2022. RMN-Grand Palais / Dist. Foto Scala, Firenze
Fig. 4: Hervé Lewandowski © 2022. RMN-Grand Palais / Dist. Foto Scala, Firenze
Fig. 5: Bridgeman Images
Fig. 6: Musée de Louviers
Fig. 7: Musée de Louviers

Samuel Raybone
Fig. 1: National Museum Wales

Chikako Takaoka
Fig. 1: Private collection
Fig. 2: Kurashiki, musée Ohara or Kurashiki, YURINKAI Ohara Memorial Foundation
Fig. 3: Kurashiki, musée Ohara or Kurashiki, YURINKAI Ohara Memorial Foundation
Fig. 4: Kurashiki, musée Ohara or Kurashiki, YURINKAI Ohara Memorial Foundation
Fig. 5: Private collection – Photo by Kojima
Fig. 6: Ohara Museum of Art

Cover
Pierre-Auguste Renoir, *Girl on a Balcony, Cagnes* (*Jeune femme au balcon, Cagnes*), detail, c. 1911, oil on canvas, 43.2 × 52.1 cm, The Barnes Foundation, Philadelphia, BF98

Back Cover
The Barnes Foundation, Philadelphia, *Ensemble*, Room 9, South Wall; at the top left, Pierre-Auguste Renoir, *Girl on a Balcony, Cagnes* (here reproduced on the cover), and in the centre, Pierre-Auguste Renoir, *Girl with a Jump Rope (Portrait of Delphine Legrand) (Jeune fille à la corde à sauter [Portrait de Delphine Legrand])*, 1876, oil on canvas, 107.3 × 71 cm, BF137

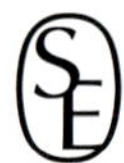

Silvana Editoriale

Direction
Dario Cimorelli

Art Director
Giacomo Merli

Editorial Coordinator
Sergio Di Stefano

Copy Editing
Carlotta Santuccio

Layout
Evelina Laviano

Production Coordinator
Antonio Micelli

Editorial Assistant
Giulia Mercanti

Photo Editor
Silvia Sala, Federica Quaglia

Press Office
Alessandra Olivari, press@silvanaeditoriale.it

Translations
Contextus, We Translate Art (Mirta Cimmino, Sandrine Merle, Laurence Monnot, Richard Kutner, Lisa Richardson, Cheli Rioboo, Calum Short)

ISBN 9788836647453

Available through ARTBOOK | D.A.P.
155 Sixth Avenue, 2nd Floor, New York, N.Y. 10013
Tel: (212) 627-1999 Fax: (212) 627-9484

Silvana Editoriale S.p.A.
via dei Lavoratori, 78
20092 Cinisello Balsamo, Milano
tel. 02 453 951 01
www.silvanaeditoriale.it

Reproductions, printing and binding in Italy
Printed by Grafiche Antiga, Crocetta del Montello (Tv)
November 2022

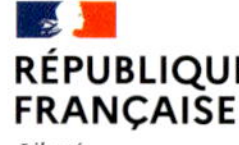

Colloque soutenu par l'État (Contrat de plan interrégional État-Régions Vallée de la Seine, fonds FNADT)

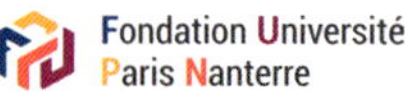

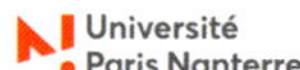

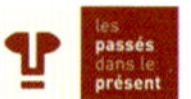

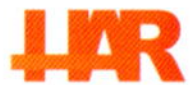

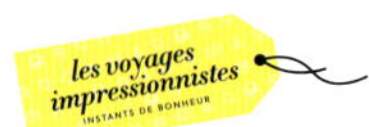

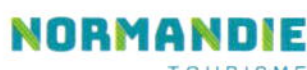

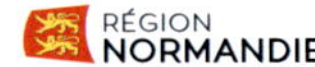

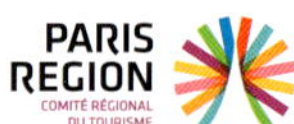

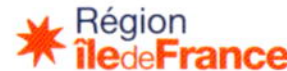

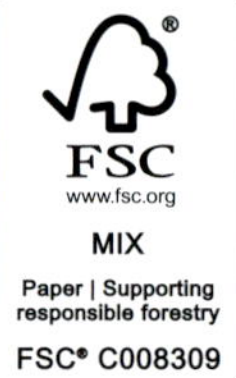